Modernity with a Cold War Face

Harvard East Asian Monographs 360

Modernity with a Cold War Face

REIMAGINING THE NATION IN CHINESE LITERATURE ACROSS THE 1949 DIVIDE

XIAOJUE WANG

Published by the Harvard University Asia Center
Distributed by Harvard University Press
Cambridge (Massachusetts) and London 2013

Printed in the United States of America

The Harvard University Asia Center publishes a monograph series and, in coordination with the Fairbank Center for Chinese Studies, the Korea Institute, the Reischauer Institute of Japanese Studies, and other faculties and institutes, administers research projects designed to further scholarly understanding of China, Japan, Vietnam, Korea, and other Asian countries. The Center also sponsors projects addressing multidisciplinary and regional issues in Asia.

Library of Congress Cataloging-in-Publication Data

Wang, Xiaojue, 1973-
Modernity with a cold war face : reimagining the nation in Chinese literature across the 1949 divide / Xiaojue Wang.
pages cm. — (Harvard East Asian Monographs ; 360)
Includes bibliographical references and index.
Summary: "Bridging the 1949 divide in both literary historical periodization and political demarcation, Xiaojue Wang proposes a new framework to consider Chinese literature beyond naitonal boundaries, as something arising out of the larger global geopolitical and cultural conflict of the Cold War."—Provided by publisher.
ISBN 978-0-674-72672-7 (hardcover : acid-free paper) 1. Chinese literature—20th century—History and criticism. 2. Cold War in literature. 3. Modernism (Literature)—China. I. Title.
PL2303.W3397 2013
895.1'090052—dc23

2013007732

Index by Anne Holmes of EdIdex

♾ Printed on acid-free paper

Last figure below indicates year of this printing
19 18 17 16 15 14 13

In memory of my brother

Wang Xiaohui 王曉暉

(1968–87)

Contents

Acknowledgments

This book would not have been possible without the support and generosity of many people and institutions along the way. I owe the deepest of debts to David Der-wei Wang and Andreas Huyssen, my advisors at Columbia University, who have been tremendous sources of stimulation and inspiration at every stage of writing this book. My gratitude goes to C. T. Hsia, Leo Ou-fan Lee, Ban Wang, and Wei Shang, who read earlier versions of the manuscript and provided invaluable comments and constructive criticism. For early inspiration, I thank Judith Ryan of Harvard University, my advisor who introduced me to Rainer Maria Rilke. I have also immensely benefited from the insights, suggestions, criticism, and camaraderie of Weijie Song, Carlos Rojas, Kirk Denton, Michelle Yeh, Ping-hui Liao, Yomi Braester, Tani Barlow, Jingyuan Zhang, Shu-mei Shih, Eric Hayot, Michael Berry, Xiaobing Tang, Yingjin Zhang, Kang-I Sun Chang, Kam Louie, Robin Visser, Andrea Bachner, Chien-hsin Tsai, Jie Li, Leslie Kriesel, Jianmei Liu, Haili Kong, Tse-lan Deborah Sang, Sheldon Lu, Xiaomei Chen, Lingchei Letty Chen, Wang Hui, Sun Fengcheng, Chen Pingyuan, and Dai Jinhua. Special words of thanks must be reserved for David Der-wei Wang, my advisor and my mentor, for his intellectual generosity, enthusiasm, and wisdom, and for his unwavering support and encouragement for my work as well as for so many things in my life.

I also wish to thank my wonderful colleagues in the Department of East Asian Languages and Civilizations at the University of

Pennsylvania: Victor H. Mair, Nancy S. Steinhardt, Paul R. Goldin, Adam Smith, Linda H. Chance, Ayako Kano, and David Spafford, who provided me with advice and support that were entirely indispensable over the course of writing this book. My colleagues in the Department of Germanic Languages and Literatures and in Cinema Studies program at the University of Pennsylvania gave me careful criticisms, for which I am very grateful. I am especially indebted to Liliane Weissberg, Karen Beckman, Timothy Corrigan, Peter Conn, Catriona MacLeod, Bethany Wiggin, and Peter Decherney, who offered invaluable ideas and comments. I am also grateful to the organizers and participants of the Race and Empire Faculty Reading Group at the University of Pennsylvania, a critical, interdisciplinary-minded group from which I have immensely benefited. In particular, I want to thank David Eng, Ania Loomba, Suvir Kaul, Amy Kaplan, Josephine Park, Deborah A. Thomas, Jed Esty, Si-yen Fei, Chi-ming Yang, and Toorjo Ghose for their incisive comments and penetrating questions. My gratitude extends to my students at the University of Pennsylvania.

I thank the Chiang Ching-kuo Foundation Inter-University Center for Sinology for a generous conference grant, which helped found the annual workshop "Modern China Seminar: Culture and Society" based at the University of Pennsylvania. The first two workshops "The Great Divide in China: Cold War Culture and After" brought together important scholars to consider cultural impacts of the Cold War, from which I benefited enormously. Small segments of the book were presented, in earlier drafts, in lectures and conferences at Harvard University, Peking University, Columbia University, Yale University, the University of Hong Kong, the Pennsylvania State University, and the University of Pennsylvania. I am grateful to the organizers for giving me the opportunity to present my work and to my audiences for invaluable feedback. Profound appreciation also goes to two anonymous reviewers for the Harvard University Asia Center for their incredibly instructive suggestions that helped improve the book in many ways. I am beholden to my editor, Kristen Wanner of the Harvard University Asia Center, who was extremely supportive, helpful, and patient when the manuscript was being prepared for publication. Special thanks also go to Robert Graham and Deborah Del Gais of the Harvard University Asia Center and Michael Haggett and Pat Cattani of Westchester Publishing Services.

An An Wang Postdoctoral Fellowship at the Fairbank Center for Chinese Studies at Harvard University allowed me to finish the final revisions for publication. I would like to express my sincere thanks to the Fairbank Center and to the office of the Dean of the School of Arts and Sciences, University of Pennsylvania, for generously enabling me to devote a year to writing. Over the years, I also received a faculty research travel grant from the Center for East Asian Studies at the University of Pennsylvania, a Chiang Ching-kuo Foundation Junior Scholar Grant, and a semester of academic leave at the University of Pennsylvania, which gave me time to write and revise large portions of the manuscript. I am grateful to all these sources for kindly supporting my work. I would also like to thank the following libraries for facilitating my research: Harvard University libraries, Columbia University libraries, Peking University libraries, University of Pennsylvania libraries, and Princeton University libraries. Special thanks go to Rongxiang Zhang, Rich Jandovitz, and Alexander Brown at the C.V. Starr East Asian Library at Columbia University for their tireless assistance.

Parts of chapter 2 appeared as "From Asylum to Museum: The Discourse of Insanity and Schizophrenia in Shen Congwen's 1949 Transition," in *Modern Chinese Literature and Culture* 23, no. 1 (Spring 2011): 133–168. Parts of chapter 6 were published as "Eileen Chang, *Dream of the Red Chamber*, and the Cold War," in *Eileen Chang: Romancing Languages, Cultures, and Genres*, ed. Kam Louie (Hong Kong: Hong Kong University Press, 2011), 113–129. Both have been revised or expanded for this book.

Finally, this book owes its existence to my family, who supported me with love, encouragement, and forgiveness. During long periods of intensive writing, my parents and my parents-in-law have shared the responsibilities of child-care and household work, for which I am forever grateful. I thank my parents for their trust and faith in me. Above all, my love and gratitude to my husband, Weijie Song, who has been my first reader and my most unflinching critic, and to my son, Patrick, who was born during the completion of this project and has taught me how to love unconditionally. They are my permanent source of inspiration and strength.

X.J.W.

Note on Romanization

All transcriptions of Chinese are provided in Pinyin, except in cases where a different system of romanization was used originally in a quoted text or where another romanization of a proper name is widely known or preferable.

Introduction

This book revisits China's 1949 division from the vantage of many twentieth-century imaginations of a Chinese modernity. It examines the competing, converging, and conflicting modes of envisioning a modern China into being, in Chinese literature on the mainland, in Taiwan, Hong Kong, and overseas, across the 1949 geopolitical fault line as well as in the global Cold War context. These investigations suggest how the Chinese divide might be understood and show how unfinished or repressed ideas and ideals of the time resurfaced with a vengeance in politics, literature, and culture of the post–Cold War era. Exploring the intricate relationship between art and politics, nation and narration, I offer a study of social and cultural responses to the Cold War state division in mid-twentieth-century China, which continues to shape political and cultural events to this day.

In 1949, the advent of Communist rule in mainland China and the retreat of the Nationalist government to the island of Taiwan marked a significant turning point. With the Bamboo Curtain sealed along the Taiwan Strait, China was ideologically and territorially divided into various political and cultural entities—the mainland, Taiwan, Hong Kong, and overseas—which displaced hundreds of millions of Chinese people. Along with the partitions that occurred in Germany, Vietnam, and Korea, China underwent a Cold War divide. In his study of twentieth-century state partitions, Robert K. Schaeffer identifies two distinct patterns: "those of British colonies—Ireland, India, and Palestine—and those subject to great or superpower military occupation at the end of World War II—Germany, Korea, China, and Vietnam."[1] Whereas the former was a unilateral division along ethnic lines, the latter, a multilateral process, was a product of the Cold War.

Although the Kuomintang (KMT) and the Chinese Communist Party (CCP) aligned themselves during the civil war (1946–49) along fields of force generated by the confrontation of the United States and the Soviet Union, it was the outbreak of another hot war—the Korean War—that ensured the formation of the Cold War bipolar constellation in East Asia and the antagonism of mainland China toward its offshore island along the Taiwan Strait. The Korean War (1950–53) caused abrupt change in the policy of the Truman administration, which previously had excluded Taiwan from the American West Pacific defensive perimeter.[2] Realizing that a Taiwan occupied by the CCP would allow the Communists to control "sea lanes between Japan and Malaya, thus threatening the Philippines, the Ryukyus, and ultimately Japan itself," and would therefore be seriously detrimental to the security of the Pacific area and American interests in that region, the United States sent its Seventh Fleet to patrol the Taiwan Strait to prevent CCP and KMT military activities shortly after the U.S. Army went to the Korean peninsula.[3] Although the entry of the newly founded People's Republic of China (PRC) into the Korean War effectively hampered Mao Zedong (1893–1976)'s plan to start another conventional war to liberate Taiwan, it also

---

1. Schaeffer, *Severed States*, p. 89.

2. See Gaddis, *Long Peace*, pp. 80–86; Gordon H. Chang, *Friends and Enemies*, pp. 72–75.

3. Chen Jian, *China's Road to the Korean War*, p. 116. This book provides a detailed analysis of the international political situation in the Pacific area in the Korean War. For the formation of the Cold War confrontation in East Asia, see Gaddis, *We Now Know*, pp. 54–84. There seems to be no scholarly consensus on the periodization of the Cold War either in the study of East Asia or in the more well-studied cases in Europe. Some scholars maintain that East Asia first entered the Cold War in 1948 (see Iriye, *Cold War in Asia,* pp. 164–165), but others suggest a much earlier start to the conflict in mid-1945. Westad, *Cold War and Revolution*, maintains that the start of the Cold War in East Asia begins with the outbreak of civil war in China. For related narratives regarding the situation of Taiwan, see, for instance, Kerr, *Formosa Betrayed*, pp. 396–397. The book was translated into Chinese by Chen Rongcheng, *Bei chumai de Taiwan* (Taipei: Qianwei chubanshe, 1991).

postponed Chiang Kai-shek (Jiang Jieshi, 1887–1975)'s restoration ambition in Chinese mainland.[4] As a result, the U.S. intervention in the Taiwan Strait not only neutralized and eventually postponed the CCP and the KMT's direct military confrontation but also imposed a Cold War conception of antagonism between a Communist mainland and a U.S.-backed "free" island along the geopolitical divide of the Taiwan Strait.

A growing body of scholarship has taken greater interest in the cultural Cold War and explores how the governments of the East and the West shaped culture and competed for ideological and cultural supremacy.[5] The U.S. Cold War operation in East Asia in the name of anticommunism went well beyond the military deployment. It also utilized ideological and media warfare—via the Committee for Free Asia (later renamed Asia Foundation), which was funded by the Central Intelligence Agency (CIA), and the United States Information Agency (USIA)—to seek cultural propaganda and domination. Jointly these U.S. Cold War organizations not only contrived to tell a story of America to the world but also sponsored a wide array of literary and cultural activities in Cold War frontier spots including Hong Kong and Taiwan. Across the Cold War fault lines, the Soviet propaganda machine waged an equally fierce war of arts and letters. Moscow's international political propaganda institutions, including the postwar Communist Information Bureau (COMINFORM), strived to persuade its Cold War rivals as well as other socialist countries that the Union of Soviet Socialist Republics (USSR) was the

---

4. It was after the U.S. intervention in the Taiwan Strait that the Republic of China (ROC) government in Taiwan started to receive massive economic and military aid, which enabled its economic rise in the following decades. For a discussion of the emergence of revolutionary movements in the early 1950s in East Asia and their challenge to the West in general and the United States in particular, see Hunt and Levine, "Revolutionary Challenge"; see also Westad, "Rethinking Revolution" and *Cold War and Revolution*.

5. For instance, see Saunders, *Cultural Cold War,* which investigates the CIA's covert sponsorship of artists and intellectuals during the Cold War to oppose communism; Cull, *The Cold War and the United States Information Agency,* which provides a full account of the evolvement of the USIA and its engagement in public diplomacy during the Cold War years; Rubin, *Archives of Authority,* which examines how the CIA's Congress for Cultural Freedom shaped a new canon of transnational world literature by championing certain writers in the name of anticommunism.

wave of the future.[6] In the years of Sino-Soviet alliance, the Soviet model of socialist realism penetrated all cultural realms in the PRC, from literature to music, from design to architecture.[7]

In his report to the U.S. Congress in April 1998, William C. Kirby asserted that China had never been more deeply involved in an international system than during the heyday of the Cold War.[8] The apparent isolation within the exclusive ideological bloc paradoxically fortifies the country's engagement in world political and cultural configurations. Accordingly, any critical considerations of Chinese politics, literature, and society since the late 1940s must take into account the Cold War discursive framework ingrained in the Chinese context. The Cold War confrontation was characterized by a dichotomous discourse propelled by the Manichaean myth of clash between the forces of good and evil, capitalism and communism, democracy and authoritarianism. Such a relentless dichotomy was amply manifested in the moral of Mao Zedong's famous New Year speech. On December 31, 1948, on the verge of the Communist victory over the Nationalists in the civil war, Mao Zedong, in an editorial broadcast by the CCP's Xinhua Press, called upon the Chinese people to propel the revolution to its very end. Adeptly using allegorical rhetoric, Mao resorted to the parable of "the farmer and the snake" to warn against "snakes" spared by working people: "Those snakes who inhabit the vast territory of China—big snakes and small snakes, black snakes and white snakes, the snakes who expose their poisonous teeth and those who incarnated into beautiful women—although they have already felt the threat of winter, they

6. Caute, *Dancer Defects,* offers an essential historical survey of cultural competitions between the Soviet Union and the West covering theater, film, music, ballet, painting, as well as exhibition. The book has an extensive account of the Soviet performance and cultural activities during the Cold War. For a discussion of Soviet international political propaganda, see also Barghoorn, *Soviet Foreign Propaganda.*

7. For Sino-Soviet relations, see Westad, *Brothers in Arms.* For Sino-Soviet cultural exchanges and relations in the 1950s, see, for instance, Shen Zhihua and Stiffler, *Cuiruo de lianmeng*, especially Volland, "Zhengzhi rentong," 93–113; He Donghui, "'Gangtie shi zenyang liancheng de,'" 114–41; and T. M. Chen, "Sulian dianying de yinjin," 142–67. For Soviet influences on the PRC architecture, see Fan, "A Classicist Architecture for Utopia."

8. Kirby, "Lessons of Modern Chinese History."

are not frozen yet." Consequently, Mao requested, "Chinese people at the peak of revolution should, in addition to remembering their friends, firmly remember their enemies and enemies' friends."[9] His talk stipulated an either/or framework: either stay within this camp, or go on the other side with the enemy. From that moment on, as Qian Liqun observed, children of the "new China" learned to classify people into two categories: "good" and "evil." When confronted with the evil, they would spare nothing.[10] The world was thenceforth separated into opposing blocs in stark binary terms.

This rhetoric of dichotomy, in which the year 1949 was widely regarded as a radical break in historical time, has taken hold and informed Cold War China studies. In the late 1980s, the dramatic geopolitical changes in the Cold War constellation—including the lifting of martial law in Taiwan and the Tiananmen Incident in the PRC—once again brought controversy over the designation of the 1949 division as the start of the Cold War era to the forefront. Scholarship in history and social sciences has started to question the conventional designation of that year as a moment of complete rupture in the continuity of Chinese history. Many historians and social scientists have ventured to bridge the dramatic breach that 1949 seemed to represent through a reconsideration of twentieth-century Chinese history and society across the whole sweep of the century.[11]

In the field of Chinese literary study, the existing paradigm conveniently bisects the trajectory of twentieth-century Chinese literature into a pre-1949 era of modern (*xiandai*) literature and a post-1949 era of contemporary (*dangdai*) literature. It regards the divide as bringing an abrupt end to the development of Chinese literary modernity and initiating an epoch of literary aberration brought about by political

9. Mao Zedong, "Jiang geming jinxing daodi" (Propel the revolution to its very end), p. 1377.

10. Qian Liqun, *1948 Tiandi xuanhuang*, p. 305.

11. In history, as Cohen, "Ambiguities of a Watershed Date," points out, the representative magazine of Chinese historical studies changed its title from *Republican China* to *Twentieth-Century China* in 1994 to reflect this trend of rethinking the 1949 divide. Other scholarly attempts include, for instance, Kirby, "Continuity and Change"; Wasserstrom, *Student Protest in Twentieth-Century China*; Perry, *Shanghai on Strike*; Philip C. C. Huang, "Rethinking the Chinese Revolution"; Hershatter, *Dangerous Pleasures*; Jeremy Brown and Paul G. Pickowicz, *Dilemmas of Victory*.

authoritarianism on both sides of the Taiwan Strait. Such a conceptualization not only writes off mainland and Taiwan writers of this transitional period as purely political victims but also consigns writers in Hong Kong and other Sinophone regions into complete oblivion. In recent years, scholars have made important efforts to reexamine the 1949 divide in Chinese literature.[12] In the PRC, Qian Liqun and He Guimei brought to the forefront the much-neglected literature of the 1940s. In North American academia, David Der-wei Wang made the initial attempts to overcome the 1949 barrier. In reconsidering 1950s communist and anticommunist fiction across the Taiwan Strait, Wang demonstrates how these two Cold War enemies used similar cultural rhetoric in demonizing each other. The recent anthology *1949 yihou: dangdai wenxue liushi nian* (After 1949: Sixty years of contemporary literature), with articles contributed by Chinese scholars in the PRC, Hong Kong, Taiwan, and overseas, seeks to rethink the impact of the 1949 division on the development of post-1949 Chinese literature.[13] However, a comprehensive examination of mid-twentieth-century Chinese literature has yet to be done.

My book shows that it is important to bridge the 1949 divide in Chinese literary study and that Chinese literature of the 1940s and 1950s provides a missing link in our understanding of Chinese literary modernity in terms of the relationship between poetics and politics, nation and narration. It rethinks mid-twentieth-century Chinese literature in the international Cold War context of state partitions such as those in Germany and Korea. By proposing this new framework, I consider Chinese culture beyond the inward-looking focus of national literatures, as something arising out of the global geopolitical and cultural conflict known as the Cold War. Most scholarship on Cold War China looks to the high politics of diplomatic influence and international history. Studies on the sociocultural dimensions of the Chinese divide remain sparse. In examining literary activities on mainland China, in Taiwan, in the British

12. For studies done by the PRC scholars, see Qian Liqun, *1948 Tiandi xuanhuang,* and He Guimei, *Zhuanzhe de shidai*. In the field of Chinese literature in North America, see Chi Pang-yuan, edited with David Der-wei Wang, *Chinese Literature in the Second Half of a Modern Century*.

13. David Der-wei Wang, Chen Sihe, and Xu Zidong, *1949 yihou*.

colony of Hong Kong, and in overseas Sinophone regions during the high Cold War—the period between the late 1940s and the early 1960s—I suggest that a study of literature better captures the capricious nature of the Cold War than does analysis of history or politics. Ever since its emergence as a modern cultural institution, Chinese literature has been deeply entangled with issues of nation, nationalism, and nation building. At no other time in the entire course of the twentieth century was modern Chinese literature endowed with a heavier political responsibility than during the Cold War. The two opposing Chinese regimes took great pains to wage a cultural and ideological war. Neither was aware that instead of representing political reality and narrating national history, literature embodied those very treacherous experiences—personal, national, and international—we call the Cold War. They are unlikely twins.

In addition, I argue that the Cold War era brings us to reconsider the concepts of nation and narration. The state divisions in China, Korea, and Germany force us to face up to the syndrome of schism and schizophrenia always already embedded in the project of naming the nation and delineating its sovereignty. Taking literature as a weapon to represent their own version of Chinese identity as the antithesis to the Cold War Other, the Communist and the Nationalist regimes are mutually implicated as much as mutually exclusive.

Beyond Cold War Ethical Sentimentalism

In this section, I question the tendency of ethical sentimentalism inherent in post–Cold War narratives of the Chinese division in academic literature as well as the general public perspective. Given their discursive framework of subjugation versus resistance, betrayal versus loyalty, two trends of criticism need to be approached with particular caution. In their reflections on the Chinese intellectual mentality in the Cold War era, these critical undertakings endeavor to overcome the Cold War binary discourse, only to reinforce it in the most unexpected ways. Bound by the same dichotomous rhetoric, they regard Chinese intellectuals at the Cold War divide as either heroic dissidents or tragic victims, or disgraceful accomplices of totalitarian power positioned at the center. I venture to call them the two sentimentalisms of Cold War "if only."

The first "if only" hypothesis was implicated in numerous reminiscent writings and academic studies about mid-twentieth-century Chinese intellectuals. A strong sentimental investment is evident in these studies' reflections on how these intellectuals spiritually and physically survived the ascending political catastrophes in the Mao era—the Anti-Rightist Campaign, the Great Leap Forward movement, and the Cultural Revolution, among others. Embedded in the consensus that these intellectuals were regrettable victims of uncontrollable political and historical contingencies is the implicit question: Would these intellectuals have made the same decision to stay in socialist China if only they had known beforehand about what was to happen? Such a question in the pluperfect subjunctive mood has its preset answer: If only they could have anticipated what would confront them after 1949, they would have chosen differently. If only so, their intellectual lives would not have terminated prematurely; if only so, the whole topography of modern Chinese literature and culture would have been redrawn; and so on.

What underlies such conditional "if onlys" is the assumption that there could have been alternative ways out of the political predicament of that time, that there existed an outside space beyond the boundary of communist authoritarianism. With the continuation of their intellectual activities and contributions elsewhere—presumably in Taiwan, Hong Kong, or overseas—the trajectory of Chinese modernity would have been different. This Cold War hypothesis, which seemingly points to time structures in the irreversible past, is in effect projected into the spatial scope: an alternative geopolitical entity, located on the other side of the Cold War fault line. Thus, in an unexpected way, such sentimentalist speculation consolidates the very dichotomous framework it set out to criticize. The practice of contemporary exorcism only conjures up and ultimately perpetuates the specter of the Cold War myth.

Charles J. Alber's significant monograph about Ding Ling's experiences in the PRC, *Embracing the Lie*,[14] demonstrates many of the feelings inherent in the post–Cold War hypothesis. Ding Ling, one of the most daring and avant-garde female writers of modern Chi-

14. Alber, *Embracing the Lie.*

nese literature before her conversion to communism, has been the favorite "literary dissident" in the study of Communist China.[15] Provoked by Ding Ling's radical leftist attitude after her recuperation from a twenty-year-long political purge, Alber writes that "my disillusion with Ding Ling was so profound I was no longer convinced that the writer deserved so much attention."[16] Basic to his complaint is the deep perplexity about how such a repressed literary dissident like Ding Ling could reemerge even more enchanted with the Maoist revolutionary discourse, the very ideology that had terminated her literary career and occasioned the most ardent experiences of disenchantment: detention, hard labor, public abuse, and humiliation. After all the ordeals, Ding Ling did not, much to the scholar's disappointment, turn into a vanguard against the evil of communist authoritarianism, making testimonies to the historical monstrosity or at least composing some sentimental writings of regret or confession, as did many of her contemporaries.[17] On the contrary, she was determined more than ever "to safeguard her political credibility and reliability, reaffirm her loyalty as a Chinese Communist Party member, and maintain her reputation as an old-line revolutionary."[18]

Alber concludes, "The tragedy of Ding Ling is that she traded her own integrity for legitimacy in the Party. . . . No reward can compensate for the loss of one's integrity; there is no honor in embracing a lie."[19] Significantly, this moralistic indictment of Ding Ling's infidelity masks a more fundamental anxiety that originates in Alber's own disillusioned presumption: if only she had expected what would be coming, Ding Ling would have done differently. The latter's ostensible "leftism," however, smashes this axiomatic hypothesis. As it turned out, Ding Ling would probably *not* have done differently, given that she chose to remain even more revolutionary in a new

---

15. One of the finest studies on these dissident leftist writers in Communist China is Goldman, *Literary Dissent in Communist China*. For a study of the relations between literature, literary policies, and political domination in the mid-1950s PRC, see Wagner, *Inside a Service Trade*.

16. Alber, *Embracing the Lie*, p. 2.

17. The most significant works in this category include, for instance, Ba Jin, *Suixiang lu*; Zhou Yiliang, *Bijing shi shusheng*; and Ji Xianlin, *Niupeng zayi*.

18. Alber, *Embracing the Lie*, p. 285.

19. Ibid., p. 287.

epoch known as a time to undo the past injustice (*boluan fanzheng*), when she was endowed with relatively more freedom of choice. It seems that there were no alternatives after all—not then, not now. Such hasty blame on monstrous political environments only consolidates the Cold War binary paradigm and justifies the critic's own position of moral righteousness. Inevitably, it leaves much uninvestigated in mid-twentieth-century Chinese literature.

Although the first type of attempt to deal with mid-century Chinese literature attributes writers' aphasia to political oppression by the authoritarian state, Maoist socialist or Nationalist, and flirts with a hypothetical outside world, thus overlooking problems intrinsic within literature itself, the second type of criticism betrays another dangerous tendency in recent scholarly undertakings.

The rationale of the second mode of Cold War "if only" is palpably caught in the deliberation by Ye Zhaoyan on the resurrection of Qian Zhongshu's novel *Weicheng* (Besieged city, 1948) since the late 1980s. Ye, a writer of the younger generation who arose in the post-Mao era, observes:

> While Qian Zhongshu's giving up fiction writing might have something to do with the transformations in 1949, Shen Congwen was already mired in stagnation before 1949. The good thing is that both of them found substitution outside literary creation in the latter half of their lives. Qian Zhongshu finished his scholarly tour de force *Guanzhui bian* (Limited views), and Shen Congwen became a pre-eminent expert in archaeology. Ba Jin and Shi Tuo didn't give up writing, to be sure. Yet they seemed to take more effort to say good-bye to their pasts and to seek to become a new type of writer that they were not familiar with. Why didn't Ba Jin continue writing down the road he trod with *Disi bingshi* (The fourth ward) and *Hanye* (Cold nights)? Why didn't Shi Tuo continue writing works like *Guoyuan chengji* (Orchard town) and *Wuwangcun guanzhu* (A master in the village of no hope)? A simple explanation is that the environment didn't allow them to continue writing like before. However, Eileen Chang escaped the mainland and had way too much free time to write, yet still she did not produce any good works. During this long period, there did not appear a single writer, like Cao Xueqin, who could have written for ten years in the most arduous times and would die for a work that could reach later generations.[20]

Ye's observation provides a useful point of departure. He maintains that political persecution was not the primary reason for dispa-

---

20. Ye Zhaoyan, "Weicheng li de xiaosheng," p. 149.

rate changes these writers went through after 1949: termination of literary life, self-transformation, and conversion to Communist writing, or forced or unforced exile. In doing that, he notably overcomes the discourse of exterior political victimization that informed the first thinking mode previously discussed. However, his reflection betrays another lure of Cold War speculations. After the careful analysis of the dilemma confronting writers after 1949, Ye asserts that "there must be something wrong with the desire and motive of literary creation embedded deep in the minds of our writers."[21] He continues to conjecture: "If only writing had become part of their biological mechanism, something involuntary, like sexual drive, like hunger, or like shitting, things would have been different."[22] If only these writers had possessed such a drive to write, they would have continued writing, even in a secret manner as accomplished by Cao Xueqin of the imperial time, for later generations.

Ye thus concludes that the writers deprived themselves of possibilities. Strikingly, he attributes the termination of literary writing to the lack of a certain kind of inner drive among Chinese writers. How to decode the political charge in this mysterious, libidolike drive of writing Ye emphasizes? Anyone familiar with cultural trends of the last decades of twentieth-century China will notice that this seemingly interior drive obviously points to something else than the Freudian drive of eating and mating. Instead, the Freudian terminology masks a deeper anxiety haunting Chinese intellectuals in the post-Mao era that was manifested in various searches for "cultural heroes" launched by the reconstruction of cultural images of Chen Yinke (1890–1969) and Gu Zhun (1915–74) since the 1990s.[23] The ideal men of letters they sought to establish amount to intellectual heroes or martyrs, like Russian writers under Stalinist authoritarianism

---

21. Ibid.

22. Ibid.

23. The most influential works in the reconstruction of historically vanished intellectuals are, among others, Lu Jiandong's *Chen Yinke de zuihou ershi nian* and Zhang Zige's *Xinxiang leiyu ji Wu Mi*. On the significance of the resurrection of intellectuals such as Chen Yinke, Gu Zhun, and Qian Zhongshu, who literally disappeared from socialist intellectual history, see Yang Zao, "Jiushi niandai wenhua yingxiong."

such as Boris Pasternak (1890–1960) and Alexander Solzhenitsyn (1918–2008), whom Ye and his generation strongly admired.

Therefore, Ye's regret that Chinese writers did not have the inner drive to write can be translated into a more accurate statement: Chinese writers did not have the guts to write. What Ye's speculation, or, more precisely, expectation, implies is that writing constitutes a way to resist the hegemonic socialist discourse. Clearly, one of the premises hidden in such thinking is that there are only two possibilities for intellectuals confronting ideological hegemony: subjugation or resistance. Inasmuch as that opposition is itself a product of the Cold War Manichaean rhetoric of exclusion, in his criticism of Cold War literature, Ye only reinforces the very dichotomous discourse he seeks to eradicate. As chapters in this book demonstrate, what these writers experienced is more complicated than just oppression or victimization. The strategy of calling on resistance is as damaging as resorting to a political outside: both obscure and even negate the real alternatives and potential agency for liberation that exist within the totality itself. Both these two critical approaches oversimplify by assuming that the intellectual field was a one-way street in which all of the traffic flowed from the hegemony above to the intellectuals below, thus perpetuating a notion of unidirectionality, so to speak.

In both types of ethical sentimentalism, the critics resorted to a simplistic dualism pitting individual moral integrity against a historical process that was presented as demonic and out of control. Ye Zhaoyan's lamenting betrays the post-1989 intellectual disillusionment prevailing in the post-Tiananmen Chinese mainland, when once again, the very state that Chinese intellectuals considered benign cracked down on democratic practice in promoting a second round of enlightenment and modernization in the post-Mao China. At this low point of morale, PRC intellectuals once again looked at the 1949 divide, when pioneers of the Republican China were confronted with the drastic turning point in the course of Chinese modernization. While they strove to praise virtues of cultural perseverance in these tragic heroes and mourned over their inevitable sacrifice in the repressive Communist or Nationalist statecraft, they might not be aware of their own ethical anxiety as a self-righteous rhetoric of resistance. Such a simplistic dualism could be as revealing as it could be obscuring in addressing issues of Chinese literary and political transformations of the modern age. This potential of Cold War criticism for turning against its own critical capacity is the foremost danger against which scholars of Cold War studies must be repeatedly warned.

To go beyond the containment of moral antithesis of good versus evil, it is pertinent to examine those elusive yet provocative moments, which were so easily wrapped up in Cold War ethical sentimentalism that the deeper implications about divergent modes of cultural imaginations of a modern nation were often obscured. When China's quest for modernity and modernization reached its mid-twentieth-century point, the revenge of the past emerged in its most intense and violent form, and resulted in the contestations of various modes of modern imaginations. The following episode occurring at the Chinese divide provides a notable case in point.

It is a story about love at first sight with "our Party" (the CCP). On July 14, 1957, during the heyday of the Anti-Rightist Campaign, the architect and architectural historian Liang Sicheng (1901–72), the eldest son of the late Qing reformist Liang Qichao (1873–1929), wrote about his affection toward the Chinese Communist Party in the official party newspaper *Renmin ribao* (People's daily).[24] In this confessional piece, Liang resorted to his first encounters with the CCP army to rationalize his decision not to leave mainland China in late 1948:

> On the third day after Tsinghua University was liberated, there came a cadre. He said if the PLA had to attack the city (Beijing), they would try to avoid destroying historical buildings. So he asked me to mark them on a map, and to make a note of their historical and artistic values. I read *Mencius* when I was a child; the words "bringing food and fetching drinks, to welcome the army of a benevolent king" were substantiated in my mind on that very day. Previously, I had known nothing about the Communist Party. I "fell in love with it" right away.[25]

One would hardly miss the moral message this narrative carries. Liang, who had had no experience with communist revolution before, started to sympathize with the Communist Party because he was persuaded by its moral integrity. Indeed, during the civil war period, the moral superiority of the CCP and its army over the

24. Liang Sicheng, "Wo weishenme."
25. Ibid., quoted in Zhang Qingping, *Lin Huiyin*, pp. 360–62.

notorious corruption of the KMT regime served as an even bigger weapon than anti-imperialist sentiment in mobilizing the masses and winning support and sympathy from the educated class. Ultimately, at the historical turning point in 1949, moral imperative played an inestimable role in drawing the majority of Chinese intellectuals to stay in or return from abroad to socialist China. In this regard, Liang's story is but one of the legendary sentimental narratives of the 1949 division.[26]

With the advantages of historical hindsight, it is now easy to point to the Cold War rhetoric of good versus evil forces effectively deployed by the CCP propaganda machine in its moralistic performance.[27] Although bearing the unmistakable imprint of the Cold War ideology, Liang's story is by no means yet another Cold War moral melodrama. In the post-Mao era, this story of love at the first sight, which had been repeated by Liang himself in his endless confessions during various political purges since the mid-1950s, returned to haunt virtually every work of reminiscent literature and academic scholarship on Liang and his wife, Lin Huiyin (1904–55), renowned poet, fiction writer, architect, and architectural historian.[28]

26. Similar stories appeared not only in confessions made by intellectuals during various political purges engulfing the mainland China since the mid-1950s but also in those of many intellectuals confronted with the same critical decision of staying or leaving at the division of 1949, such as Shen Congwen and Chen Zhanxiang. Chen Zhanxiang (a.k.a. Charles Chen, 1916–2001) was a renowned scholar of architecture and city planning educated at the University of Liverpool and University College London. After witnessing the disciplined Communist army in Shanghai, he tore up the airline tickets to Taiwan the night before his planned departure and remained on the mainland with his whole family. He was famous for proposing and constructing the Liang-Chen project with Liang Sicheng to renovate Beijing while preserving its ancient cultural and historical features in the 1950s. Together with Liang, he was purged for his reactionary ideas. Allyn Rickett, in his famous memoirs of life in prison in socialist China, described an interesting encounter with Chen at a party at the British embassy in the 1950s, which was characterized by the schizophrenic existence of Chen between his Western educated lifestyle and his adjustment to the new socialist ideology. See Allyn and Adele Rickett, *Prisoners of Liberation*.

27. For a discussion of Cold War discourse, see, for instance, Carmichael, *Framing History*, esp. the first chapter, "Cold War Frame Narrative," pp. 3–48.

28. See, for instance, Zhang Qingping, *Lin Huiyin*; Lin Shan, *Yidai cainü Lin Huiyin*; Wilma Fairbank, *Liang and Lin*.

What kind of cultural politics and psychological economy is still circulating in the post–Cold War era? By invoking the moral imperative and emotional investment in Liang's story, contemporary reflections on the cultural psychology at the critical 1949 transition seek to expose the ominous lure of morality wrought by the Cold War ideology. Yet, the repetitive elaboration of Liang's moral drama only serves to conjure up the specter of the Cold War ethical antithesis, thus fortifying the very ideology it sets out to exorcise. On the other hand, the dissipation of moral sentimentalism blinds the readers to other important aspects of Liang Sicheng's experiences and hence precludes critical examination of cultural and aesthetic responses by like-minded Chinese intellectuals to the mid-twentieth-century division.

What is often overlooked in Liang's story is that his compassion toward the CCP stemmed from his belief that the party paid great attention to the cultural and artistic value of historical buildings and cities, which, according to his previous experiences as an architectural historian, were often neglected by the KMT government.[29] Liang saw the possibility of cooperation with the new regime to preserve and rejuvenate ancient cultural cities such as Beijing on the way to modernization. In his considerations of European and Soviet urban developments around the same time, Liang observed that the totalitarian socialist system might also have advantages for modern architecture and urban planning.[30] Planned by the state at large, a rational urban transformation and modernization would be feasible in the new China and would greatly benefit the modernization of the ancient city of Beijing.

Therefore, what the moral melodrama of good versus evil has displaced is the intriguing lure of modernization: a vision of urban renovation and imagination in the upcoming socialist state. If moral imperative influenced Liang's choice between the two parties, which I believe was true among the majority of intellectuals of the time, then the politics of modern imagination was of equal, if not greater, importance in his ruminations at that transitional moment. Liang's

---

29. In those years, Liang was disappointed with the KMT's neglect of historical buildings, for instance, in Shenyang, where he and Lin established the first department of architecture in China. See Lin Zhu, *Kunhuo de dajiang*.

30. Wang Jun, *Chengji*.

story of apparent moral sentimentality indicates that the socialist discourse, which was itself born out of the process of Chinese modernization, had distinct attractions even for those intellectuals who did not belong to the left wing. Accordingly, the mid-twentieth-century transitional experiences of these intellectuals cannot be simplified as the drama of repression and subjugation. Although the divergence between Liang's conception of modern urbanity and the Maoist vision of urban industrialization soon became clear in the project of socialist reconstruction and modernization of Beijing, the anticipation at the 1949 turning point of potential, even if only partial, convergence of modern imaginations between the new Communist regime and the nonleftist intellectuals cannot be ignored. The survey of the mid-twentieth-century Chinese literary and cultural topography is incomplete without investigating such moments of convergence, however vulnerable and elusive they may ultimately turn out to be.

Given that Liang's vision of urban modernization foregrounds the harmonious combination of preserving the historical city and constructing modern urban space, it was bound to conflict with the Maoist picture of industrial urbanity based on a complete obliteration of the past. Inasmuch as the Maoist notion of modern Beijing imagines modernity as constituting a radical break, a tabula rasa, it stands closer to the modern vision as manifested in Georges-Eugène Haussmann's Paris project in 1848, which "bludgeoned the city into modernity,"[31] or to Moscow's version of squeezing modernity into the present unity of urban traditionality.[32] Consequently, it was the clashes between different modern imaginations that led to Liang's inevitable deviation from the mainstream discourse and the ensuing purges after 1949. Although his dream of modern Beijing was considerably damaged by the Maoist urban planning, especially with the

31. For an analysis of how Haussmann's project of urban modernization in Paris corresponded to the specific vision of modernity as evidenced in Paris of the mid-nineteenth century, see Harvey's seminal work, *Paris, Capital of Modernity*, esp. pp. 93–116.

32. In the 1950s, before the relationship between the PRC and its socialist ally deteriorated, urban planners sent from the Soviet Union played a crucial role in the modernization project for Beijing. For the conflicts between the Soviet and Chinese architects, Liang Sicheng and Chen Zhanxiang in particular, see Wang Jun, *Chengji*, pp. 73–96.

destruction of ancient city walls and gate towers, the legacy of Liang's urban planning found its way back into the post–Cold War modernization plan of Beijing.

Such ambivalent moments when different orders of modern imaginations were in competition or complementation at the 1949 Chinese division are what this book sets out to explore. These intriguing instances of deviations and convergence, which cannot be included in the clear-cut rubric of political antagonism, have been largely overlooked. And they have remained unresolved even in the presumed post–Cold War era. Even today, the prevalent thinking often implies that the overcoming of the oppressive totality or hegemony is a flight to the opposite side, the other side of the shore. As discussed previously, this type of criticism still lingers within the constraints of Cold War rhetoric, which favors conceptualization in terms of binary oppositions and often privileges one over the other. As this book reveals, there has never been any innocent laissez-passer to a better world. Or, to begin with, there exists no better world beyond, nor redemption on the other shore. Instead, efforts can only be made from within. As Walter Benjamin pointed out in his examination of Charles Baudelaire's lyricism in the late capitalist period, the best means of resistance for intellectuals might be their function as "secret agent" within the existing system: "There is little point in trying to include a Baudelaire in the fabric of the most advanced position in mankind's struggle for liberation. From the outset it seems more promising to investigate his machinations where undoubtedly he is at home—in the enemy camp. Very rarely are they a blessing for the opposite side. Baudelaire was a secret agent—an agent of the secret discontent of his class with its own rule."[33] Indeed, these interior fragmented activities do not point to a world beyond, nor do they intend to effect yet another apocalyptical revolutionary turnover. Rather, through political penetrations into the totalizing control, these intellectual agencies render the alleged iron cage a porous space.

The collapse of the Communist regimes in Eastern Europe in 1989 is generally regarded as marking the end of the Cold War. Francis

---

33. Benjamin, *Charles Baudelaire*, p. 104n1.

Fukuyama's notion of the "end of history" suggested a universal, liberal democracy instituting the ultimate form of human society. However, socialism as a form of government remains resilient in the People's Republic of China. Across the Taiwan Strait, the Cold War ideological antagonism along the Bamboo Curtain lingers on. The recent economic growth in mainland China seemed to reinforce the myth of China's rise, which triggered the debate about a "China model." From the official government discourse—socialism with Chinese characteristics endorsing a "harmonious society"—to popular culture—such as the mega-epic film *The Founding of a Republic* (2009), mainland Chinese society seems to indulge in triumphalism about Chinese socialism, which has at least some of the critics in ecstatic rapture. Theories have emerged on the governance of "socialist benevolence" beyond democracy that best epitomizes the Beijing Consensus, which conjures up the specter of a nationalist cultural renaissance à la Confucian ethics, on which the Cold War KMT regime in Taiwan claimed its legitimacy, or a not-so-far-fetched "capitalist Confucianism" prevailing at the peripheries of a "Greater China" in the 1980s.[34] Such praises of socialism seems to differ drastically from the harsh denunciation of Maoist socialist practice (1949–79) by the PRC "Second Enlightenment" intellectuals of the 1980s, which disavowed the experiences of the first three decades of socialist China as a demonic historical aberration and the realization of the worst nightmare of Chinese feudalism. Although their political or cultural positions might be starkly different, both discourses lack serious reflections on Chinese socialist legacy at the political, cultural, or economic levels.

Today, as the ideologues of the Taiwanese independence movement are preoccupied with a mission of desinicizing nation building, the forces of globalization are smoothing over the PRC's socialist industrial wastelands. None is willing or able to curb the process whereby the two formerly hostile regimes are busy making friends across the Taiwan Strait. How to come to terms with the adamancy of Chinese state socialism in the post–Cold War era? How to approach disintegrated Chinese polities, cultures, and modern imaginaries that

34. For the conception of "cultural China" as related to a new type of capitalism in periphery states such as Singapore, see Tu Wei-ming, "Cultural China."

resulted from the Cold War divide and remain severed in a post–Cold War "borderless world"? It is high time to revisit the 1949 Chinese Cold War division, which is not quite history yet, to examine how a modern nation was being imagined and put into practice in disparate political entities across geographical and ideological fault lines.

How did literary narratives of the 1940s and 1950s help ratify or contest the division? How did people deal with the diverse intellectual activities and competing imaginations of a modern nation in the era of ideological despotism? How did unfinished or repressed ideas and ideals of Chinese modernity resurface with a vengeance in politics, literature, and culture of the post–Cold War era? To address these questions, I examine the interplay of multivalent modernities across generic, gender, disciplinary, linguistic, and ideological boundaries in Cold War China. I study writers who had been major figures in Chinese literature prior to the 1949 divide and underwent dramatic changes in their careers during the Cold War era in multiple Chinese political entities: Shen Congwen (1902–88), Ding Ling (1904–86), Wu Zhuoliu (1900–76), Feng Zhi (1905–93), and Zhang Ailing (Eileen Chang, 1920–95). By examining their major works of the 1940s and 1950s as well as their intellectual, artistic, and ethical choices at the Chinese severance, I explore how their cultural endeavors revealed disparate visions of Chinese modernity that competed and converged with the overriding political discourses and attested to the poignant and treacherous experiences called the Cold War.

My book therefore considers the Chinese Cold War divide not just as a consequence of domestic or international ideological antagonism but also as an emanation from the unsettled, competing modes of envisioning a modern Chinese nation. This view helps us understand Chinese modernity as an incomplete cause that resurfaced forcefully in post–Cold War politics, literature, and culture in Greater China, manifested in the People's Republic of China's socialist triumphalism that heralds a model of "Confucian socialism" as well as Taiwan's independence-versus-unification controversies.

Chapter 1 examines how the discipline of modern Chinese literature (*xiandai wenxue*) was invented during the early Cold War years in mainland China, Hong Kong, and Taiwan, in conjunction with a critical reading of three foundational treatises that informed the political and cultural policies in these divided entities: Mao

Zedong's 1940 "Xin minzhu zhuyi lun" (On new democracy), the New Confucianists' 1958 "Wei Zhongguo wenhua jinggao shijie renshi xuanyan" (A manifesto to the world on behalf of Chinese culture), and Chiang Kai-shek's 1953 "Minsheng zhuyi yule liangpian bushu" (Supplementary treatises on education and recreation to the "Principle of Livelihood"). I consider how the ascendancy of modern Chinese literature registered different imaginaries of a modern literature, culture, and nation at the onset of the political division and argue that the notion of Cold War Chinese modernity was produced through various active relations among these diverse loci of modern imaginaries.

Chapters 2 through 6 represent five entry points to explore the multiple modes of imagining a modern nation at the Chinese division. Chapter 2 deals with an aesthetic of the fragment and fragmentation by examining Shen Congwen's reflections on literature, art, antiquity, museum work, and the discourse of insanity. I seek to interpret Shen's schizophrenic breakdown around 1949 and his subsequent conversion from fiction writing to research on antiquities and art, and suggest that by conceptualizing a form of history written with artistic fragments and details of the materialist past, Shen presents an alternative vision of modernity to the monumental socialist revolutionary history. In his post-1949 work, including his *Zhongguo gudai fushi yanjiu* (Studies on traditional Chinese costumes), Shen turns to the multitude of fragmented historical artifacts and episodic art historical accounts as a means of breaking with the monolithic socialist ideology.

Chapter 3 explores the clashes between feminist consciousness and socialist revolutionary discourse in Ding Ling's work after the late 1940s. Through an analysis of two socialist realist works—the Stalin literary prize–winning *Taiyang zhaozai sangganhe shang* (The sun shines over the Sanggan River, 1948), and "Du Wanxiang" (Du Wanxiang, 1979), a belated degendered model work of socialist realism published after Ding Ling's political recuperation—this chapter examines a woman writer caught between the Communist mandates and her feminist consciousness. Incapable of carving out a feminist space in the socialist discourse of gender and sexuality, Ding Ling fought vainly against her antagonist undead other to prove her leftist revolutionary loyalty.

Chapter 4 inquires into the entangled problematic of colonial modernity, nationalism, and cultural identification ingrained in mid-twentieth-century Taiwanese literature, which was repressed by the dominant anticommunist ideology of the Nationalist regime in Taiwan. Taking Wu Zhuoliu's postwar Taiwan narratives as a point of departure, this chapter first discusses ethnic confrontations in post-retrocession years that obscure more convoluted clashes between nationalistic sentiments and Japanese colonialism, modernization's prosperity promise and destructive potentiality. It then analyzes various historical and theoretical narratives of the 1895 Taiwan Republic to probe the limitations of modernization theory fashioned in Cold War America and argues that modernity has never been singular. By exploring the political, cultural, and linguistic implications of "orphanization" in Wu Zhuoliu's novel *Yaxiya de gu'er* (Orphan of Asia) and its criticism, I argue that the concept best conveys a split modern Taiwan subjectivity between Chinese culturalism and Japanese colonialism, between traditional and modern forces. Unresolved problems also resulted in opposition between the independence and unification campaigns.

Chapter 5 focuses on Chinese intellectual endeavors to reconcile the aesthetic and the political, modernist poetry and socialist ideology, European humanism and Maoist class discourse across the mid-twentieth-century divide. Socialist concepts of national collectivity had a strong appeal to writers who sought a positive relationship between aesthetic autonomy and social commitment. To consider this poignant process of reconciliation, I discuss the transition of Feng Zhi, a prominent modernist poet and a significant German literature scholar, from poetry to politics in socialist China. Feng's disavowal of his pre-1949 modernist aesthetics has often been regarded as a cultural and ethical betrayal. An examination of his ideas of poetic solitude, analogy, metamorphosis, and social engagement formed in his study of Rilke, Goethe, and other European humanists reveals that Feng's concept of relationality converges with the socialist idea of collectivity. In his efforts to bridge art and politics, Feng forges a notion of affirmative socialist affinity, which enables the bourgeois aesthetic self to overcome its finitude by positioning itself within a larger Whole of socialist kinship.

Chapter 6 concerns the intricate relationship between culture and polity, the left and the right, and enlightenment and entertainment that played out conspicuously in Cold War Hong Kong in the interstices of the British colony and the two competing political regimes across the Taiwan Strait. When anticommunist fiction met New School martial arts romance in newspapers, the arbitrariness in politics and the permeable boundary between ideological rivals found a most compelling manifestation. To consider these issues, I investigate Eileen Chang's post-1949 diasporic, translingual, and cross-media literary and cultural practices, which were deeply embedded in the Cold War history of the East Asian front, including Hong Kong and Taiwan, and of the United States. In her 1950s political fiction and two endeavors to rework the Qing dynasty classic novel *Honglou meng* (Dream of the red chamber) in her late career, I argue, Chang's political and artistic ambiguity and her compulsive rewriting across disparate languages, genres, and media problematized the binary ideological confrontation and provided a way to break out of political domination in the age of Cold War antagonism. The epilogue considers the possibilities of constructing a de-Cold War critical consciousness.

In the main, these six chapters touch upon various moments of convergence and/or divergence in China's modern imaginations across the 1949 divide. Together they attest to the dynamic configuration of Chinese modernities in the Cold War era's literary and cultural productions, thus constructing a special kind of modernity with a Cold War face. The discourses of modernity and the Cold War are mutually imbricated. Like the modernity project, the Cold War is also Janus-faced, enacting and embodying modernity's liberating and destructive potentials. As it excludes the enemy and bifurcates the globe, the Cold War also reconfigures borders, forms allegiances, and opens up new routes of transnational flow. As it furnishes modernity's new stage with a Manichean face-off, this Cold War face obscures issues related to gender, race, ethnicity, colonialism, diaspora, and diverse cultural practices behind the mask of communism or anticommunism. In this petrified, frozen face of modernity, everything about separation, loss, assimilation, or rehabilitation is expressed and, at the same time, concealed. As this book demonstrates, even in the most rigorous period of ideological despotism, those modern visions manifested in Chinese literature and culture never ceased to compete and to negotiate. Such contestations and competitions informed the Cold War binary discourse, yet simultaneously undermined it and anticipated its ultimate disintegration.

CHAPTER 1

Literature, Nationhood, and the Cold War: How Was Modern Chinese Literature Invented?

The 1949 Chinese divide constitutes both a nation-building and a destabilizing instance: geographically, it unified the Chinese mainland once again under one government but entailed a Cold War partition of the Chinese nation into multiple polities and many more diasporic Chinese communities within other nations; culturally, it triggered even more dispersed and dynamic versions of Chinese national and cultural imaginaries. Although diasporic and exilic dislocation triggered poignant nostalgia toward a lost or displaced home/land and feelings of estrangement, loss, and marginalization, it also mobilized deterritorialized self-reflection and new ways of conceiving nation and national culture.

Both socialist China and the Nationalist regime in Taiwan made a great deal of effort to represent their own version of Chinese identity as the antithesis to the other as a result of the mutual hostility that characterized the Cold War period. Through cultural constructions, each of the two governments sought to articulate conceptions of Chinese national identity and consciousness. In this chapter, I examine how political dominance proceeded via the construction of cultural hegemony in the severed polities after the 1949 divide, through the prism of the ascendency of modern Chinese literature as a discipline. I look at several discourses about the institutionalization of modern Chinese literature in post-1949 mainland China, Hong Kong, and Taiwan, and how they registered different imaginaries of a modern literature, culture, and nation at the onset of the Chinese division. The notion of Cold War Chinese modernity was produced through various active relations among these diverse loci of modern imaginaries.

The discipline of modern Chinese literature came into its own during the Cold War. Born out of the May Fourth New Culture Movement of the 1910s, modern Chinese literature as a subject of study was not institutionalized until the early years after the Chinese division. I examine how modern Chinese literary study was invented in the Cold War PRC, Hong Kong, and Taiwan in conjunction with a critical reading of three foundational treatises that not only informed the political and cultural policies in these divided entities but also shaped their respective cultural mentalities during the Cold War years: Mao Zedong's 1940 "Xin minzhu zhuyi lun" (On new democracy), the New Confucianists' 1958 "Wei Zhongguo wenhua jinggao shijie renshi xuanyan" (A manifesto to the world on behalf of Chinese culture), and Chiang Kai-shek's 1953 "Minsheng zhuyi yule liangpian bushu" (Supplementary treatises on education and recreation to the "Principle of Livelihood"). By doing so, I seek to demonstrate that the institutionalization of modern Chinese literary study was entailed by the Cold War confrontations between various Chinese political entities. Just like the modernization process itself, modern Chinese literature is a contested subject, perpetually unfinished and subject to constant interpretations and reinventions.

The Institutionalization of Modern Chinese Literary Study in the People's Republic

The new subject of modern Chinese literature was first introduced in the People's Republic of China in the early years after its foundation in 1949. Although modern Chinese literature was taught a couple of times during the Republican period, it was never institutionalized in the university curriculum.[1] In 1950, the Ministry of Education of the newly founded socialist state issued a national curriculum program for institutions of higher education and designated the history of modern Chinese literature as a mandatory course for all Chinese majors. The following year, the "Pedagogical Outline for the History of New Chinese Literature" (draft) [*Zhongguo xin wenxueshi jiaoxue dagang (chugao)*] was composed collectively by Lao She, Cai Yi, Wang Yao, and Li Helin overseen by state bureaucracy: it stipulated the nature, methodology, and teaching plans of modern Chinese literature.[2] To meet the need for a textbook for this young discipline, Wang Yao rushed to complete a literary history, which was published with the title *Zhongguo xin wenxue shigao* (A draft history of new Chinese literature, 1951–52). More literary histories followed. By the outbreak of the Cultural Revolution, there were altogether thirty works of literary history published, all serving as college textbooks. In the process of the reorganization of colleges and departments (*yuanxi tiaozheng*) from 1953 to 1957,[3] the national curriculum program created a specialization in modern Chinese literature in the Department of Chinese Language and Literature with a requirement of a total of thirty-five units, which completed the institutionalization

---

1. Zhu Ziqing (1898–1948) taught the first modern Chinese literature course at Tsinghua University in 1929. It was offered only once before it was forcibly dropped from the curriculum. Shen Congwen offered courses on modern Chinese literature during 1930–31 at Wuhan University. See Chen Pingyuan, *Zuowei xueke de wenxueshi*, pp. 392–409.

2. The outline was first published in the magazine *Xin jianshe* (New construction) 4, no. 4 (July 1951) in Beijing, later collected in Li Helin et al., *Zhongguo xin wenxueshi yanjiu*, published the same year, pp. 1–18. The selection of group members is noteworthy. The group consisted of the veteran writer Lao She, who was at the time considered a progressive and patriotic writer; Li Helin, the scholar who composed a leftist literary history reflecting Mao Zedong's revolutionary historical view in the 1940s; Wang Yao, professor of Chinese literature at Tsinghua University who was at the time writing a literary history; and Cai Yi, the Party literary theorist. See Huang Xiuji, *Zhongguo xin wenxueshi bianzhuanshi*.

3. For a discussion of the formation and transformation of the higher education system in the People's Republic of China, see Hayhoe and Zhong, "University Autonomy and Civil Society," pp. 99–123; Hayhoe, *China's Universities, 1895–1995*, pp. 71–110.

of modern literary study. Modern Chinese literature thus appeared in the PRC curriculum as a fundamental branch of knowledge.

Why, we might wonder, did the young socialist state give such great urgency and priority to constructing modern Chinese literary study? Why literature? As is well argued by theorists of nationalism, cultural forces played a central role in the building of the nation-state, which helped to produce a sense of national consciousness and national identity.[4] Upon the founding of the People's Republic, the state-administered construction of a national literature was no doubt a significant part of the process of nation building and of claiming cultural and political legitimacy for the Communist Party. For the last couple of decades, scholars of Chinese literature have started to pay attention to the sociopolitical circumstances under which modern Chinese literature as a discipline emerged in the early years of the PRC. In his significant article "'Dangdai wenxue' de gainian" (The concept of "contemporary literature"), Hong Zicheng discusses the ideological implications inherent in the seemingly transparent disciplinary concepts *xiandai wenxue* (modern literature) and *dangdai wenxue* (contemporary literature). In a series of articles, He Guimei examines the creation of modern Chinese literature as a new discipline and its cultural significance in the establishment of the PRC's pedagogical system of higher learning during the 1950s and 1960s.[5]

However, the ascendancy of modern Chinese literature has hardly been treated in the context of the global Cold War geopolitical order. It is my contention that the establishment of a national culture at the 1949 divide must be understood as conditioned by the Cold War cultural politics. Facing the formation of the bipolar world order, the Chinese Communists had decided to join the socialist camp led by the Soviet Union even before they seized state power. The PRC's self-assertion in the Eastern bloc created a dual dimension for this body of literature: at once socialist and national. This literature was envisioned as representing both distinctive national features and the international position of the new nation. Confronted with the Na-

4. The most important thesis can be found in Benedict Anderson's seminal work, *Imagined Communities*.

5. Hong Zicheng, "'Dangdai wenxue' de gainian"; He Guimei, "Xiandai, dangdai, wusi" and "'Xiandai wenxue' de queli."

tionalist regime's "free China" situated on the other shore, the socialists had to construct a national literature from a body of works that had its very roots in bourgeois enlightenment formed in the Republican era. How to transform the Republican literature (new literature) into a Communist literature (modern literature, or new democratic literature) was a question of utmost urgency. The invention of modern Chinese literature as a literature of "new democracy" led by the Communists laid the foundation on which the People's Republic could claim a new China as an antithesis to its Cold War other, the Nationalists who had just retreated to Taiwan.

In considering the ascendency of modern Chinese literature in the PRC, it is pertinent to examine the role of state power in the construction of a humanistic program and, in particular, the literature curriculum. Since the 1970s, scholars in the sociology of knowledge and education, such as Michael F. D. Young, Basil Bernstein, and Pierre Bourdieu, have sought to treat the curriculum critically not as absolute and value neutral, but as "the organized and codified reflection of societal and ideological interests."[6] Building on works in educational sociology, Gauri Viswanathan, in her influential book *Masks of Conquest*, examines the institutionalization of English literature in colonial India in the nineteenth century to elucidate the relationship between the process of curricular selection and the exercise of colonial power. In exploring the masking effects of the curriculum in the institutionalization of modern Chinese literature, it is well to recall Viswanathan's argument that "the curriculum is conceived here not in the perennialist sense of an objective, essentialized entity but rather as discourse, activity, process—as one of the mechanisms through which knowledge is socially distributed and culturally validated."[7]

One important step in the establishment of a modern Chinese literary curriculum was the renaming of the subject: replacing the original term *xin wenxue* (new literature) with *xiandai wenxue* (modern literature). In literary criticism and literary history during the pre-1949 period of the Republic of China, the term *xin wenxue* was used to designate the new type of literature born out of the May

---

6. Sadovnik, *Knowledge and Pedagogy*.
7. Viswanathan, *Masks of Conquest*, p. 3.

Fourth movement, as opposed to *jiu wenxue* (old or traditional literature), which was considered as archaic and hindering the modernization of the Chinese nation.[8] The compilation of the ten-volume *Zhongguo xin wenxue daxi* (Compendium of new Chinese literature, 1935–36) edited by Zhao Jiabi (1908–97), marked an early canonization of new Chinese literature and laid the foundation for modern Chinese literary historiography.[9] The assertion of the term *xiandai wenxue* occurred around 1956, the same time when the CCP declared that the country had completed its socialist transformation and was entering an epoch of socialism. Therefore, the renaming signified not only a reinvention of modern Chinese literature within the time frame of new democracy but also the necessity to make room for a new literature of the highest order—socialist literature named *dangdai wenxue*, as has been well pointed out by the PRC contemporary literary historian Hong Zicheng.[10]

The transition from "new literature" to "modern literature" does not merely reflect a change name. Rather, these labels are more concerned with disparate ways of conceptualizing literary modernity in Chinese literature between 1919 and 1949. The distinction is conspicuously elucidated in the "Pedagogical Outline for History of New Chinese Literature (draft)," which stated that new literature is "literature of new democracy" (*xin minzhu zhuyi wenxue*), not "ver-

---

8. "New Literature" appears in book titles including Zhou Zuoren's *Zhongguo xin wenxue de yuanliu* (Sources of new Chinese literature) (Beijing: Beiping renwen shudian, 1932); Lu Yongheng's *Zhongguo xin wenxue gailun* (A brief study of new Chinese literature) (Guangzhou: Kewen yinwuju, 1932); Wang Zhefu's *Zhongguo xin wenxue yundong shi* (A history of the movements of new Chinese literature) (Beijing: Beiping jiecheng yinshuju, 1933); Wang Fengyuan's *Zhongguo xin wenxue yundong shupin* (On new Chinese literary movements) (Beijing: Xinxin xueshe, 1935); and so on. For a discussion of these early works on modern Chinese literature, see Huang Xiuji, *Zhongguo xin wenxueshi bianzhuanshi*; also see Zhang Yingjin, "Institutionalization of Modern Literary History."

9. *Zhongguo xin wenxue daxi* (Compendium of new Chinese literature), 10 volumes, ed. Zhao Jiabi (Shanghai: Liangyou, 1935–36). For a discussion of the compilation of the *Compendium of New Chinese Literature* and its role in canonizing modern Chinese literature, see Lydia H. Liu, *Translingual Practice*, pp. 214–38.

10. As Hong Zicheng argues, it was the creation of *dangdai wenxue* (contemporary literature) that gave birth to the subject of *xiandai wenxue* (modern literature); see Hong, "'Dangdai wenxue' de gainian."

nacular literature (*baihua wenxue*), nor literature in the national language (*guoyu wenxue*), nor human literature (*rende wenxue*), nor plebeian literature (*pingmin de wenxue*)."[11] Ideas such as individualism, vernacular language, and egalitarianism, which had been foregrounded in new literature narratives of the Republican era, were disavowed as bourgeois and reactionary. For the young socialist state, it was the revolutionary Marxist view "combined with specific national characteristics"[12] rather than the humanistic values of enlightenment that rendered Chinese literature distinctively new and modern.

In this foundational writing of the modern Chinese literature curriculum, the main historical and cultural thesis was formulated by Mao Zedong in his January 1940 essay, "On New Democracy." In this seminal essay, written at a time when the Communists and the Nationalists still formed a united front against Japan in the Second Sino-Japanese War (1937–45), Mao charts the essential course of development of Chinese revolution, society, and culture through three distinctive phases: old democracy, new democracy, and ultimately socialism. Accordingly, he designates three different types of culture: the old democratic literature that served the semifeudal, semicolonial Nationalist regime; the new democratic literature that had emerged since the May Fourth movement under the leadership of the Communist Party; and the Chinese socialist literature that was yet to come upon the success of the Chinese Revolution. After the founding of the People's Republic, Mao's cultural blueprint was finally materialized and institutionalized through the intervention of the state apparatus. Party theorists and literary scholars of the young socialist state made every effort to come up with a modern Chinese literary history that fit into the conceptual framework of Mao's theory laid out in his theses such as "On New Democracy" and "Talks at the Yan'an Forum on Literature and Art."[13]

---

11. Li Helin et al., *Zhongguo xin wenxueshi yanjiu*, pp. 3–4.

12. Mao Zedong, "Xin minzhu zhuyi lun," p. 707.

13. Mao's revolutionary historiography lays the foundation for the historical view of the leftist camp. Through various interpretations by leftist and party theorists such as Zhou Yang (1908–89), Mao Dun (1896–1981), and Guo Moruo (1892–1978), who presented talks at the first congress of Chinese writers, the framework was set for the new conceptualization of modern Chinese literature.

For example, Wang Yao's *A Draft History of New Chinese Literature*[14] is generally regarded as the first academic attempt to apply the Maoist historical outlook and methodology to reconstructing modern Chinese literary history. It explicates modern Chinese literature as "the reflection of the Chinese new democratic revolution in the literary field. It's a way to utilize the weapon of art to fight against imperialism and feudalism, and to educate the people; therefore, it is bound to be part of the Chinese new democratic revolution, and is closely connected with political struggle."[15] Presented in strict conformity with the periodization of modern Chinese revolutionary history outlined in Mao's "On New Democracy," the history of modern Chinese literature was conceived as a linear process spearheaded by Communist revolutionary ideology and moving toward the telos of socialist realism.

In "On New Democracy," which lays the foundation for the CCP's nation-building theory, Mao went to great lengths to envision a national literature for a new nation and gave a special significance to cultural construction, as has been noted repeatedly in the extensive scholarship on Mao's revolutionary theory. In this regard, it is pertinent to highlight an embedded controversy in Mao's theoretical formulation of culture. Embracing Karl Marx's (1818–83) idea that culture is determined by politics and economy, Mao explicated that "any given culture (as a culture of ideology) is a reflection of the politics and economy of a given society, and the former in turn has a great influence and effect upon the latter."[16] However, Mao also granted culture a substantial role in the process of establishing political domination, which resonated with Antonio Gramsci's notion of hegemony that argues for a close connection between political and intellectual

---

14. Although the term "modern Chinese literature" was officially adopted in literary history in 1956, the basic rationale of this new body of knowledge had already been set out in literary criticism and history in the early years of the People's Republic. In 1956, the CCP declared that the social transformation into socialism has finished, thus ending the phase of new democracy. Therefore, it became urgent to make room for a new type of literature for socialist China, the *dangdai wenxue*. This is one reason why the term *xiandai wenxue* was officially adopted for works of literary history thereafter.

15. Wang Yao, *Zhongguo xin wenxue shigao*, p. 2.

16. Mao Zedong, "Xin minzhu zhuyi lun," p. 663–64.

dominance. Both thinkers regarded culture as a constituent element of social life, thus deviating from the classic view of Marxist historical materialism that "it is not the consciousness of men that determines their being, but, on the contrary, their social being that determines their consciousness."[17] Scholars such as John Cammett, Nigel Todd, and Jerome Karabel have drawn extensive attention to striking similarities between Mao and Gramsci on Marxism.[18] For our purposes, it is well to recall Arif Dirlik's observation that for both Mao and Gramsci, "the cultural and the educational task appeared as a prerevolutionary rather than a postrevolutionary task."[19] In his *Selections from the Prison Notebooks* written during the 1930s, Gramsci argues that cultural domination works by consent and can precede seizure of governmental power by armed force: "the supremacy of a social group manifests itself in two ways, as 'domination' and as 'intellectual and moral leadership.'"[20] Any politically dominant class is also ideologically dominant. In his efforts to control the field of literature and art and to seize the power of narration toward nation building, Mao was well aware of the importance of moral and intellectual suasion in matters of governance. "On New Democracy" is hence both a political thesis and a cultural manifesto, ascertaining the Communists' political dominion and intellectual superiority. In this perspective, just as Raymond Williams observes in his reading of Gramsci, hegemony is "in the strongest sense a 'culture.'"[21]

The institutionalization of modern Chinese literary study in the People's Republic was a significant part of establishing cultural and political legitimacy of the Communist Party, which reveals the important relationship between cultural hegemony and political coercion.

---

17. Karl Marx, "Preface to 'A Contribution to the Critique of Political Economy,'" in *Karl Marx: Selected Writings*, ed. David McLellan (Oxford: Oxford University Press, 1977), p. 181.

18. John Cammett, *Antonio Gramsci and the Origins of Italian Communism* (Stanford, CA: Stanford University Press, 1967); Nigel Todd, "Ideological Superstructure in Gramsci and Mao Tse-tung," *Journal of the History of Ideas* 35 (Jan./Mar. 1974): 148–56; Jerome Karabel, "Revolutionary Contradictions: Antonio Gramsci and the Problem of Intellectuals," *Politics and Society* 6, no. 2 (1976): 123–72.

19. Dirlik, "Predicament of Marxist Revolutionary Consciousness," p. 185.

20. Gramsci, *Selections from the Prison Notebooks*, p. 57.

21. Williams, *Marxism and Literature*, p. 110.

Whereas the construction of modern Chinese literature as a new disciplinary branch of knowledge has been part of the process of building a Chinese national literature on the socialist mainland, in Hong Kong it bespeaks cultural nationalism and cultural deterritorialization, which I consider in the following section.

Fashioning Cultural Authenticity in Hong Kong

After the Chinese mainland turned Communist and the Nationalists retreated to Taiwan, many Chinese intellectuals and writers migrated to the British colony of Hong Kong, where most of them stayed. This section considers three instances that reflect deterritorialized cultural imaginations of a modern China in post-1949 Hong Kong. First, the colonial government's institutionalization of traditional Chinese culture cast a modern Chinese identity in the abstract. Second, the so-called *nanlai zuojia* (writers coming to the south) formed a conception of modern Chinese literature that envisioned a Chinese national identity with pure national language and lyrical authenticity. Third, the New Confucianism in exile fashioned a modern Chinese nation in nationalist culturalism marked by a Confucian democracy.

In Hong Kong, modern Chinese literature did not appear as a subject in the curriculum until the 1960s. The first university course in modern Chinese literature was offered by Li Huiying (1911–91) in 1967 at the United College of the Chinese University of Hong Kong. In the late 1960s, Xu Xu (1908–80) and Sima Changfeng (1920–80) started to teach modern Chinese literature at Hong Kong Baptist College. At the University of Hong Kong, the official university of the colony, courses on modern Chinese literature were not offered until the mid-1970s. Even then, it was never a favored subject in the colonial curriculum. The virtual absence of a modern Chinese literature is the flip side of the emphatic promotion of traditional Chinese culture by the colonial government since the 1920s to balance against contemporary Chinese nationalism.

After the Cold War Bamboo Curtain was sealed along the Taiwan Strait, this educational ideology took on yet another dimension that was epitomized by the secondary school curriculum for Chinese studies. For Chinese culture classes before 1949, Hong Kong schools used the same textbooks and syllabi prescribed by the Nanjing government for mainland Chinese schools. Such a Hong Kong–China continuum on the educational front terminated with the 1949 divide. Although Hong Kong now served as a crucial link on the Cold War East Asian frontiers for the containment of communism, its colonial rulers considered both Communist propaganda and Nationalist ultranationalist anti-Communist convictions detrimental. Consequently, Hong Kong schools did not regard textbooks on Chinese studies newly published on both sides of the Taiwan Strait as suitable. Facing the urgent need to reconstruct the curriculum and produce its own textbooks on the subject of Chinese culture, the Education Department of the Hong Kong government appointed a Committee on Chinese Studies in 1952 to review the questions of Chinese language, literature, and history in the curricula of primary and secondary schools. The committee denounced previous versions of Chinese studies for "producing ignorant and bigoted Chinese nationalists" and set a new goal for Chinese studies in Hong Kong: by acquiring proficiency in the Chinese language, literature, and history, Hong Kong children should be able to communicate between China and the West. Only then could they "become modern Chinese, conscious of their own culture and at the same time having a liberal, balanced and international outlook."[22]

In the statement of this goal, the subject of Chinese studies was cast as a fortress to dissociate Hong Kong from both Communist and Nationalist ideologies and to foster "modern Chinese" with a cosmopolitan view. It is ironic that the British colonial power now turned into the most diligent Cold War sponsor of the same cultural tradition whose demise it had triggered a century before, in a primal moment that initiated the poignant process of Chinese modernization. Paradoxically, being "modern" and "Chinese" is measured by proficiency in a Chinese cultural tradition that is frozen in a time capsule of the past and by a liberal, international outlook that is oriented toward the modern, the global, and the present. The colonial educational discourse implied that instruction in Chinese cultural traditions would lead to a benign cosmopolitanism among modern Chinese, whereas modern Chinese language, literature, and history that evolved from

22. Luk, "Chinese Culture in the Hong Kong Curriculum," pp. 659–60.

the same cultural sources should be dismissed for producing xenophobic narrow nationalism. This logic came to the conclusion that Chinese nationalism could be contained by teaching the Chinese their own cultural tradition in order to prop up their cultural confidence and national pride. It is impossible not to be struck by its inherent contradiction: How was a national identity without the substance of the nation ever possible? Was the emperor wearing any clothes, after all? Ironically, with the rise of decolonization and nationalism in the Cold War era, the colonial education administration countered by institutionalizing Chinese culture, a formula that, as Bernard Luk observes, aimed "for Chinese culture and British colonialism to survive together in the shadow of Communist threat."[23] The alliance in Hong Kong generated a Chineseness in the idealized national culture severed from any tangible political reality, "a Chinese identity in the abstract."[24]

The entangled relations of culturalism and nationalism, culture and polity take different forms in two fields that are intricately related with the official colonial educational ideology: that of modern Chinese literature and that of New Confucianism in Hong Kong. Among the handful of works of modern Chinese literary history written and published in Hong Kong, all by "writers coming to the south," Sima Changfeng's three-volume *Zhongguo xin wenxue shi* (History of new Chinese literature, 1975, 1976, 1978) was the most influential and controversial.[25] Given the poor market for modern Chinese literary history in Hong Kong, the book sold surprisingly

23. Ibid., p. 667.

24. Ibid., p. 668.

25. Very few works on modern Chinese literature were written and published in Hong Kong. In his study of modern Chinese literary historiography in post-1949 Hong Kong, Wong Wang-chi lists Cao Juren's *Wentan wushi nian*; Li Huiying's *Zhongguo xiandai wenxueshi* (History of modern Chinese literature) (Hong Kong: Dongya shuju, 1970); Sima Changfeng's three-volume *Zhongguo xin wenxue shi* (History of new Chinese literature) (Hong Kong: Chiu Ming Publishing House, 1975, 1976, 1978); Xu Xu's *Xiandai Zhongguo wenxue guoyan lu* (Reflections on modern Chinese literature) (Taipei: Shibao wenhua, 1991). See Wong, *Lishi de ouran*. All four of these authors were exiled writers who came to Hong Kong after the 1949 divide. Initially, literary history books published in the PRC were still available in Hong Kong. However, after the border completely closed in 1951, it was no more the case.

well, with three reprints.[26] It exerted a huge impact in post–Cultural Revolution mainland China and propelled PRC scholars to approach modern Chinese literature beyond the strictures of socialist realism. However, it was heavily criticized by a number of scholars for its lack of academic rigor and careless scholarship.[27] What is striking about Sima's *History of New Chinese Literature* are two central themes, literariness and Chineseness, and how their conceptualization in the unique sociopolitical context of Hong Kong raised interesting questions about nationalism, aesthetic autonomy and authenticity, and Cold War cultural politics. With its contentious conception of literary and national purity, Sima's work presents an intriguing notion of literary modernity in the interstices of the British colony and the two competing political regimes across the Taiwan Strait.

Sima delineates the rationale of his literary history as follows: "First, this is a new literary history that breaks any political shackles and takes purely literature as the guiding principle; second, this is a new literary history written from a pure Chinese heart."[28] His conception of modern Chinese literature is characterized by its pure literariness and Chineseness. His strong stance against political control of literature, especially by communism, led him to a notion of literary autonomy as an oppositional space. Anything bearing the taint of political contamination was suspicious. By this criterion, Lu Xun's "Guxiang" (My hometown) and "Zai jiulou shang" (In the wineshop) deserved higher regard than the writer's commonly acclaimed "Kuangren riji" (Diary of a madman) or "Ah Q zhengzhuan" (The true story of Ah Q). Whereas the latter carried heavy-handed political

---

26. Sima Changfeng wrote the *History of New Chinese Literature* when he taught modern Chinese literature at Hong Kong Baptist College in early 1970s. In a way, it was conceived as textbook for his course. It was published by Chiu Ming Publishing House, the leading education publisher in Hong Kong known for its publication of textbooks and supplementary materials for college admission examinations.

27. C. T. Hsia, "Xiandai zhongguo wenxue shi." Similar criticisms are also offered by Wong Wang-chi. Kwok Kou Leonard Chan, on the contrary, argues that Sima's work provides an alternative writing of literary history. On his part, C. T. Hsia laid the groundwork for modern Chinese literature as a discipline in the United States with the publication of his *History of Modern Chinese Fiction* in 1961.

28. Sima, *Zhongguo xin wenxueshi*, p. 324.

messages, the former were characterized by their "sincere feelings and poetic sentiments."[29] Ba Jin's *Hanye* (Cold nights, 1947) was a much finer work than his early *Jia* (Family, 1933), for by the late 1940s, "his narrative skills had reached perfection, and he had developed a sense of sincerity and piety toward literature and art and got rid of politics completely, thus turning into an utterly independent writer."[30]

Sima's vigilance against political encroachment upon literature might not seem far from the prevalent notion of depoliticized art promoted by the Western bloc of the Cold War, such as "high modernism," which was canonized as official American culture in the 1950s to show that "the United States was the bastion of liberal ideals in a world threatened by Communist totalitarianism."[31] In this sense, despite the unfavorable position of modern Chinese literature, Sima's notion of literary autonomy might have been a good fit in Cold War Hong Kong, a strategic outpost of democracy in the containment of communism. The notion of aesthetic autonomy has been nothing new any more since the birth of modernism. What is distinctive in Sima's conception of authentic autonomy, however, is his emphasis on emotional sincerity. In Sima's evaluations of modern Chinese writers and their works, one can hardly miss the frequent usage of notions such as "sincere feelings," "lyrical nature," "authentic emotion," and so on. For him, the literariness of a work lies in its capacity to reflect on the times with profound lyricism. He terms this capacity *jixing de yanzhi*, which he delineates as "the finest faculty of a creative mind" that "articulates one's mind without falling prey to political instrumentality or suppression of one's thought and emotion."[32] Sima derives this notion from Zhou Zuoren's classification of literature into *yanzhi* (literature to articulate aims) and *zaidao* (literature to convey the Way).[33] Inspired by late Ming literature, Zhou maintains that "literature only has *ganqing* (emotions) and no *mudi* (aims)," hence close

29. Ibid., pp. 107–8.
30. Ibid., p. 72.
31. Harvey, *The Condition of Postmodernity*, p. 37.
32. Sima, *Zhongguo xin wenxue shi*, p. 110.
33. Zhou Zuoren, *Zhongguo xin wenxue*, pp. 17–27.

to the "lyrical" in European literary traditions.[34] The lyrical is precisely the aesthetic quality that Sima emphatically expounds in his narrative of modern Chinese literature. Such a propensity should not be dismissed as merely the excessive "sentimentalism" of an émigré. As Kwok Kou Leonard Chan reminds us, Sima's lyricism was intended to "create a connection with the real world, and to contest the political view in the dominant discourse of modern Chinese literary history."[35]

Lyrical authenticity marked an essential element in Sima's conception of Chineseness in modern Chinese literature. Furthermore, he maintained that a pure national identity was embodied in a pure national language. Whereas the construction of a vernacular language (*baihua*) was one central task of the May Fourth New Culture Movement, Sima went much further to pursue a pure modern national language uninflected by either European languages or regional dialects. In his view of the development of modern literature, this pure Chinese language, freed from arduous Europeanized or dialect expressions, finally appeared during the Second Sino-Japanese War, when nationwide migration brought about the merging of regional tongues and facilitated the birth of a "new rich national language."[36] Critics were upset by his linguistic obsession and dismissed it as a mere "formalistic view."[37] K. K. Leonard Chan, however, points out that it must be considered in the linguistic and cultural context of Hong Kong, where Sima arrived as a migrant after the 1949 divide. Considering the dominance of English and local Cantonese, it is difficult and contentious to promote a particular Chineseness, literary or linguistic, in the British colony. Sima was himself aware of such an awkward cultural position. In reflecting on the competition between classical Chinese and the vernacular in imperial China, he makes an analogy with the linguistic rivalry between Chinese and

---

34. Ibid., p. 14. For a discussion of the lyrical attribute in Zhou Zuoren's work, see Pollard, *A Chinese Look at Literature*.

35. K. K. Leonard Chan, *Wenxueshi shuxie xingtai*, p. 227.

36. Sima, *Zhongguo xin wenxue shi*, p. 156. Such a view was shared by recent mainland Chinese scholarship on modern Chinese literature, such as Qian Liqun's *Duihua yu manyou*, which foregrounds the pure linguistic quality of works in the 1940s by Sun Li, Xiao Hong, Shen Congwen, among others.

37. Wang Jiancong, "Ping Sima Changfeng," p. 40.

English in Hong Kong: although Chinese was one official language in Hong Kong, it could not compete with English as the dominant language in a British colony.[38] However, for that very reason, such a linguistic and cultural resolution held sway all the more absolutely and meaningfully. Sima's insistence on a pure vernacular Chinese betrayed his determination to cling to a national consciousness outside of the Chinese mainland.

By defending the linguistic and lyrical bona fides of modern Chinese literature, Sima constructs a narrative of modern Chinese literary history that was an alternative both to the mainstream one freshly produced in the PRC, also available at the time in Hong Kong, and to those written in other political entities during the Cold War years. In a reminiscent essay on Tang Junyi (1909–78), the New Confucian scholar who also came to Hong Kong after 1949, Sima remarks that Tang's post-1949 writings were marked by a deep lyrical sentiment that resulted from his grief about the motherland. Sima's own writings in Hong Kong, including his history of modern Chinese literature, are also shot through with nostalgic lyricism. In his recharting of modern Chinese literature, lyrical sincerity constitutes the foundation of an authentic Chineseness. Authenticity is thus deployed in this exiled invention of modern Chinese literature nostalgically and lyrically. Sima's literary history can thus be regarded as having constructed an alternative lyrical modernity in Cold War Hong Kong, an invention that created a significant space for the unwelcome subject of modern Chinese literature in the colonial curriculum.

Such a heartfelt effort to fashion a cultural armor can also be found in the cultural statement coauthored by Tang Junyi, Zhang Junmai (a.k.a. Carsun Chang, 1886–1969), Mou Zongsan (1909–95), and Xu Fuguan (1902/03–82), later regarded as the foundational declaration of the overseas New Confucianism.[39] Like the scholars

---

38. Sima, *Zhongguo xin wenxue shi*, p. 25.

39. Tang et al., "Wei Zhongguo wenhua" (A manifesto to the world on behalf of Chinese culture). Let's map out the exilic routes of the four signatories of the New Confucianism Manifesto, which is important to consider its cultural and political implications. After the 1949 divide, Tang Junyi fled from Chinese mainland to Hong Kong, where he founded *Xinya shuyuan* (New Asia College) together with Qian Mu and Zhang Peijie, as a cultural fortress to study and promote Chinese culture. New Asia College later became one of the colleges of the Chinese Univer-

of modern Chinese literature discussed previously, New Confucianists in Hong Kong endeavored to construct a national culture beyond mainland China. On January 1, 1958, this group of New Confucianists issued "Wei Zhongguo wenhua jinggao shijie renshi xuanyan" (A manifesto to the world on behalf of Chinese culture), which was published simultaneously in the Hong Kong journal *Minzhu pinglun* (Democratic criticism), founded by Xu Fuguan, and the Taiwan journal *Zaisheng* (Rebirth).[40] That Confucianism found a place of rebirth in Cold War Hong Kong, under the British imperial power whose aggression partially forced Confucianism out of the Chinese mainland, is ironic yet poignant.

This manifesto provides yet another intriguing imaginary of a modern China with a distinctive national culture. It summons Confucian values as a means of building a culturalist modern China. Its appeal to Confucianism, however, does not make it less modern or progressive than the cultural propositions concerning modern Chinese literature. In effect, distinctions between notions of conservative and progressive, modern and antimodern, are redundant in discussions of Chinese cultural imaginations at the Cold War divide. In her study of the National Essence movements of the early twentieth century, Lydia H. Liu argues that those scholars who advocated a revival of the traditional learning should not be viewed simply as antimodern conservatives.[41] In emphatically asserting a universal humanistic value in Confucianism and locating in it a national essence of the Chinese, they shared the same discursive ground as their opponents, the May Fourth New Culturalists, and were active participants in the same national-building and cultural-modernization project of which the latter claimed to be the sole legitimate champions. The same can be argued about post-1949 New Confucianism. In the manifesto, the four signatories envision a modern Chinese

---

sity of Hong Kong established in 1963. Tang Junyi became the head of the Philosophy Department. Mou Zongsan first came to Taiwan, then moved to Hong Kong two years after signing the Manifesto. Carsun Chang lived in the United States after a short stay in Hong Kong and India. Xu Fuguan chose to flee to Taiwan, where he stayed politically critical of the Nationalist Party.

40. Ibid. Carsun Chang's English translation of the manifesto, "Manifesto for a Re-appraisal," outlines the main issues of the Chinese original.

41. Lydia H. Liu, *Translingual Practice*, pp. 239–64.

nation predicated on the establishment of a democratic polity and a Confucian philosophy.

However, the New Confucianism's emphasis on traditional Chinese learning made it a relatively safe cultural bastion in the interstices of British colonial rule and the binary ideological antagonism of the East Asian Cold War. The agenda of promoting Confucian values was ironically complementary to the colonial government's accommodative cultural policy that attempted to fabricate a China of antiquity, inoculated against real politics. Accordingly to the 1841 Elliot proclamation, the inhabitants of Hong Kong were to "be governed, pending Her Majesty's further pleasure, according to the laws, customs, and usages of Chinese." The colonial government's principle of positive noninterventionism in Hong Kong opened up a space for the preservation and promotion of a national culture for exiled intellectuals. As long as they were not menacing the British authority directly, they were tolerated and enjoyed some freedom of speech and publication. On this point, it is pertinent to note the crucial geopolitical position of Hong Kong as a Cold War free port in alignment with the United States in the containment of Communist China.[42] Just like the notion of literary autonomy highlighted by modern Chinese literary scholars in Hong Kong, the cultural authenticity of Confucianism rendered the construction of a cultural China a seemingly apolitical cause within the sphere of toleration of the colonial government. Aesthetic autonomy and cultural traditionalism are redeemed as politically immune notions promoted by the Cold War cultural policy and sanctified in academies in other parts of the free world. The canonization of high modernism in the United States during the Cold War era is a salient example.[43]

The manifesto sought to undertake a cultural reflection aspiring to a Chinese nation building. The four signatories lament that almost a half century after the downfall of the Qing dynasty and the Republican Revolution, the Chinese nation has not yet completed its

---

42. For a discussion of Hong Kong's geopolitical position in the relationship between the KMT government and the United Kingdom during the Cold War years, see Tsang, *Cold War's Odd Couple*, pp. 165–84.

43. For a discussion of the rise of high modernism in the United States during the Cold War period, see Huyssen, *After the Great Divide*.

nation building.[44] They posit that neither the Nationalist nor the Communist regimes has succeeded in realizing a modern Chinese nation. They argue that a modern Chinese national citizen must be first of all a moral and cultural sovereign before becoming a political and epistemological subject. Only a national sovereignty based on citizens with characters of all these four aspects can be viewed as genuinely modern and democratic. They observe that Confucian learning has already borne primitive forms of democracy and science. The Confucian moral self-cultivation not only furthers modern political and technological developments but also, more importantly, is able to overcome their drawbacks as exposed in recent histories of modern Western countries. Therefore, the signatories assert that the prerequisite of modern nation building is the moral perfection of individual citizens and the cultivation of the national spirit.

Scholars have questioned the manifesto's problematic identification of Chinese national culture with Confucianism, the *xinxing* (mind and nature) Confucian tradition in particular.[45] Although its conceptualization of Chinese culture or of Confucianism might be debatable, its determination to preserve Chinese cultural heritage outside of the mainland is unmistakable. In locating in Confucian tradition as the foundation for establishing a democratic polity and a scientific philosophy, the New Confucianists attempted to construct a Chinese national consciousness as an essential force in nation building. The democratic Confucian sociopolitical imaginary projected onto the Chinese motherland bespeaks not only a sense of "emotional nostalgia," as Arif Dirlik notes in his article "Confucius in the Borderlands,"[46] but also, more importantly, that of cultural nationalism.

In the manifesto's statements such as "a nation's culture is the expression of its spiritual life,"[47] we can hear a definite echo of the notion of *Volksgeist* (the spirit of the folk, or nation) developed by Johann Gottfried Herder (1744–1803), the German philosopher who laid the groundwork for what would later be called cultural nationalism.

44. Tang et al., "Wei Zhongguo wenhua."

45. See, for instance, Hao Chang, "New Confucianism and the Intellectual Crisis."

46. Dirlik, "Confucius in the Borderlands," p. 234.

47. Carsun Chang, "Manifesto for a Re-appraisal," p. 465.

Considering the world as consisting of interrelated organisms, Herder defines "culture" as a unique entity and maintains that any legitimate political or social association must be a product of natural growth out of a common culture with a specific language and literary tradition.[48] Herder's theory of culture and *Volksgeist* was developed in late eighteenth-century Germany in the absence of a unified state, when a German nation was, as Johann Gottlieb Fichte (1762–1814) describes, held together "almost solely by the instrumentality of the man of letters, by speech, and writing."[49] Drawing strong inspirations from Herder and early Romanticists, the German historian Friedrich Meinecke (1862–1954) coined the term *Kulturnation* (cultural nation) as independent of *Staatsnation* (political nation) in the early twentieth century.[50] By appealing to the idea of a cultural nation, Meinecke distinguishes between two categories of nationalism, the political and the cultural. Cultural nationalism strives for a national consciousness based on its distinct culture, language, and tradition. When Prussia under Otto von Bismarck (1815–98) strove to form a unified German Reich in the late nineteenth century, a German cultural unity had already preceded and prefigured a political unification. As Peter Uwe Hohendahl argues, "guiding principles for the legitimation of the new Reich were discovered more in the history of literature than in the history of politics, where Prussians, Saxons, Holsteiners, and Württembergers could hardly be said to have a common fund of experience."[51]

Such a notion of a cultural nation was conspicuously missing from the intellectual discussions at the Cold War German division. As critics have pointed out, nation and nationalism became politically suspicious ideas as a result of the Nazi abuse of German nationalism. During the peak of the Cold War, writers in the Federal Republic of Germany such as Günter Grass even defended *Zweistaatlichkeit* (division into two states) predicated on substituting a cultural nation for a political one. Upon the German reunification that marked the end of the Cold War, the contradictory conception of *Kulturnation* vis-à-vis

48. Herder, *Outlines of a Philosophy.*
49. Fichte, *Addresses to the German Nation*, p. 217.
50. Meinecke, *Cosmopolitanism and the National State.*
51. Hohendahl, *Building a National Literature,* p. 196.

Staatsnation found its postnationalist variation in Jürgen Habermas's *Verfassungspatriotismus* (constitutional patriotism), which contends for a citizenship freed from its conventional ties to a specific nation: "the nation of citizens does not derive its identity from ethnic or cultural properties, but from the praxis of citizens who actively exercise their civil rights."[52]

At the 1949 Chinese state division, however, cultural nationalism took on a significant position in foreseeing a modern nation beyond the strictures of the Communist and Nationalist ideologies. In a national culture, exiled scholars such as the New Confucianists saw an alternative space to "transcend the split in the Chinese nation state between two competing regimes,"[53] as Elaine Yee Lin Ho observes in her reading of the manifesto from the discursive spaces of diaspora and nation. In his discussion of postcolonial India, Partha Chatterjee argues that the spiritual sphere that contained imprints of cultural distinctiveness was declared sovereign, hence beyond the control of colonial power.[54] In this regard, the construction of national culture served as a site of opposition to foreign rule. In his defense of nation and cultural nationalism in *The Necessary Nation*, Gregory Jusdanis extends Chatterjee's argument to "belated societies," including Greece, and argues that cultural nationalism is of utmost importance in nationalist and modernization programs because it promotes modernization while maintaining national identity and cultural distinctiveness.[55] For the New Confucianists in their diasporic sojourn in Hong Kong, cultural nationalism was conceived as a means to resist not so much the colonial rule in Hong Kong in particular, but the dominion of foreign ideologies, including Marxism and fascism, in recent Chinese history. The construction of a cultural nation was intended to promote both national sovereignty and modernization.

Severed from its motherland geographically, New Confucianism was the way of reaffirming Chinese cultural identity outside of China.

---

52. Habermas, "Citizenship and National Identity," p. 3. For a discussion of debates on nation, postnationalism, and normalization upon German reunification, see Huyssen, *Twilight Memories*, pp. 67–84.

53. Elaine Yee Lin Ho, "China Abroad," p. 17.

54. Chatterjee, *The Nation and Its Fragments*, p. 6.

55. Jusdanis, *The Necessary Nation*.

Envisioning a national identity in and through culture, New Confucianists conceived a "cultural nationalism in exile." However, such a geographical severance calls up questions about culture and polity, ethnos and topos. That the New Confucianists invoked an authentic culturalist China in Hong Kong, a colony under British sovereignty, raises questions about their own cultural positions: Can a cultural nation without political boundaries really exist?[56] How would cultural transmission without a national polity be possible and meaningful? Its Confucian utopian cosmopolitan evocation of *tian xia yi jia* (one family under heaven) notwithstanding, its central focus on a modern Chinese nation is unequivocal. On this point, it is well to recall the notion of *yimin* (loyalists) at dynastic transitions in Chinese history, which also bespeaks the ambiguous relations of cultural and political identification. Loyalists claimed to stay faithful to a lost dynasty and refused to acknowledge the legitimacy of the new conqueror. In insisting on the legitimate orthodox culture of the former dynasty, they helped preserve and transmit cultural heritage. However, in clinging to a lost time, they deprived themselves and the culture of which they claimed to be the sole legitimate bearers of an existing territory and lineage of transmission. The New Confucianists were not unaware of the lure and snare of loyalism. Mou Zongsan in his later years warned his fellow scholars not to turn into yet another Zhu Shunshui (1600–82), the controversial Ming loyalist exiled to Japan and who never again set foot on his native soil.

Modern Chinese Literature: The Negative Space in Taiwan

In Cold War China, modern Chinese literature and its historiography were employed as constituent parts of the production of national history and national imaginaries. Whereas the institutionalization of modern Chinese literature in the PRC acted as a pedagogical appara-

---

56. In her reflection on the dilemma of moving between essential and flexible citizenship in an age of transnationalism, Aihwa Ong questions the intrinsic entanglements of the neo-Confucianist notion of "cultural China" with Asian nationalism and capitalism. She contends that the Confucian revival since the 1980s in peripheral states of "a Greater China" reconnected Confucianism with the state power. Ong, "Chinese Modernities"; see also her book *Flexible Citizenship.* For the concept of a "cultural China," see Tu Wei-ming, "Cultural China."

tus to teach a national narrative about the rise of modern China along the path of socialist revolution, in post-1949 Taiwan such a narration of national history proceeded by eliminating the same subject and promoting anticommunist fiction that purported to rationalize the loss of the national land and to project its restoration. Accusing modern Chinese literature of being an ideological incubator for the rise of communism, the KMT regime censored all Chinese literature between 1919 and 1949. Virtually all writers were banned for their alleged complicity in advancing or conforming to communism. Two who survived the KMT's new literature paranoia were Xu Zhimo (1897–1931) and Zhu Ziqing (1898–1948), who were considered politically neutral and passed away "luckily" before the Communist takeover.[57] However, even virtually nonexistent, modern Chinese literature exerted a presence, occupying the negative space defined by the boundaries of the official culture in postwar Taiwan.

Realizing that the failure of the Nationalists was not just a military one but also a cultural one, the KMT regime stridently tightened its cultural policies shortly after its move to Taiwan. In 1950, the Committee on Chinese Literature and Art Awards (*Zhonghua wenyi jiangjin weiyuanhui*) was established under the directorship of Zhang Daofan (1897–1968), head of the Legislative Yuan, followed by the Chinese Literature and Art Association (*Zhongguo wenyi xiehui*) to implement the official "anti-Communist and counter-Soviet" (*fangong kang'e*) literary policy. The same year, in response to the slogan "Literature and Art into the Military" (*Wenyi dao junzhong qu*), the Ministry of National Defense founded a literary prize and a number of literary magazines to foster writers in the military service. Through literary publications and awards, these two cardinal institutions, among others, administered and sponsored the production of anticommunist fiction.[58] Reflecting on the KMT's defeat at the Communists' hands shortly after he assumed the presidency, Chiang Kai-shek stated that "the bandit communists painstakingly harnessed literature and the arts, instilling ideas of class struggles and class consciousness to the minds of the citizens through literature and drama.

57. Lü Zhenghui, *Zhanhou Taiwan wenxue jingyan*, pp. 185–96.

58. For a more detailed outline of the literary institutions in 1950s Taiwan, see Ying Fenghuang, "Fangong+xiandai."

As a result, the general public was impaired by either the yellow menace or the red poison."[59] A Cultural Hygiene Campaign (*Wenhua qingjie yundong*) was launched in 1954 to follow Chiang's admonition to ensure a mentally and morally healthy national body.[60]

Evidently, anticommunism was the top priority of KMT cultural policy in Taiwan. Within the decade, more than fifteen hundred writers engaged in the battle against communist evil in the republic of letters. Chen Jiying's *Dicun zhuan* (Fool in the reeds) and *Chidi* (Red land), Wang Lan's *Lan yu hei* (Blue and black), Pan Renmu's *Lianyi biaomei* (My cousin Lianyi), and Jiang Gui's *Xuanfeng* (Whirlwind) are among the best achievements. Although disregarded in later literary criticism as "eight-legged literature" that gave rise to the "white wasteland" of Taiwan literature, anticommunist fiction, as the defining literary genre of 1950s Taiwan, cannot simply be dismissed.[61] By emplotting the Communist rise and the defeat of the Nationalist regime on mainland China, this anticommunist *littérature engagée* practiced something no less serious than constructing a national history for the recently exiled Republic of China. Anticommunist writers endeavored to explain how the spread of communist ideology in Chinese society accelerated its moral, economic, and cultural collapse and ultimately resulted in the Nationalist debacle. However, the raison d'être for this kind of political fiction is not just to rationalize the Nationalist defeat but also to predicate the redemption of the lost mainland and the restoration of the Nationalist regime, which carried the mandate of history and culture. In other words, the rationalization of the national failure provides spiritual preparation and a weapon for the national resurrection.

Anticommunist literature was generally dismissed for its propagandist indoctrination and artistic ineptitude. Recent scholarship,

---

59. Chiang, "Minsheng zhuyi," p. 67.

60. For a discussion of literary policies in 1950s Taiwan, see Zheng Mingli, "Dangdai Taiwan wenyi zhengce."

61. Ye Shitao, *Taiwan wenxue shigang*, pp. 88–89. In recent years, a number of scholars in Taiwan and the United States including Jiang Baochai, Fan Mingru, Ying Fenghuang, Yvonne Sung-sheng Chang, and Mei Jialing have begun to reconsider Taiwan literature of the 1950s and to probe alternative literary writings to question the monophonic domination of anticommunist literature.

however, has started to reconsider this important genre.[62] Nostalgia and diaspora provided interlocked perspectives to examine this important literary genre born in a time of disintegration. The KMT regime's retreat to Taiwan after the loss of the civil war to the CCP brought millions of people to the island province. Such an unprecedented demographic migration caused traumatic separation in families, polities, and cultures. In dealing with temporal and spatial displacements, the anticommunist *littérature engagée,* which was saturated with nostalgic sentiments, fed the tremendous hunger of mainland expatriates for justice in both personal and national terms. Such an excessive sentimentality characterized other types of mainstream literature in the 1950s. Michelle Yeh observes that the new regulated verse of the 1950s was marked by its "sentimentality and shallow lyricism."[63] Essayistic writings proliferated during the 1950s Taiwan, permeated with literati sensibility and nostalgic sentiments, which were harshly attacked by the modernists rising in the 1960s. Sung-sheng Yvonne Chang attributes the boom of stylistic, traditionalist prose partly to "the dominant culture's selective emphasis on the lyrical strand of New Literature from the pre-1949 era."[64] The unbalanced selection of works by Xu Zhimo and Zhu Ziqing for middle-school textbooks contributed to the popularity of the former's flamboyant poetry and the latter's genteel prose.

General scholarship ascribes the failure of anticommunist literature to its artistic mediocrity, melodramatic maneuver, and emotional immoderation. David Der-wei Wang argues that those features might well be considered the virtue of any political fiction. He suggests that the impasse of this impossible genre lies in its "suicidal" tendency. Because anticommunist literature was intended to fight a war against communism, it was bound together with the success or the defeat of the Communist power, which was the very reason for its existence. Therefore, Wang notes that "vacillating between these two poles, anti-Communist literature became caught in existential indeterminacy;

62. Mei, *Xingbie, haishi jiaguo?*; David Der-wei Wang, *Monster That Is History*, pp. 148–82.

63. Yeh, "'On Our Destitute Dinner Table,'" p. 122.

64. S. Y. Chang, *Modernism and the Nativist Resistance*, p. 25.

either its success or its failure would obliterate it."[65] It is well to observe that this "existential indeterminacy" also attested to a temporal impasse, where it was stuck in an atrocious past, with no present, and with a future only attainable by more atrocity. More important, the predicament of this literary genre also originated from its inability to construct an alternative moral and cultural order. In its rage to expose the morbid social reality corroded by communist evil, it failed to realize that it actually demolished the very moral and cultural ground on which the Nationalist regime claimed its legitimacy. Or, even more dangerously, with works such as Jiang Gui's *Whirlwind*, which declares that it would "recount evils so as to admonish,"[66] history was presented in a cyclical course "drenched in buffoonery."[67] Such dissipation in anomaly did not leave any room for norms and the orthodox. If the Nationalist regime had existed on the same bedrock of historical monstrosity that was decayed through and through, how could an imminent rehabilitation on the same foundation be possible or desirable? In the process of witch-hunting, anticommunist work was too eager to identify and blame the Other before it could establish a proper moral or cultural foundation for the restoration of the Nationalist regime. Therefore, despite their strident anticommunist commitment, these political writers failed to project a national restoration.

In this regard, Chiang Kai-shek's 1953 "Minsheng zhuyi yule liangpian bushu" (Supplementary treatises on education and recreation to the "Principle of Livelihood") can be read as the archetype of anticommunist literature that served both purposes: to fight against communism and to imagine a restored nation. In this article, which spells out the theoretical foundation for the KMT cultural policies in Taiwan, Chiang not only asserts the political legitimacy of the Nationalist regime as the genuine inheritor of Sun Yat-sen's "Three Principles of the People" but also envisions a modern China with a moral and cultural renaissance. Chiang proposes that the improvement of people's livelihood must be based on cultural and moral constructions of the nation. Accordingly, he sets out to delineate in a

---

65. David Der-wei Wang, *Monster That Is History*, p. 159.
66. Jiang Gui, *Xuanfeng*.
67. C. T. Hsia, *History of Modern Chinese Fiction*, p. 631.

fastidious manner the "correct" types of culture, literature, arts, music, film, and theater, among other things, for modern Chinese citizens after the imminent restoration of the mainland temporarily occupied by the Communists. Chiang spares no effort to contend that cultural and moral cultivation are fundamental to the realization of a modern nation. In order to become a qualified citizen of a modern China, "he/she must obtain four types of education: moral, intellectual, physical, and social," with moral and social being the top priorities.[68] To that end, Chiang urges a revitalization of traditional moral and cultural values based on the ethics of Confucianism as a means to enhance the KMT's political and cultural legitimacy. He then lays out the blueprint for attaining a modern China through three steps: the anticommunist revolution, the construction of the people's livelihood, and the ultimate realization of "a free, secure society that is the *datong* world."[69] A modern nation was therefore envisaged on the foundation of traditional morality and conflated with a Confucian *datong* (utopian) world. Chiang continues an argument he made during the 1934 New Life movement (*Xin shenghuo yundong*), which reasserted traditional Confucian values to combat communist ideas. In his speech, "Essentials of the New Life Movement," Chiang stipulates that the four virtues, namely, *li* (ritual/decorum), *yi* (rightness or duty), *lian* (integrity or honesty), and *chi* (sense of shame), are "the essential principles for the promotion of morality," which is vital to save the nation from the precipice of irrationality.[70] In 1966, as a response to Mao's Great Proletarian Cultural Revolution, Chiang restated the same notion of building a traditional cultural bastion in his launch of the Chinese Cultural Renaissance movement (*Zhonghua wenhua fuxing yundong*), which was to reinstate the Nationalist regime as the legitimate carrier of Chinese culture.

Such cultural and moral conservatism constituted the base of the KMT's anticommunist policy. Indeed, the KMT waged a war for cultural and moral supremacy during its Cold War confrontation with Communist China. Ironically, the cultural heritage that the

---

68. Chiang, "Minsheng zhuyi," pp. 39–40.

69. Ibid., p. 86.

70. Chiang, *Xin shenghuo yundong yaoyi*. English translation comes from *Sources of Chinese Tradition*, p. 342.

KMT strove compellingly to defend was precisely the one disavowed by its antagonist across the Bamboo Curtain as feudal remnants curbing socialist modernization. The official ideology of "anticommunism and restoring the lost land" actually consisted of two different types of conflict: the war against communism and the war to reunite a severed nation. At the political strategic level, anticommunism and civil war were bound together. However, at the cultural level, they were not always without contradictions. Whereas the anticommunist mission pitted East against West and authoritarianism against democracy, the war to reunify a divided nation was a continuation of an anticolonial nationalist program aiming at building a modern China. Whereas *fangong kang'e* launched a war of arts and letters to rescue the nation from the enslavement of communism, the nationalist mission of *geming jianguo* (a revolution to build a nation) swore to realize a national renaissance to save a cultural heritage severely impaired by foreign encroachment ever since the May Fourth New Culture Movement. The two objectives that the Nationalist government sought to accomplish—anticommunism under Cold War American patronage and a nationalist moralist renaissance with a poignant anticolonial tenor—did not always make a perfect match. The chasm between these two orders contributed to the inherent predicament of anticommunist literature. The conflict would soon flare up more intensely in the crackdown on two magazines: *Ziyou Zhongguo* (Free China fortnightly) in 1960 and *Wenxing* (Literary star) in 1965, where liberal intellectual voices were smothered to maintain the KMT's nationalist program.

Although concepts of the European Enlightenment such as democracy and individualism sat high on the priority list of the Cold War anticommunist war of ideas, for the KMT government, the promotion of those ideas might not always be desirable. This inconsistency could be discerned in the KMT's ambivalent attitude to the May Fourth New Culture Movement. In reflecting on its debacle on the Chinese mainland, the KMT official discourse condemned the May Fourth movement for its excessive promotion of Western ideas of democracy and science at the cost of radical renunciation of Chinese cultural tradition. In *Zhongguo zhi mingyun* (China's destiny), which was first published in 1943 and reprinted numerous times in Taiwan, Chiang rebukes the May Fourth movement for bringing in two precarious Western ideas—"individual-oriented liberalism and Communism with a focus on class struggle."[71] The breach in the traditional culture and morality created a vacuum that allowed the invasion of foreign ideas and eventually the failure of the Nationalist cause. The 1934 New Life movement marked an early effort to challenge the May Fourth discourse for cultural hegemony. The production of the *Compendium of New Chinese Literature,* which involved the majority of May Fourth pioneers, was, as Lydia Liu suggests, a response to the repressive cultural policy stipulated by the New Life movement.[72] In modifying its cultural policy after retreating to Taiwan, the KMT government restated that the nationalist struggle to reunify the divided nation would only be successful if a national cultural heritage and morality could be restored. In a 1952 speech, Chiang remarked:

> I have once talked about the serious malady of the May Fourth Movement: although it raised two slogans of "democracy" and "science," it didn't touch upon the essential problem of national salvation. The slogans of "democracy" and "science" have been thrown around for over thirty years; were they capable of resolving the crisis of our country? Had these two slogans done anything effectively to improve our nation? In my point of view, "democracy" and "science" are necessary for our nation building, to be sure; however, without the "culture" of our nation serving as the foundation for democracy and science, these two slogans would not only be incapable of saving our country but also exacerbate our country's crisis. This is a lesson drawn from the recent defeat of our revolution.[73]

In response to Chiang's statement, Gao Xuhui, a Nationalist party liner, remarked that "many people think that the anti-Communist and counter-Soviet cause is a battle between democracy and totalitarianism. They don't realize nationalism is important and essential to anti-Communism."[74] He then concluded that democracy and freedom were not a panacea to counterattack communism. Instead, nationalism guaranteed success. Chiang felt so compelling a need to claim the high ground of Chinese cultural tradition that he proposed to add the concept of *lunli* (morality) to democracy and science to

71. Chiang, *Zhongguo zhi mingyun*, p. 71.
72. Lyida H. Liu, *Translingual Practice*, p. 217.
73. Chiang, "Dangqian jige zhongyao wenti," p. 49.
74. Gao Xuhui, "Fayang 'wusi' de minzu sixiang," p. 5.

rectify the erroneous cultural trajectory advocated by the May Fourth movement. Forbidding books of modern Chinese literature was only too foreseeable.

The banned writers of modern Chinese literature shared the negative space with Taiwan writers from the Japanese colonial era. Whereas the former were eradicated for suspicious ideological inclinations, the latter were repressed in the immediate postwar years, which bespoke an even more complicated dilemma in which discourses of modernization, colonialism, and nationalism competed and contested. After the retrocession, Taiwanese writers who grew up under the Japanese colonial rule had to reckon with problems of different orders that were layered together. Although the transition of written language from Japanese to Chinese certainly posed a serious challenge for these men of letters, the historical and political complications of the time further exacerbated their dilemmas. Zhang Wenhuan (1909–78) had to give up his writing career completely because he was not able to grasp the new language.[75] Language was not just a medium for literature but also served as a means of asserting cultural identity. Yang Qianhe (1921–2011), the first female professional writer and journalist in the Japanese colonial period, stopped her active writing career during the KMT's White Terror. The decisive, painful silence not only attested to the linguistic barrier but also made a subversive gesture against the newly imposed cultural and political oppression. More intriguingly, forty years later, when Yang resumed writing in her diasporic life in the United States, she chose Japanese to compose her autobiography, *Jinsei no purizumu* (Life's prism, 1993), to express "her dissatisfaction with the Chinese regime."[76] Writers such as Lü Heruo (1914–51) and Zhu Dianren (1903–51) determined to stop writing due to deep disappointment with Chinese political and cultural realities after Taiwan's retrocession. Both became Communists after the February 28 Massacre in 1947. Lü Heruo, who wrote four short stories in Chinese between 1945 and 1949, was driven into exile in 1949 because of his engagement in the leftist *Guangming bao* (Guangming daily) and was alleg-

75. Chen Jianzhong, "Bei zuzhou de wenxue?" pp. 49–52.
76. Yang Qianhe, *Rensheng de sanleng jing*, p. 10.

edly poisoned to death by a snake in Lugang in 1951. Zhu Dianren, who was regarded as the most talented writer (*qilin'er*) because he had written in beautiful Chinese even before 1945, was executed during the White Terror as a dangerous Communist at the Taipei Ma-chang-ting. Wang Shilang (1908–84) and Yang Yunping (1906–2000) switched from literary writing to academic research after the retrocession, in search of a seemingly safe niche separate from politics.[77] Indeed, as the choices of these writers demonstrated, language and literature functioned as a political means by which a distinctive cultural and political consciousness was formed and expressed, even when they chose the silence of nonwriting.

The following chapters will provide five entry points to the dynamic configuration of Chinese modernities represented in literature and culture across 1949. The writers I have chosen contributed important visions of a modern nation and national culture. The selection, which aims at composing a topography of Chinese intellectual mentality at the crossroads, is not intended to be in any way comprehensive. Many equally important writers whose works are symptomatic of the mid-twentieth-century experiences of severance have only been touched upon or have to be done without: Qian Zhongshu (1910–98) and his *Weicheng* (The besieged city, 1947); Lu Ling (1923–94) and his *Caizhu de ernümen* (Children of the landlord, 1945 and 1948); Zhao Shuli (1906–70) and his novellas and short stories; Liu Yichang (1918–) and his *Jiutu* (Drunkard, 1956); Chen Jiying (1908–97) and his *Dicun zhuan* (Fool in the reeds, 1951), to name just a few. By choosing this group of writers—Shen Congwen, Ding Ling, Feng Zhi, Wu Zhuoliu, and Eileen Chang—as subjects, I do not suggest that because they were purged or persecuted, they are better representatives of the Chinese intelligentsia or cultural martyrs. In those transitional years, they were as confused and spiritually besieged as most Chinese people; if any different, then, they were more persistent, more strenuous, and had therefore confronted more profound agonies.

---

77. For studies on Taiwan writers during Japanese colonial rule and in the immediate years after the retrocession, see, for instance, Peng Ruijin, *Taiwan xinwenxue yundong sishi nian*; Xu Junya, *Riju shiqi Taiwan xiaoshuo yanjiu*; Lü Zhenghui, *Zhanhou Taiwan wenxue jingyan*.

CHAPTER 2

Fragments of Modernity: Shen Congwen's Journey from Asylum to Museum

In July 1949, the First All-China Congress of Literary and Art Representatives (Zhonghua quanguo wenxue yishu gongzuozhe daibiao dahui) was held in Beijing in the newly founded socialist state. Shen Congwen (1902–88), one of the most prominent writers of modern Chinese literature, was conspicuously absent from the roster of writers. At this conference, which marked the starting point of "contemporary literature," Guo Moruo (1892–1978), leader of the left camp, and Zhou Yang (1908–89), head of the Communist Party writers, issued guiding reports, entitled, respectively, "Wei jianshe xin zhongguo de renmin wenyi er fendou" (Fighting to construct people's literature and art of new China) and "Xin de renmin de wenyi" (New people's literature and art).[1] This conference not only defined the function, content, theme, and form for literature and art but also mapped out social and administrative networks for writers and artists. As a result, the National Association of Literature and the Arts and the Writers' Association were established. Every intellectual was

---

1. Hong Zicheng, *Zhongguo dangdai wenxueshi*, p. 14. Guo Moruo, "Wei jianshe xin zhongguo de renmin wenyi er fendou" (Fighting to construct people's literature and art of new China); Zhou Yang, "Xin de renmin de wenyi" (New people's literature and art), both articles were collected in Hong, ed., *Zhongguo dangdai wenxueshi shiliaoxuan 1945–1999*, pp. 172–78; also see pp. 150–61.

to be assigned to a socialist "work unit" and a household registration, a new system of control and surveillance under the new socialist regime,[2] which proved to be extremely effective in the ominous political campaigns that would soon engulf the whole country. Not positioned in any work unit associated with literature, Shen Congwen was no longer recognized as a writer in the socialist regime.

More devastatingly, in 1953, when Shen had already begun working at the National Museum of History, he was informed by the Kaiming Press in Shanghai that all extant copies and printing plates of his works had been destroyed. Meanwhile, his works were also proscribed on the other side of the Taiwan Strait for his perceived "communist tendency" because he had decided to remain in mainland China. With his works thus purged, Shen effectively disappeared from the Chinese literary world and from its literary canon.

Shen Congwen was not unaware that something like this might happen when he rejected the invitation to go to Taiwan and decided to remain in mainland China. Anticipating the inevitable political change that would come to China beginning in 1949, he wrote in 1948: "For these twenty or thirty years my writing has been based on *si* (contemplation). Now, however, one has to start everything from the perspective of *xin* (conviction). I might not be able to accomplish such a transformation. Before long, I would eventually stop writing, even if not forced to. This is the predestined consequence of certain people of our generation."[3] The shift from thinking to believing, a product of a monumental social transformation, symbolizes a shift from individual agency to monolithic collectivity, which confronted all the intellectuals of this transitional period with great urgency. In addition, the inevitable interruption of intellectual life foreshadowed Shen Congwen's own destiny after the 1949 transition. Like many

---

2. For a study of the evolution and function of the system of work units in China, see Yang Xiaomin and Zhou Yihu, *Zhongguo danwei zhidu*.

3. Shen Congwen, "Zhi Jiliu—Gei yige xiewenzhang de qingnian" (To Jiliu: A letter to a young man who writes), *SCWQJ* 18: 519. This letter was never published. Shen's work is cited according to *Shen Congwen quanji* (Complete works of Shen Congwen), abbreviated as *SCWQJ*. References are given in a format with volume number followed by page number. All English translations of Shen Congwen's work cited in this book are my own unless otherwise noted.

Chinese intellectuals of that generation, Shen experienced poignant changes in both his career and his personal life.

From the end of 1948, when Communist troops besieged Beijing, Shen Congwen was besieged by increasingly vehement leftist attacks. In an essay titled "Chi fandong wenyi" (A denunciation of reactionary literature and art), Guo Moruo, who at the time was the leader of the leftist camp in Hong Kong, denounced Shen as a pornographic, "peach-pink" writer who was "always active as a conscious counterrevolutionary."[4] The most devastating attack came a few months later from Shen's own students at Peking University, where he held a teaching position.[5] The leftist students petitioned the university to dismiss him, copied Guo's article on massive wall posters, and reviled Shen as "a member of the Crescent Moon Society, the Modern Critique Society, and the Third Road."[6]

Shen Congwen's transition to the new regime, meanwhile, started with a bitter mental breakdown that began before Beijing was taken over by the Communist army. In March 1949, Shen attempted suicide in his small apartment at Peking University. After his life was saved, he gave up his writing career for good and instead chose to work in the National Museum of History, where he would copy catalogues for the museum collection.[7] During his thirty years there,

---

4. Guo Moruo's article was published in the first issue of the journal *Dazhong wenyi congkan* (Mass literature and art collection) in March 1948 in Hong Kong. Shen Congwen did not take Guo's article seriously until late 1948 when the political pressure from the leftist camp started to intensify. This special issue, entitled "Wenyi de xin fangxiang" (The new direction of literature and art), includes two additional articles refuting Shen Congwen and his writings: "Dui dangqian wenyi yundong de yijian" (Opinions of the contemporary literature and art movement) written by Shao Quanlin, this journal's fellow traveler, and "Lüeping Shen Congwen de 'Xiong gongguan'" (A brief take on Shen Congwen's "The Xiong family mansion") by Feng Naichao. For a study of the founding of the journal and its cultural and political significance, see Qian Liqun, *1948 Tiandi xuanhuang*, pp. 21–47; Zeng Lingcun, "1948–1949: *Dazhong wenyi congkan.*"

5. See Zhang Zhaohe's recollections, in Chen Tushou, "Wumen chengxia de Shen Congwen," p. 13. Also see Wang Zengqi, "Shen Congwen zhuanye zhimi," pp. 139–42.

6. See Ling Yu, *Shen Congwen zhuan*, p. 421.

7. When Mao Zedong launched the *shuangbai* movement (blooming of a hundred flowers and schools) in 1956, Shen was also lured by the apparent freedom in the intellectual world, so much so that he attempted to write fiction again. How-

Shen, an art collector and connoisseur long before he was employed at the museum, dedicated himself to research on Chinese art and art history. His greatest contribution to the field was his *Zhongguo gudai fushi yanjiu* (Studies on traditional Chinese costumes), the manuscript of which survived the Cultural Revolution and was subsequently published in Hong Kong.[8]

Shen Congwen's suicide attempt and his conversion thereafter from fiction writing to research on antiquities and art remain a puzzle for his contemporaries as well as for Shen scholars in the mainland and abroad.[9] It was viewed as either a result of Communist political persecution or a tragic self-refusal. Interpreting Shen's critical transition provides a key to his aesthetic vision and may also illuminate his unique notion of modernity and historical consciousness at the sociopolitical transitional period around 1949.

Decades later, Shen Congwen's disciple Wang Zengqi would remark melancholically: "Our country thus gained a connoisseur by losing a novelist. But from a cultural-historical perspective, wasn't that a great loss? But then, whose loss?"[10] At the same time, however, Shen's post-1949 oeuvre has hardly received the attention it deserves. The aesthetic and historical visions he constructed in his art scholarship, which continued and further developed his previous artistic imaginations and propositions, have for too long been ignored. Is this consignment of Shen Congwen the art historian to oblivion not another great loss for the Chinese intellectual world? Shen's 1949 transition has thus been made bitterer because all the hard work he dedicated to his new career has not been taken seriously. Despite all

---

ever, he soon realized he was not able to fit into the framework of socialist discourse and gave up. Yet, his classical poems and letters to Zhang Zhaohe in the post-1949 years should be regarded as a unique genre in contemporary Chinese literature.

8. Shen Congwen, *Zhongguo gudai fushi yanjiu* (Studies on traditional Chinese costumes), *SCWQJ*, vol. 32.

9. Jeffrey C. Kinkley, for instance, points to pressures coming from leftist intellectuals around 1948 and also to familial pressures, as a result of Shen's wife Zhang Zhaohe's enthusiasm toward socialist ideology, after 1949. However, he does not completely explore the aesthetic and political importance of Shen's conversion to art history after his failed suicide. See Kinkley, *Odyssey of Shen Congwen.*

10. Wang Zengqi, "Shen Congwen zhuanye zhimi," p. 144.

his post-1949 contributions to art history, Shen is still regarded as the already-sacrificed and, as such, the virtually nonexistent writer. In the collective mourning over Shen the writer, Shen the art historian strangely vanished.

By examining Shen Congwen's 1949 transition from literature to art history, from asylum to museum, this chapter considers his unique aesthetic of the fragment and fragmentation, and his notion of rethinking history by means of collecting and reassembling artistic fragments and cultural details. I argue that Shen's conceptualization of modernity in fragments of artistic creation presents a cultural and historical alternative to the monumentality and totality of the socialist revolutionary ideology that has taken hold in mainland China since the 1949 divide.

The first part of this chapter reviews Shen's meditations on antiquities, cultural heritage, museum modernization, and urban planning in conjunction with the debate on the preservation of the besieged city of Beijing during the civil war, in order to explore his efforts to bring together the traditional and the modern in regard to art and culture. The second part of this chapter deals with the divergence of Shen's cultural and historical imaginations from the dominant Maoist ideology through an examination of key concepts in his aesthetic reflections: art, beauty, life, the divine, and history. I suggest that Shen was "the collector and the historian" who, dedicated to art historical research, assembled antiques and cultural artifacts discarded as feudalist relics by the storm of socialism. By investigating Shen's 1949 psychological crisis, the third part explores the political and cultural implications of insanity and schizophrenia in the context of the Cold War Chinese division and considers how the discourse of fragmented subjectivity might provide a means of breaking with the overpowering ideological authority. The final, fourth part of the chapter looks at Shen's distinctive aesthetic of the fragment and fragmentation as manifested in his post-1949 art historical scholarship, in particular *Studies on Traditional Chinese Costumes*. Hidden behind Tiananmen Square, Shen Congwen, the survivor or, perhaps, the specter of history, haunted the isolated Wumen Gate of the National Museum of History, where the past imperial history resided, adding an invisible dissonance to the grand socialist mise-en-scène of post-1949 China.

Whither Beijing? "Socrates Talks about What Beijing Needs"

He asked Jesus, "Domine Quo Vadis?" (Lord, whither goest thou thus) and Jesus replied, "To Rome to be crucified anew."

—M. R. James, *The Apocryphal New Testament*

Two million people are waiting silently for the event on the horizon. It is truly the most uncanny and profound chapter of history.

—Shen Congwen, Letter to Shen Yunlu, November 28, 1948

Thus Shen Congwen described the standstill in Beijing in November 1948, with the impending calamity of the ancient capital becoming the next battlefield of the civil war between the KMT and the CCP troops. In December 1948, Beijing was besieged by the Communist army. For their own interests, both the KMT regime and the opposing CCP rushed to rescue cultural treasures, artistic works, and intellectuals from the city. Beijing would be the greatest booty, not only in a geographical and political sense but also as the capital of culture. Even before the battle broke out, a fierce fight for cultural resources had already been launched. At this critical moment, the ancient city of Beijing, which had survived numerous battles in modern history, was confronted with yet another catastrophe.

This was surely not what Shen Congwen had expected when he returned to Beijing from exile in Kunming after the Second Sino-Japanese War. He came back with plans to accomplish overdue literary writings, including another seven stories about West Hunan cities, which, together with *Biancheng* (Border town, 1934), "Xiaozhai" (Little stockade, 1937) and "Yunlu Jishi" (Yunlu chronicles, 1947), would compose *Ten Stories of Hunan Cities*. Even in July 1948, when the hope of fiction writing seemed dimmer and dimmer with the worsening civil war, Shen still promised his son that he had yet to achieve "dozens of books."[11] Shen never had a chance to actualize his writing plans. His literary career had come to an unexpected halt.

---

11. See a conversation between Shen and his son recorded in his letter to his wife, in Shen, "A letter to Zhang Zhaohe, 1948, 07, 30, Summer Palace," *SCWQJ* 18: 504.

Between 1946 and 1948, in addition to teaching creative writing at Peking University, Shen edited literary supplements for four major newspapers: *Dagong bao, Pingming ribao, Jingshi bao,* and *Yishi bao.* In his editorial work, he devotedly helped and endorsed "a group of bold, tender, enthusiastic, and courageous young and vital people"[12] to implement aesthetic explorations and experiments. This younger generation of writers, poets, literary translators and critics, including Wang Zengqi, Yuan Kejia, Mu Dan, and Zheng Min, to name a few, "used their vigorous and youthful hearts and hands to compose mature and experienced writings,"[13] thus forming a promising circle in the northern literary arena of the late 1940s, with Shen Congwen as the mentor and the core. Meanwhile, Shen also wrote a great number of feuilleton articles. One of the major concerns in these writings is how to treat antiques and cultural relics as well as how to rebuild the historical city of Beijing. The deficiency of literary creation of the time can of course be attributed to the aesthetic dilemma Shen encountered during his experimental writing of "Kan hong lu" (Gazing at the rainbow).[14] However, his shift from literature to art was also a direct consequence of the urgent political situation of the civil war. With the Battle of Beijing looming large, how to protect cultural relics, historical buildings and sites, as well as the ancient imperial capital itself as a historical structure, inevitably became the focal point of intellectual reflections.

Inasmuch as researchers on Shen Congwen tend to restrict their focus to the literary realm, they fail to come to terms with Shen's writings on art, architecture, and art preservation, which were completed a couple of years before his psychological breakdown. In this part of the chapter, I shall read Shen's writings between 1946 and 1948 in conjunction with his aesthetic conceptualization and with the specific historical constellation in Beijing. As will be explained, these articles on antiquities and art not only recapitulate his previous

---

12. Shen, "Tan xiandai shi" (On modern poetry), in "Xinfeiyou cundi xubian" (New letters never mailed), *SCWQJ* 17: 478.

13. Shen, "Zhi Ke Yuan xiansheng" (To Mr. Ke Yuan), in "New Letters Never Mailed," *SCWQJ* 17: 475.

14. Shen Congwen, "Kan hong lu" (Gazing at the rainbow), *SCWQJ* 10: 327–42.

aesthetic meditations developed during the Kunming exile but also assume unique significance in the debate on the preservation of cultural relics in the besieged city of Beijing. Furthermore, Shen Congwen's artistic considerations of the time also foreshadow the shift of his career to art and art history in the post-1949 era. To investigate Shen's writings in that critical moment, one should not overlook that, though they are a constitutive part of his artistic vision, they also contribute to a body of polemic writings on the significance of antiques and of Beijing as a historical work of art. Accordingly, one must take into account the particular historical bearings of Shen's ideas concerning art, urban planning, and restoration, which were formed in Beijing in the darkest years of the civil war.

How to salvage cultural relics and antiquities from the violence of war? Were they worth saving at a time when the whole nation was enduring poverty, famine, and inflation? This was a critical issue facing intellectuals both inside and outside the besieged city. Should cultural relics be preserved and restored as part of the national essence, or be disposed of as corpses and fossils blocking the road toward modernization and ossifying the mind of reform? Ever since the onset of Chinese modernization in the late Qing dynasty, the debate on the preservation of *wenwu* (cultural relics) and *guocui* (national essence) has had great significance among Chinese intelligentsia. Although the historical contingencies might change, the demarcation of national identity is constantly at stake. More important, the debate on national essence is nothing less than the old yet resilient opposition between the traditional and the modern, which, not surprisingly, constantly emerges at political crisis points in modern Chinese history. After its defeat in the Battles of Huaihai, the ultimate downfall of the KMT government was imminent. What triggered the pre-1949 intellectual reflections on antiquities, historical sites, and urban restoration was, therefore, not only the looming destruction of Beijing as a sacrifice to the civil war but also the subsequent political and cultural transformations, which would usher in an uncertain future for China. What strikes me about this particular polemic around 1948 is its deep anxiety about the fate of intellectuals and the elite culture in the approaching regime with its socialist ideology, which makes it a poignant new phase in the trajectory of the century-long polemic.

To deal with the configuration of tradition and modernity has been the central task of every modernization movement. In the battle between the old and the new, *wenwu* has been a convenient and enduring trope for cultural heritage and history, which are regarded as impeding the progress of modernization. *Wenwu* epitomizes a body of knowledge called "tradition." Lu Xun (1881–1936) once mocked those who rejected modern things and ideas as "wearing glasses of *guocui*."[15] Preferring ancient Chinese bronze mirrors to Western glass mirrors, these people were convinced that the latter could not reflect images as accurately as the former. By condemning the past as ossified and dead, modernity seems to have been marked by its absolute break with the past. However, this break has never been unambiguous. As demonstrated in the 1948 debate on the preservation of Beijing and its cultural treasures, the attitude toward cultural relics and historical sites was highly controversial. Although cultural relics embodied the timeless, suffocating tradition, the advocates of preservation did not necessarily reject the modern.

A great number of intellectuals supported a peaceful surrender of Beijing to the Communist army in order to avoid a tragic ruination of the historical city.[16] The following remarks by the historian Xiang Da (1900–66), appealing for immediate protection of the cultural relics, represent their concerns:

> The civil war is a tragedy of the nation; although it doesn't seem likely to end soon, the historical relics are truly innocent. And in the light of the current war situation, the location of the cultural relics can't hinder the victory of either side. They are the public heritage of the whole nation, and cultural evidence of human intelligence, emotions, and work. Those that have been already ruined are irremediable; the rest of them must not be destroyed![17]

However, this preservationist attitude was by no means unanimous. Zhu Ziqing's article "Wenwu, jiushu, maobi" (Cultural relics, ancient books, writing brush), published in *Dagong bao* on March 31, 1948, pronounced intriguing dissonance. With regard to the Febru-

---

15. Lu Xun, *LXQJ* 1: 200.

16. See Wang Jun, *Chengji*, esp. pp. 58–61.

17. Xiang Da, quoted in Shen, "Shoushi canpo: Wenwu baowei de yizhong kanfa" (Restoring the damaged and the ruined: A view of protecting the cultural relics), *SCWQJ* 31: 293.

ary proposal by the Beijing Committee of Regulation of Cultural Relics for funding toward supervision and preservation of historical buildings and sites, Zhu Ziqing, a major figure of the May Fourth generation and at the time a professor of Chinese literature at Tsinghua University, stated that such a financial investment when famine and war were devastating the country was unnecessary and inappropriate. He observes: "Cultural relics, ancient books, writing brushes, are all the same. They are all heritage, history, and old culture."[18] In his view, these are already "fossils," and "that which is bound to pass away will eventually pass away."[19] Hence, there is no need for redemption: "Although I agree about the need to preserve historical relics, I definitely think it is not worth restoring and rescuing them. The truth is that it would not be late to preserve historical relics after there are sufficient clothes and food. Even if it was too late, we could only be sorry for it, for clothes and food are after all the fundamentals."[20]

Upon reading Zhu's article, Liang Sicheng and his wife Lin Huiyin were deeply upset. In rebuttal, Liang wrote the essay "Beiping de wenwu bixu zhengli yu baocun" (The cultural relics in Beijing must be restored and preserved) to elucidate the urgency of the issue from the perspective of architecture. He argues that Zhu's idea of conserving historical relics as "fossils" is clearly a prejudice of the nonprofessional, indicating his lack of knowledge concerning architectural engineering and construction science. Beijing is unique in its historical and artistic significance as well as in its urban construction and planning; however, if its historical relics and buildings cannot be restored in time, they will be completely jeopardized and out of repair in only decades, thus becoming real burdens for the city's inhabitants. Consequently, Liang asserts, "At any rate, unless we deny art, deny history, or deny the artistic and historical value of Beijing's cultural relics, they must undoubtedly receive our appreciation and preservation."[21]

Whereas Liang Sicheng is certainly insightful with respect to the preservation of cultural and historical relics, he may well have missed

---

18. *Zhu Ziqing sanwen quanji* 3: 517.
19. Ibid., p. 518.
20. Ibid.
21. Liang Sicheng, "Beiping de wenwu bixu zhengli yu baocun."

the implicit point of Zhu Ziqing's essay. Although Zhu seems to be against the restoration of cultural relics at this particular historical juncture, he does not mean to discard traditional culture. In fact, a frequent customer in Liulichang, the hub of antique stores in Beijing, Zhu was himself a passionate collector of antique books. The last writing he left behind was a letter to order a rare edition of a book from one of the Liulichang stores.[22] I suggest that for Zhu Ziqing, the crux of the matter is how the intellectuals should confront the tremendous social and political transformations resulting from the collapse of the KMT regime. Therefore, Zhu's *wenwu* is never just cultural objects *per se*. His true concerns lie, first and foremost, in what "cultural relics, ancient books, writing brush" embody, namely, intellectuals and the culture they construct. Having acutely sensed the bitter fate of the intellectuals left behind by the old regime and the choices they had to make under the upcoming political authority, Zhu argued that the only solution out of the status quo was to discard their elite identity and the elitist culture. This notion comes across most clearly in his article "Lun buman xianzhuang" (On being discontent with the status quo), published a year earlier, in which he perceptively reflects on the situation facing the intellectuals: "In the current years, the ivory tower has turned into the crossroad, and this tower is being torn down. Thus, they have no other choice but go outside of it, go among the masses."[23] With this attitude, Zhu Ziqing could well have joined Baudelaire's crowd of modern times who trample the halo fallen from the head of the poet on the muddy pavement.

Accordingly, behind Zhu's advocacy for abandoning "cultural relics, ancient books, writing brush" is his determination to annihilate the bastion of the old. In such statements, one will not miss a familiar echo of Lu Xun's hailing of the collapse of Leifeng Pagoda in Hangzhou some twenty years earlier. In his 1924 article "Lun Leifangta de daodiao" (On the collapse of Leifeng Pagoda), Lu Xun enthusiastically embraces the ruination of the ancient Leifeng Pagoda: "Now, it has collapsed, and people all over the world, how happy

---

22. Lei Mengshui, "Zhu Ziqing xiansheng maishu ji."

23. Zhu Ziqing, "Lun buman xianzhuang," originally published in *Guancha* (Observation) 3, no. 18 (1947), collected in *Zhu Ziqing sanwen quanji* 3: 509.

they must be!"[24] Similarly, Lu Xun uses the collapse of Leifeng Pagoda as a metaphor to appeal for the abolishment of the traditional social system, which discriminated against women.[25]

However, Lu Xun's powerful adversary position on the preservation of cultural relics in this essay may have caused people to bypass his second essay on Leifeng Pagoda, which presents a new perspective on the same issue. This second article, "Zailun Leifengta de daodiao" (Another thought on the collapse of Leifeng Pagoda, 1925), is much more complicated than the first one. A year after his famous celebration of the collapse of Leifeng Pagoda, Lu Xun began to lament it. Yet, what upset him was not so much the destruction of a building as a deeper message this event carried. Ironically, the collapse of this historical construction was a direct result of the superstitions of local people, who over the generations stole bricks from the body of the pagoda, in the belief that keeping a brick at home would bring the family good fortune. Lu Xun observes sadly, "The reason for the destruction, however, is neither the destroyers' intention to sweep away the old nor the bandits' intention to rob or destroy. It is merely due to the current tiny, selfish interest that they would like to secretly harm the complete massive object."[26] Indeed, ignorance and superstition, rather than enlightenment, occasioned the demolition of the old.

Thus, as Lu Xun compellingly illuminates, destruction will not necessarily lead to enlightenment and a better future. Then, one might wonder: Zhu Ziqing remarked on the eve of the downfall of the old political regime, "They (the people) might not know how to change the current conditions, but they smash them down anyway,

---

24. Lu Xun, *LXQJ* 1: 172.

25. Leifeng Pagoda was built in 975 AD. It was one of the ten sights in Hangzhou. It is also famous for its appearance in the popular folktale "Legend of White Snake." In the story, Madame White Snake marries a mortal scholar. They lead a happy life until a Buddhist monk interferes motivated by the belief that human beings and spirits should not marry. The monk uses the pagoda to imprison the white snake and eventually breaks up the marriage. When Lu Xun remarked, "Why didn't they think of the collapse of the pagoda when they built it? It served them right!," he might not have considered that one day the pagoda would be rebuilt. Ironically, the Leifeng Pagoda was reconstructed in 2002.

26. Lu Xun, *LXQJ* 1: 194.

believing that after destruction there would be hope"[27]; could there really be hope after the collapse of Leifeng Pagoda? Zhu worried about the social welfare after the calamities of the civil war, whereas Shen Congwen took the lack of spiritual enlightenment and historical consciousness into consideration, thus furthering Lu Xun's reflections.

"Beijing might be destroyed in the disaster of the civil war of this couple of years; even if not, the antiques will still be scattered and lost, nothing can be preserved,"[28] Shen expressed his concern in a letter to his friend Ling Shuhua (1900–90), a female writer who was a member of the Investigation Committee for Calligraphy and Painting of the Museum of Gugong (the Forbidden City) and at the time lived in Paris with her husband Chen Yuan (1896–1970), the KMT's permanent representative to the United Nations Educational, Scientific and Cultural Organization (UNESCO). Evidently, what concerns Shen is not only the jeopardy in which culture was placed during the war but also the lack of historical consciousness among both intellectuals and common people. Around 1948, Shen wrote a series of articles about the status of research on antiquities and the construction of museums in China in the previous thirty years. Confronting the destruction the civil war has brought to cultural relics, Shen's considerations go far beyond the scope of preservation and restoration, thus contributing an intriguing voice to the 1948 debate about cultural heritage. In "Shoushi canpo: Wenwu baowei de yizhong kanfa" (Restoring the damaged and the ruined: A view of protecting the cultural relics), an article written in October 1948, Shen remarks, "Talking about the preservation of cultural relics, what matters is not 'the respect' of powerful personages, nor 'the appreciation' of the people. Most important is the broad and profound 'understanding' of history and culture by the majority of intellectuals of our society."[29] What is at stake is less the conservation of the concrete cultural objects than the enlightenment of the people, through the building of strong historical and cultural awareness.

---

27. Zhu Ziqing, "Lun buman xianzhuang," *Zhu Ziqing sanwen quanji* 3: 509.
28. Shen, "A letter to Ling Shuhua, 1948, 10, 16, Beiping," *SCWQJ* 18: 512.
29. Shen, "Shoushi canpo: Wenwu baowei de yizhong kanfa" (Restoring the damaged and the ruined: A view of protecting the cultural relics), *SCWQJ* 31: 294.

Fundamentally, the museum serves as a significant institutional organ for that purpose. However, as Shen criticized, since its establishment in 1924, the Museum of the Forbidden City only focused on "classification," "preservation," and "exhibition," and was barely qualified to perform the function of enlightenment. The emergence of the museum in modern times is a direct effect of the process of modernization. As Andreas Huyssen puts it, "A traditional society without a secular theological concept of history does not need a museum, but modernity is unthinkable without its museal project."[30] Like the Louvre in Paris, the Forbidden City, the former palace of the Qing dynasty, was opened to the public as a museum as a result of modern revolution. The Forbidden City is unrivaled in its collection of thousands of years historical relics and cultural treasures; however, given the severe lack of art historical research at the time, it was nothing better than a warehouse. Accordingly, the staff in the exhibition rooms was rather a "police force keeping watch on visitors to prevent them from touching or stealing the artworks than professionally trained guides there for the purpose of explanation and illumination."[31] The irony of history is that, a couple of years later, after the 1949 divide, Shen would appear voluntarily as such a museum guide.

Viewed in this light, Shen concludes that the Museum of the Forbidden City was evidently incapable of fulfilling the function of modern museums. He proposes cooperation among museums, university departments of literature, history, anthropology, sociology, architecture, and archaeology, and schools of arts in Beijing to promote academic research as well as new concepts of classification and exhibition, and ultimately, "to build an all-new country in the ruins."[32] By illuminating the connotation of the article title, Shen recapitulates his project at the end, "I chose the title 'Restoring the damaged and the ruined,' hoping that in doing so, we can bring a true 'renaissance' to our country. This renaissance is not for the

30. Huyssen, *Twilight Memories*, p. 15. Huyssen's work provides an insightful analysis of the memory boom and the museum as mass medium in contemporary Western societies.

31. Shen, "Restoring the damaged and the ruined," *SCWQJ* 31: 295.

32. Ibid., 31: 294.

decoration of any political hegemony, but a guarantee and a symbol of the combination of intelligence, morality, and hard work aiming at an accurate evolution of the life of the human being."[33]

Shen's argument for the modern museum is also intriguing for his notion of a new configuration of the traditional and the modern. As scholars have pointed out, though it was born out of the movement of modernization, the museum "has become the privileged institutional site of the three centuries old 'querelle des anciens et des modernes' (quarrel of the ancients and the moderns)."[34] What concerns Shen Congwen in mid-twentieth-century China is not merely the old *querelle*, but more important, how the apparently exclusive opponents, the old and the new, can be effectively welded together to propel a new productivity. Only then is it possible to realize both the restoration of cultural relics and the modernization of the museum. The best way, Shen suggested, is to facilitate collaboration between the museum and the production of modern handicrafts. After visiting the Exhibition of Beijing's Special Handicrafts in the Museum of History in 1948, Shen lamented the degeneration of manufacture and production of traditional handicrafts in Beijing, such as porcelain, ivoryware, jade sculpture, and lacquerware. In "Guanyu Beiping tezhong shougongye zhanlanhui yidian yijian" (My opinion concerning the exhibition of special handicrafts in Beijing, 1948), an article he wrote shortly after the exhibition, Shen argues that the improvement of handicraft production is not just an economic and technological problem. More significantly, "there lies a deeper level, namely, an issue of the encounter of the new and the old as well as that of reconstruction."[35] The relics of high artistic achievement cannot be buried in a mummifying status in museum collections, transforming the museum into a splendid mise-en-scène of death. Art historical research will not only broaden the horizon of and provide new perspectives on modern art, but also greatly contribute to the revitalization of contemporary handicraft production. In this man-

---

33. Ibid., 31: 298.

34. Huyssen, *Twilight Memories*, p. 13.

35. Shen, "Guanyu Beiping tezhong shougongye zhanlanhui yidian yijian" (My opinion concerning the exhibition of special handicrafts in Beijing), *SCWQJ* 31: 301.

ner, " 'modern culture' and 'classic civilization' can be fused into a new constellation."[36] Its impact on art will be as profound as that of the literary revolution on modern Chinese literature. This, Shen is convinced, provides the very prerequisite of the claim, "Beijing must not be destroyed."[37]

Indeed, Beijing must not be destroyed; beyond that, Beijing should be reconstructed and rejuvenated. For Shen Congwen, the ancient city itself represented a historical work of art. In 1947 and 1948, he composed his own version of *Lettres de Pékin* using the pen name "Lord Balu," in which he conceptualized a reconstruction of his favorite city. In "Sugeladi tan Beiping suoxu" (Socrates talks about what Beijing needs), the most important in the series of letters from Beijing, Shen evokes the ancient sage Socrates to build his own "Republic of Art." His utopia is to be planned and regulated on the principles of art, literature, and music. As for the municipal administration, the head of the city police will be a theater director, orchestra conductor, or horticulturalist; the department of education will be managed by artists of applied arts; last but not least, the deputy mayor of this art city should be assumed by architect Liang Sicheng, who helped design the headquarters of the United Nations. The combination of art and science will constitute the basis of a new religion, and accordingly, its citizens will be endowed with aesthetic education.[38] On this point, the imprint of Cai Yuanpei (1868–1940)'s notion of aesthetic education is unmistakable. Furthermore, given the Greek origin of the word "museum" denoting a place associated with the Muses, and thus with the arts, Shen's "Republic of Art" posits Beijing as the ideal art museum. However, under the political circumstances of the time, neither side of the civil war would even bother with such utopian ruminations, which elaborated Shen Congwen's last idealist vision before the great divide.

Liang Sicheng was indeed invited to participate in the urban planning and reconstruction of Beijing after the founding of the People's Republic. However, his proposals to build a new political center in

---

36. Ibid., 31: 303–4.

37. Ibid.

38. Shen, "Sugeladi tan Beiping suoxu" (Socrates talks about what Beijing needs), *SCWQJ* 14: 370–81.

western Beijing to accommodate all the departments of administration of the new regime and to restore the ancient city and its historical buildings were ruthlessly rejected by the new people's state. History is never short of irony. Beijing was not ruined in the civil war after all. However, in accordance with the Maoist version of the "modern," the city was gradually deprived of its historical features and was soon transformed into a spectacular socialist monument. The irony of history was carried further. Shen Congwen, who employed literary imagination to envision his ideal city of art with its ideal museum, or the city *as* museum, ultimately ended in the post-1949 era as a museum worker at the Wumen Gate of the Forbidden City, a place which had once witnessed the establishment of the Association of Architecture (Yingzhao she), a society aiming at the research and preservation of traditional Chinese architecture, by his friend Liang Sicheng, and which now became the National Museum of History of the new socialist regime, where a monumental history of revolution was about to be constructed.

The Collector and the Historian

> A *Lumpensammler* early in the morning twilight after the day of revolution.
> —Walter Benjamin, "Politisierung der Intelligenz"

Art connoisseurship and collecting were constitutive parts of Shen Congwen's aesthetic world. His post-1949 choice of art and art history is by no means a coincidence. In an essay titled "Wo weishenme shizhong bulikan lishi bowuguan" (Why I determined not to leave the historical museum), written in 1968 as one of the many confessions he had to submit during the Cultural Revolution, he calmly recollected the changes he was confronted with after 1949:

> On the surface of life, it can be said that I "was completely doomed, wrecked." Everything was done for. Because in comparison, my old colleagues, my previous old friend Ding Ling, for instance, seems now like God's privileged; even friends like Mao Dun, Zheng Zhenduo, Ba Jin, and Lao She have turned into illustrious figures and become very active, going abroad and being treated like distinguished guests. As for me at that time, I left home before dawn, and bought a roast yam in Beixin qiao to warm up my hands. When I arrived in Tiananmen by trolley bus, the gate was not yet open. I sat down on the ground looking at the sky, stars, and moon, waiting

> until the gate was open. When I went home in the evening, sometimes the rain poured; I then wrapped myself up with a ragged gunnysack.[39]

Reading such reminiscences, one cannot help asking what passion enabled him to survive the forced termination of his literary career and supported him through all the political pressures. Was it just the obsession of a collector, or passionate devotion to arts and antiques? How should we read this lonely figure wandering in the dawn in Tiananmen, the socialist revolutionary center? Is he just another Cousin Pons figure, who, as in Balzac's nineteenth-century Paris, endures meanness and contempt only to satisfy his insatiable desire for fine food while preserving his art collection, accumulated with another insatiable desire, in his shabby apartment? Or is he "a *Lumpensammler* (a trash collector) early in the morning twilight of the day *after* the revolution"?[40] Shen might never be one of those proud owners of a *Wunderkammer* (curiosity cabinet) to begin with. In the post-1949 era, he was not even a collector in the strict sense any more, for no private ownership of collection would be possible in a society where communism was the ideal. However, it was precisely at this historical turning point that the collector in Shen Congwen gained its full importance. What characterizes Shen Congwen the collector in a society of collectivity? In this section, through a critical reading of his essayistic writings around 1949, most of which were never printed in his lifetime, I examine Shen Congwen's distinctive aesthetic and historical vision as a pioneer of modern collector.

The collector has always been an intriguing figure in both Eastern and Western culture. Chinese literati are more or less art collectors. The ability to identify and appreciate good calligraphy, painting, and other cultural artifacts was essential for traditional Chinese literati.[41]

---

39. Shen, "Wo weishenme shizhong bulikan lishi bowuguan" (Why I determined not to leave the historical museum), *SCWQJ* 27: 247.

40. Benjamin, "Politisierung der Intelligenz," p. 428 (my emphasis).

41. One of the most famous literati collectors is Zhao Mingcheng (1081–1129), who not only gained great collections of *tapian* (rubbings from inscriptions or pictures on stone tablets or bronze vessels), but also made catalogues titled *Jinshilu* (Records on metal and stone). It is well-known for its preface by his wife, Li Qingzhao (1084–1155). For an interpretation of Li Qingzhao's preface and the

Among modern intellectuals as well, there are numerous collectors, such as Lu Xun, Zhu Guangqian, Zheng Zhenduo, and Lin Huiyin, to name a few.

No one would doubt Shen Congwen's position as one of the most prominent writers in the history of modern Chinese literature. However, few are aware of Shen as a significant art collector and connoisseur. His practice of collecting and connoisseurship started even before his career in literature, which eventually became his true métier. As early as the 1930s, Shen Congwen was one of the few art collectors who paid attention to the value of *qinghua ci* (blue-and-white porcelain), before it gained recognition in the art market. His collection also included silk and embroidery, ancient papers, and lacquerware. In this sense, Shen Congwen has good standing in the genealogy of collecting and connoisseurship of Chinese literati. In another sense, however, he completely rejects the traditional notion of connoisseurship, which regards culture as something pleasurable, something to be enjoyed in leisure time. In Shen's view, art represents beauty, life, and the divine. Art and its creative inspiration constitute the major content of history. The pathos that runs through Shen's understanding of art is the notion of history. In this latter sense, Shen Congwen asserts that "my understanding of and interest in arts are evidently different from both art theory in general, and common connoisseurship."[42] One can see the collector not only in Shen the antiquarian but also in Shen the writer. Walter Benjamin states that a collector is someone who wanders in the field of ruins and fragments from the past, in which the wish images of the past appear in the present.[43] In Shen Congwen's literary world, the wish images of Qu Yuan and the ancient Chu culture appear repetitively in the present, mixed up with his construction of a contemporary yet timeless utopian world Xiangxi (West Hunan). In this sense, his literary delineation of Xiangxi in its content and form is permeated with the spirit of collecting, wandering in the field of historical fragments.

---

connection between collection and recollection, see Stephen Owen, *Remembrances*, pp. 80–98.

42. Shen, "On Lacquerware of Southwest China and Others," *SCWQJ* 27: 23.

43. Benjamin, "Eduard Fuchs: Collector and Historian," p. 227.

Shen Congwen's main aesthetic contemplations are to be found in his essayistic writings during his wartime exile in Kunming, the eight years of the Second Sino-Japanese War (1937–1945), which he described as the fourth phase of his life, "very long, very lonely, and very hard."[44] Shen's aesthetic system consisted of his creative renderings of Taoist, Buddhist, and Confucian notions of art and life, and his peculiar interpretations of Immanuel Kant's (1724–1804) idealism and Friedrich Nietzsche's (1844–1900) Dionysian will of life. For Shen Congwen, things are essential for the reason that Beauty (*mei*) is located in them. And in the things that are beautiful exists Life (*shengming*). Consequently, in the fleeting moments of Life and Beauty, the Divine (*shen*) is captured. Things that are beautiful include both natural phenomena, such as stars, clouds, and plants, and artificial objects such as porcelain, brocades, music, literature, and so forth. In "Zhuxu" (Illuminating the abyss, 1941), the most important among his philosophical writings, he observed:

> This beauty perhaps has been produced by the creating hands of God. A slab of bronze, a piece of rock, a bundle of threads, an arrangement of sounds—though they are small as matter, [in them] may be seen the vastness and completeness of the world. Perhaps it is "creation" (*zaowu*), [or] most directly, most simply, "man." A shooting star or a lightning flash is gone in a transient moment; in this it manifests a beautiful sacredness, and man is the same. A smile, a frown—nothing is incapable of manifesting this sacredness.[45]

Beauty is both physical and abstract. It is tangible because it is crystallized in the distinct colors, forms, and arrangements of things. Shen Congwen states, "I found 'Beauty' in living things, whose forms and shapes in themselves represent the greatest virtue. One would love to be under its supremacy and domination. All wisdom originates from its influence."[46] On the other hand, Beauty is abstract in that it is close to the Divine, the formless principle that surpasses concrete time and space. In "Qianyuan" (Hidden profundity),

---

44. Shen, "Cong xianshi xuexi" (Learning from reality), *SCWQJ* 13: 389. This notion was repeated in the essay "Wode xuexi" (My study), his first essay published in the post-1949 years. It was originally written as a report during his political education in the Revolutionary University, where he was sent after his stay in the mental hospital.

45. Shen, "Zhuxu" (Illuminating the abyss), *SCWQJ* 12: 23–24.

46. Ibid., 12: 23.

he sees it as "a synthesis of endless things in endless spatialities and temporalities."[47] Beauty is eternal yet emerges in transient moments. It is a condition reminiscent both of the Kantian notion of the sublime and of the Buddhist concept of *dunwu* (sudden illumination). Again, in "Zhuxu," Shen describes it as a state in which it is "as if [one is] poisoned, or hit by lightning. Someone in such a state is deprived of any ability of language, paralyzed, and loses all his beliefs."[48]

Only things that are beautiful have Life. Life and Beauty are inseparable. Shen defines *shengming* as the opposite of *shenghuo*. *Shenghuo* indicates men's physical living, a degraded form of existence based on "the principle of animals," "seeking the satisfaction of food and sex."[49] *Shengming*, on the other hand, is an exalted form of *shenghuo*, seeking the Divine, "a spiritual activity with higher ideals and virtues."[50] With the increasing urbanization and commodification in modern times, people are more and more degraded into existence as animals. Although Life is not possible without basic physical existence of living, such "living" without Life is a biological degeneration. Accordingly, one has to transcend the physical living to approach the Beauty, the Abstract.[51]

Shen Congwen believed that among all the attempts to approach the Divine, art, be it applied arts, painting, music, or literature, is the most important way to capture and represent such ephemeral moments. Creativity is thus a divine expression of Beauty and Life. "Everything that is able to capture these beautiful, mystical fleeting moments will preserve these moments in life forever. Dante, Goethe, Cao Zhi, and Li Yu are among those who have kept these moments by forming them with words."[52] Thus, art is not only the way to maintain the Beautiful and the Divine but also the way to transcend the physical aspect of living, to reach the sublime form of Life. Literature, to be sure, is a significant way to represent Beauty and there-

---

47. Shen, "Qianyuan" (Hidden profundity), *SCWQJ* 12: 34.
48. Shen, "Illuminating the Abyss," *SCWQJ* 12: 24.
49. Shen, "Xiaoshuo de zuozhe yu duzhe" (The authors and readers of fiction), *SCWQJ* 12: 70–72.
50. Shen, "Hidden Profundity," *SCWQJ* 12: 34.
51. Shen, "Shengming" (Life), *SCWQJ* 12: 42–45.
52. Shen, "Illuminating the Abyss," *SCWQJ* 12: 24.

fore to achieve immortality; however, since Beauty is abstract and in constant metamorphosis, Shen comes to the conclusion, reminiscent of Kant, that it is "better captured in painting than literature, in mathematics than painting; better still, in music."[53]

In Shen Congwen's aesthetic reflections, art represents Beauty, Life, and the Divine, which make up the Abstract—the very essential Shen attempted to convey by means of literary and artistic experiments. This concept is emphasized once again in "Guanyu xinan qiqi ji qita" (On lacquerware of southwest China and others), an essay Shen wrote during a time of excessive political pressure in 1949 as a part of his autobiography, which was never completed. Focusing on his collecting of lacquerware in wartime Yunnan and how such activity contributes to the construction of Chinese cultural history, Shen evaluates the influences of music and art upon him from early childhood through every phase of his literary experimentation. He claims that the most essential of all arts, including music, fine arts, and literature, is no less than "human nature," which is intrinsic in the artwork.[54] Accordingly, he states, "what I must stress in particular is that what I love is not just art, but more important, the soul, which has created poignant artworks, a simple soul of a true 'human being.'"[55] Collecting becomes for him a way of capturing life and getting in touch with the subjectivity inscribed into the artwork.

If art is where the true life is located, then, it is the artwork and the life crystallized in it that constitute the history of humanity. From Shen's point of view, history is never the monumental history composed of wars or political conspiracies. Instead, it appears in the form of art and culture, whose essence remains unchanged through thousands of years, namely, Beauty and Life, which are embedded in the artwork. These objects of eternal beauty carry bits and pieces of history and construct the body of real history. They function as connections between different ages and enable the past to live in the present and extend into the future. This conception of history informed Shen's first contact with Chinese art, which can be dated

53. Ibid., 12: 25.

54. Shen, "On Lacquerware of Southwest China and Others," *SCWQJ* 27: 21. This article was never published during Shen's life time.

55. Ibid., 27: 23.

back to his early years in the West Hunan army. When he was a secretary for Chen Quzhen (1882–1952), the reformist warlord in West Hunan, Shen catalogued Chen's collection of old books, paintings, porcelain, and other antiques, an experience that Shen later identified as "a time and place to learn history." These artistic objects were the source of memory, that is, of cultural memory of the past. "This was truly a turning point for me. As a result, I was endowed the opportunity to know and approach the brilliance of various ages and various aspects of the whole history."[56] In these artifacts, he saw scraps and ruins of bygone years, the true essence of human history. After witnessing the decapitation of thousands of innocent people, Shen came to believe that history is composed not of war and politics but of various arts, consisting of "a slice of color, a bundle of threads, a slab of bronze or a pile of earth and an arrangement of words, combining with the life of the artist,"[57] a point Shen further elaborated about ten years later in "Illuminating the Abyss" during his aesthetic contemplation in wartime Kunming.

Shen's conception of history is underscored in his writings from the subsequent civil war period. Confronted with nearly eight years of war with the Japanese and with the ongoing civil war between the KMT and the CCP, Shen Congwen was determined to counter political violence with art and creativity, which he thought could enlighten the nation and prevent further destruction. Not surprisingly, his emphasis on art and literature was criticized and condemned as an untimely aestheticist gesture of "l'art pour l'art."[58] Accused of being indifferent to reality, Shen Congwen wrote "Cong xianshi xuexi" (Learning from reality), in which he stressed that the "reality" that had been exposed to him over the years was actually "completely different from what is understood by the intellectuals who grew up in a hothouse environment, as well as from what is imagined by those who grew up in small cities but claim to be members of the proletariat."[59] The reality he witnessed was that of military force, vi-

56. Shen, *Congwen zizhuan* (Congwen's autobiography), *SCWQJ* 13: 355.

57. Ibid., 13: 356.

58. Shen was criticized as being an aestheticist by Shiyi in his article "1948 nian xiaoshuo chuangzuo niaokan," quoted in Qian Liqun, *1948: Tiandi xuanhuang*, p. 255.

59. Shen, "Cong xianshi xuexi" (Learning from reality), *SCWQJ* 13: 373.

olence, and political conspiracies, which he felt would eventually destroy the country. He even composed a Buddhist chant to describe this sentiment: "Everything is like a theater, decorating politics. Everything is like a dream, it cannot be taken seriously. Every reality has a vacuity behind it. Looking at it carefully, I am filled with grief and compassion."[60] In order to save the whole nation from a tragic self-destruction, one has to deny and reject such a concept of reality and reconstruct a new and reasonable reality based on conceptions of art and beauty.

Such a pacifist historical and political vision inevitably diverges from the teleological notion of history-as-revolution held by the leftist camp, which, with the severe corruption of the KMT government and the predictable victory of the Communists, gradually became the dominant political force. At a time when the majority of intellectuals and students were becoming increasingly sympathetic to the Communist Party, Shen was one of the few to be suspicious and to express his concerns without any reservations. Not surprisingly, he became the major target of the leftist camp, and his "Learning from Reality" and other writings of the time were fiercely attacked. Guo Moruo sensed the dangerous message in Shen Congwen's distinctive notion of literature and history, and therefore when Guo condemned Shen's writings as "evil, wrong, and antirevolutionary," what provoked him was not only the seemingly "peach-pink" erotic description in "Kan hong lu" (Gazing at the rainbow),[61] but, more important, Shen's nonconformist attitude and his antipolitical and anti–civil war writings at a time when "the people's revolutionary force and anti-people's reactionary force are engaging in a face-to-face fight."[62]

In the fall of 1949, Shen began to work at the National Museum of History. Although his official job was to write labels for the museum collections, Shen in his fifties determined to start another course of self-education, this time in art history. The majority of his collection had already been donated to Peking University, where he

---

60. Ibid., 13: 388.

61. Guo Moruo misread "kan hong lu" (gazing at the rainbow) as "kan yun lu" (gazing at the clouds).

62. Guo, "Chi fandong wenyi," pp. 19–22.

helped to found the Department of Museum Studies in 1948.[63] The rest of his accumulations were brought to his work unit, the National Museum of History, during the 1950s and 1960s. Hence, he turned into a collector without collection, or more precisely, he became the collector and the historian in the National Museum of History. He visited provincial museums and archaeological excavations and used his antiquarian and historical knowledge to distinguish and purchase objects for the museum's collection. Before long, corroborating literary and archaeological evidence, he completed articles on textile designs, Tang and Song mirrors, Ming brocades, and other types of artworks. When the second All-China Congress of Literary and Art Representatives took place in 1953 in Beijing, Shen Congwen, who was not allowed to be present as a writer at the first congress, attended as a member of the fine arts sector.[64]

To be sure, Shen would never mean to live intentionally as a dissident in the PRC. Jenny Huangfu's 2010 article discusses how Shen sought to adjust to the new state, as his participation in the criticism against Xiao Qian (1910–99) showed. However, although he attempted to fit into the new political and social environments, he hardly changed his views in the field of literature and art.[65] Beneath this seemingly mutual accommodation of Shen and the new regime lay the greatest clash, between Shen's conception of history and the dominant historical vision. At the time, Maoist historiography was sanctioned as the only legitimate conception of history. With full conviction in his version of art and history, Shen dedicated himself to the study of Chinese art and art history and attempted to compose art histories of silk, lacquerware, porcelain, and so on. Even during the most agonizing years of the Cultural Revolution, Shen still claimed that historical progress "must be reflected in individual events, with it, everything in the history of production development, in the history of technological invention, and in the history of mate-

---

63. Shen, "Why I Determined Not to Leave the Historical Museum," *SCWQJ* 27: 242.

64. Ling Yu, *Shen Congwen zhuan*, p. 441.

65. Jenny Huangfu, "Roads to Salvation." Shen was invited a couple of times in the 1950s to resume creative writing. However, this prolific writer prior to the 1949 divide was never able to complete any fiction.

rial culture."[66] Whereas Shen believed that a museum of history constituted a site where people could get to know Chinese history through cultural artifacts and artworks, the Maoist vision of the National Museum of History was as a place to document and display peasants' rebellions and class struggles through different dynasties and different historical stages, which should form a historical continuum of revolutions leading to the ultimate socialist revolution.[67]

Among modern intellectuals, Walter Benjamin proposes the most illuminating concepts of collector and collecting. When Benjamin nostalgically hails the figure of the collector in modern society in a series of articles in the 1930s,[68] the historical conditions to which he was responding were threefold: the increasing commodification and reification in capitalist society, the tightening Nazi oppression and its barbaric threats to human civilization, and last but not least, the authoritative historicism and cultural history that turned knowledge into a burden "piled up on humanity's back."[69] In the positive type of collector and collecting, Benjamin sees the possibility of breaking through the frozen world of commodities and the parasitic conformism of tradition, and thus the hope of redemption. Whereas Benjamin's notion of collector was developed on the capitalist eve of revolution, Shen's collector achieved its full power in the dawn, after the socialist revolution that annihilated a short-lived capitalism in China. The historical situation Shen faced was the threat of another barbarism, the socialist historicism looming large, which forged a Maoist

---

66. Shen, "Huida" (Response), *SCWQJ* 27: 177.

67. According to the former museum director Chen Qiao, the guiding principle for the National Museum of History is to put class struggle first and to examine historical figures strictly; Chen Qiao, quoted in Chen Tushou, "Shen Congwen under the Wumen Gate," p. 24. Shortly after the establishment of the PRC, the National Museum of Revolution was built at the Tiananmen Square. This new building is completely dedicated to a creation of a visual official history of Chinese revolution following Mao's historiographical periodization. For a study of the Museum of Revolution, see Kirk A. Denton, "Visual Memory and the Construction of a Revolutionary Past."

68. These articles include Benjamin, "Unpacking My Library: A Talk about Book Collecting," in *Illuminations*, pp. 59–68; "Eduard Fuchs: Collector and Historian," "Surrealism: The Last Snapshot of the European Intelligentsia," and "Paris, Capital of the Nineteenth Century," in *Reflections*, pp. 146–62; among others.

69. Benjamin, "Eduard Fuchs," p. 234.

historical vision whose ultimate course comes from class struggles. The significance of Shen as collector thus lies in the alternative notion of culture and history that it provides. Rey Chow argues that one reason Benjamin's work is so powerful is that "he manages to turn this entrenched discursive stereotyping of love-of-things-as-selfishness around by arguing that collecting, however private and selfish it may seem, can also be understood as a kind of historical-materialist practice."[70] Significantly, Shen's art historical practice provides an ironic twist to Maoist historical materialism, which is nothing but a *métarécit* of revolution and class struggle and regards material culture and history as decadent and reactionary. Therefore, whereas Benjamin attempted to redeem and reassemble fragments and scraps of history from their dead status within commodity fetishism and conformism of tradition, Shen Congwen, who himself had already been discarded by canonical literary history, metamorphosed into an actual *Lumpensammler*, a collector of trash, who accumulated the ruins and debris of Chinese tradition that were ruthlessly shed and smashed in the storm of progress named socialism.

The Delirious Mind of the Cold War: The Discourse of Schizophrenia

> Recollecting the scene in *Quo Vadis*, in which a group of people about to be sacrificed in the Colosseum were waiting in the basement, I feel gentle and peaceful.
>
> Shen Congwen, Diary entry, April 6, 1949

In a brief note that she contributed to the *Complete Works of Shen Congwen*, Shen Congwen's wife Zhang Zhaohe states: "Shen Congwen eventually succumbed to mental disorders (*jingshen shichang*) in January 1949, and tried to kill himself in March. After he was saved, he was sent to a mental hospital. . . . His mental condition gradually improved that same fall and winter."[71] What Zhang describes here as "mental disorders" was later referred to as "schizophrenia" (*jingshen*

70. Rey Chow, "Fateful Attachments," p. 290.
71. Shen, *SCWQJ* 27: 2.

fenlie).[72] Whereas it remains arguable whether the term "schizophrenia" accurately diagnoses Shen's mental disorders, the discourse of schizophrenia conceived both as a pathological term and a cultural and political metaphor helps us to consider Shen's psychological and cultural crisis in a time of political indeterminacies.

Modern psychiatry has considered schizophrenia—characterized by disintegration of personality expressed as blurred boundaries between the self and the external world, emotional disturbances, delusions, and hallucinations—to be one of the most severe and enigmatic illnesses. Even today, the illness is not fully understood. Given its elusiveness, schizophrenia is sometimes regarded as "the sacred symbol of psychiatry"[73] or "madness *par excellence*."[74] The French psychiatrist Bénédict Augustin Morel (1809–73) coined the term *démence precoce* (dementia praecox) in 1856 to describe a condition of mental deterioration. Emil Kraepelin (1855–1926) revitalized the term "dementia praecox" in 1896 to conceptualize a set of psychiatric disorders manifested in this mental disease. The diagnostic category was later refined by Eugen Bleuler (1857–1939) in his significant monograph *Dementia Praecox or the Group of Schizophrenias* (1911), in which he coined the term "schizophrenia" and redefined it as dynamic psychophathology. In the understanding and treatment of schizophrenia, there have been two major theories: Kraepelin proposed in 1919 that schizophrenia was caused by pathological, anatomical, or chemical disturbance in the brain, or mental deterioration[75];

---

72. According to Shen Longzhu, Shen Congwen's eldest son, after Shen Congwen was saved during his attempted suicide, he was sent to the Beijing Anding Hospital, the first national institution for mental health, by Zhang Zhonghe, his wife's brother. No medical diagnoses are available. In recollections of his relatives and also in Shen's letters to relatives and friends around the time of his nervous breakdown, the notions *jingshen fenlie zheng* and *renge fenlie* (schizophrenia) often appeared to describe his mental illness; see Huang Yongyu, "Zheyixie youyu de suoxie," p. 480; see also, for instance, Shen's letter to Ding Ling dated September 8, 1949, *SCWQJ* 19: 48. As scholars have noted, mental illness might have run in the Shen family. Shen Yuemeng, Shen's younger sister, for instance, suffered from schizophrenia in middle age; see Kinkley, *Odyssey of Shen Congwen*, p. 292; Huang, "Zheyixie youyu de suoxie," pp. 442–47.

73. Thomas Szasz, *Schizophrenia*, p. 18.

74. Michel Foucault, *Order of Things*, p. 375.

75. Kraepelin, *Dementia praecox and Paraphrenia.*

Sigmund Freud (1856–1939) approached the disorder psychoanalytically and regarded it as a regression to the primitive stage of "infantile auto-erotism" dominated by an archaic mode of experience, and accordingly he held that it was the result of a deficiency of the psyche.[76] Thus the debate among early theorists centered on whether schizophrenia was a disease of the mind or that of the emotions.

The schizophrenic has been a central figure in literary, artistic, and intellectual imagery and discourses of modernism and the avant-garde, often valorized for his or her unfettered passion, desire, and vitality, and for a corresponding ability to break through what R. D. Laing refers to as the "appalling state of alienation called normality."[77] As Laing stresses, "What we call 'schizophrenia' was one of the forms in which, often through quite ordinary people, the light began to break through the cracks in our all-too-closed minds."[78] Laing, one of the most iconoclastic antipsychiatrists of the twentieth century, is the prominent advocate of this conceptualization of schizophrenia as being a state of a "divided self."

Influenced by the Nietzschean Dionysian model, with its emphasis on excessive passion, imagination, and vitality, Gilles Deleuze and Felix Guattari developed this positive notion of schizophrenia into a powerful theoretical discourse. In *Anti-Oedipus*, the first volume of their collaborative work *Capitalism and Schizophrenia*, they launched a forceful thought experiment they called "schizoanalysis," which seeks to bring historical materialist and psychoanalytic dynamics together in the analysis of sociohistorical and cultural changes. Like Laing, Deleuze and Guattari understood the schizophrenic beyond its usual clinical implications. Regarded as a "revolutionary materialist psychiatry,"[79] their work constructed the term not only as a frontal attack on the established institution of psychoanalysis epitomized by the Freudian Oedipus complex but also as a powerful critical method for analyzing cultural and sociopolitical texts under any repressive psychosocial mechanisms.

---

76. Freud, "Psychoanalytic Notes," p. 153.
77. Laing, *Politics of Experience*, p. 167.
78. Ibid.
79. Holland, *Deleuze and Guattari's Anti-Oedipus*, p. viii.

With schizophrenia, Freud argues, the libido leads back to the self, resulting in regressive narcissism. Therefore, the disease cannot be decoded in psychoanalytical terms and engenders an irresolvable psychiatric complex. However, it is precisely in schizophrenia's resistance to decoding—or its "resistance to being oedipalized,"[80] in schizoanalytical terminology—that Deleuze and Guattari find its essential revolutionary potential. In the breakdowns of the schizophrenic, they discern the possibility of counterhegemonic "breakthroughs," arguing that "madness is a radical break from power in the form of a disconnection."[81] Schizoid desires can unravel artificial categories such as those of the nation, ethnicity, party, and family, together with their underlying repressive social mechanisms. In this way, the schizophrenic opens up "lines of flight" to smash the hegemonic system. Recent critical thinking on imperialism continues Deleuze and Guattari's theoretical thrusts, applying notions of schizoid resistance—the schizophrenic, lines of flight, and deterritorialization—to a new multitude breaking through the impending reterritorialization of empire.

Inasmuch as this notion of schizoid political agency opens up new possibilities of subversion against political hegemony, it is of particular importance to my examination of intellectual activities in mid-twentieth century China for writers like Shen Congwen. Whereas the discourse of the schizophrenic process finds emancipatory potentials to overcome the cultural oppression of late capitalism in schizoid openings, fragments, and flows, it helps elucidate schizophrenic intellectual agencies within the overriding ideological dominance in Cold War China and, of particular relevance to Shen's case, the monolithic totality of Chinese socialism. Shen's 1949 transition started with a schizophrenic breakdown and ensuing suicide attempt—a personal crisis that literally and figuratively constituted a turning point for Shen's survival within the Maoist authoritarian era. As I argue in this chapter, in his post-1949 work as cultural historian, Shen found in the multitude of fragmented historical artifacts and

---

80. Deleuze and Guattari, *Anti-Oedipus*, p. 23.
81. Ibid., p. xxiii.

episodic art historical accounts a possible escape from socialist totalitarianism.

Schizoid deterritorializations enable forms of resistance to and subversion of the totalizing structure of socialist socio-symbolic orders, but avoid yet another apocalyptic vision of revolution to take its place. As Jean Franco has pointed out in her mapping of Cold War Latin American literature and culture, "resistance is not putting up a fight to the death but the detection and intensification of 'lines of flight' that transform individuals."[82] In the emphatically binary environment of the Cold War era, the splitting schizophrenic process provides a way of overcoming the propensity for apocalyptic thinking, which foregrounds the redemptive and transfiguring power of war, revolution, or any other form of political violence.

However, although the discourse of insanity and schizophrenia as positive political agencies may open up new perspectives on political and cultural hegemony, it nevertheless tends to underplay the pain and paralysis induced by schizophrenia as a pathopsychological disease that afflicts both the individual psyche and the national body politic. Reflecting on the politics of everyday life in postwar Munich shortly after the political and territorial division in Germany, the German writer Wolfgang Koeppen (1906–96) perceptively observes, "TENSION, CONFLICT, you lived in a field of tension, eastern world, western world, you lived on the seam, perhaps just where the seam would split open."[83] Indeed, such was the inevitable existential reality keenly felt by everyone in the age of Cold War division. The same issues of how to survive and to confront political and social transformations were at stake in China, the Cold War's frontier in East Asia, which was itself divided into disparate geographical and ideological entities. At the 1949 divide, for Shen Congwen and his fellow Chinese, this was a pain that would never vanish.

At the dawn of modern Chinese literature, Lu Xun, with his short story "Kuangren riji" (Diary of a madman, 1918), introduced a case of mental illness, in particular, "a form of persecution complex."[84]

---

82. Franco, *Decline and Fall of the Lettered City*, p. 265.

83. Koeppen, *Tauben im Gras*, p. 8.

84. Lu Xun, *LXQJ* 1: 9. English translation is from Lu Xun, *Selected Stories of Lu Hsun*, p. 7.

Employing a schizophrenic voice, the forefather of Chinese literary modernity examined the pathology of Chinese history both metaphysically and metaphorically. Thirty years later, amid the political and ideological division of the mid-twentieth century, Shen Congwen, the most significant short story writer after Lu Xun, was actually living such a psychiatric illness. Reflecting on the sociopolitical condition in socialist China, Cao Juren (1900–72) recalls a remark in 1950 by Ai Siqi (1910–66), the Communist party theorist, who urged liberal intellectuals to transform themselves: an intellectual is "like a brick, if it was built into a wall, it could no longer move; if not, and dropped to the foot of the wall, it would be kicked away."[85] Unwilling to be built into the wall or disposed of, Cao determined to leave mainland China for Hong Kong shortly after the establishment of the People's Republic. Shen Congwen, who decided to stay, soon became one of the discarded bricks. Although Cao was right about the inevitable elimination of insubordinate individuals, the actual process was much more complicated than even he could have imagined. Abandonment was just the first step. What then happened to these discarded bricks that could not fit in?

The case of Shen Congwen is surely illuminating. Given that there are no detailed medical diagnoses of Shen's illness, the collection of his letters, diaries, and other texts written during his psychological crisis provide important clues to investigate his state of mind. In "Yige ren de zibai" (One man's confession), an article written one month before his attempted suicide in March 1949, Shen observes that his purpose in composing these confessional writings was to provide "a case file for pathology (*bingli xue*) or abnormal psychology (*biantai xinli xue*)."[86] Examples include the following passages written when Shen lived at Liang Sicheng and Lin Huiyin's house at Tsinghua University where he sought refuge from the excessive political pressures upon him:

> Give me less painful rest, and no need to wake up, it would then be fine. Everything I say, nobody understands. Not even one friend is willing to understand, has the courage to understand that I am not mad. They all just hedge and dodge the issue, afraid of getting involved. It doesn't matter, one

85. Cao Juren, quoted in Li Wei, *Cao Juren zhuan*, pp. 333–34.
86. Shen, "Yige ren de zibai" (One man's confession), *SCWQJ* 27: 3.

> is bound to rest, why is it not proper to put oneself in order? Even Wang Xun, who has studied philosophy, didn't understand, and regarded me truly as a madman. I think a lot of people have a hand in the persecution; there will be fun to watch.[87]
>
> Nobody is willing to understand, and just elides the issue. I am in complete isolation. Isolated and desperate, I have never had any illusive hope of survival. I should rest![88]
>
> I should rest, my nerves have reached the utmost I can bear. I would go mad even if I were not to be destroyed.[89]
>
> The world is moving, everything is moving. Yet, I remain still and look at it sympathetically. I am not part of it, not part of anything. I am not insane! But, why does my family remain the same, whereas I exist in such an utterly alienated and helpless way. Why? Why on earth? Answer me.[90]

Words such as "rest" and "liberation" arise frequently in Shen's vocabulary of the time and function as euphemisms for "taking one's own life." Profound feelings of isolation and of not being understood permeate his writings following the siege of Beijing by the Communist army in December 1948. A couple of days after the 1949 wall poster incident at Peking University, Shen wrote a letter to his nephew Huang Yongyu, a woodcut artist who was in Hong Kong at the time, in which he observes that "the city will be conquered in a couple of days. Given all those complicated interpersonal relationships in my past, I am ready for the gallows."[91] Shen Congwen was caught in a Kafkaesque state of anxious alienation—an implosion of the inner self. The themes of death—the "rest"—and insanity constantly arise in his writings before the attempted suicide. When Shen says, "Nobody is willing to understand, and just elides the issue," what was it, precisely, that people were ignoring? Furthermore, the indisputable and transparent use of the term "madness" in the discussions of Shen's mental illness leaves unaddressed issues that are crucial to the interpretation of Shen Congwen's case. What are the politics of mental health? What particular functions and implications

---

87. "Zhang Zhaohe to Shen Congwen, and Shen Congwen's Remarks in Response to Zhang Zhaohe, 19490130, Beijing, Tsinghua Yuan," *SCWQJ* 19: 9.

88. Ibid., 19: 11.

89. Shen, "Remarks on *Green Nightmare*," *SCWQJ* 14: 456.

90. Shen, "Wuyue sanshi xiawu shidian Beiping sushe" (10 p.m. May 30 in the Dorm in Beijing), *SCWQJ* 19: 43.

91. Huang Yongyu, "Zheyixie youyu de suoxie," p. 465.

does the concept of madness assume in the social and historical context of 1949?

To address these questions, I begin by returning to the wall posters displayed at Peking University in January 1949. What message was delivered when young students pasted Guo Moruo's article "A Denunciation of Reactionary Literature and Art" on campus walls? After all, this was not the first time Shen was attacked from the left. In the 1930s, he had been repeatedly assaulted for his liberal, noncommunist stance. In the early 1940s, Shen was accused of being a member of the pro-fascist Zhanguo ce clique because of his editorial role in the journal *Zhanguo ce* (Annals of the warring states), founded by a group of the National Southwest Associated University professors in Kunming. Shen Congwen saw in *Annals of the Warring States* a venue to create a liberal intellectual forum independent from both Nationalist and Communist forces. Although his contributions to the journal show that he hardly shared the notions of hero worship and militarism advocated by key editorial members including Chen Quan (1903–69), Lin Tongji (1906–80), and Lei Haizong (1902–62), his involvement with the journal implicated him in dubious political activities. In the early years of socialist China, this affiliation seriously jeopardized his chances of political survival.[92] In an interview, Xia Yan recalled that one major reason Shen was excluded from the First All-China Congress of Literary and Art Representatives was his suspicious affiliation with *Annals of the Warring States*, which "promoted fascism."[93] At the request of Xiao Qian, Shen Congwen in 1948 endorsed *Xinlu* (New road), a journal that was soon denounced as anticommunist and embarking on a "third road," thereby further endangering his already precarious political standing.[94] In her examination of Shen Congwen's and Xiao Qian's disparate strategies of accommodation to the new socialist regime, Jenny Huangfu discusses

---

92. For a good study of *Annals of the Warring States*, see Wu Shiyong, "Wei wenxue yundong de chongzao." Although Shen never endorsed the militarism or fascist authoritarianism advocated by some members of the journal, he still felt a need to disavow his connection with the journal and, in fact, would later deny he had ever had an editorial role with it; see Kinkley, *Odyssey of Shen Congwen*, pp. 253–54.

93. Wu Shiyong, "Wei wenxue yundong de chongzao," p. 19.

94. Xie, "Xinlu yu Guancha."

Shen's denunciation of Xiao during the Anti-Rightist Campaign and argues that it was Shen's involvement with Xiao in the establishment of *New Road* that partly caused the post-1949 rupture between the two.[95]

The original publication of Guo Moruo's article, "A Denunciation of Reactionary Literature and Art," which should be read as political denunciation rather than as literary criticism, did not attract much attention from Shen. On the eve of the Communist takeover, however, the posting of Guo's article on Peking University's campus came to signify nothing less than a totalistic denunciation of Shen's entire literary oeuvre, thereby guaranteeing Shen's final withdrawal from literature. Later, in the mental hospital, Shen understood his vulnerability in the new political climate: "Meanwhile, I found out that literature is bound to be identified with propaganda; only then can it take on the significance and effect of edifying the majority. . . . It completely demolished my previous ideas of literature. Relentlessly demolished. I am bound to, have to stop writing."[96] And his anticipation turned out to be well founded.

Like other intellectuals aboard the "sinking ship"—a metaphor he repeatedly invokes in his writings from this period—of the Nationalist regime, Shen was surely aware that individual agents would inevitably be sacrificed to the looming force of collectivity in the form of the Communist political authority. However, whereas his colleagues started to modify their aesthetic conceptions, Shen remained one of the very few who publicly expressed deep suspicion toward the imminent new ideology. On November 7, 1948, at a forum convened at Peking University entitled "The Direction of Today's Literature," Shen questioned whether literature should be controlled by politics. Using the trope of traffic signals to discuss the interaction between literature and politics, he asked, "What if the traffic lights were manipulated?" "Literature is confined by politics, to be sure; however, is it possible for literature to maintain some right of criticism and amendment?"[97] How to defend an independent space for

95. Huangfu, "Roads to Salvation."

96. Shen, "19490406," *SCWQJ* 19: 25.

97. The transcript of the discussions was first published in *Dagong bao* 107, November 14, 1948. Reprinted in Hong Zicheng, *Zhongguo dangdai wenxueshi shiliaoxuan 1945–1999*, pp. 143–49.

art and literature? How is writing still possible after politics dominates all? On the verge of the Communist triumph, Shen insisted on literary autonomy untrammeled by politics, whereas his colleagues attempted to sound out a new relationship between politics and literature.

Shen Congwen's insistence on artistic autonomy and individual agency led inevitably to his political ostracism and isolation in the transitional period. When he describes how a "certain feeling of vacuity and dissociation emerged from deep in my heart; it was as if I were completely isolated in the world, as if I were completely severed from the sadness and happiness of the masses,"[98] what unsettles him is not so much the alienation of the elite class of intellectuals from the masses, which, as discussed previously, Zhu Ziqing forcefully implicated in his symbolic rejection of cultural relics. Rather, what *liqun* (separation from the masses) means for Shen Congwen is the inexorable sacrifice of the individual agent to the fanatical masses worshiping a political idol—a process he was about to witness at Tiananmen Square, near which he would spend the next thirty years of his professional life.

In a sense, Shen's aesthetic determination in an age of political fanaticism turned him into yet another tragic madman in a lineage that, as Shen himself observed, traces back to Qu Yuan, his spiritual forefather. "The only sober person while everyone was drunk" (*zhongren jiezui wo duxing*), this minister of the ancient Chu kingdom was banished from the imperial court, committed suicide in protest, and was eventually transformed into the eternal image of "the madman in Chu," an image that Shen Congwen constantly evoked during his psychological crisis. Like Qu Yuan, Shen would rather end his own life than compromise his cultural and political positions to ensure his survival in a new regime. In this light, madness can be viewed as a form of determination to stand by one's purity and principles. Shen's mental illness, meanwhile, also bespeaks the volatile boundary between madness and sanity, and therefore could be understood in Foucauldian terms as an illustration of how concepts of insanity and reason are inseparably intertwined. In the age of reason, the lunatic must be separated from the

---

98. Shen, "10 p.m. May 30 in the Dorm in Beijing," *SCWQJ* 19: 43.

social mainstream, either in "ships of fools" cast off in the sea or in an asylum segregated from the rest of the world, so that rationality can be maintained.

Some thirty years before Shen's breakdown, a positive vision of madness was presented by Lu Xun in his short story "Diary of a madman." Examining Chinese society within the context of the suffocating years of stagnation following the 1911 Revolution, Lu Xun portrays his madman as a Cassandra-like figure who, tirelessly warning of the cannibalism lurking beneath the veneer of traditional Chinese moralism, stands "invariably ahead of [his] time, [and thus] must suffer the fate of being misunderstood and persecuted by the very people whom [he wishes] to serve."[99] Just as Laing argues, in the same intellectual zeitgeist as Foucault, "Madness need not be all breakdown, it may also be break-through."[100] In Lu Xun's literary modernity, madness constitutes a particular social institution of confinement where the dangerous prophet is banished so as to safeguard the social order out of politically reactionary motives. As Antonin Artaud explains with regard to the insanity of intellectuals such as Vincent van Gogh (1853–90), Ludwig van Beethoven (1770–1827), and Friedrich Hölderlin (1770–1843), "So a sick society invented psychiatry to defend itself against the investigations of certain visionaries whose faculties of divination disturbed it."[101] Viewed this way, madness is revealed to be yet another "iron house,"[102] though now the iron house is being used to bolster the legitimacy of medical discourse.

At the turning point of 1949, Shen Congwen was trapped in just such an iron house, no matter what scientific name it bears—madness, depression, schizophrenia, or paranoia. Being cast off into complete isolation, Shen and his idea of artistic autonomy could no longer cause any "harm" to the normality and rationality of the newly founded socialist state. "I am very tired, very tired. I heard the dog barking incessantly. Why do you still bark? You would be quiet if you ate me. I offer myself indifferently, whether to feed the

---

99. Leo Lee, *Voices from the Iron House*, p. 54.
100. Laing, *Politics of Experience*, p. 110.
101. Artaud, "Van Gogh: The Man Suicided by Society," p. 135.
102. Lu Xun, *LXQJ* 1: 9.

dog or the tiger, it's the same. The society is progressing; will these noises end in a couple of years?"[103] Using images of dogs and tigers to embody the beastly nature of potential persecutors, Shen presents his vision of cannibalism to expose social oppression. Such delirious remarks are astounding in their conspicuous similarity to those of Lu Xun's madman. Indeed, the Chinese society that Lu Xun diagnosed as ill has never ceased searching for modernization. However, after forty years, the vicious "dog" in Lu Xun's "Diary of a Madman" is still menacing, wild for a taste of human flesh.

Although Shen's mental breakdown can be attributed to the enormous political pressure of the time, critics lately have suggested that it may be more a process of "self-destruction" (*zihui*) rather than simply political persecution.[104] Indeed, Shen's tenacious insistence on artistic autonomy when he knew such a position would incur fierce reprisals suggests an act of self-sacrifice or self-negation. Furthermore, I would argue that it also includes an element of schizophrenia. At a clinical level, schizophrenia is basically understood as a disorder of self-identity and self-experience, typically manifested through a fundamental uncertainty regarding the boundaries of the self. The schizophrenic treats his or her self as both subject and object, with the relation between them being "so severely disturbed that it takes the form of an intrapsychic splitting."[105] The uncompromising contestations between schizoid identities can reach the most exacerbated stage of self-negation. At the same time, Shen's nonconformist pursuit of the true meaning of literature and art through arduous self-reflection is a pursuit of self or at least a restoration of a precarious self-identity.

Given the implications of self-consumption and self-interrogation in the discourse of schizophrenia, Shen Congwen's self-negation via insanity suggests not only Lu Xun's madman and the allegory of cannibalism but, more poignantly, the grotesque imagery of eating one's own flesh found in Lu Xun's prose poem "Mujie wen" (Epitaph), from his collection *Yecao* (Wild grass, 1927). The frag-

103. Shen, *SCWQJ* 19: 11.

104. Zhang Xinying, "Cong 'chouxiang de shuqing' dao 'yiyu kuangyan' "; He Guimei, *Zhuanzhe de shidai*, pp. 82–133.

105. Zahavi, "Schizophrenia and Self-Awareness," p. 340.

mentary inscription on the front of the epitaph reads, "There is a wandering spirit which takes the form of a serpent with poisonous fangs. Instead of biting others, it bites itself, and so it perishes," whereas the inscription on the back of the tablet takes a first-person narrative stance and elaborates on the act of cannibalism in devouring his own heart:

> I tore out my heart to eat it, wanting to know its true taste. But the pain was so agonizing, how could I tell its taste? . . .
>
> When the pain subsided, I savored the heart. But since by then it was already stale, how could I know its true taste?[106]

With his body mutilated, how could the I-narrator be capable of perceiving and conceiving the psychic, epistemological, or aesthetic truth? By depicting a dismembered body using textual fragments, Lu Xun reflects on the paradox that the search for the true meaning of life and of selfhood can only be conducted through the destruction of the body, through the eradication of the self.

As Leo Ou-fan Lee points out, at the time Lu Xun was writing *Wild Grass* he was influenced by the aesthetic and psychological theories of Kuriyagawa Hakuson, whose writings highlight the connection between artistic creativity and repressed life forces.[107] Like Lu Xun, who translated Kuriyagawa's *Kumon no sōchō* into Chinese with the title *Kumen de xiangzheng* (Symbols of anguish, 1924), Shen Congwen was an enthusiastic reader of Western psychology and psychoanalysis.[108] According to Jingyuan Zhang's research, psychology and Freudianism were introduced to China during the early years of the twentieth century, along with other important philosophical schools such as social Darwinism, Marxism, and pragmatism, and

---

106. Lu Xun, *LXQJ* 2: 202.

107. Leo Lee, *Voices from the Iron House*, pp. 92–97.

108. Shen Congwen read widely in psychology; see Kinkley, *Odyssey of Shen Congwen*, pp. 111–13. According to Zhang Zhaohe, he loved reading the book *Abnormal Psychology*; see Shen, *SCWQJ* 19: 22. Ironically, Shen himself conjectured that he might have fallen victim to his profound interest in Western psychology, just like his neighbor, the president of an asylum, who eventually went crazy due to his dedication to psychiatric study and killed himself by jumping into the path of a train; see Shen, *SCWQJ* 19: 31.

they exerted a profound impact on modern Chinese intellectuals.[109] Shen Congwen's exposure to Western psychology and Freudian theories was mostly through translations and Chinese criticism. As early as the 1920s, Shen Congwen had embraced Zhou Zuoren's ideas about psychosexuality that Zhou had developed from his reading of Havelock Ellis's *Studies in the Psychology of Sex*. Zhou once described this reading experience as a process of enlightenment, which steered him to a new understanding of man and society. In her analysis of Ellis's influence on Zhou's notion of humanism, Susan Daruvala states that at the core of Zhou's reception of Ellis's work on sex is the idea of human sexuality as "a mark of civilization," rather than of barbarianism.[110] Critics have noted Shen Congwen's efforts, in his romanticization of West Hunan regional and minority cultures, to create an idealized combination of divine (*shenxing*) and animalist instincts (*shouxing*) for humanity, through which to revitalize a decrepit Chinese civilization.[111]

Shen Congwen was certainly no stranger to the notion of schizophrenia. By the early 1930s, he had already read Zhang Dongsun's *Jingshen fenxi xue ABC* (The ABCs of psychoanalysis, 1929) and Zhu Guangqian's *Biantai xinli xue paibie* (Schools of abnormal psychology, 1930), which introduce Freud's notion of *dementia praecox* as a form of psychosis.[112] On his way to Yunnan as part of the massive inland migration during the Second Sino-Japanese War, he reflected on a "man-made psychotic disorder":

> I've recently been reading the book *Abnormal Psychology*, and realized that one who is able to write about a different person in a different society is bound to reconstruct and rearrange his neural system in order to place him-

---

109. Jingyuan Zhang, *Psychoanalysis in China*.

110. Daruvala, *Zhou Zuoren*, pp. 207–10. Zhou Zuoren compiled some of his favorite passages from Ellis's work into "Ailisi *Ganxiang lu* chao" (Copied from Ellis's *Impression and Comments*) published in *Yusi* (Threads of talk), vol. 30 (1925).

111. For instance, Su Xuelin argues that Shen tends to beautify Miao minority culture in order to locate a new vitality for an aged Han Chinese civilization. See Su, "Shen Congwen lun."

112. During an interview conducted by Kinkley in the 1980s, Shen Congwen recalled reading Zhang Dongsun's book in 1929–30; see Kinkley, *Odyssey of Shen Congwen*. Zhu Guangqian coined the term *tongdian* (premature insanity) to translate *dementia praecox*. See Zhu Guangqian, *Biantai xinli xue paibie*, p. 137.

> self in the reactions of that other person, that other social environment. So this person gets to be "mentally ill." This can be taken as a joke, but there is also truth in it.[113]

What impresses Shen is the writer's schizophrenic state of mind—a divided personality produced by a process of artistic creation. This notion is repeatedly evoked in his writings of the subsequent Kunming years, during which Shen struggled strenuously, even to the point of insanity, to create a new literary form to convey an idea he later called *chouxiang de shuqing* (abstract lyricism):

> I'm in a state of mental derangement. I'm crazy for the Abstract. I saw an utterly complete form of life, which is present in the Abstract, but vanished in the face of facts.[114]

> Obviously, all my neural organs are fully exhausted, and my mental and neural systems have lost clarity and flexibility. Therefore, all I want now is rest. Or only if I could escape, escape from "the Abstract" that invades my heart and devours my intelligence, an abstract of beauty that is composed of endless spaces and times. However, since life and the Abstract cannot be separated, the only escape means nothing but death. Indeed, rest in my vocabulary signifies death in that of others.[115]

Although the way in which he uses those scientific terms obtained from his reading of Western psychology is idiosyncratic, they evidently helped to shape his aesthetic explorations.

Shen's reflection on madness takes on yet another dimension in his socio-anthropological study of West Hunan. In "Fenghuang" (Fenghuang) from 1938, Shen elucidates the "regional neurosis"[116] firmly embedded in his hometown and to which he returned over and over again in his psychological self-dissections during his 1949 mental crisis. He attributes the West Hunan myth of insanity to a

---

113. Shen, *SCWQJ* 18: 318. Based on Jingyuan Zhang's appendix of Chinese publications on Freud before 1949, the book Shen is referring to here must have been his friend Zhu Guangqian's recent publication, *Biantai xinli xue* (Abnormal psychology) (Shanghai: Shangwu yinshuguan, 1933). It is later included in *Zhu Guangqian quanji*, vol. 2, pp. 103–208.

114. Shen, "Shengming" (Life), *SCWQJ* 12: 43.

115. Shen, "Qianyuan" (Hidden profundity), *SCWQJ* 12: 34.

116. Shen, "Fenghuang" (Fenghuang), in *Xiangxi* (West Hunan), *SCWQJ* 11: 393.

local "belief in ghosts and sorcery,"[117] which he later defines as "the regional mental illness."[118] To shed light on this regional mental illness, Shen offers a creative psychiatric case study of three mysterious phenomena as examples of abnormal psychology resulting from repressed sexual desires: *wu* (witchcraft), *gu* (a process of bewitchment by means of instilling noxious insects into the victim's mind), and *shaonü luodong* (girls who imagine themselves lovers of the god of the mountain cave). Shen argues that all three conditions originated from the same root—from "a concoction of humans and gods, an abnormal consequence of emotional depression."[119] Taking God as the object of her neurotic or erotic yearnings, the lunatic "unified religious and romantic susceptibilities, thus convinced that God cares for her. She is wild and crazy, delirious; from heaven to earth, she is able to get anywhere."[120] In Shen's analysis, madness and femininity are the two central loci of *wu*, *gu,* and *shaonü luodong*, which are rituals that help release suppressed feminine susceptibilities. Thus, madness is used to present that which cannot be faced directly, that which is inexpressible, uncontrollable, and unresolved—in a word, that which has been repressed.

Devoted to his aesthetic Divinity of Beauty and Abstract Lyricism, Shen himself became the lunatic he analyzed. In a set of diary entries written during the time he spent at the sanitarium, he wrote: "I am now precisely caught in a kind of mental disorder, and enacting the tragedy of three psychological experiences of *wu*, *gu* and *shaonü luodong*."[121] His aesthetics embodied precisely that which the socialist political ideology sought to control, and so Shen Congwen had to be declared insane.

Sent to a mental asylum after a failed suicide attempt, Shen Congwen was completely consumed with his own fantasies and neuroses. The phantasms of paranoia and imprisonment come across in a dramatic moment when Shen, after being saved from suicide, wakes up in the clinic. Seeing doctors and nurses in white uniforms

---

117. Ibid.
118. Shen, "19490406," *SCWQJ* 19: 31.
119. Shen, "Fenghuang," *SCWQJ* 11: 395.
120. Ibid.
121. Shen, "19490406," *SCWQJ* 19: 32.

surrounding him, he cries out loud that he is in prison.[122] His son later recalled that Shen exclaimed: "It's so terrifying! You could hardly imagine." He continued with his recollection:

> Father grabbed my hand and pressed it up to his chest, lowering his voice. He saw the man with a mask, wearing a white uniform and pretending to be a doctor, gazing down at him to determine whether or not he was dead. . . . "I recognize that the others were doctors, but he is not." Father saw people tightening the net, rehearsing a drama that pushes him, step by step, toward ruin. Someone always appears in his hallucinations.[123]

What imagery could better illustrate the logic of the asylum than that of a prison? The mechanism of social exclusion and confinement easily won. For Shen's eradication from modern Chinese literature, no political campaign was necessary, as it was for those such as Ding Ling, Hu Feng, and many other Chinese intellectuals in the subsequent decades. Yet, as Shen stated in one of the diary entries during his stay in the asylum, "the sense of persecution would haunt me the rest of my life."[124]

Family and friends were relieved when Shen recovered in the fall of 1949 and chose to work for the National Museum of History. The madman seemed to have recovered sanity and survived the severe psychological crisis. Zhang Zhaohe, his wife, recollected decades later:

> At that time, we thought *he was backward, and held us back* [my emphasis]. It was a mess in the family. Now, in retrospect, I think I didn't fully understand his agony. . . . Han Shouxuan was then the director of the department of museum studies at Peking University, and Congwen went to help him and donated quite a lot to the exhibition hall. Thus, naturally, he converted to the profession of antiquities and stopped teaching at Peking University. Luckily he made the switch. During his conversion, there were pains and struggles. He indeed thought that literary writing was not easy any more, very difficult.[125]

Most striking in this passage is that the source of family worries during Shen's nervous breakdown was not simply his physical and spiritual suffering, but the jeopardy in which his political and aesthetic

---

122. Ling Yu, *Shen Congwen zhuan*, p. 470.
123. Shen Huchu, "Tuanju," p. 510.
124. Shen, "19490406," *SCWQJ* 19: 24.
125. See Chen Tushou, "Wumen chengxia de Shen Congwen," pp. 13–14.

nonconformism put his family. Therefore, in the eyes of his family, Shen's conversion to art history signified his accommodation to the new social system. In this aspect, Shen seems to have experienced the exact same process of convalescence as Lu Xun's madman. In the well-quoted frame narrative of "Diary of a Madman," which is written in classical Chinese to distinguish it from the diary entries in the modern Chinese vernacular, the madman's older brother told the first-person narrator that the madman has been recovered for a while and has taken on an official position somewhere else.[126] This informed assimilation into the social system the madman condemned in his diary seems to shatter the whole idea the diary attempts to assert. Or does it? Why does this message have to be conveyed by his older brother and then again transmitted by a narrator under the cloak of classical Chinese? In that context, the recuperation of the madman comes across as rather suspicious.

Similarly, the social accommodation of Shen Congwen is unsettling. Up to this point, critics have attempted to read Shen's turn from literature to the study of antiquities in the binary terms of resistance versus subordination, but in so doing they have left unexplored the relationship between the discourses of the asylum and those of the museum.

Fragments of Modernity: Studies on Traditional Chinese Costumes

Emerging in the age of modernity, the museum has often been condemned as an institution of "cultural ossification."[127] The museum is at the center of tensions between tradition and modernity, between processes of maintaining the past and of innovation. Placing art and artifacts in the museum tears them from their material and historical contexts, leading to a kind of mummification and virtual death. It is not surprising that the museum has often been described with metaphors of death and decay. The best-known remarks on death and museums come from Theodor W. Adorno. In his analysis of the ex-

126. Lu Xun, *LXQJ* 1: 9.
127. Huyssen, *Twilight Memories*, p. 15.

periences of Paul Valéry (1871–1945) and Marcel Proust (1871–1922) at the Louvre, Adorno maintains, "The German word museal [museumlike] has unpleasant overtones. It describes objects with which the observer no longer has a vital relationship and which are in the process of dying. They owe their preservation more to historical respect than to the needs of the present. Museum and mausoleum are connected by more than phonetic association. Museums are the family sepulchers of works of art."[128] In this sense, the museum is yet another modern institution of enclosure, which, as Douglas Crimp suggests, should be subjected to the sort of archeological examination that Foucault applied to the clinic, the prison, and the mental asylum.[129]

Yet, the process of musealization does not stop with the works of art that are incarcerated in the museum collection. The museal mortality is simultaneously spread to people who work in the museum. Looking back at his 1949 transition, Shen stated in his speech at St. John's University decades later, "According to the social customs, if one enters the historical museum, it means he himself has become history, which indicates that he has been wrecked."[130] Similarly, like museum collections, people who work in the museum are frequently regarded as "no longer [having] a vital relationship" to the society and "in the process of dying."[131]

Born out of the surge of modernity after the Revolution of 1911, the Museum of History was the first public museum in China. It was initially located in the former Imperial College, but was subsequently transferred to the Forbidden City in 1918, occupying the halls between Duanmen and Wumen gates. After the founding of the socialist regime in 1949, the museum was renamed as the National Beijing Museum of History, and in 1959 it was raised to national status and was renamed the National Museum of History. It was relocated to a gigantic new museum building—one of the "ten great buildings," which was constructed to celebrate the tenth anni-

128. Adorno, "Valéry Proust Museum."

129. Crimp, *On the Museum's Ruins,* pp. 44–65.

130. Shen, "Cong xinwenxue zhuandao lishi wenwu" (Conversion from new literature to historical relics: Speech on November 24, 1980, at St. John's University in the USA), *SCWQJ* 12: 386.

131. Ibid.

versary of the new socialist state and which it shared with the National Museum of Revolution—on the east side of Tiananmen Square. When Shen was first assigned there, the museum was like a mausoleum, located in an enclosed space inside the Forbidden City, a space buried in imperial history. Therefore, in moving from the asylum to the museum, Shen experienced a transition from one institution of social imprisonment to another—a logical step in the process of social sanitization and punishment.

In "Huanghun he wuye" (Twilight and midnight), a poem written after his hospitalization, Shen meditated on the ambiguous historical implications of the former imperial palace:

> The applause quieted down, people were dismissed. In a while, the gate tower
> Was restored to the loneliness and vacuity arranged by History,
> With shadowy dust and the drum and the bell facing each other.
> Seen from the crenellations of the gate tower
> The dark green Jingshan Hill in front is extremely quiet,
> All of Beijing is extremely quiet in the twilight dusk.
> All life
> Seems all very quiet and still.
> The golden roofs and red walls of the palace became mere symbols of
> feudalism,
> Nothing else.
> . . .
> Only red walls and the twilight, in the long silence,
> Looking at the vicissitudes of people and things, the decline and the rise.[132]

Although discarded by the socialist state as a symbol of feudalism, the former Imperial Palace seems to be where the true history and historical memories reside.

The Museum of History—the mausoleum of art—occupied an intriguing position in the political and cultural topography of the socialist capital in the 1950s. The museum stood inside the Forbidden City, behind Tiananmen Gate, on top of which Mao Zedong had declared the founding of the People's Republic, and was a landmark that appears prominently on all Chinese national insignia. Consequently, Tiananmen Gate symbolizes the political power of the socialist regime. In the first few years of the People's Republic, the space in front of the gate was transformed into a vast public

---

132. Shen, "Huanghun he wuye" (Twilight and midnight), *SCWQJ* 15: 225–28.

square "large enough for a million people to gather en masse."[133] From atop the Tiananmen Gate, Chairman Mao would watch parades of his revolutionary people. In the following decades, the massive Tiananmen Square imposed in front of the former Imperial Palace, designed as the center of world revolution, would witness a sea of fanatic Red Guards enacting rituals of political worship of Mao Zedong.

Hidden behind this revolutionary arena, the Museum of History seemed to be an ideological vacuum. Within this virtual prison or sepulcher, however, Shen Congwen found a great opportunity to "systematically and thoroughly examine Chinese antiquities of six thousand years."[134] More important, it was here that he eventually had the opportunity to implement his aesthetic ideas—not by means of literary experiment as such, but rather through an art historical and material study combining literature, historical and archaeological documents, art history, and material artifacts.[135] One main result is Shen's *Studies on Traditional Chinese Costumes*. In the preface, Shen remarked that although individual chapters of the book focus on shared subject matters, the explanatory and commentary parts lack a sense of system and wholeness. He continued to observe, "The book seems to have the scope of a full-length novel; in actuality, it is rather a collection of prose narratives of various styles and on various topics."[136] The book is composed of 179 sections structured in chronological order by dynasty. Each section bears a specific title, which depicts individual daily scenes, social events, or moments related to topics as diverse as satire, hair styles, ornaments, dishes, furniture, means of transportation, water supplies, and so forth. Section 109, titled "Song cuntong naoxue tu" (A Song dynasty picture of village children's mischief at school), for instance, starts out with a brief interpretation of the eponymous Song dynasty painting. Shen then introduces references from contemporary paintings, poems, vernac-

---

133. See Wang Jun, *Chengji*, pp. 271–72.

134. Shen, "Conversion from new literature to historical relics: Speech on November 24, 1980, at St. John's University in the USA," *SCWQJ* 12: 386.

135. Shen, "Wenshi yanjiu bixu jiehe wenwu" (The study of literature and history must be combined with that of cultural artifacts), *SCWQJ* 31: 311–17.

136. Ibid., 32: 10.

ular fictions, and anecdotes to consider not only features of furniture and children's garments of the time, but also how Song dynasty painting and literature are characterized by their passionate yet realistic portrayal of everyday life of ordinary people.[137] Such an aesthetic of the fragmentation also marks Shen's pre-1949 literary creations such as *Xiangxing sanji* (Random sketches on a trip to Hunan) and *Xiangxi* (West Hunan), which feature casual depictions of local customs, landscapes, biographical accounts, anecdotes, and legends. In this sense, his remarks in the preface to his *Studies on Traditional Chinese Costumes* can be understood: "There might still be correspondences between this work and the literary creation of the first half of my life in terms of approaches and viewpoints."[138] David Der-wei Wang argues that the trivial, fragmentary narrative in *Random Sketches on a Trip to Hunan* best characterizes Shen's native soil writings and "serves as a synecdoche, suggesting what the missing whole might have been as well as the impossibility of restoring it."[139] Shen Congwen's fascination with constructing fragmentary imageries into an epic narrative of Chinese culture and civilization is an important part of his conception of collecting. His large numbers of essays, letters, and diaries are all various forms of literary fragmentary compositions. Collecting is related not only to his interests in art and art history but also to his literary creation and aesthetic reflections. Although the figure of incompleteness in Shen's West Hunan narratives may well evoke the deep nostalgia toward a lost utopia, the aesthetic of the fragment appropriated in his post-1949 studies on fashion and material culture does not suggest similar regrets for a missing totality that might correspond to the dominant Maoist teleological historical view.

With the growing industrialization and commercialization in capitalist society, the notion of things as inanimate objects takes up a significant position in the discourse of modernity.[140] Dead, inorganic,

---

137. Ibid., 32: 353–54.

138. Shen, Preface, *Zhongguo gudai fushi yanjiu* (Studies on Traditional Chinese Costumes), *SCWQJ* 32: 10.

139. David Der-wei Wang, *Fictional Realism in 20th Century China*, p. 257.

140. In the Chinese context, for instance, Craig Clunas's *Superfluous Things*, which deals with late Ming artistic modernity, is important.

and artificial things are viewed in the mystical form of commodities, a thesis primarily elaborated by Karl Marx in *Capital*. According to Marx, commodity fetishism leads to alienation of human labor in the industrial society. In his classic Marxist study, *History and Class Consciousness*, Georg Lukács extends Marx's argument of alienation and commodity fetishism to the domain of human subjects and formulates his famous concept of the reification of human consciousness.[141] Reification of the subject appears as a direct result of the commodification and fetishization of the object. Both are symptoms of a pathological condition that is often described as modernity. Socialism takes on yet another form of object-phobia. Historical antiquities together with other forms of cultural heritage have been relentlessly rejected and smashed into piles and piles of ruins by the storm of socialist modernization, by the Maoist iconoclastic determination to wipe the historical-cultural slate clean. In this storm of progress, Shen Congwen the *Lumpensammler* (trash collector), however, dedicated his art historical research to those antiques and cultural artifacts labeled as feudalist relics. Thus, in a way, in his distinctive fetishism, Shen proposed a significant alternative aesthetic of fragments to the socialist cultural hegemony.

During his thirty years in the museum, Shen completed numerous articles and books on topics ranging from embroidery and textile designs, to lacquerware, ancient bronze mirrors, Ming dynasty brocades, and so forth. In celebrating those antiques and cultural artifacts that had been excluded as relics of feudalism and capitalism by state political discourse, Shen constructed an alternative aesthetic to socialist cultural hegemony. Through his dedication to traditional artworks, Shen forged a novel materialist history, ultimately breaking with the grand narrative of socialist revolutionary history. As his nephew Huang Yongyu, the woodcut artist, asserts, Shen Congwen was the true historical materialist.[142]

Shen Congwen's *Studies on Traditional Chinese Costumes*, which was completed in 1964 but was not published until 1981, is the first work delineating and examining Chinese fashion history. Why write a his-

---

141. Lukács, *History and Class Consciousness*.

142. Huang Yongyu, *Changhe bujinliu*, pp. 484–85.

tory of clothes and ornaments? Why focus on fashion in an era of collectivity and uniformity, at a time when politics rules all, when the only legitimate history was the history of revolution? What could be more disconnected from and discordant with the zeitgeist than a study of things as "trivial" as fabrics, clothing ornaments, and other accessories? In the context of post-1949 China, Shen Congwen's *Studies on Traditional Chinese Costumes* appears squarely irrelevant and untimely. Not surprisingly, during the Cultural Revolution, his research on fashion was criticized as a reactionary *heishu ducao* (a black book and a poisonous weed) that praises "emperors and generals" and "scholars and beauties" of the imperial past.[143]

However, it is exactly in these aberrations that the historical significance of Shen's work becomes apparent. From patterns of embroidery, collars, silk buttons, and sleeves, to jewelry and ornaments, hairstyles, and shoes, Shen Congwen turned to cultural details as a means of rethinking history. In his view, fashion and clothing come to define the parameters of human existence in history. As Mark Anderson remarks with respect to Franz Kafka's (1883–1924) obsession with fashion, clothing is "the hieroglyph of material existence, the mysteriously ineradicable sign of the human world, mortality, and history."[144] For Shen, history similarly lies in the material artifacts and details of everyday life; no matter how irrelevant and minute they might appear, they are the foundation of real history. Culture itself originates in the superficial textures and surfaces of objects from the past. Shen's post-1949 writings such as his art history works and hundreds of letters to home include constant reflections on history and Chinese civilization, suggesting that the Chinese cultural heritage could not be eliminated by Mao's "iconoclastic desire to wipe the historical-cultural slate clean"[145] or appropriated simply to showcase a Maoist vision of history, which emphasizes the economic and revolutionary transformation of the Chinese people from primitive society, through feudalism, to socialism.

With the flamboyance of past fashions buried in the historical abyss (or stored in museum warehouses), socialist China was dominated by

---

143. Chen Tushou, "Wumen chengxia de Shen Congwen," p. 38.
144. M. M. Anderson, *Kafka's Clothes*, p. 4.
145. Meisner, *Mao's China and After*, pp. 316–17.

rationalized and revolutionized clothing—navy blue or gray Mao suits, largely devoid of any individual or gender distinctions. Just as the consciousness of the new citizen was to be reeducated, the human body also had to be disciplined. Behind the ubiquitous cotton uniform in Tiananmen Square, however, lurked a spectacular mise-en-scène of thousands of years of diversity and individuality in texture, color, pattern, and style. The aesthetic of the fragment and fragmentation that characterize Shen's history of fashion and material culture thus designate a cultural and historical alternative to the monumentality and totality of the socialist revolutionary history. In this light, Shen's poetics of the material cultural history echoes Eileen Chang's efforts in the early 1940s to register the correspondences between fashion and history. In 1943, Chang wrote an essay, "Chinese Life and Fashions," for the English-language journal *The XXth Century* and rewrote it in Chinese with the title "Gengyi ji" (Changing clothes). Written in occupied Shanghai during the Second Sino-Japanese War, this meditation on various changes in fashion from the Qing dynasty to the 1940s Republic of China is yet another untimely undertaking. In Chang's analysis, fashion in China is not "an organized, planned, business venture"[146]; thus, it does not generate the "commodity phantasmagoria" described by Benjamin in his study of nineteenth-century Paris. Rather, Chang argues that fashion, which seems to be inconsequential—"as Liu Bei once said, 'Brothers are like hands and feet; wives are like clothes' "[147]—should be considered as part of the social and historical conditions, and thereby she concluded that "During times of political turmoil, people are not capable of improving their environments. They can only create their immediate and intimate milieu—their clothes. We live in our clothes."[148]

As Chang points out, societal and political frustrations might actually cause intellectual and artistic energies to flow into domains as seemingly superficial as fashion; therefore, the proliferation of details

146. Eileen Chang (Zhang Ailing), *Liuyan*, p. 74.
147. Ibid., p. 75.
148. Ibid., p. 73.

might sometimes be a sign of social stagnation.[149] In Chang's conceptualization of fashion lies her understanding of history, in which men and women in fashionable clothes are the protagonists and the material details of everyday life are the very foundation: "They are not heroes, yet, they are the carriers of the burden of this age. For, although they are not absolute, they are serious after all. They have no tragic grandeur; they only have desolation. Tragic grandeur is a form of closure, but desolation is illumination."[150]

In 1951, Shen Congwen was sent to Sichuan to participate in the local land reform movement. In a letter to his wife written on his trip to Sichuan, he expressed a similar notion of history:

> What especially moved me are those mountain villages preserving ancient features, and those boats sailing up and down the river. A few boat trackers walked on the rocks. Everything maintains its form of two or one thousand years ago. One can imagine how little the way of life has changed. But all this exists in this changing world. The transformation of the world is proceeding in a planned way. Yet, all this naturally forms a harmonious whole together with fishes in the water and trees on the mountain, and exists in this changing world, very quietly. Positioning these two in correspondence, how could I not be moved? . . . It is as if I were alone, yet, not alone. Because all this forges a certain kind of knowledge, of illumination in my life, —later, it will be projected into words, thus becoming a form of history.[151]

---

149. Just as Chang observed, the political ambiguity in occupied Shanghai was so pervasive that the writers of this particular chronotope dedicated much of their energy to the most sensuous, minute, and trivial details of life. Su Qing, who emerged as a star in the literary field in Shanghai, like Eileen Chang herself, achieved her reputation through detailed descriptions of the everyday life of her marriage in her novel *Jiehun shinian* (Ten-year marriage) (Shanghai: Sihai chubanshe, 1944). The culture administrators in the Wang Jingwei puppet regime, such as Zhou Fohai (1897–1948), turned themselves into traditional literati and founded aesthetic journals, which published essays describing all kinds of culture, such as traditional opera, calligraphy, paintings, food, etc. Eileen Chang enthusiastically indulged in describing the development of fashion of modern China and contributed to modern Chinese literature with great works characterized by decadent and desolate fascinations with sensual details.

150. Eileen Chang, *Liuyan*, p. 19.

151. Shen, "Zhi Zhang Zhaohe, 1951, 11, 01, Huayuan lun, Wushan" (To Zhang Zhaohe, November 1, 1951, Huayuan Boat, Wushan Mountain), *SCWQJ* 19: 139–40.

For Shen, historical illumination does not come from monumentality. Seeing in the artistic fragments and the materialist past a possible way to write "a form of history," to break the hold of the hegemonic discourse of history that proceeds "in a planned way," Shen resembles some European cultural critics of the early twentieth century who reflect on strategies of cultural resistance against oppressive orders of capitalism. The political potential of the fragment has been a cardinal concept among artists and theorists of modernism and especially of the avant-garde.[152] Walter Benjamin, for instance, foregrounds the "profane illumination, a materialistic, anthropological inspiration" of French surrealism as a way to break out of the frozen world of capitalism. Benjamin considers surrealism a more political than "artistic" or "poetic" movement, in the sense that the surrealist perceives revolutionary energies concealed in isolated and disjointed objects, understands how to bring these energies to the "point of explosion," and thus transforms them into revolutionary experiences.[153] In those moments when temporal and spatial fragments are torn out of their irremediably enslaved existences, when the potential energies concealed in them are unleashed, Benjamin sees revolutionary hope and the possibility of politicizing art. Therefore, when Benjamin's "Angelus Novus" stares at piles of historical debris at his feet, his mission is not to restore them to their original sequence, to an ultimate totality.[154] Rather, any redemption is hidden in the very scraps of the past. In considering Shen Congwen's post-1949 intellectual practice, the discourse of schizophrenia as evidenced in fragmentation in art history writings opens a remarkable site for a potential aesthetic break from the socialist cultural hegemony.

Shen Congwen overcame his psychological crisis through a conversion from literature to art history. Enclosed in the mausoleum-like Museum of History, haunting the graveyard of Chinese imperial history, and buried among all those dead and inanimate things, Shen the cultural historian was like a specter of history. If we follow

---

152. My reference to the avant-garde comes from Peter Bürger, *Theory of the Avant-garde*. Bürger argues that what distinguishes the avant-garde movement from "institution art" is the intention of the former to reintegrate art into the praxis of life.

153. Benjamin, "Surrealism," pp. 178–86.

154. Benjamin, "Theses on the Philosophy of History."

the specter's eyes, what do we see from within the fallen Imperial Palace? The sea of the masses in uniform in Tiananmen Square paying tribute to their god, their chairman? The uncanny political or religious carnival, a parade of ghosts, like the phantasmal Labor Day parade in 1950s Shanghai described by Eileen Chang in her novel *Chidi zhilian* (Naked earth)?[155] Perhaps the specter of history is not Shen Congwen the art historian, but rather the figure of Chairman Mao himself, standing atop Tiananmen at every national parade, waving his hand and accepting the worship of his revolutionary people. Even after Mao died, he remained there, transformed into the huge portrait hanging at Tiananmen, facing the vast square forever.

"Standing alone atop the Wumen Gate, I look at the city of Beijing in the twilight,"[156] murmured Shen Congwen at the Museum of History in his utter isolation after 1949. Facing Beijing and the entire nation caught in the post-1949 fanaticism of socialist modernization, Shen Congwen, with all his ability to endure anguish and pain—physical, psychological, and cultural—presented a unique aesthetic and historiographical conceptualization and opened a gap in the monolithic totality of socialism.

155. Eileen Chang, *Chidi zhilian*, pp. 121–26.

156. Chen Tushou, "Wumen chengxia de Shen Congwen," p. 16.

CHAPTER 3

Over Her Dead Body: Ding Ling's Politicization after the Socialist Revolution

What happened to revolutionary literature and revolutionary writers after the socialist revolution? Although sanctioned as the overriding model of literature of the People's Republic, was socialist realism gendered? How could writers negotiate a feminist space in the socialist imaginations of modern womanhood? In studying Ding Ling in her post-1949 political and literary rises and falls, this chapter explores the clashes between feminist consciousness and socialist discourse of gender and sexuality. Unable to suture feminist critical fissures in her socialist writings, Ding Ling ultimately chose to disavow literature for politics. However, the irony of history is that, in spite of her determination to demolish her critical edges for the sake of her political identity, the Communist Party refused to cover her body with a Party flag at her funeral. Hence the fracture between literature and revolution was forever sealed over her dead body.

From "Shafei nüshi de riji" (Miss Sophie's diary, 1927) to "Wo zai xiacun de shihou" (When I was in Xia Village, 1940), from *Taiyang zhaozai Sangganhe shang* (The sun shines over the Sanggan River, 1948; abbreviated as *Sanggan River* in the following discussions) to "Du Wanxiang" (1979), Ding Ling embodied the most exciting moments in the trajectory of modern Chinese literature.[1] The 1949

1. Ding Ling, "Shafei nüshi de riji" (Miss Sophie's diary), *DLWJ* 2: 45–86; "Wo zai xiacun de shihou" (When I was in Xia village), *DLWJ* 3: 221–42.

great divide in China coincided with the highest point of her literary and political career. Her novel *Sanggan River*, published after the Yan'an rectification, was highly acclaimed by the CCP. By September 1954, there were 300,000 copies in print. Ding Ling soon took on a number of principal positions in the new socialist political and literary apparatus. Honored as female cultural envoy of the new China, she was sent to a series of congresses and celebrations in the Soviet Union and other East European socialist states.[2] Whereas Shen Congwen was driven to the edge of psychological breakdown under intense pressure from the leftist camp, which led to the end of his literary career and his bitter dislocation to the field of art and archaeology, his old friend Ding Ling rose to become a most illustrious cultural celebrity in the socialist limelight. As Shen bitterly described, she was "God's privileged one, . . . going abroad and treated like distinguished guests."[3]

In 1951 and 1952, Kaiming Press published a series of compilations of modern Chinese literature. In *The Anthology of New Literature* (Xin wenxue xuanji), the term of *xin wenxue* (new literature) is defined as realistic literature, which is further subdivided into critical realism and revolutionary realism, and the historiography of modern Chinese literature is represented as a process of escalation from critical realism to revolutionary realism. For this highest stage of Chinese new literature, Mao Zedong's 1942 "Talks at the Yan'an Forum on Literature and Art" are stipulated as the supreme political and theoretical guiding principle.[4] *The Anthology of New Literature* signifies a new literary canon and also establishes a ranking of writers in the new political and cultural order.

The Anthology of New Literature consists of two parts of compilation. The first includes twelve writers who died before the founding of the People's Republic—Lu Xun, Qu Qiubai (1899–1935), Yu Dafu (1896–1945), Wen Yiduo (1899–1946), Zhu Ziqing, Xu Dishan (1893–1941), Jiang Guangci (1901–31), Wang Luyan (1901–44), Rou

2. For instance, Ding Ling attended the World Congress of Defending Peace in Czechoslovakia and headed the Chinese delegation to celebrate the thirtieth anniversary of the Bolshevik October Revolution. See Ding Ling's *Ouxing sanji* for her own descriptions of the experiences of attending international socialist meetings.

3. Shen Congwen, *SCWQJ* 27: 247.

4. See Ye Shengtao, *Ye Shengtao xuanji*, pp. 5–6.

Shi (1902–31), Hu Yepin (1903–31), Hong Lingfei (1902–34), and Yin Fu (1909–31). Remarkably, for the first time in Chinese literary history, these twelve writers were grouped together under the same rubric of "revolutionary writers." Evidently, the process of classification observed political rather than literary criteria. Zhu Ziqing's canonization is particularly intriguing. In post-1949 Taiwan, Zhu is among the very few writers who survived the KMT's obliteration of modern Chinese literature. Across the Cold War divide, Zhu was also sanctioned as a patriotic revolutionary writer and included in the new literary canon. On the verge of the Communist victory on the mainland, in a sarcastic article "Biele, Situ leideng" (Farewell, John Stuart Leighton), Mao Zedong praised Zhu for his moral integrity: "Zhu Ziqing was seriously ill; however, he would rather starve to death than receive American relief grain."[5] Thus, Zhu was elevated as the ideal patriotic heroic Chinese intellectual who would not bow to the KMT authority supported by American imperialism. The second part includes another twelve writers, who were still alive at the advent of the socialist state—Guo Moruo, Mao Dun (1896–1981), Ye Shengtao (1894–1988), Ding Ling, Tian Han (1898–1968), Ba Jin (1904–2005), Lao She (1899–1966), Hong Shen (1894–1955), Ai Qing (1910–96), Zhang Tianyi (1906–85), Cao Yu (1910–96), and Zhao Shuli (1906–70). Whereas the first twelve writers stand for the "blood and ink" history of the accomplished socialist revolution, the second group has been endorsed not only as devoted revolutionary writers, but more importantly, as the epitome of the new socialist literature.

However, Ding Ling fell from her glorious position before long. From the end of 1955, various purges began to hurl accusations at her, which eventually led to more than two decades of exile and imprisonment. In 1958, five years after Shen Congwen's works were eliminated by Kaiming Press, Ding Ling's works met the same fate. The advent of communism might have killed Shen Congwen the writer; however, he opened up a new aesthetic space in art historical research right in the heart of Tiananmen Square—the red revolutionary center. In

---

5. For a discussion of Zhu Ziqing's death, see Qian Liqun, *1948 Tiandi xuanhuang*, pp. 148–64.

contrast, the literary and political mechanism of the socialist state suffocated Ding Ling the writer, not because it made her more a culture cadre than a writer, but because her self-transformation was so sincere that finally the revolutionary discourse took on a life of its own and necessitated the death of a writer and an intellectual with conscience and critical consciousness. In this light, the postrevolutionary fallout for Ding Ling is even more dramatic and devastating. If we say that Shen Congwen the writer was destroyed because he was not a revolutionary or leftist, then, ironically, Ding Ling the writer vanished precisely because she was too determined to be proletarianized and politicized. Hence, after her political rehabilitation, Ding Ling reappeared as the most obstinate revolutionary. As Chen Tushou describes, "After this old woman came back from her self-transformation in the Great Northern Wasteland, her countenance became dull, she spoke cautiously, acted sluggishly, and echoed other people's thoughts. It was virtually impossible to hear her own insightful voice. One could rarely see her past invincible gesture in the literary arena, her fierce and forceful working style, and her frank and open personality."[6]

This chapter focuses first on Ding Ling's socialist realistic novel, *Sanggan River*. I will read *Sanggan River* first and foremost as a political event, tracing its history of production, publication, and distribution against the backdrop of the formation of the Cold War. Emerging on the modern Chinese literary stage in the 1920s as the most avant-garde woman writer, how did Ding Ling seek to negotiate her feminist consciousness in the predominant Maoist literary ideology? In this land-reform novel, where the class struggle has been elevated to the highest order, does gender identity interfere at all with socialist class solidarity? Could gender problems still be addressed in the "unhappy marriage of Marxism and feminism"?[7] In short, is socialist realism gendered? In questioning the suspicious discrepancies in Ding Ling's depiction of women personae in this model work of socialist realism, I will show how Ding Ling, stranded between gender and

6. Chen Tushou, "Ding Ling de beidahuang rizi," p. 154.

7. Here, I borrowed the notion coined by Heidi Hartmann in "Unhappy Marriage of Marxism and Feminism."

class, literature and revolution, danced on the edge of political and ideological antagonism at the mid-twentieth-century transition.

Although *Sanggan River* had a great reputation in the post-1949 regime, this novel, together with some of her early writings, caused harsh persecution of Ding Ling during the numerous political campaigns after the mid-1950s. After her rehabilitation in the late 1970s, rather than offering any new avenue to reflect on the recent political and cultural catastrophes, Ding Ling presented "Du Wanxiang" (1979), a degendered model work of socialist realism, which apparently sutures the feminist fissures intrinsic in *Sanggan River.* In the second part of this chapter, I will investigate an uncanny anachronism in Ding Ling's socialist realist fairy tale. In "Du Wanxiang," a story of land reclamation in the Great Northern Wasteland, the Great Leap Forward and the resultant Great Famine have been transformed into a glorious epic of socialist agricultural modernization.

Furthermore, this socialist fairy tale was written and rewritten at a time when the Maoist socialist utopia had completely collapsed. The last part of this chapter will examine Ding Ling's orthodox revolutionary gesture at a time of political disenchantment. Without inquiring into her ostensibly retrograde obsession with Maoist revolutionary discourse in the 1980s, one cannot fully evaluate the revolutionary and postrevolutionary effects on Ding Ling. In particular, I will analyze her vehement attack on Shen Congwen's *Ji Ding Ling* (Remembering Ding Ling, 1934),[8] and decode her reaction as a disavowal of a literary representation of her prerevolutionary history. From literary revolution to revolutionary literature, in the path of politicization, Ding Ling wound up defending her revolutionary stance by disavowing her literary creation.

Is Socialist Realism Gendered? The Sun Shines over the Sanggan River

> When will it no longer be necessary to attach special weight to the word "woman" and raise it specially?
>
> —Ding Ling, "Thoughts on March 8"

8. Shen Congwen, *Ji Ding Ling*, *SCWQJ* 13: 49–128.

> The "Marriage" of Marxism and feminism has been like the marriage of husband and wife depicted in English common law: Marxism and feminism are one, and that is Marxism . . . we need a healthier marriage or we need a divorce.
>
> —Heidi Hartmann, "The Unhappy Marriage of Marxism and Feminism"

A NOVEL AS A POLITICAL EVENT

Taiyang zhaozai Sangganhe shang (The sun shines over the Sanggan River, 1948) marks the peak of Ding Ling's literary career after Mao Zedong's Yan'an Talks. The novel was applauded by contemporary Chinese Marxist critics as the model work of Chinese socialist realism and won the Stalin Prize for literature in 1951. However, as is the case with many socialist realistic works, *Sanggan River* is not just a literary achievement of an individual writer, but more remarkably, a political event. The book not only greatly affected its author's literary and political career throughout the rest of her life, but its intriguing history of production, publication, and distribution also demonstrates the complex and unpredictable relationship between politics and fiction, between ideology and narrative, and thus best represents the fate of a writer skirting the political and ideological antagonism of the transitional era of the mid-twentieth century.

Sanggan River is a novel on land reform, a mass movement initiated by the CCP in 1946, shortly after the end of the Second Sino-Japanese War, and through which the party attempted to mobilize the peasantry to support its war against the Nationalist government. Ding Ling started to write immediately after her participation in the work of land reform in southern Chahar in 1946 and finished the manuscript in August 1947. However, the novel had to wait another year for approval for publication. During that year, it was not only intensively revised by its author in accordance with the changing land reform policy, but also thoroughly examined by the party authority. There may be no other literary work in all of modern Chinese literary history that required scrutiny and sanction by the most prominent party theorists and authorities, including Mao Zedong himself.

The years 1947 and 1948 witnessed the most significant transitions in the modern Chinese and international historical landscapes. American General George C. Marshall's mission to mediate between the Nationalist and Communist parties failed, and China was on the eve of the Communist victory that would ultimately draw the Bamboo Curtain of the Cold War in Asia, whereas in Europe, the Marshall Plan was about to speed reconstruction and economically seal the Iron Curtain between the West and the Eastern bloc. At this critical moment, Chinese Communists made every effort to seek their own incorporation within the socialist world. That Mao Zedong—at the time commanding the People's Liberation Army in the decisive war against the Nationalist government—bothered to turn his attention to a work of fiction demonstrates exactly the new political function imposed on literature and art since the Yan'an Talks. In 1948, the CCP sent a delegation to the Second Congress of the International Democratic Women's Federation held in Hungary. In a photo taken before the delegation left for Budapest, Ding Ling stands among other proud women representatives of an approaching new China.[9] Her prominence as an internationally known woman writer is one of the major reasons Mao and other party authorities approved the publication of *Sanggan River* after more than a year's suspension.[10] According to the memoir of Gan Lu, who was present in the final discussion regarding *Sanggan River*, Mao and other party theorists authorized that the novel be published immediately so that Ding Ling, female cultural envoy of the new China, could take her representative work to the international conference.[11]

---

9. The Second Congress took place between December 1 and 6, 1948, in Budapest, Hungary. For her experiences there, see Ding Ling's *Ouxing sanji*, and her diary entries between October 25 and December 3, 1948 (*DLWJ* 10: 259–73), which presented two intriguingly different versions of her reflections on attending this conference. She was also invited to participate in the International Congress of Peace in Paris in 1949. However, as Chinese delegation members could not get visas to France, they attended the Peace Conference provisionally arranged in Prague, along with members from other socialist states. The split between the free world and the Communist Bloc was already manifested there.

10. In 1940s Yan'an, Ding Ling was a favorite personality of the foreign media. Some scholars maintained that her international reputation helped her avoid the cruelest persecution during the Yan'an rectification campaign. During the same campaign, writers such as Wang Shiwei were harshly censured, whereas Ding Ling, who held a similarly critical stance toward the hierarchy and bureaucracy in Yan'an, was spared of further purges.

11. Gan Lu, "Ding Ling yu Mao zhuxi ersan shi." Gan Lu was the wife of Xiao San, a prominent Communist theorist.

A few months after its publication in Manchuria, just before the Communist victory in China, *Sanggan River* was translated into Russian and published by the Foreign Literature Press in Moscow. In 1952, the novel won the Stalin Prize in literature for the year 1951. In light of the Sino-Soviet Treaty signed by Beijing and Moscow in 1950 to assure military alliance against imperialist countries in the world,[12] the bestowing of this literary honor is not all that surprising; it represented not simply the recognition of aesthetic achievement of a certain individual but also part of the strategic culture of Soviet foreign politics responding to the East/West antagonism of the Cold War.

This honor surely guaranteed Ding Ling's literary and political position in the newly founded socialist state. She was appointed vice-president of the National Association of Literature and Art and headed the Bureau of Literature and Art of the Party Central Propaganda Department, in addition to other prominent positions in the PRC's cultural bureaucracy.[13] In the famous caricature "Wanxiang gengxin tu" (A new manifestation) published in *Wenyi bao* (Literary gazette), among the writers choosing to remain in mainland China, those who were qualified as "literary workers" were given their portraits and positions in the cultural hierarchy of the new socialist state. Ding Ling's big smiling face emerged in the middle of this Chinese socialist Hall of the Saints.[14] She is shown walking on the road toward the countryside, holding a permit of residence registration change, which symbolizes her famous manifesto urging writers to live among *gongnongbing* (workers, peasants, and soldiers) as stated in her talk "Dao qunzhong zhong qu luohu" (Go make your dwelling among the masses, 1953). The notion of the proletarianization of intellectuals clearly echoes Mao's Yan'an Talks, and with it, Ding Ling

12. For the signing of the Sino-Soviet Treaty, see Shu Guang Zhang, *Deterrence and Strategic Culture*, pp. 30–31.

13. Ding Ling was also director of the Central Institution of Literary Research and a member of the standing committee of the Women's Association, the Chinese People's Political Consultative Conference, and the National Committee of Culture and Education. In addition, she was editor-in-chief of *Wenyi bao* (Literary gazette) and *Renmin wenxue* (People's literature), two leading literary periodicals in the PRC.

14. See *Wenyi bao*, no. 1 (1956).

implies that she herself has already achieved the transformation from a petit bourgeois writer into a proletarianized literary worker. The irony of history is that this idea was indeed materialized during the Cultural Revolution and that Ding Ling was one of the intellectuals forced to go to the countryside for a reeducation among peasants.

The irony of history was, however, to be carried further. This "grand land reform epic"[15] had not only won Ding Ling high esteem but also brought upon her the charge of "one-bookism." Together with other accusations of antiparty crimes, this criticism led to her purge during the Anti-Rightist Campaign launched in 1957 and ultimately to her exile to Beidahuang. Ironically, this Great Northern Wilderness of Heilongjiang province lies not far from the Soviet border. Thus, Ding Ling and her works disappeared from the PRC cultural stage as well as Chinese literary history for the next two decades.

IS SOCIALIST REALISM GENDERED?

Mao Zedong's Yan'an Talks constitute a dividing line in Ding Ling's literary career. At their core, the talks assert that the political classification of "people who are for us" and "those who are against us" is the fundamental prerequisite for any literary production.[16] Consequently, the purpose of literature is to praise the bright side of the masses. In such a dominant binary rhetoric of class antagonism, was there any space for gendered experiences and female consciousness? How could literature conceptualize and articulate women's problems and gender issues? Was gender identity possible at all in such socialist literature?

These problematics are particularly intriguing in view of Ding Ling's conversion from a feminist writer to a Communist literary worker and bureaucrat. Ding Ling made her literary debut in the late 1920s as a distinctive modern woman writer with a sharp feminist consciousness. With works such as "Miss Sophie's Diary" (1927), which frankly dealt with the sexual anxiety and depression of

---

15. Feng Xuefeng, "*Taiyang zhaozai Sangganhe.*"

16. Mao Zedong, "Zai Yan'an wenyi zuotanhui" (Talks at the Yan'an forum on literature and art). English translation in Mao Zedong, *On Art and Literature*, p. 19.

xinnüxing (new women or modern women) grounded in commercialized cities, she shocked the contemporary literary arena with her audacious sexual description and won instant fame. Compared with the first May Fourth generation of women writers, such as Bing Xin and Ling Shuhua, Ding Ling is characterized by her profound exploration of subjects such as female sexuality that had rarely been approached by any May Fourth literati, male or female.[17]

She turned to the leftist writings and joined the Communist Party after her first husband, Hu Yepin, along with four other Communist writers, was executed by the Kuomintang government in 1931. They were posthumously honored by the Communist Party as the Five Martyrs of the League of Left Wing Writers. Ironically, as later documents show, they were in fact betrayed to the KMT secret police by their own comrades as a result of factional conflicts.[18] After a three-year house arrest (1933–36), Ding Ling managed to escape to the Communist base area.[19]

Although her literary concerns shifted from problems of urban young women to issues of the socialist cause, Ding Ling never lost her acute critical consciousness regarding women's problems in the revolutionary area. In her short stories and critical essays written around 1940, she criticized various kinds of oppression, sometimes in the name of revolution, that women still had to confront even in the revolutionary Communist regions. Her short stories "When I was in Xia Village" (1940) and "Zai yiyuan zhong" (In the hospital, 1940), and her critical essay "Sanbajie yougan" (Thoughts on March 8, International Women's Day, 1942) not only were used by the propaganda department of the KMT government in Chongqing as exemplary anticommunist materials but also were reprimanded by the Communist

---

17. See Mao Dun, "Nüzuojia Ding Ling."

18. See T. A. Hsia, *Gate of Darkness*, pp. 163–233.

19. About her house arrest years, see Ding Ling, "Wangliang shijie (Nanjing yuju huiyi)." Ding Ling never wrote a complete autobiography. The only autobiographical writings she left are "Wangliang shijie" and "Fengxue renjian" (Blizzard world), which were themselves never completed. *Ding Ling zizhuan* (Autobiography of Ding Ling) (Nanjing: Jiangsu wenyi chubanshe, 1996) is a quasi-autobiography edited by Xu Yangqing and Zong Cheng, in an attempt to describe Ding Ling's life based on these two autobiographical writings and her other writings such as prefaces, epilogues, diary entries, letters, and recollection essays.

Party for inappropriately exposing the dark side of the sacred revolutionary capital of Yan'an and almost wrecked her literary and political career.

As a result of her disobedience, she was sent to the party school and then to the countryside to learn from the rural masses, who, as Mao asserted in his Yan'an Talks, were much cleaner, both spiritually and physically, than the intellectuals who had not yet been cleansed of their bourgeois sins.[20] After a two-year self-transformation, Ding Ling reemerged on the Communist literary scene with *Sanggan River,* her full-length novel on land reform in a northern Chinese village, which was applauded by Feng Xuefeng (1903–76), a leading party literary theorist, as the inaugural work of Chinese socialist realism.

Ding Ling scholarship notes that her writings after the Yan'an Rectification Campaign reflect her complete subordination to the party doctrine at the expense of her independent voice, thus dismissible as ideological clichés. When reading *Sanggan River,* the major oeuvre of the latter half of her life, critics of the post-Mao period tend to focus on one of two aspects of this work: first, the ideological message the novel carries and consequently the deteriorating "Mao style" (*Mao wenti*) it produces and reproduces, which dominated PRC literature and art for the next three decades and has not yet totally disappeared[21]; or second, the degeneration of humanity represented in the detailed descriptions of bloody scenes of violence, which often culminate in confrontation between the peasants and the landlord.[22] I am not suggesting that the aesthetic or ethical aspects are not crucial to the interpretation of this novel. However, it seems equally relevant to examine the elusive space women occupy in this model

20. See Mao, "Talks at the Yan'an Forum." Mao's notion of spiritual and physical hygiene was implemented during various political campaigns targeted at Chinese intellectuals, of which the 1942 rectification campaign was only the beginning. This sanitary obsession is best manifested in the "sixiang gaizao" (thought reform) campaign launched in early 1950, which was mocked as "xizao" (taking a bath) among intellectuals. This effort, based on self-criticism and public confession, aimed at eliminating Western influences. It became all the more urgent with the PRC's involvement in the Korean War. See Yu Fengzheng, *Gaizao.*

21. Li Tuo, "Ding Ling bu jiandan."

22. For instance, see the article coauthored by Liu Zaifu and Lin Gang, "Zhongguo xiandai xiaoshuo."

work of Chinese socialist realism, which these interpretations have left largely unexplored. In my reading of *Sanggan River*, I consider the most important and sophisticated perspective throughout Ding Ling's literary life, that is, gender consciousness, and I propose that even in her most overtly Communist work, she never totally lost sight of her critical feminist perception. Moreover, given the predominant discourse of rigid class polarization in land reform, Ding Ling's exploration of gender issues becomes all the more potent.

My reading of *Sanggan River* does not aim at reversing the image of Ding Ling as an unyielding Communist writer or proposing instead that she was a dissident who would sacrifice her life to challenge the party orthodox for the feminist cause. No doubt, Ding Ling made a great effort after the Yan'an rectification to mold herself into a literary worker as defined by the Yan'an Talks. In her preface to the reprint of *Sanggan River* in 1979, she stated that this novel came to fruition under the guidance of Chairman Mao and as a result of her self-transformation among the revolutionary people in the Communist base area. We must take seriously her determination to transform herself through the practice of writing, when reading her recollections of her physical and political trial: "At the time I was writing that novel, I suffered from blinding pain in my abdomen. Nevertheless, I bent over my desk, writing word by word, as if I were a soldier on the front line, charging toward the enemy crying out his [Mao Zedong's] name. It was out of my gratitude to him and for those people in the novel that I could continue writing."[23]

However, as we shall see, the more serious Ding Ling's Marxist self-transformation, the more difficult it was for her to deal with gender issues as an indispensable part of any social movement—a subject that she persistently emphasized at all stages of her literary life and that constitutes the very origins of her writings. In the socialist revolution, does women's liberation merit special attention? When the revolutionary goals are realized, does this in itself guarantee a solution of women's problems? Do marital and economic equality, in particular, necessarily mitigate sexual oppression and conflict? In a historical context, where class struggle takes precedence over other forms

23. Ding Ling, *Sanggan River* (1997), pp. 2–5. My own translation.

of social conflict, is the gender problem allowed to interfere with class solidarity, and to what extent would sexual differences be addressed? Furthermore, when gender and class differences are both at stake, how is the relationship between feminism and class struggle played out?

These are the questions Ding Ling the feminist takes up in her socialist novel, which was endorsed by party authorities—significantly, all male—as a representative work about class struggle in the Chinese countryside. As the most avant-garde woman writer of the May Fourth generation, who contributed to modern Chinese literature a series of defiant, resolute women characters, Ding Ling knew all too well that class is never the only possible framework within which to consider women's identities. In the dominant discourse of class struggle, women are inevitably stranded between two incommensurable entities, gender and class, that Ding Ling is at pains to bridge. Given the profound contradictions between feminist consciousness and the gender-blind Marxist theory of class struggle, Ding Ling's efforts to negotiate between gender and class are almost predestined to fail.

And it is precisely this inherent conflict between gender and class, I will argue, that generates a gap between the open endings of women's stories in *Sanggan River* and the apparent full closure of the novel itself with the victory of the land-reform movement. Both affirmative and negative critiques of this novel are politically keen enough to recognize that *Sanggan River*'s depictions of female figures betray narrative discrepancies with ambivalent messages not in accord with the official literary and political norms. Although supportive critics clarify these discrepancies as unintentional vestiges of "bourgeois realism, or, critical realism,"[24] which characterized Ding Ling's early writings, her detractors seize them upon as evidences of her anti-party crimes during the Anti-Rightist Campaign. These elusive loci of dissonance, in my point of view, are precisely the space that Ding Ling's feminist consciousness occupies. And it is these narrative discrepancies and the underlying clash between Ding Ling's party iden-

24. Feng Xuefeng, "*Taiyang zhaozai Sangganhe shang*," p. 337.

tity and feminist consciousness that make *Sanggan River* an intriguing case in our investigation of gender issues in socialist literature.

THE SCHIZOID IDENTITY: GENDER AND/OR CLASS?

The story of *Sanggan River* takes place in a small village of northern China during the early phase of land reform (1946–47). In a time span of a little over a month, the villagers have been mobilized to confront the local landlords and accomplished the redistribution of land under the leadership of the village cadres and a CCP land-reform team. What these peasants gain through this mass movement are not only their own shares of land, implements, and other material possessions but also, more important, a new political and class consciousness, which will serve as the ideological basis for the socialist revolution and for the new socialist state to come. In thematizing this vital transition, Ding Ling greatly contributes to the new state's symbolic politics of power. Feng Xuefeng asserts that *Sanggan River,* the first success of Chinese socialist realism, presents "the epic of land reform" to socialist literature.[25]

The village constitutes a microcosm of the socialist state, as Yi-tsi Mei Feuerwerker points out in her discussion of *Sanggan River.*[26] In this Maoist cosmology, everyone's political position and class identity should be clearly delineated, and so should their interpersonal relationships. However, as existing scholarship makes great efforts to tackle, there are some dubious figures in the novel, and they are, paradoxically, more vividly depicted than the model characters who should be the focus of socialist realistic literature, as the Chinese Marxist conceptualization of Friedrich Engels (1820–95)'s notion "typical characters in a typical environment" prescribes.[27] Besides Ding Ling's evident sympathy with these ambiguous figures, what

---

25. Ibid., p. 340.

26. Feuerwerker, *Ding Ling's Fiction.*

27. The introduction and interpretations of Engels's notion of typical characters and typical environments in realism in China are of great controversy. The major debate on how to create typical characters in realist literature occurred between two leading leftist theorists, Hu Feng and Zhou Yang, during the late 1930s. For a discussion of the Chinese realist debate, see Chen Shunxin, *Shehui zhuyi xianshi zhuyi,* esp. pp. 112–44. On how the original notion of typical characters had been

concerns her critics are also those suspicious "intellectual" or bourgeois sentiments displayed by model village cadres. Failing to explain why these suspicious elements virtually all relate to women characters and women's spaces, these critiques betray, I would argue, the blind spot in Communist gender politics.

Since at least the mid-nineteenth century, Chinese political and cultural movements have held out explicit promises of women's equality and liberation as an integral part of their respective reform or revolution agendas. In the Chinese Communist movement, women's emancipation is basically grounded on two main principles: first, the May Fourth discourse of smashing the cannibalistic Confucian familial norm, which relegates women to an inferior social position and restricts them in the domestic sphere and in the Confucian morality of chastity; second, a Marxist historical and material analysis of women's oppression drawn from Friedrich Engels's *The Origin of the Family, Private Property and the State* (1884), which locates the roots of women's oppression in a marriage system enshrining and protecting private property and opens it to political intervention.[28]

However, although Chinese Marxism signals its commitment to women, it subsumes their liberation as a dimension of the universal social revolution. As early as February 1927, when the CCP and the KMT were still allied during the national revolution called the Northern Expedition, Mao Zedong formulated the root theory of the Chinese Communist agenda of woman's emancipation in his "Report on an Investigation into the Peasant Movement in Hunan." This treatise provided a vision and a theory of a Chinese revolution based on the peasantry, the largest portion of its population, which was fulfilled twenty-two years later with the establishment of the PRC. Mao's report asserts that the problems of patriarchy, superstition, and the oppressive relationship between husband and wife "will

---

transformed into that of socialist model characters since the 1950s, see Ye Jibin, *Zhongxi dianxing lilun shuping*.

28. Friedrich Engels, *The Origin of the Family, Private Property, and the State* (New York: International Publishers, 1942; originally published by Hottingen-Zürich: Volksbuchhandlung, 1884). For a thorough investigation of how the woman question has been addressed in major works of Marx and Engels, see Landes, "Marxism and the 'Woman Question.'"

be automatically abolished as a natural consequence of the triumph of the political and economic revolution."[29] Similarly, Deng Yingchao (1904–92), the leader of the Communist women's movement, explicitly declares, "Women's emancipation can only be achieved after the realization of social and national liberation."[30] Clearly, the Communist project believes that the socialist revolution in political and economic terms will necessarily solve the question of women. Thus, from its inception, the agenda of the Chinese Communist women's movement is defined within the framework of male-dominated social and national discourse.

Consequently, women's interests are conceived as a subset of political and class interests. As contemporary feminist critics well observe regarding women's liberation under socialism, "the Woman Question would be answered by socialism along with all other social problems. Women as a category had nothing to contribute to the theory of socialism."[31] During the Communist land-reform movement, the key strategy of women's emancipation depended on their participation in revolutionary socialist movements and their endowment with land as a way to achieve economic independence. In the rigid discourse of socialist revolution, all social distinctions are subordinated to the dominant paradigm of class. Women are political and economic, therefore genderless. As Heidi Hartmann observes in her influential article "The Unhappy Marriage of Marxism and Feminism," the Communist woman question has never been the "feminist question."[32] As a result, women's experiences and problems that are not directly subsumed to class often remain omitted or at best, only indirectly articulated.

The critics have been preoccupied with exactly those loci where the woman question and the feminist question are being contested and negotiated. How do women try to carve out their own space in the male-dominated revolutionary discourse? How are women's experiences differential and unique under socialist revolutionary directives?

---

29. Mao Zedong, "Hunan nongmin yundong kaocha baogao."

30. Deng Yingchao, "Kangri minzu tongyi zhanxian," p. 26.

31. Kruks, Rapp, and Young, eds., Introduction to *Promissory Notes: Women in the Transition to Socialism* (New York: Monthly Review Press, 1989), p. 8.

32. Hartmann, "Unhappy Marriage of Marxism and Feminism," p. 3.

It is my purpose to explore the narrative discrepancies where Ding Ling vacillated between the party mandate and the feminist consciousness. As my reading shall reveal, it is not simply a dichotomy between repression and resistance. Rather, it is at the sites where Ding Ling tries to contain or even repress her feminist consciousness that the problems within the socialist gender politics are most severely exposed. In the following discussion, I examine the cases of two women characters of different social status in *Sanggan River*, to see if it is possible to construct female space and consciousness in a socialist revolution.

KNOWLEDGE AND THE FEMALE SPACE: WHEN THE HEAD OF THE WOMEN'S ASSOCIATION IS A WOMAN

In a famous article criticizing *Sanggan River* during the Anti-Rightist Campaign, Zhu Keyu reprimands Ding Ling for the scene where Dong Guihua, the head of the women's association, suddenly feels alienated from other women in the literacy class. He questions, "How could this poor peasant woman all of sudden look at the literacy class (*shizi ban*) and other young women in the village *from the viewpoint of an intellectual?*"[33] He then imputes the aberrant emergence of intellectual consciousness in a peasant woman to the incorrect political position of the author. Indeed, this scene is very disturbing, if not downright absurd, in this socialist realistic depiction of the land reform movement. Zhu Keyu is keen enough to diagnose the suspicious symptoms of feminist narrative, which expose Ding Ling's "petit bourgeois" literary roots. However, by handling it solely from a political perspective, he misses a significant dimension of this problematic scene: Why did Ding Ling choose a female character, the head of the women's association, as the carrier of this bourgeois perception? And, most significantly, why did she arrange the women's literacy class (*funü shizi ban*), a special female institution and space, for this suspicious sentiment to take place?

Why the head of the women's association? Why the literacy class, and moreover, how to define this special space? Less than ten years ago, shortly after she arrived in Yan'an, Ding Ling wrote a short story

33. Zhu Keyu, "Lun 'Taiyang zhaozai sangganhe shang,'" p. 367. My emphasis.

entitled "In the Hospital," using hospital as a special institution to address existent problems within the Communist system. In his significant reading of this story, Huang Ziping takes the spatial setting of the story, namely, the hospital, to task to illustrate the complexity of Communist "social hygiene." He calls attention to the fact that Communist intellectuals have to confront not only the ignorant, narrow-minded, and backward villagers but also the modern institution of the hospital. Their suggestions to improve the conditions in the hospital, albeit reasonable, have been regarded as "heterodox," therefore "unclean."[34] In the subsequent Yan'an Rectification Campaign, Ding Ling paid dearly for her "heterodoxy" and her "unclean" description of the sacred revolutionary base area in stories like "In the Hospital." Compared with the hospital, a modern institution of science, the women's literacy class in *Sanggan River* is a more complicated space. It is not only an institution of education but also a gendered space, where women seek to create a female public space outside both the domestic space and the male-centered ideological domain.

The Communist literacy classes are, in the first place, a modern political institution. According to the "Directive on the Work of the Literacy Class" issued in 1933, political education is the primary task of the literacy classes, and the ability to read is of second rank.[35] Compared with the May Fourth embrace of new knowledge with Enlightenment ideals, the Communist literacy movement attempts to inculcate authoritative ideology in the peasantry.[36] More intriguingly, the literacy class is primarily directed at rural women. It aims at women's solidarity and emancipation. Through participation in the literacy class, women are encouraged to step out of their traditional familial space and learn how to read and write. However, in this apparently transparent institution of education, the women are in effect put into an even denser network of surveillance: only the patriarchal

34. Huang Ziping, *Geming, lishi, xiaoshuo*, pp. 141–58.

35. See Gao Hua, "Zhonggong cong wusi jiaoyu." The literacy movement was of vital importance in the agenda of the Chinese Communist revolution. From the beginning of the Chinese Soviet Republic (1931–37), literacy classes targeted at illiterate women had been set up in rural areas.

36. According to the statistics in Gao Hua's "Zhonggong cong wusi jiaoyu," the majority of the texts used in literacy classes are charged with political ideas.

figure of husband or father is replaced by the omniscient political authority, the CCP. In the women's association and in the women's literacy class, women are institutionalized, and thus more effectively manipulated and monitored. As Zhu Xiaodong maintains, "this effort to get women out of the domestic space does not mean that the revolution wanted women to establish their own public space, which was not wanted by the revolution; what it really wanted was to posit the body of the woman outside the screen of the family, to disperse it and expose it in the surveillance of the revolution."[37]

The women's literacy class, intended as an essential institution of political education and surveillance, must be considered as a modern space. However, Ding Ling's description of the women's literacy class in Nuanshui Village reveals the much more paradoxical nature of this modern institution. In *Sanggan River*, the literacy class is a field where the political machinery and the women's public space, the male-centered Communist ideology and the female knowledge, encounter, clash, and contest for power. To be sure, in Ding Ling's description of this special space, there is hardly the kind of defiant criticism presented in "In the Hospital" or other of her early 1940s writings. Nevertheless, in spite and because of Ding Ling's resolution to transform herself, her contained portrait of the literacy class only makes the ambiguous nature of this women's space and the elusive woman question in the socialist revolution all the more conspicuous. Indeed, it is precisely at this locus of contestation and negotiation that the double-edged "intellectual" sentiment of Dong Guihua, the head of the women's association, inevitably emerges, and behind it, a Ding Ling caught between the Communist mandates and her feminist consciousness.

The women's literacy class of Nuanshui Village is located in the large hall of the house of the former landlord Xu Youwu, who fled when the village was liberated. This specific setting suggests that women, as a result of liberation, are able to obtain their own space within the traditional patriarchal territory. However, the author's nuanced description invites yet deeper consideration. "This was a fine building, originally exquisitely furnished but now in a state of disre-

37. Zhu Xiaodong, "Tongguo hunyin de zhili," pp. 64–65.

pair and disorder."[38] The emphasis on residential well-being and sanitation is intriguing. Similar concerns appear several times in the novel indicating the obvious destruction the peasant revolution has brought to the originally clean and well-preserved space of the wealthy landlords. Some twenty years earlier, in "Report on an Investigation of the Peasant Movement in Hunan" (1927), Mao Zedong described the carnivalesque scene of peasant revolution in a state of ecstasy:

> Crowds of people swarm into the homes of the local bullies and bad gentry who oppose the peasant association, slaughtering their pigs and consuming their grain. They may even loll for a minute or two on the ivory beds of the young mesdames and mademoiselles in the families of the bullies and gentry. . . . Doing whatever they like and turning everything upside down, they have even created a kind of terror in the countryside. . . . A revolution is not the same as inviting people to dinner, or writing an essay, or painting a picture, or doing fancy needlework; it cannot be anything so refined, so calm and gentle, or so mild, kind, courteous, restrained and magnanimous. A revolution is an uprising, an act of violence whereby one class overthrows another. A rural revolution is a revolution by which the peasantry overthrows the authority of the feudal landlord class.[39]

Ding Ling's spatialization of transgressing class boundaries in *Sanggan River*, however, betrays a tangible regret and upset, at the risk of taking the wrong side in the class struggle. Furthermore, it is the literacy class—a place to eliminate illiteracy and ignorance—that becomes one of the main causes of the contamination of the previously fine building. Hence, the multilateral dialogues at the levels of gender, class, and knowledge form an intriguing configuration of discursive tensions. Buried deep in Ding Ling's obsessive conceptualization of contamination, I argue, lies doubt about the ultimate triumph of the socialist revolution, which would require the proletarianization of all social classes, particularly the intellectuals like herself who originated in the gentry class, belonging to the same social stratum as the landlords.

What characterizes the women's literacy class in Nuanshui Village? And how to account for the strange "intellectual" sentiment

---

38. Ding Ling, *Sun Shines over the Sangkan River*, p. 28. The English translations of *Sanggan River* come from Yang Hsien-yi and Gladys Yang's rendition with minor revisions.

39. Mao Zedong, *Selected Works of Mao Tse-tung*, vol. 1, pp. 28–29.

that Dong Guihua, the head of the village women's association and the organizer of the class, suddenly feels in that particular afternoon? In Ding Ling's depiction, the literacy class, which is originally created as an institution where women are enlightened with ideas of solidarity, revolution, and liberation, turns out to be a space of female leisure and feminine knowledge. The favorite topics of the young women there include "the embroidered pillow-case" and "the prices of threads and laces."[40] Accordingly, the classroom for revolutionary knowledge turns into a female public space where female experiences are exchanged. Ironically, this female knowledge seems even more relevant for these women than the political concepts of class struggle or equality with men, about which Dong Guihua, the head of the association, is obliged to enlighten them. As a matter of fact, the students could not care less about these political ideas. "By coming to this lively place to exchange news of their neighbors and joke together, these women could throw off their family yoke and boredom."[41] Therefore, Dong Guihua the political messenger is bound to feel distanced from this feminine slot of time and space: "These young women certainly did not need her, and she was not sure they did not despise her, yet she wasted three hours a day sitting here."[42]

Dong Guihua's feeling of isolation is also a result of the awakening of her female self-consciousness. On that particular afternoon, Dong, for the first time, looks at her fellow people in the literacy class from the standpoint of a woman, not that of a cadre. Although she is poor and worn out from years of hard work, she still harbors her feminine side. As the narrator emphasizes, every time Dong went to the literacy class, she "combed her hair and fastened it firmly, then changed her tattered blue cotton jacket for a new white blouse."[43] But in contrast to the young wives and girls, who are comparatively well off and who enjoy and cherish the leisure time and the female space in the literacy class, Dong is preoccupied with the financial burden of her family. Hence, "for the first time she realized with amazement how out of place she was here. Although neither old nor withered, she was

---

40. Ding, *Sun Shines over the Sangkan River*, p. 28.
41. Ibid.
42. Ibid., p. 29.
43. Ibid., p. 28.

coarse and weather-beaten. Good as she was at dealing with people, still she lacked interest!"[44] Dong's perception of alienation is double-edged, rooted in her identity both as a poor peasant and as a young woman. Gender, as a specific form of social determination, is thereby always already interwoven with class discourse.

The complex entanglement of gender and class consciousness is manifestly thematized in Dong's resentment toward Heini, the niece of a landlord, who volunteers to serves as teacher for the literacy class. As Heini is illustrating the meaning of the word "prosperous" with examples of beautiful clothes and abundant food, Dong Guihua cannot hold back any longer. This young, pretty, and well-educated teacher only reminds Dong of her impoverishment and her abashed situation in this feminine community. Leaving the class early for the first time, she "cast a look of dislike at Heini with whom she was usually on excellent terms," feeling "as if she had had a surfeit of something, and at the same time, an emptiness as when she had gone hungry too long."[45] Obviously, her aversion to Heini results not only from class differences but also from the feminine appeal of this young girl with "silvery tones."[46]

Therefore, the combination of "surfeit" and "emptiness" Dong entertains is composed of the intermingled feelings of class conflicts and her awakening female self-consciousness. These "intellectual" sentiments originate in the contestation of her political and female subjectivity, of the political machinery and the female space of the literacy class. Ding Ling's opponents perceptively spot the suspicious political indeterminacy inherent in Dong's psychological battle. However, given their political reading under the strictures of Mao's doctrine on literature, they have unavoidably missed the gender implication. And it is exactly in such elusive sites that Ding Ling's keen feminist consciousness can be recognized.

To be sure, in this model work of socialist realism, the writing of which constituted an essential part of Ding Ling's political rehabilitation in the late 1940s, these gendered alternative experiences, which cannot fit into either the discourse of class struggle or the discourse

44. Ibid., p. 29.
45. Ibid.
46. Ibid.

of women's liberation, must be carefully contained or repressed. In effect, Dong Guihua never again voices such contradictory feelings throughout the rest of the novel. With these heterodox sentiments silenced in the wake of the tremendous success of land reform, Dong has become a strong but genderless cadre leading village women in the struggle against the evil landlords. As Tani Barlow observes, in socialist works, "all stories about women were stories about political subjects."[47] Nonetheless, the dissonance in the psychology of the head of the women's association represents one of the most suspicious yet fascinating moments of Ding Ling's socialist realist novel. In such moments, we can still locate the shadow of Ding Ling's feminist consciousness, which is diminishing yet has never ceased to produce its effects.

HOW TO MAKE LOVE POSSIBLE IN CLASS SOCIETY: THE STORY OF THE LANDLORD'S NIECE

No doubt, Heini is a highly controversial figure in the novel: first, because of her "original sin"—she is the niece of the landlord Qian Wengui, the chief target of the land reform struggle in Nuanshui Village; second, because of the liaison between her, a member of the exploiting class, and Cheng Ren, a hired laborer and later the head of the peasants' association—which is considered politically improper in this new societal order. Therefore, how to deal with, or more precisely, to legitimize this problematic love relationship becomes the core issue of the story of Heini and her beloved.

At the outset of the novel, the liberation of the village by the Communist army has also liberated Heini from her arranged marriage and thus kindled hope for her love with Cheng Ren. However, in this new Communist region with its dominant class ideology, the relationship becomes even more problematic as a result of their different class origins. "Now as chairman of the peasants' association, Cheng Ren ought to identify himself with the masses and not go marrying Qian's niece, while an affair with her would be even worse. He feared this connection might damage his position and set tongues wagging. . . . Hence he must harden his heart. Although his deliber-

---

47. Barlow, *I Myself Am a Woman*, p. 42.

ate coldness to Heini was very painful to him, and he felt not a little ashamed of it, still he was a man, he could set his teeth and stick it out."[48] Before the liberation, her uncle did not allow her to marry Cheng Ren, a poor laborer; now, her lover intentionally avoids her to protect his political reputation. In this conjuncture, the order and hierarchy in the new class society seems more omnipotent and sinister than that of the traditional patriarchy.

The story of Cheng Ren can be seen as an archetypical Communist bildungsroman in socialist realist literature. The name "Cheng Ren" means in Chinese "to become a human being," or "to become a man with lofty ideals and morality." In political terminology, "human being" means a man with correct class standpoint, and "ideals and morality" refers to the Communist ideology. In order to become a true human being in a new class society, Cheng Ren has to experience the painful formative process toward a mature and pure political morality. The author uses a whole chapter (chapter 46) to describe the transformation of his class consciousness. In this chapter, Cheng struggles to overcome his personal feelings and reject Heini as an exchange offer to spare her uncle's life the very night before the public struggle against the latter, the landlord Qian Wengui. And intriguingly, Ding Ling names this chapter "Liberation," which clearly indicates the ultimate fulfillment in Cheng's self-transformation: he was freed from his old self for the larger-than-life socialist cause. With this political rebirth accomplished, Cheng Ren, a true revolutionary human being, is able to take the initiative in the public humiliation of and struggle against Qian Wengui the next day.

Compared with the arduous spiritual catalysis Cheng Ren had to experience, Heini's story of transformation seems much simpler. After Qian Wengui is arrested and repudiated in public, Heini moves to live with her other uncle, Qian Wenfu, who is a poor peasant. Accordingly, her identity instantly turns from being the niece of a landlord to being the niece of a peasant, and thereby becoming politically correct and secure. In contrast to the strenuous psychological battle of Cheng Ren, Ding Ling hastily closes Heini's story with a physical relocation, which apparently solves her class problem. In chapter 55,

48. Ding, *Sun Shines over the Sangkan River*, pp. 18–19.

"The Happiness of *Fanshen*," when the villagers are distributing their land-reform gains, Cheng Ren suddenly realizes the changing class identity of Heini and sees a new hope for their love relationship. He helps Heini and her poor peasant uncle to carry the big urn that was distributed to them as the result of the land reform. A happy ending of this love story is implied.

However, this seemingly clear-cut narrative closure leaves certain entanglements unexplored. An essential question that arises is why Heini does not experience a *rite de passage* toward a genuine Communist citizenship similar to Cheng Ren's. Until the very end of the novel, Heini does not feel the imperative to separate from her landlord family, much less to break with and accuse her landlord uncle. Given her vivid description of Cheng Ren's mental remolding, Ding Ling must have been aware of the importance and necessity of this Communist rite of passage. Why did she leave a suspicious blank in the political resume of the female character, but not the male one? What is implied in this lacuna of class consciousness in Heini? This missing story must point to something that the author could not articulate directly, or could not work through. I propose that a feminist message was implied by this empty political locus, and that Heini's hollow and superfluous transformation in class identity points to the dilemma for women from landlord households in the class struggle of the socialist revolution.

A number of critics pointed out that the character of Heini is not fully developed, especially in the second half of the novel. However, they did not realize that it is actually this suspicious blank in Heini's political psychology that constitutes the missing part of her story. Feng Xuefeng, Ding Ling's best friend and the most sincere critic of her works,[49] hinted at this omission when he observed that Ding Ling "didn't pay sufficient attention to and make incisive analysis of the contradictory relationships between Heini and her uncle and the social relationships within which Heini's psychology was grounded."[50]

---

49. On the romance and friendship of Feng Xuefeng and Ding Ling, see, for instance, Shen Congwen, *Ji Ding Ling* (Remembering Ding Ling, 1934), *SCWQJ* 13: 51–128; Ding Yanzhao, *Zai nanren de shijie.*

50. Feng Xuefeng, "*Taiyang zhaozai Sangganhe shang*," p. 331.

He then attributed this failure to Ding Ling's having not described her "in a socialist realistic manner." In Feng's analysis, we can fathom his deep concern, which was actually caused by the lack of transformation of Heini's class consciousness. He was worried that Heini appeared to be too aloof or transcendental to the class struggle during the land reform. Having hinted at the heroine's missing political engagement, Feng Xuefeng, however, leaves the intriguing linkage between the political and the gender questions unexplored.

Given her elaboration of the formative story of Cheng Ren, Ding Ling understood all too well what kind of trials a person had to go through in order to be qualified in the Communist world. She omitted this rite of passage in Heini not because she failed to use the socialist realistic techniques or could not shake off the debris of bourgeois realism, as Feng Xuefeng conjectured. To be sure, one can always attribute to the constraints of the party literature doctrine Ding Ling's incomplete exploration of the situation of women from the opposite class background in the socialist revolution. Then why did she not just delete this character, instead of describing her with such great sympathy? As her notes clearly say, in order to keep the portrait of Heini politically unproblematic, Ding Ling even changed her identity from the daughter to the niece of the landlord. Hence, what is happening in regard to Heini's character development is not merely an expedient strategy to stay within the party line. Rather, the suspicious absence of political consciousness in Heini suggests how deeply aware Ding Ling was of the intricate dilemma for women in the socialist class struggle, especially for those with problematic class origins.

Unlike Cheng Ren or Dong Guihua, Heini was not born with the right class roots. Therefore, any momentary hesitation or even mistakes in political stance cannot be rectified through the prescriptions of class ideology alone. Evidently, Ding Ling did not think a clean break with the landlord family could be the solution for the woman question represented in Heini. Heini's predicament results not only from her identity as niece of the landlord but also from the fact that she is an independent, strong-willed, and beautiful modern woman. In either the traditional or the Communist society, she is unorthodox. Before the village has been liberated, she is accused by her family for her romance with a hired laborer from a lower social class. Although the liberation of the village frees her from the fate of an arranged marriage, it does not spare her puritanical criticism from other village women for her "excessive" freedom and "modern" style.[51] To be sure, Heini is ostracized from the village women's association primarily because of class differences. However, she is also rejected because she is young, pretty, and feminine. Even when she voluntarily teaches the women's literacy class, she cannot "altogether avoid cold stares, envy and hatred. Even the instinctive hatred which her youth and beauty aroused was considered reasonable by those to whom she was a temptress or monster or something despicable."[52] She is condemned by people of the same sex as "bitch" and "frivolous,"[53] words aimed at her female sexuality, not her class categorization. Paradoxically, characteristics of gender and sexuality such as "femininity" and "beauty" become tropes for her "heterodox" and "contaminated" political identity.

The land-reform movement, as William Hinton points out in his work on north China, *Fanshen*, was essentially a revolution in the class consciousness of the peasantry, not merely an economic revolution.[54] In *Sanggan River*, even the mother of Gu Changsheng, who is depicted as a selfish "middle peasant" (*zhongnong*), has come to realize that land reform is in the interests of all.[55] After obtaining his share of land, the stubborn peasant Hou Zhongquan, who has lived his whole life in utter destitution and believed that was his preordained fate, has finally been awakened and starts to worship Mao instead of God.[56] Among this happy mass of people who have been economically and socially *fanshen* (turned over), Heini is the only one virtually untouched by any of these transformations or historical violence of the land reform. Even when she sees the big urn distributed to her poor peasant uncle, she innocently recognizes it as the belongings of her landlord uncle and yells out, "This container be-

51. Ding, *Sun Shines over the Sangkan River*, p. 76.
52. Ibid., p. 155.
53. Ibid., p. 78.
54. Hinton, *Fanshen*.
55. Ding, *Sun Shines over the Sangkan River*, p. 330.
56. Ibid., pp. 313–15.

longed originally to our family. I know it, my uncle bought it from the town last year, a good container."[57]

In her analysis of Ding Ling's 1940 short story "When I Was in Xia Village," Barlow keenly emphasizes the contradiction between the discourse of gender and that of anti-Japanese nationalism in the case of Zhenzhen, the female protagonist who has been brutally exploited by both sides in the war—the physical use by one is a means of gaining information for the other.[58] After returning to her village, this unyielding girl is despised for her "contaminated" body and for offending the normative of chastity. However, Zhenzhen refuses to be defined by either the patriotic or the patriarchal code. When talking about her decision to employ her own body to do intelligence work for the Communist Party, Zhenzhen expresses a clear resolution to live a sensible and meaningful life. In revising the story after the establishment of the PRC, Ding Ling added particular political and nationalist motivations,[59] but in both versions, Zhenzhen is determined to go to Yan'an for further education and embark on a new path in search of her true self. Although not as resistant as Zhenzhen, Heini also declines to be contained in either the class or the female identity assigned to her in the second liberation brought about by land reform. The missing political transformation in Heini suggests that she is not seeking a correct class identity, so as to be qualified as the lover of a Communist cadre, but rather her female subjectivity. Although Zhenzhen might be assimilated into the political hierarchy through her education in the sacred Communist capital, Heini's

---

57. Ibid., p. 331

58. Barlow, *I Myself Am a Woman*.

59. In the original version, Zhenzhen told the narrator, "I've got to find a way to live, and to live in a way that makes sense." After the revision, it reads, "Later I made connections with our own people and was even less afraid. When I saw the Japanese devils getting beaten because of the tricks I played, the guerrillas active all over, and everyone feeling better every day, it's worth it. I've got to find a way to live, and to live in a way that makes sense, unless it's absolutely impossible. So when they said they would let me have medical care, I thought, that's fine." The revisions made here are mostly concerned with Zhenzhen's revolutionary consciousness. According to Feuerwerker, the 1945 English edition of the story published by Kutub Publishers, Bombay, translated by Kung Pu-sheng, was different from the 1951 revised edition. The former has a particular emphasis on Zhenzhen's understanding of her work. See Feuerwerker, "Ting Ling's 'When I Was in Sha Chuan.'"

apolitical passage into the opposite class category only precludes the possibility of placing her on a pedestal of class ideology, thereby making her more independent of the dominant political discourse.

Accordingly, Heini's missing political bildung renders the entangled question of class and gender in the socialist revolution even more important. Ding Ling's refusal to sublimate or displace the female identity creates a gendered position that unsettles an ideological discourse that the novel aims to establish. Indeed, Heini's silence on political and class issues provides a highly upsetting reply to the existing policy regarding class struggle and women's emancipation and renders the question of women in the socialist revolution all the more compelling. By staying away from political engagement, Heini rejects any fixed identity that would situate her in a preexisting grid of meaning, patriarchal or Communist. Viewed in this light, this strategy of absence indicates an even more obscure future for the realization of female consciousness in the socialist state.

As if that silence was not provocative enough, Ding Ling gives another twist to the seemingly happy ending of the love relationship between Heini and Cheng Ren by creating a powerful trope between Heini the woman and the urn as the trophy of class struggle. In the scene of distributing land-reform gains, Cheng Ren realizes that it is politically safe to maintain the liaison with Heini now that she has become the niece of a poor peasant and offers to carry the big urn for her. Like the container, Heini the woman becomes the prize that Cheng Ren wins for his relentless self-transformation. The reader has every reason to doubt whether this politically correct love relationship will end in a happy marriage, considering the fierce critique Ding Ling made about a decade earlier in her essay, "Thoughts on March 8," on the problematic situation of marriage in which women of the Communist area were trapped.[60] Ding Ling might not have been aware of the parallels between the woman's body and the urn as a hollow receptacle, as psychoanalytical critics would note; nevertheless, the trope indicates that women, like the land or farming implements, are distributed or assigned as spoils for revolutionary peasants. Consequently, the seemingly happy ending for Heini

60. Ding, *DLWJ* 4: 388–92.

anticipates an uncertain future for women within the constraints of socialist ideology.

Thus, *Sanggan River*'s apparent formal closure actually leaves open an urgent question regarding the destiny of Heini, which, as the PRC history in the following decades proves, was an enormously bitter one. Heini and her fellow Chinese from problematic class backgrounds—above all, the Chinese intellectuals like Ding Ling herself who were educated in the so-called "old" and "reactionary" society—would be purged over and over to atone for their original sin, for which, of course, they could never truly be redeemed. Walter Benjamin, pondering the perplexing situation of the European left intelligentsia of the 1930s, describes it so well:

> The solidarity of the specialist with the proletariat . . . can only be a mediated one. . . . [T]hey could not do away with the fact that even the proletarianization of an intellectual hardly ever makes a proletarian. Why? Because the bourgeois class gave him, in the form of education, a means of production that, owing to educational privilege, makes him feel solidarity with it, and still more it with him. Aragon was thereby entirely correct when, in another context, he declared, "The revolutionary intellectual appears first and foremost as the betrayer of his class of origin."[61]

"Du Wanxiang": The Anachronism of a Socialist Realist Fairy Tale

During the Anti-Rightist Campaign, many of Ding Ling's writings were subjected to a harsh new scrutiny and reinterpreted in the light of her alleged antiparty treachery. Thus a series of women characters in her fiction became incriminating "self-portraits." "Miss Sophie's Diary," "When I Was in Xia Village," and "In the Hospital" were singled out as targets for the most ferocious condemnation and often absurd literary and political reading and misreading. Even her socialist realistic work *Sanggan River,* with its description of Heini, among others, could not avoid such a tragicomic fate of "recritique." A collection of such problematic works was even published by *Wenyi bao* (Literary gazette), with the title *Zai pipan* (Re-critique), which, sanctioned by Mao Zedong himself, purported to lay bare the evil thoughts

61. Benjamin, "The Author as Producer," p. 237.

of those heterodox intellectuals.[62] Ding Ling's essay "Thoughts on March 8" and short story "In the hospital" were among the writings that were urged to be denounced a second time. In the preface to this special edition of *Literary Gazette*, whose former editor-in-chief was none other than Ding Ling, Mao Zedong, who twenty years earlier had welcomed her to Yan'an and praised her as a "general with a pen"[63] in the poem he sent her via military telegram, now condemned her as a "poisonous weed" who "wrote antirevolutionary articles in the guise of a revolutionary."[64] Among such criticism by her antagonists, the following remarks by Zhou Yang, her colleague and major enemy in her later life who was assigned the vice cultural minister after the establishment of the PRC, are surely representative: "For quite a few years, the phantom of Miss Sophie has haunted Ding Ling, but later she wore the Communist uniform, and therefore, her countenance was not so easy to be identified."[65] Thus, regarding different aspects of her characters, such as Miss Sophie in "Miss Sophie's Diary," Zhenzhen in "When I Was in Xia Village," Lu Ping in "In the Hospital," and Heini in *Sanggan River*, all were viewed as reincarnations of a cunning and evil femme fatale, Ding Ling herself. These works constituted different yet complementary palimpsest layers of a body text called Ding Ling.

All the criticism of bourgeois aesthetics in her works notwithstanding, the primary reason for her purge, however, was the suspicious three-year house arrest (1933–36) by the KMT government, before Ding Ling fled to Yan'an. Feng Da, her second husband, allegedly betrayed Ding Ling to the KMT secret police.[66] As a result, she was kidnapped and put under house arrest. Although she had never done

62. "'Zai pipan' bianzhe anyu" (Editors' words to *Re-critique*), *Wenyi bao*, no. 2 (1958). See Hong, *Zhongguo dangdai wenxueshi shiliaoxuan*, pp. 430–31.

63. Mao Zedong, in Ding Yanzhao, *Zai nanren de shijie li*, pp. 246–47.

64. "'Zai pipan' bianzhe anyu," p. 431. Although the initial draft of this article was not written by Mao Zedong, Mao made substantial revisions.

65. Zhou Yang, "Wenyi zhanxianshang de yichang."

66. Ding Yanzhao, *Zai nanren de shijie li*, esp. pp. 157–99. According to Ding Yanzhao, Feng Da did not intentionally betray Ding Ling. When he was arrested by the KMT secret police, he claimed he was not a Communist but just an ordinary family guy. When the police ordered a search of his apartment, Feng brought them home believing that Ding Ling would be gone by then, as they had originally

anything harmful to the party during the detention years, she was accused of treason.[67] Ironically, the fact that she lived together with Feng Da, a traitor to the party, and even had a daughter with him, during her house arrest became part of the substantiation of her betrayal. As early as 1940, Ding Ling was investigated by the Central Ministry of Organization of the Communist Party regarding her confinement by the KMT police. In the Ding Ling archive, a crucial piece of evidence against her reads, "Ding Ling still lived with her husband Feng Da, who had already turned traitor, after she was arrested in 1933 and until October 1934."[68]

Strikingly, the accusation of treachery is based not only on her "contamination" of Communist purity but, more importantly, on the fact that she slept with the enemy—Feng Da the traitor. Here, the Communist ideal of purity signifies the chastity norm for women. The charge was directed first and foremost against the woman who violated the code of chastity, casting female sexuality as evil. Ironically, such a femme fatal is exactly what Ding Ling set out to investigate in her Yan'an fictional version of "sleeping with the enemy," "When I Was in Xia Village." The heroin Zhenzhen, a name that literally means "chastity," who was raped by Japanese invaders and later worked as a spy for the Communists as a Japanese army prostitute, is detested by her fellow villagers after she returns from the frontier. Feuerwerker is surely right in pointing out that the miseries Zhenzhen has to confront are "fully 'available' only to women: arranged marriage, rape by enemy soldiers, exploitation of her body by both armies and, after her return to the village, ostracism for violating the chastity code."[69] To push Feuerwerker's feminist critique one step further, I would stress that such sexual abuse and discrimination become all the more violent when intertwined with a political discourse of revolution and women's emancipation that is marked by a

---

planned. However, when they arrived at the apartment, both Feng and the secret police unexpectedly found Ding there with another Communist.

67. Zhou Liangpei, *Ding Ling zhuan*, pp. 217–346.

68. "Zhongyang zuzhibu shengcha Ding Ling tongzhi beibu beijing jingguo de jielun" (The conclusion of the investigation of Comrade Ding Ling's arrestment and confinement), in *DLWJ* 8.

69. Feuerwerker, *Ding Ling's Fiction*, p. 114.

Communist code of sexual puritanism. Although this revolutionary discourse repudiated love and sexuality as decadent and evil, it paradoxically developed a certain kind of political voyeurism. Exposing someone else's love affairs or sexual lives had been a powerful means to fight against him or her during the political purges ever since the Yan'an Rectification Campaign of the early 1940s. Sexual accusations often became evidence in political censure. Such voyeurism came across as all the more sadistic in various post-1949 political campaigns. The purge Ding Ling suffered as a result of her tainted history—the suspicious three years under house arrest—can be brought to bear effectively on the gendered discourse of revolution, in which female sexuality has to be contained and repudiated. Such a strict sexual politics makes up a significant part of the agenda of social hygiene discussed earlier in this chapter. What forces are then at stake in this distinctive Communist sexual puritanism—political, ethical, gender, and/or sexual? Remarkably, gender- or sexuality-related problems are often displaced into the so-called lofty, larger-than-life domain of nation or revolution. Thus, the political charge of being "antiparty" and "treacherous" obscured the urgent question of gender and sexuality.

Whereas Zhenzhen in the story can still go to a certain sacred place, Yan'an most probably, to cure her disease and pursue revolutionary ideals, no matter how ambiguous this place could be, Ding Ling in postrevolutionary China had nowhere to run and had to pay dearly for breaking the chastity code and her antiparty "crime." Not unlike Heini in *Sanggan River*, who is a victim of her familial origin, a sin inerasable and unforgivable, Ding Ling was haunted by this transgression for the rest of her life. From fiction to history, from socialist realism to socialist purge, political and gender issues entangled and interacted with each other. Ding Ling was condemned in 1955 for her 1930s antiparty crime of *zishou bianjie* (surrendering to the enemy and defecting) and accused subsequently of being a rightist. Deprived of all official positions and ultimately of her party membership, she spent twelve years (1958–70) in exile in Beidahuang on the remote northern border of Manchuria and was then put into Qincheng prison (1970–75) in suburban Beijing as a traitor. After she was released, she and her third husband, Cheng Ming, were banished to a remote village in Shanxi province (1975–79). Not until 1979 were they allowed to return to Beijing.[70]

Strikingly, after more than two decades of ordeals, Ding Ling reemerged on the PRC literary stage with the most sincere model work of socialist realism, "Du Wanxiang" (1979). The heroine, who transforms from an ignorant village girl into a model Communist worker, conforms to every Communist norm, political or ethical, gender or sexual, with a moral certainty and humbleness never truly achieved by any of her female predecessors in Ding Ling's fiction. As Barlow points out, Du Wanxiang's story "is a parable of Chinese women's liberation."[71] In her last representation of Chinese womanhood, Ding Ling finally managed to suture the gap between the political subject and the female subjectivity, and thereby completed her own transformation from the avant-garde woman writer who claimed "what I sell is my writings, not my identity as woman"[72] when first entering the literary arena in the late 1920s, into the genderless political writer of a true socialist realism.

"Du Wanxiang," which Ding Ling viewed as the best work she had ever written,[73] is a portrait of a Communist model worker in Beidahuang. Du Wanxiang, daughter of a poor farmer in northwest China, lost her mother when she was still a child and was mistreated by her stepmother. She was sold as a child-adoption wife to the Li family for fifty dollars when she was thirteen years old and soon became the major labor in that household. Shortly after the liberation of their village by the Communist army, Wanxiang is enlightened by a female land-reform cadre and becomes head of the women's association. Soon she joins the Communist Party. After her husband, demobilized from the anti-American Korean War, is transferred to Beidahuang as a farm worker, Du Wanxiang follows him to the farm. Although neglected by him as merely a housewife, she nevertheless takes every opportunity to work selflessly for the farm and finally is glorified as the epitome of the socialist model worker. Wanxiang's

70. See Wang Hong, *Zuoyou shuo Ding Ling*, pp. 311–20.
71. Barlow, *I Myself Am a Woman*, p. 45.
72. Mao Dun, "Nüzuojia Ding Ling," pp. 204–8.
73. See Wang Meng, "Wo xinmuzhong de Ding Ling," p. 204.

final remarks in her speech in the Palace of Culture, which accept "applause as loud as spring thunder," can be exactly read as Ding Ling's own confession to the party after all the pain she had gone through since her banishment:

> I am an ordinary person. I have done nothing more than what ordinary people do. The little I've understood, the reason why we're all here today, is because of you. You, my hardworking comrades, you people with ideals, you've prompted my mental development, encouraged me. We've all been educated and nurtured by the Party. All I want is to stay under the Party's leadership forever, acting with practical wisdom, honestly carrying out the Party's directives, and struggling for our Communist enterprise for the rest of my life.[74]

In spite of Wanxiang's complex identities as orphaned stepdaughter, child-adoption daughter-in-law, and neglected wife, which could have made her a figure no less intriguing than Zhenzhen in "When I Was in Xia Village" or Dong Guihua, also the head of the women's association, in *Sanggan River,* Wanxiang's interior psychology are left unexplored. Instead, she is a socialist Cinderella salvaged and turned into "a Communist princess" of model worker by the omniscient messiah, embodied by the party. If there are still feminine energies and sensibilities to be perceived in characters such as Dong Guihua and Heini in *Sanggan River,* which nevertheless are eventually rechanneled toward the larger goals of the party, then, in Du Wanxiang, even these faint sparks are completely erased. Deprived of any female gender characteristics, Wanxiang is not identifiable with any female role—mother, daughter, or wife. In the working collective, the female subjectivity vanished; purified and deified in disenchanted postrevolutionary China, it becomes a desexualized woman. The birth of a new socialist woman occasions the desexualization and defeminization of the gendered woman.

In a classical bildungsroman as represented by Johann Wolfgang von Goethe's (1749–1832) *Wilhelm Meister's Apprenticeship, Bildung* (education) is a socio-aesthetic process to produce an ideal bourgeois human being who is at the same time a good citizen of an ideal state. In contrast, Ding Ling's socialist story of initiation is more concerned about the disavowal of the individual human being in order

74. Ding Ling, trans. in Barlow, *I Myself Am a Woman,* p. 353.

to create an "every wo/man" who embodies the collective social and political body of the People. The significance of this short story goes beyond its eventual suture of the feminist gap, which has been the central theme in Ding Ling's writings. "Du Wanxiang" is not only a story about the transformation of a hu(wo)man being into a socialist new citizen, but also about the transformation of a waste land into a socialist paradise. Ding Ling made the Great Northern Wasteland from 1958 to 1964, the exact time and place where she spent her internal exile, as the site of rebirth for Du Wanxiang. What is interesting on this point is how she set about to write a tale of the metamorphosis of a land into the socialist base of agriculture. "To compel the land to offer grain, to transform the notorious Beidahuang (Great Northern Wasteland) into rich Beidacang (Great Northern Barn),"[75] as Ding Ling enthusiastically described when she first arrived in Beidahuang, indicates the land reclamation and agricultural mechanization in the Great Wasteland in northern Manchuria. From 1958 on, Mao Zedong urged millions of young people, most of them soldiers recently returned from the Korean War, to fight yet another battle to conquer nature—to reclaim the vast wilderness and accomplish agricultural modernization in north Manchuria. This project constitutes the best example of the socialist utopia of industrial and agricultural modernization launched in the Maoist China.

Remarkably, what Ding Ling witnessed in the Great Northern Wasteland was in fact disillusionment with this socialist utopia and its catastrophic consequences. Du Wanxiang's story spans from 1958 to 1964, approximately the time of the Great Leap Forward, the enactment of the Maoist utopian plan for economic modernization. Aiming at "catching up with and surpassing England and America" (*ganying chaomei*) and "leaping into Communism" (*paobu jinru gongchanzhuyi*), this pseudo-modern and false scientific program became stuck in an economic and political hysteria and resulted in the unprecedented famine that plagued China between 1958 and 1962, with at least 30 million people starving to death.[76] In every corner of

75. Ding *DLWJ* 5: 336.

76. The Great Famine caused by the Great Leap Forward is attributed to *sannian ziran zaihai* (a three-year natural disaster) in Chinese official statements. In the last few decades, scholarly research has gradually come to the conclusion that it was

China, people perished for their Communist fanaticism. Nothing could better prove the absurdity and catastrophe of the irrational Maoist vision of modernization. Ding Ling, in exile on a remote farm of the Great Northern Wasteland, could not have been unaware of the harsh situation. However, in her socialist realist fairy tale,[77] which deals with the exact same historical time period, the hysterical Great Leap Forward has been displaced by a glorious socialist epic of mass farming. In such uncanny anachronism, the Great Famine vanishes like a ghost.

In research on the Great Leap Forward, scholars such as Yang Dali argue that the irrational consumption system, particularly the construction of free dining halls in each People's Commune (*gongshe shitang*), is one of the major causes of the Great Famine.[78] If the dissipation of food resulted directly in the devastating mass starvation, then, remarkably, the ideological dissipation of Communist enthusiasm and optimism led to another form of famine in language and literature.[79] With the disappearance of feminist or any other sort of critical space, Ding Ling's writing is dominated by the stereotypical Maoist political vocabulary. Hence, Ding Ling presented her last incarnation in Du Wanxiang: a pure, desexualized, and politicized socialist model woman. A decade before Ding Ling was glorifying her socialist fairy tale in the time of the Great Famine, Eileen Chang,

---

rather a man-made catastrophe. See, for instance, Ding Shu, *Renhuo*; Becker, *Hungry Ghosts*; D. L. Yang, *Calamity and Reform in China*; and the special edition on the Great Leap Forward, *Twenty-First Century*, no. 48 (August 1998). Intriguingly, the program of the Great Leap Forward was carried out in the name of science. Even Qian Xuesen, the famous nuclear physicist, wrote articles to claim that the crop yields of every acre of land could reach 5,000 kilograms as long as the solar energy was to be fully employed. See Becker, *Hungry Ghosts*, p. 62.

77. According to Ding Ling's epilogue to "Du Wanxiang," she first wrote this short story in the spring of 1966, and the manuscript was destroyed during the Cultural Revolution. She recomposed it in 1978 as the first work she contributed to the post–Cultural Revolution Chinese literature.

78. Yang, "Cong dayuejin jihuang dao nongcun gaige," pp. 4–13.

79. The Great Leap Forward was by no means just an economic project. It simultaneously launched a cultural leap forward with its campaign of *quanmin xieshi* (all people write poetry), *quanmin xiexiashuo* (all people write fiction), etc. For a discussion of the cultural aspects of the Great Leap Forward, see Qian Liqun, "Tan zuomeng."

another significant modern Chinese woman writer, explored the theme of hunger in a completely different manner during her exile in Hong Kong. In her novel *Yang ge* (The rice-sprout song),[80] Chang addressed another famine plaguing the Chinese countryside right after the establishment of the socialist state. Tan Yuexiang in *Yang ge* gathers every bit of her energy to fight for survival in the natural and man-made famine. After her husband is killed by the village cadres, she sets the village barn on fire as a desperate way of taking revenge and burns to death. Du Wanxiang, on the contrary, during the famine, which is never directly spoken of in the story, only mentioned in an obscure manner as "a year of below-average yields,"[81] gleans grain left behind on the farm and turns it over to the government, despite the resentment of her own starving family. A happy cog in the socialist machinery, she completely loses her subjectivity in the socialist collectivization. Thus, whereas Eileen Chang contributed an epic of hunger to modern Chinese literature, Ding Ling could not realistically represent the insatiable spiritual hunger for the socialist revolution in "Du Wanxiang" without turning it into a colossal socialist realistic monument that entirely screens the real physical starvation swallowing up the land of famine.

The irony of history is that the damage caused by the Maoist fantasy of socialist modernization did not stop with the end of the Great Famine or the Cultural Revolution. When the twentieth century neared its close, the Great Northern Wasteland, which was suffering from the environmental deterioration caused by the irrational and aggressive large-scale reclamation of Du Wanxiang's time, was requested by the post-Mao government to be reconverted to its original status of "Wasteland"—forest, pasture, and wetlands—to restore the ecological balance. With the bankruptcy of the state-owned factories, the three provinces of northeastern China, the last bastion of industrial modernization of the state socialism, turned into a gloomy rust belt, a landscape bearing testimony to the failure of the Maoist socialist utopia.[82] Could the natural and economic disaster in effect be undone? Even if so, what about the political and cultural, moral

80. Eileen Chang, *Yang ge*.
81. Ding Ling, "Du Wanxiang," trans. in Barlow, *I Myself Am a Woman*, p. 348.
82. See Zhang Jing, "Wilderness to Reclaim Farmland."

and psychological calamities? Could they be undone with Deng Xiaoping's policy of *boluan fanzheng* (set wrong things right)?

In retrospect, the implications of Ding Ling's case become all the more poignant. If the socialist fairy tale of land reclamation and mechanized agriculture in a time of famine and crisis generates the uncanny anachronism in "Du Wanxiang," then another striking anachronism lies in the fact that it is a socialist fairy tale written and rewritten at a time when the Maoist socialist utopia was completely disillusioned, when the scar literature was burgeoning to ponder the socialism gone awry. Since the manuscript of "Du Wanxiang" had been lost during the Cultural Revolution, Ding Ling recomposed it in 1978 and published it as the first and the best writing she could ever contribute to modern Chinese literature. After decades of political perdition, Ding Ling seems to have been no longer capable of expressing herself other than in the revolutionary vocabulary that had haunted her ever since the Yan'an Rectification Campaign.

Another important case of political aphasia is Lu Ling (1923–94). The most talented and passionate writer of the leftist *Qiyue* (July) School with Hu Feng (1902–85) as spiritual leader, Lu was driven mad by the never-ending political torture after he was charged as a member of the "Hu Feng reactionary gang" and put into prison in the 1950s. The tragedy is that when he was finally released in the 1980s, the psychologically damaged Lu Ling was unable to speak other than in the political jargon and rhetoric that he internationalized through numerous self-criticisms and public confessions.[83]

Whereas the schizophrenic Lu Ling, who, after all, had never become a high culture official as had Ding Ling, could not expel the revolutionary vocabulary that took root in his subconscious, the politically rehabilitated Ding Ling was never able to exorcise the revolutionary specter. Or was she? Has she really been liberated in her revolutionary passion and converted into a politicized being? Or were the traumatic experiences induced by numerous political purges so devastating that she finally learned a lesson and became politically strategic? As stated in her diary entries in 1978, "'Thoughts on March 8' brought me decades of agony. The old wound is still present, how

83. Li Hui, "Linghun zai feixiang."

can I seek trouble again and harm my future generations!"[84] In order to address this problem, a close look at the years after Ding Ling's rehabilitation is necessary.

Over Her Dead Body: Ding Ling's Leftist Loyalism in the 1980s

The postrevolutionary imprint on Ding Ling cannot be fully evaluated without taking into consideration her ostensible retrograde obsession with Maoist revolutionary discourse in the 1980s. Instead of providing critical reflections on the political and cultural catastrophes since the 1950s, Ding Ling became even more revolutionary than ever. In this time of political disenchantment, Ding Ling's insistence on the Maoist revolutionary theory constrained her under the proletarian cultural revolutionary spell.

When she returned to Beijing in the late 1970s, her untimely "radical leftist" behavior and writings provoked an upsetting discord in the literary and cultural domain. She discarded her early works, such as "Miss Sophie's Diary," "When I Was in Xia Village," and "In the Hospital," which made her literary reputation and later brought her political doom, and declared that "Du Wanxiang" was her best work. She claimed that a writer should be above all politicized, and harshly rebuked scar literature, which dealt with the psychological damage caused by radical leftism since the mid-1950s.[85] Consequently, Ding Ling was named *zuopai* (leftist), and labeled " 'orthodox,' 'conservative,' and even 'Cardinal,' 'whipping stick.' "[86] Her alteration from "rightist" to "leftist" after her political rehabilitation became a controversial subject matter in the post–Cultural Revolution intellectual domain. Yet, as Li Tuo insightfully comments, "In effect, she didn't change her political stance. Because compared with the Ding Ling from Yan'an rectification to the 1950s, the Ding Ling of the 1980s had hardly changed. The vocabulary of her discourse

---

84. "1956–1979nian shenghuo pianduan," "October 8, 1978," *DLWJ* 10: 330.

85. For discussions of Ding Ling's post-Mao leftist stance, see, for instance, *Zuoyou shuo Ding Ling*, edited by Wang Hong; Alber, *Embracing the Lie*; and Barlow, "Woman under Maoist Nationalism in the Thought of Ding Ling."

86. Zhang Yongquan, "Zoubuchu de guaiquan," p. 231.

remained the same as what she had learned during the Yan'an rectification. It is precisely her determination and insistence on the Maoist style that conditioned her color-changing like a chameleon."[87] Indeed, her theses in articles such as "Gaizao" (Transformation, 1943), "Dao qunzhong zhong qu luohu" (Go make your dwelling among the masses, 1953), and "Zuojia shi zhengzhihuale de ren" (Writers are politicized people, 1980) are emphatically consistent, carefully shaped in accordance with the literary norm prescribed by Mao Zedong's Yan'an Talks. Hence, the changing label of "leftist" or "rightist" should not obscure Ding Ling's sustained effort at self-transformation after the Yan'an Rectification Campaign.

This sustained effort leads to a most cynical question: What occasioned Ding Ling's obsessive investment in the discourse of revolution in a time of revolutionary disenchantment? To be sure, as some critics have argued, Ding Ling's revolutionary insistence must be considered in conjunction with the fierce rivalries among Communist cultural cadres, especially between Ding Ling and Zhou Yang, which did not cease with the end of the Cultural Revolution.[88] Some other critics have imputed it to the fact that Ding Ling had finally learned a lesson from the harsh political purges resulting from her "politically incorrect" writings. Wang Meng was surely right when he maintained that Ding Ling had to act according to the Maoist norm in order to prove that compared with Zhou Yang, she was the true revolutionary.

Yet, beyond the internecine power struggles and the CCP's literary control, how can we explain Ding Ling's apparent retrograde romance with the revolution? I suggest that her determination to politicize and recuperate herself was so strong that she stuck to it even when the political and ideological machinery went awry. After decades of self-transformation, she had become overly dependent upon the Maoist discourse, so much so that she was never able to find an alternative. Indeed, she endorsed the discourse of the revolution so

---

87. Li Tuo, "Ding Ling bu jiandan."

88. See, for instance, Zhang Yongquan, "Zoubuchu de guaiquan," in which Zhang argues that it was the conflicts between Ding Ling and Zhou Yang that forced Ding Ling to take a radical leftist stance: "It is exactly Zhou Yang's continuous attacks that drove her into an uncanny circle" (p. 241).

completely that she remained attached to it, not in spite of but because of its failure. Therefore, when this discourse was reevaluated in the post–Cultural Revolution era, her political commitment took on an absurd and bitter cast, so meaningless yet meaningful. The revolutionary passion seemed to expand beyond its original ambition of social and cultural redemption to take on a ghostly life of its own.

Ding Ling's condemnation of Shen Congwen's *Ji Ding Ling* (Remembering Ding Ling, 1934) is to be understood in this context. *Remembering Ding Ling*, a fine and sympathetic account of the years before Ding fled to Yan'an, is a memoir Shen Congwen finished after learning that she had been kidnapped in 1933. Assuming that she might have been executed by the KMT government like her former husband Hu Yepin two years earlier, Shen Congwen, the best friend of this couple in their early literary careers, composed this work to memorialize a talented female writer and, in case Ding Ling was still alive in one of the KMT prisons, to arouse public indignation, which might forestall her execution.[89]

Ding Ling, who claimed not to have known about this book until a Japanese sinologist brought it to her as a gift in 1979, was immensely provoked by it. In the article "Yepin yu geming" (Yepin and the revolution), published in *Shikan* (Poetry) in 1980, Ding Ling reproached the book as "a badly fabricated 'fiction'" and denounced Shen Congwen as a "philistine with vulgar tastes" for his "distorting and ridiculing revolutionaries."[90] Why did Ding Ling choose this book written by Shen almost half a century earlier as the target of her one and only aggressive public attack after her political restoration? Why her old friend Shen Congwen, who helped rescue Hu Yepin and later Ding Ling herself during their confinement by the KMT secret police in the 1930s, and who accompanied the widowed Ding Ling and her infant son from Shanghai back to Hunan during those hazardous wartime years after Hu was executed?[91] Moreover, the post-1949 experiences of Shen Congwen, whose literary life was terminated at the mid-twentieth century, were no less trying than her

---

89. Kinkley, *Odyssey of Shen Congwen*, pp. 205–6.
90. Ding, *DLWJ* 5: 165–68.
91. See Ling Yu, in *Shen Congwen zhuan*, pp. 287–98.

own. Considering all these, Ding Ling's vindictive attitude seems rather perplexing.

To be sure, the unquenchable fury that suddenly burst out toward Shen Congwen vented some of the resentment Ding Ling had to suppress to protect herself from possible further political censure. However, such psychological displacement cannot fully account for her unusual behavior. Critics have sought possible rationalizations for it. There are, in particular, two major conjectures worth noting here. On the personal level, Ding Ling was irritated because this book touched upon her love affair with Feng Da, which led to her house arrest in Nanjing by the KMT government and eventually to the charge of treason during the Communist political campaigns.[92] On the political level, she could not bear Shen Congwen's disrespect toward the Communist revolution to which she and her martyr husband Hu Yepin had been dedicated. Indeed, Ding Ling's attack on Shen is a performance of the "ritual of offering sacrifice" to her recuperated political and literary career and a reinforcement of her unyielding political commitment.

Whether Ding Ling's charges against Shen's book can be validated remains a moot question; however, they reveal certain significant dimensions of this event. Instead of venturing yet another conjecture of Ding Ling's antagonism, I would rather call attention to a simple fact that has so far been neglected. Ding Ling's reaction to Shen's book is first of all the response of a reader confronting a literary text, who happened to be its main persona. *Remembering Ding Ling* provides an account, no matter how fictional or real, of Ding Ling in her youth, a brave yet sensitive, passionate yet sometimes naïve and bourgeois individual. Reading Shen Congwen's remembrances of a young Ding Ling was for the senior Ding Ling an uncanny encounter

---

92. This explanation was also provided by Shen Congwen himself. In a letter to Xu Chi dated July 2, 1980, which was published in *Changjiang wenyi* (Literature and art of Yangtze River) in 1989, Shen assumed that his account of Ding Ling and Feng Da in *Remembering Ding Ling* was one main reason Ding Ling attacked him so vehemently. See Shen, "19800702 Fu Xu Chi" (Re: Xu Chi), *SCWQJ* 26: 112–16. Another reason might be that Shen may have hinted that Ding Ling and Hu Yepin belonged to the faction of Li Lisan, which was soon purged by its rival, the Wang Ming sect. For a discussion of the League of Left Wing Writers and the CCP's Li Lisan line, see T. A. Hsia, *Gate of Darkness*, pp. 163–233.

with her ghostly alter ego across the monumental division of the Yan'an period, the civil war, and the ominous political campaigns in post-1949 Communist China. This small book forced her to confront her own prehistory, a prerevolutionary history of Miss Sophie, of her strenuous yet passionate life of a writer in small Shanghai apartments, and of her Nanjing house arrest. *Remembering Ding Ling* brought to the fore this elusive prerevolutionary history, which led to her traumatic indictments and which she was determined to shield from public view and disavow.

Given Ding Ling's conformity since her political recovery, which in effect preclude any possibility of working through her traumatic experiences in verbal or written manner, the shock of this unexpected encounter with her past—a tainted past in the Communist political sense—through reading *Remembering Ding Ling* was, not surprisingly, devastating. Therefore, I suggest that Ding Ling's antagonism must be decoded both politically and textually. She was alarmed that Shen's biographical representation of her past would only substantiate the charges made against her by her party foes. For a Communist as loyal as Ding Ling, who so painstakingly recuperated her political and literary life and had yet to purify her contaminated Nanjing history,[93] what could be more dangerous? Indeed, the battle she ignited against her old friend Shen Congwen is nothing less than a battle against the representation of her prerevolutionary history, or more tragically yet accurately, an allegorical battle against literature—within or beyond the constraints of Mao's Yan'an Talks, which won her fame but also triggered her perdition. In this light, Wang Meng's argument, though perhaps too cynical, is perceptive: "When she blew at Shen Congwen, she aimed at *wuhao* (font size five, which indicates writings in print, herein, literary publications), which has always led to her political depreciation."[94]

---

93. Although the antiparty charge against the Ding Ling and Chen Qixia gang had been redressed, and Ding Ling's official positions and her party membership had been restored by 1980, it was not until 1984 that the CCP finally authorized the rectification of her charge of treason during the Nanjing confinement. See Wang Zengru, *Wunai de niepan*, pp. 2–8.

94. Wang Meng, "Wo xinmuzhong de Ding Ling," p. 208.

From a revolution in fiction advocated by late Qing intellectuals to the formation of a new literature ensuing from the May Fourth movement, from the revolutionary literature set forth by Mao Zedong's Yan'an Talks to the implosion of revolutionary poetics of post-1949 socialist China, modern Chinese history witnessed an intriguing topography of literature and revolution. And Ding Ling, who achieved twin peaks in her literary career as the most avant-garde May Fourth writer and the epitome of the literary worker of Chinese socialist realism, devoted her whole life to literary revolution and revolutionary literature and ironically wound up defending her revolutionary stance by renouncing her literary creations. From implosion of revolutionary poetics to the eventual disavowal of literature, the literary modernization of socialist China leaves us a most compelling trajectory. As early as 1942, right after Mao's Yan'an Talks, Ding Ling remarked on the self-transformation of bourgeois intellectuals, "Transformation, first of all, is to surrender and hand over all your arms. Since you are a capitulator, and surrendered from that class to this class, you must trust and honor this new class . . . even if you have prolific works, you have to regard them as nothing, to eliminate your self-confidence and pride."[95] When she talked about self-transformation as capitulation to the proletariat, she might not have anticipated that the politicization of Chinese intellectuals would actually lead to their disarmament by not only discarding their works but also abolishing their critical consciousness.

It is precisely in conjunction with such a resolute literary disavowal that Ding Ling's presentation of "Du Wanxiang" as the model work to stage her rehabilitation must be understood. It is a revolutionary declaration rather than a literary work. Some critics have pointed out that Ding Ling led a double life in her later years by maintaining her intellectual conscience in her diary entries or some private letters. This is true. However, what is most important, I argue, is that Ding Ling eliminated all the critical space in her verbal and written public performance, which she had never done before, even in her socialist realistic *Sanggan River*. Yet, paradoxically, when she finally surrendered to the Maoist revolutionary discourse, it had

95. Ding, *DLWJ* 6: 21.

been hollowed out to a mere ritual rhetoric sanctioned to be abolished. Indeed, as He Guimei concludes in her study of Ding Ling, "She eventually couldn't go beyond the discursive boundary set by the system, and was forever fixed in a vacant discursive site in her obsessive endeavor."[96] Indeed, the tragedy of Ding Ling lies not only in the bitter anachronism of revolutionary discourse, but more powerfully, in the fact that she could never accomplish an effective configuration of literature and revolution, even if the Maoist revolutionary discourse could be entirely eradicated.

The irony of history is that, even though Ding Ling was determined to disavow literature for politics, her final identification by the Communist Party was as a writer. On July 6, 1984, the charge of treason against Ding Ling in her Nanjing house arrest was finally redressed. Learning the news, Ding Ling sighed, saying "Now, I can die."[97] This signified her ultimate moment of nirvana—the final purification of her identity as a Communist. Not surprisingly, two years later, when Ding Ling passed away, her husband Chen Ming asked that her dead body be covered with a party flag for her funeral ceremony. Evidently, the flag would reassure her purity and immortality as a Communist Party member. At the ceremony, the last moment for her to be presented and represented, the party flag over her dead body would function like a labeled frame or a sealed signature, indicating her political identity and precluding any future negation. However, this request was resolutely rejected, for the party decided "she was just a writer, not a significant Party leader."[98] Could there be anything that is more tragic yet meaningless than the tiring negotiations between Ding Ling's family members and the CCP over a party flag, a memorial ceremony, and members of the funeral committee?[99] Eventually, Ding Ling was covered by a red flag with the words "Ding Ling busi" (The immortal Ding Ling), offered by Beidahuang ren

96. He Guimei, *Zhuanzhe de shidai*, p. 287.

97. See Wang Zengru, *Wunai de niepan*, p. 8.

98. Ibid., p. 128.

99. According to Wang Zengru, given the deep hostilities between Ding Ling and Zhou Yang, Chen Ming fought vehemently against Zhou Yang to be included in Ding Ling's funeral committee. Even over her dead body, Ding Ling did not forgive Zhou Yang. See Wang Zengru, *Wunai de niepan*, pp. 46–53.

(People of the Great Northern Wasteland). Thus, the tension between literature and revolution was forever sealed over her dead body. How then is Ding Ling to be memorialized—a writer, an intellectual in the endless labor of self-transformation in the Great Northern Wasteland, or a Communist Party member? Ding Ling's retrograde revolutionary obsession in her later years, her final effort toward intellectual politicization, only deepened the intrinsic fissures in the trajectory of Chinese literary modernization.

CHAPTER 4

Wu Zhuoliu, Orphanization, and Colonial Modernity in Taiwan

In the last decade of the twentieth century, with the disintegration of the former Soviet Union and the fall of the Berlin Wall, the Cold War seemed to have ended. However, given the tenacious confrontation between mainland China and its offshore island, the Cold War remains an unresolved issue in East Asia. With controversies over Taiwan's independence versus unification remaining fervent, it is pertinent to revisit the mid-twentieth-century transition, the formative moment of the bipolar Cold War structure in East Asia. After its retreat to Taiwan, the Nationalist regime took great pains to create its own version of national history and national identity as the antithesis to its socialist Other in the cultural field. Given the oppressive political regulation of literature and art under the official ideology of "anticommunism and restoring the lost land," modern Chinese literature of the pre-1949 ROC period was largely eradicated or marginalized along with works by Taiwanese writers from the Japanese colonial era.

Ever since the establishment of Taiwan as the last province of the Qing dynasty in the late nineteenth century, its political significance has been deeply intertwined with the modernization process in China, Japan, and East Asia, which was inextricably entangled with impeding European imperial expansions in the Far East. A critical engagement with the issue of Taiwan cannot merely depart from an internal perspective of China, no matter what "China" indicates—the Ming dynasty, the Manchurian Qing dynasty, or the modern nation-states of the (Nationalist) Republic of China or the (Communist) People's Republic of China. Taiwan is a Chinese issue that has never been solely a domestic issue. It must be approached from an intra-Asian and international perspective, no matter what international forces are involved—the Dutch colonizers, Meiji Japanese colonial ventures, or the U. S. West Pacific "defensive perimeter" of the Truman administration. Furthermore, the issue of Taiwan has been from the very beginning embedded in the contestation and negotiation of multiple forces: tradition and modernity, Chinese culturalism, Japanese colonialism and imperialism, and finally, Japanese and Chinese modernization. As Edward W. Said points out, empire, imperialism, and culture have always been intertwined.[1] Any study of Taiwan must take into account both the history of imperial expansions and the history of Chinese modernization.

Before the KMT regime claimed Taiwan as its territorial retreat and transitory anti-Communist base, the island, whose cultural complexity appeared in its very historical origin, had already been deeply inscribed by cultural and racial clashes during its Japanese colonial history. The KMT's anti-Communist Cold War discourse added yet another layer to its already controversial and shattered political and national identity. The tangled problematic of colonial modernity, nationalism, and cultural identification found a violent way out in the form of ethnic conflicts, culminating in the February 28 Incident in 1947 shortly after the retrocession. The unresolved problems also resulted in the contemporary oppositions between the campaigns of Taiwan's independence and China's reunification.

This chapter does not intend to construct a comprehensive literary topography of Taiwan literature, nor does it seek to define or redefine Taiwaneseness or Chineseness. Such notions, together with those of sovereignty and nationalism, are modern constructions introduced and translated into China during its process of modernization. Rather, by reading the works of Taiwanese writer Wu Zhuoliu (pseudonym of Wu Jiantian, or Go Daku-ryu in Japanese, 1900–76)

---

1. Said, *Culture and Imperialism*, esp. pp. xi–xxvii.

published between the 1940s and the 1960s, this chapter considers issues of cultural China, colonialism, and modernization that together shaped the formation of modern Taiwanese consciousness. At its best, Wu's work complicates the dominant Cold War ideological discourse by evoking alternative ethnic, national, and modernization imaginations. A critical consideration of mid-twentieth-century intellectual conditions in Taiwan helps better comprehend the unique modern subjectivity of the island stranded between China, Japan, and the Western powers with their disparate ideological and sociopolitical agendas.

The first section of this chapter sets out to read Wu Zhuoliu's postwar short story "Potsudamu kachō" (Bocitan kezhang, Director Potsdam) to consider the ethnic clashes between the Taiwanese and the mainlanders in the immediate years after Taiwan's retrocession.[2] I argue that ethnic difference is itself a suspicious notion that easily and powerfully obscures all the interrelated and convoluted problems in the historical reality: nationalistic anxiety about being contaminated by the force of Japanese imperialism and colonialism, disillusionment about an imagined authentic and homogeneous Chinese culture, modernization's Janus faces of prosperity and destructive potentiality. This entangled complex of modernization, colonialism, and nationalism has been entrenched in the formation of modern Taiwan literature.

The next section of the chapter returns to Taiwan's colonial past and analyzes various historical and theoretical conceptualizations of Taiwan Minzhuguo (Taiwan Republic, 1895), in order to reconsider the limits of modernization theory, which not only overshadowed the scholarship on the Taiwan Republic but also haunted key imaginations of nation, sovereignty, and national culture across the 1949 Chinese divide through today's independence-versus-unification debates. The intriguingly controversial inception of modern Taiwan history blurs the putatively strict boundaries between traditionality

2. Most narrative works by Wu Zhuoliu were written in Japanese. The discussion of Wu's work in this chapter was based on its Chinese translation. For consistency, the first appearance of titles of Wu's writings is in romanized Japanese, immediately followed by the proper Pinyin and Engish translations in parentheses.

and modernity and demonstrates that modernity has never been singular.

By historicizing and contextualizing Wu Zhuoliu's *Ajia no koji* (Yaxiya de gu'er, Orphan of Asia, 1943–45), the third section of the chapter considers the conception of orphanization as not only a trope of the stranded condition of the modern subject between Chinese culturalism and Japanese colonialism, between tradition and modernity, but also a narrative strategy that bespeaks the always already fractured notions of nation and national culture. The final section further examines the notions of division, orphanization, and cultural loyalism in Cold War Taiwan. Today, when the Cold War phase seemed passé, among the intensifying conflicts between pro-independence and pro-unification and some pro-Japan waves, there is no place secure and unambiguous. The orphan, or to be more precise, the orphan of Asia who now turns into the child of Taiwan, remains caught in a split subjectivity.

The Tale of Tap Water: The Contestation among Nationalism, Colonialism, and Modernization

The mid-twentieth-century Taiwan experience was marked by confusion, frustration, and resentment. After half a century of Japanese colonial rule, Taiwan was returned to China's Nationalist government in 1945, shortly after Japan made its unconditional surrender in World War II. Hardly had the Taiwanese people had time to get adjusted to the retrocession, or reassimilation to the motherland, than the KMT government crumbled and retreated to the recently regained island as its last territory and anti-Communist bastion. In the dividing year of 1949, the Chinese Communists won control of the whole mainland, and the Nationalists continued their regime in Taiwan.

The short story "Director Potsdam" by Wu Zhuoliu, one of the few Taiwanese writers who continued writing after the retrocession, registered the socio-historical and emotional confusion and anxiety of this transitional time. Born in Xinzhu County five years after Taiwan was ceded to Japan, Wu belonged to the generation who had received both traditional Chinese and Japanese colonial education.[3] He was a member of the fifth generation of a Hakka family, who moved to Taiwan from Guangdong in the ninth year of the Jiaqin reign (1804 AC) of the Qing dynasty. After he graduated from the Taipei Normal School, Wu worked as a teacher in the Japanese primary schools for twenty years and later as a newspaper journalist until the retrocession of Taiwan in 1945. He started his literary career rather late and made his debut with a short story entitled "Shuiyue" (Shuiyue) when he was thirty-six years old. Followed by a few other short stories, "Shuiyue" was published in the magazine *Taiwan xinwenxue* (Taiwan new literature), which promoted mainly literature in Japanese written by Taiwanese writers.[4]

"Director Potsdam" describes the first encounter of Taiwan people with their compatriots from mainland China:

> The autumn sun sizzles as if it's stinging one's skin. About three or four hours had passed, and the army of the motherland was finally coming. Cheers of "Long live!" suddenly burst out, and lasted for a long time. People waved the national flags in their hands. The troops processed along for quite a while, every soldier carried an umbrella on his back. . . . Some of the soldiers carried iron pots, dinnerware, or quilts. Yulan had once seen the procession of a touring Taiwan opera troupe when she was a kid; and the procession of these troops was just like that. She felt bad, but didn't want to show it in the presence of the Japanese. It's not that she was obsessive, but some blood of self-esteem was storming in her which she couldn't quite understand. . . . It was as if an adopted child were meeting his blood parents, even if they were beggars.[5]

The façade of tangible nationalist sentimentalism cannot, however, conceal a deep disappointment and embarrassment at confronting

---

3. On the life of Wu Zhuoliu, see, for instance, Lü Xinchang, *Tiexue shiren Wu Zhuoliu*.

4. The short stories Wu Zhuoliu published before *Orphan of Asia* include "Shuiyue," "Nizhao zhong de jinliyu" (The golden carp in the mud), "Bijian de shuidi" (A drop of water on the tip of the pen), and "Guixi ziran" (Return to nature). There are two other short stories written during the Japanese rule, "Wumaoqian de ganzhe" (Fifty cents sugar) and "Gonggou" (A distinguished dog), which were not published. All short stories are collected in *Gonggou*.

5. Wu Zhuoliu, *Bocitan kezhang*, pp. 6–7. The disillusionment with the poverty-stricken KMT troops was a shared experience among most of Wu's contemporaries. Similar stories are, for instance, also described by Lin Boyan in his article "Wu Zhuoliu de dalu jingyan," p. 335.

the shabby troops of the motherland. Two decades later, in his autobiographical fiction *Wuhua guo* (The fig tree), Wu still struggled to deal with such an ineffaceable dissatisfaction: "I felt very odd: Is this General Chen's Corps No 70? I curbed my strong discontent, and explained to myself: it's just the appearance that is not so good, but they were the ones who fought bravely against Japan during the last eight years. So brave! This justification made me feel better, yet, this is merely a way of deceiving myself."[6] With the gap between mainlanders and Taiwanese widening, suppressed frustration was soon replaced by public derision, manifested in the notorious story of piped water that Wu continued to narrate after the opening scene: soldiers from *tangshan* (mainland China) were amazed by the miracle that water ran out of the wall. But when they tried to install the water tap into another wall, no water came out.[7]

This story, which at first sounds like nothing more than one of those tales in which civilized city dwellers mock countrymen from backward rural areas, purported to convey a message that the motherland was more backward in its economic development than its once abandoned island province. Since Taiwan has been ceded to Japan as a result of the First Sino-Japanese War (1894–95), mainland China and Taiwan had taken on disparate trajectories of economic and political development. By mid-twentieth century, they were at different stages of modernization. Obviously, the tap water story, with the poorly equipped soldiers and their amazement at the miracle water from the wall, lays bare the conspicuous differences in modern infrastructure between mainland China and Taiwan at the time of the latter's retrocession.

The sharp contrast in economic structure between the continent and its offshore island was surely one of the most salient elements that stirred resentment among Taiwanese at the mid-twentieth-century transition. Lieutenant General Albert C. Wedemeyer gave a brief delineation of Taiwan's socioeconomic status in the "Wedemeyer Report" he submitted to the U.S. Department of State after his short visit, which was kept secret and shelved for several years before being included in the famous *China White Paper* published on August 5,

---

6. Wu, *Wuhua guo*, pp. 147–48.
7. Wu, *Bocitan kezhang*, pp. 47–48.

1949.[8] After General George C. Marshall returned from his failed China mission in January 1947, convinced that there was no possibility of bringing the Communists and Nationalists together, Wedemeyer was sent to China for a last assessment of the military and political situation, so that the United States could decide whether or not to continue its commitment to the Nationalist regime. Wedemeyer also paid a visit to Taiwan. In his report, he wrote:

> The island is extremely productive in coal, rice, sugar, cement, fruits and tea. Both hydro and thermal powers are abundant. The Japanese had efficiently electrified even remote areas and also established excellent railroad lines and highways. Eighty per cent of the people can read and write, the exact antithesis of conditions prevailing in the mainland of China.[9]

In effect, such "urbanites and farmers" stories about modern life or technology channeled feelings of frustration and resentment among Taiwan people who went through the first few years of retrocession. Behind them were serious problems looming in postrestoration Taiwan: the deterioration of the economy with grave inflation; the political authoritarianism, corruption, and bureaucracy of the temporary KMT administration in Taiwan; the ban on the Japanese language in official ministries and press and the implementation of Mandarin Chinese as the standard national tongue, which inevitably entailed the marginalization, if not the exclusion, of local Taiwan elites from significant positions; and so on. The unease and anxiety were transmuted into a large rubric of ethnic conflicts, the putative differences between ethnic groups.

Indeed, something more intricate than the modernization claim is at stake. As implied in Wu Zhuoliu's story, to measure the backwardness of the motherland, one has necessarily to refer to the colonial metropolitan state as the criterion of modernity. Given that Taiwan's modernization was accomplished under Japanese colonial rule, the situation is far more urgent than the ostensibly transparent discourse of modernity. In Wu's story, where is the Taiwanese storyteller culturally and politically positioned when ridiculing his compatriot from mainland China at the time of the retrocession—as an inhabitant

---

8. The document was known officially as *United States Relations with China, with Special Reference to the Period 1944–1949* (Washington, DC: U.S. Government Printing Office, 1949), based on the files of the Department of State.

9. Wedemeyer, quoted in Kerr, *Formosa Betrayed*, pp. vii–viii.

of a specific Chinese province, a colonized Japanese subject, or a Chinese awaiting return to the motherland?

In setting forth these stories, what concerned Wu Zhuoliu is clearly the destabilized cultural identity of Taiwan people caused by the island's special colonial experiences rather than mere issues of modern economics and technology. However, at a time when ideological antagonism was accelerated to the utmost mission of a regime, that colonial history was hastily dismissed. When Taiwan was taken as the last bastion from which to fight to restore the lost land, its special cultural consciousness, which resisted to any inclusion in the KMT's dominant discourse of anti-Communism, was easily overlooked. Moreover, given the just-ended war against Japanese imperialism and the campaign against Japanese collaborators, Wu's insistence on a special Taiwan consciousness at that particular moment appears especially vulnerable. After all, the common "urbanites and farmers" joke can be easily read as a politically suspicious statement of the superiority of Japanese colonial modernity in Taiwan over the underdeveloped motherland; or, even worse, be decoded as nothing less than a "mockery by a progressive modernized Japan at a conservative backward China."[10]

The failure of the KMT regime on the mainland made reform in its cultural policies urgent, which encouraged the unique genre of anti-Communist literature. This body of realistic literature was mostly composed by émigré writers from the mainland, aiming to provide a narrative rationalization of the KMT's recent debacle. Representative works included Chen Jiying's *Dicun zhuan* (Fool in the reeds), Pan Renmu's *Lianyi biaomei* (Cousin Lianyi, 1952), and Jiang Gui's *Xuanfeng* (Whirlwind, 1959), among which the last work deserves special attention. Although it was acclaimed by literary scholars as the best achievement among "the host of cliché-ridden anti-Communist novels,"[11] the difficulty *Whirlwind* went through to find a publisher even in the heyday of anti-Communist literature attested to its unorthodox and unwelcomed political agenda.[12] The novel seeks to

10. Zheng Hongsheng, "Taiwan de dalu xiangxiang," p. 34.

11. C. T. Hsia, *History of Modern Chinese Fiction*, p. 556. For a study of this novel, also see David Der-wei Wang, *Monster That Is History*, pp. 183–223.

12. According to his preface to the English translation of *Whirlwind*, Jiang Gui finished the novel in 1952, but could not find a publisher for the book. He had

bear witness to Communist atrocity by depicting how Communist forces took hold in Fang Town of Shandong province between the May Fourth movement and the early years of the Second Sino-Japanese War. Fang Xiangqian, who is a mixture of Confucian and Marxist ideals, makes great efforts to impel people in his hometown to Communist reforms and revolutions. With the help of his nephew Fang Peilan, a local hooligan, they succeed in inciting a Communist insurrection, only to see it end up in chaos and themselves liquidated as counter-revolutionaries. What Jiang Gui ambitiously seeks to reveal is not only the violence and grotesquerie of Chinese Communism but also an intrinsic dilemma in the discourse of revolution and modernization, which was at the core of twentieth-century Chinese intellectual movements. Envisioning a strong and modern nation, Fang Xiangqian sees in Communist revolution the hope for a national rebirth out of moral degeneration, the tiger's leap into a bright future. Paradoxically, as *Whirlwind* portrays, not only did the old evil—dressed up in progress and modernity—tenaciously continue to thrive, but also the project of Chinese enlightenment and modernization with its promise of rationality unleashed even stronger forces of irrationality. The modern monsters of history that went awry embody not only the Communist revolution but also China's modernization project. Hence, the novel takes the contradictions of the ideological discourse—Communist and anti-Communist—with its underpinning modernization rationale to the extreme.

Given this tightening cultural politics during the anti-Communist White Terror in Taiwan, the modern Taiwanese literary tradition formed by writers like Wu Zhuoliu who grew up under Japanese colonial rule was easily repressed. At Taiwan's transition from Japanese colonialism to reterritorialization as the anti-Communist bastion of the Nationalist government, ethnic antagonism between mainlanders and Taiwanese seems to have been pushed to center stage.[13]

---

the novel printed at his own expenses in 1957, which bore the new title *Jin taowu zhuan* (A tale of modern monsters). The novel was finally published under its original title, *Whirlwind,* with the help of the United States Information Service in Taipei in 1959.

13. In this chapter, "mainlander" refers to Chinese immigrants who came to Taiwan after 1949, and "Taiwanese" indicates earlier Chinese settlers.

Ethnicity, a notion that stresses boundaries and territoriality, masked all the problems related to politics, economics, culture, and other areas. There are two tendencies embedded in such tensions between the expectations of mainlanders and Taiwanese. First, from the perspective of the motherland, there was the demand for an anticolonial nationalism uncontaminated by Japanese imperialism and colonialism, which was inherent in the campaign to cleanse the minds of Taiwan people. Its most radical form was blaming the formerly colonized for being morally affected by Japanese colonialism and thus nothing more than mere consumers of colonial modernity. On the other hand, the Taiwanese people were disappointed to see a motherland not at all stronger than or superior to the colonial metropolitan culture or economics. Instead of a powerful thousands-of-years-old civilization, they found a culture that was itself caught in a moment of semicolonial existence. Therefore, their dream of an authentic native culture was far from fulfilled.

The tangled complex of modernization, colonialism, and nationalism has informed modern Taiwan literature from its beginning, and any consideration of Taiwan history and culture of the mid-twentieth century has necessarily to deal with this. Embedded in the apparent ethnic conflicts between the Taiwanese and the mainlanders is the anxiety and uncertainty of cultural identification. Precisely this complex of ethnic conflicts triggered the February 28 Incident in 1947, which included the military oppression and massacre of local Taiwanese elites by the KMT regime.[14] A consideration of this entanglement of nationalism, colonialism, and modernization must start with a serious examination of Taiwan's colonial past.

The idea that the motherland is backward, compared with colonial Taiwan in the process of modernization, betrays the constraints of a modernization and convergence theory that assumes that all non-Western societies will take the same route to modernization and reach the same telos of capitalist modernity. The theory of modernization and convergence aimed to prescribe an "evolutionary model of growth" for non-Western societies to guarantee a peaceful realization of capitalism and political democracy. Formed by scholars in the

---

14. For a study of the February 28 Incident, see Lai Zehan, *Ererba shijian yanjiu baogao*; Ping-hui Liao's "Rewriting Taiwanese National History."

field of area studies during the Cold War era, this discourse also provided the basis for postcolonial studies. As H. D. Harootunian summarizes, its essential notions include "society as coherently organized systems whose subsystems were interdependent; historical development (periodized into traditional and modern) that determined social subsystems; modernity meant rational, scientific, secular and Western; the process of modernization was historically evolutionary; and, lastly, traditional, nonmodern societies could successfully modernize if evolution had already demonstrated a process of adaptive upgrading of social and cultural values."[15] The stark contrast between modernity and tradition and the putative claim of a singular homogeneous form of modernization level out historical specificities in societies with different historical and cultural forces.

Such limits echo in the reflections on the establishment of the short-lived Taiwan Minzhuguo (Taiwan Republic) at the starting point of Taiwan's cession, which inaugurated its history of colonial modernization half a century earlier. In the following section, I analyze various historical and theoretical discourses on the Taiwan Republic by scholars in the field of area studies since the 1960s and by contemporary Taiwan historians, in order to reveal the constraints of an overarching modernization theory. The inception of modern Taiwan history, which is shot through with contradictions and ambiguities, challenges and contests the prevailing Western concept of modernity and demonstrates that modernity is multidimensional.

An Authentic Modernity: Taiwan Minzhuguo (Taiwan Republic)

> Four million (Chinese) people cried together
> For the cession of Taiwan on today of last year.
>
> —Qiu Fengjia, "Chunchou"

One year after Taiwan and the Penghu Islands (Pescadores) were ceded to Japan by the Treaty of Shimonoseki signed on April 17, 1895, Qiu Fengjia (1864–1912), a Hakka Taiwanese gentry-scholar, in a

15. Harootunian, *Learning Places,* p. 158.

bitter poem "Chunchou" (Grief in the spring), mourned his home island. Such poetic expression of anguish and lament over a lost territory is not unprecedented in Chinese literature.[16] However, in this particular historical conjunction, Qiu was talking in a new language—not in terms of literary form or genre, but in that the momentum of the poem moves toward a new era. The historical occasion Qiu Fengjia had to reckon with, articulate, and subdue was of new historical relevance. The defeat of China in the First Sino-Japanese War (1894–95) at the hands of the "dwarf bandits" of Japan,[17] a country that had lived in the shadow of Chinese civilization, and the consequent territorial cession marked the most devastating humiliation China had to confront in its modern age. It resulted in more petitions to accelerate economic and military reforms in the late Qing Empire.

Indeed, the trauma of 1895 ushered in a new era of Chinese modernization. One year before writing the poem, Qiu Fengjia started recruiting a volunteer troop in mid-Taiwan to keep the island from falling victim to Japanese imperialism. Meanwhile, he appealed to Western political notions of "international law, popular rule and parliamentary government"[18] to solicit Western intervention, notions that had been recently introduced into late nineteenth-century China and helped establish Asia's first republic—Taiwan Minzhuguo (Taiwan Republic). His determined endeavor of resistance notwithstanding, the republic collapsed shortly after Japanese military forces landed on the insular province of the Qing Empire.[19] When he wrote

---

16. In Chinese history, belligerent territorial cession happened various times. The scholar to whom Qiu Fengjia paid most respect is Wen Tianxiang (1236–83), who experienced the unhinged collapsing period of the Southern Song dynasty, which was overthrown by Mongol troops and succeeded by the Mongol Yuan dynasty.

17. On the contemptuous designation of Japan as a country of "dwarf bandits" and China's attitudes toward Japan in the late Qing, see S. C. Chu, "China's Attitudes toward Japan," pp. 74–95; also see Dikötter, *Race in Modern China,* p. 62.

18. Lamley, "1895 Taiwan Republic," p. 740.

19. It was a short-lived republic. Tang Jingsong fled to the mainland on June 5, 1895. The republic was revived in Tainan by General Liu Yongfu of the famous Black Flag force, who successfully defeated the French invasion in Annam in the Sino-French War, in late June and endured until October 21, 1895, when Tainan was conquered by the Japanese after eight days of fierce fighting. For research on the Taiwan Republic, see, for example, Lamley, "1895 Taiwan Republic"; Huang

"Chunchou," Qiu had already left his home island for exile in Guangdong.[20] The concise form of classical Chinese poetry might not allow much space for the emerging global consciousness and modern experiences. Yet, at this historical juncture, the poet, his hometown Taiwan, and China in its last imperial moment were all caught in modernity's inescapable and violent momentum.

Upon learning that Taiwan was about to be ceded to Japan, the whole island was aroused and despaired. Qiu Fengjia and his followers addressed several petitions to the Qing court, pleading that Taiwan not be subjected to Japan without resistance. On the petition dated April 19, 1895, Qiu declared decisively, "this is our homeland, with which we are bound to live and die. Together with the Governor we will defend it even if it takes our lives. If we fight and fail, then you can speak of ceding it."[21] Although never assigned an official position in the republic, Qiu was among the group of scholars who actually helped Tang Jingsong (1841–1903), the last Governor of Qing's Taiwan province and the President of the Taiwan Republic of 1895, forge the idea of a self-ruling republic. In his endeavor to save Taiwan, Qiu resorted to the idea of plebiscite arrangement he learned from his readings in international law and other Western political works.[22] The notion was recorded in *Gongfa huitong*, the 1880 Chinese translation of the German work on international law by Johann Kaspar Bluntschli, originally entitled *Das moderne Völkerrecht der civilisierten*

Xiuzheng, *Taiwan gerang yu yiwei*; Wu Micha, "1895nian 'Taiwan minzhuguo.'" Through an examination of historical documents—telegram exchanges between Tang Jingsong, Zhang Zhidong (1837–1909), and Zongli Yamen, in particular—Wu's article focuses on how the idea of establishing a republican government in Taiwan ultimately emerged from the specific political circumstances after the Qing defeat in the First Sino-Japanese War.

20. For a study of Qiu Fengjia's life in exile on the mainland, see Chen Pingyuan, *Dangnian youxia ren*, pp. 86–112.

21. Qiu, quoted in Qi Qizhang, "Qiu Fengjia litai neidu kao."

22. Lamley raised an interesting speculation about this notion in international law. He thought that it was Wang Chih-chun, then in Paris, who called attention to the idea of a plebiscite as sanctioned by international law and informed Zhang Zhidong. Zhang then passed it on to Tang Jingsong, who in turn circulated it to Qiu Fengjia and other intellectual elites. See Lamley, "1895 Taiwan Republic," p. 750n47.

Staaten, als Rechtsbuch dargestellt (1868).[23] According to international law, the inhabitants of a ceded territory have the right to vote on the change of sovereignty,[24] and "if the inhabitants don't want to be subject to the occupying country, they can declare self-independent (*zili*) and popular rule (*minzhu*)."[25] Consequently, in the petition of May 16, which was wired to Zhang Zhidong, the Governor of Liang Jiang and the Minister of Nanyang (Southern Ocean), Qiu proposed to establish a *daoguo* (island-state), aiming to strategically protect Taiwan. On May 25, 1895, the Taiwan Republic was founded, with Tang Jingsong its first president. The announcement of the inauguration reads:

> The gentry and commoners in Taiwan are hit by grief and fury. Now that we are not able to rely on heaven's mandate or the court, our Taiwan people decided to call for autonomy and create a *minzhu zhi guo* (republic, state of popular rule)[26]. . . . The territory of Taiwan has been civilized by the Qing

---

23. It was rendered into Chinese as one of the books on international law in the late Qing period. This book was translated from the French rendition of the original German work. For more information, see, Lydia H. Liu, *Clash of Empires*, pp. 108–39.

24. Qiu Fengjia alluded to the idea taken from *Wanguo gongfa* (International law, 1864) that a sovereign state could not be ceded by another nation—in this case, the Qing Empire. As for the introduction of international law in nineteenth-century China, the missionary W. A. Martin with the help of four Chinese scholars—Chen Qin, Li Changhua, Fang Junshi, and Mao Hongtu, translated Henry Wheaton's *Elements of International Law* into classical Chinese under the title *Wanguo gongfa* (literally, The public law of nations). And intriguingly, a Japanese *kambun* transcription of *Wanguo gongfa* appeared as early as the next year, and had an immense impact on the 1874 expedition and the conclusion of the Shimonoseki Treaty. For a discussion of the translation history of *International Law* and its historical and political significance, see Lydia H. Liu, *Clash of Empires*, pp. 108–39.

25. Sitong zi, *Taihai sitong lu*, p. 7.

26. *Minzhu*, which means in modern Chinese "democracy," means in classical Chinese "*zhu*" of "*min*" (the ruler of the people). Yet, in late Qing context, *minzhu* means "people's rule," after it was first used by W. A. Martin in his translation of *Wanguo gongfa* to translate the word "republic." Therefore, Qiu Fengjia and Tang Jingsong's intention is to establish a state of popular rule (*minzhuguo*), which is equivalent to the notion in *Wanguo gongfa*, "republic." As imperial China approached its end, during the 1911 Revolution, the word "republic" was changed from "*minzhuguo*" to "*gongheguo*," via Japanese translation. Whereas Qiu proposed a *minzhuguo*, Sun Yat-sen employed the notion "*gongheguo*" in his establishment of "Republic of China" after the 1911 Revolution.

> Empire for over two hundred years. Therefore, although it declared itself a state, in gratitude to the previous favor of all sacred emperors, Taiwan will stay loyal to your authority, and form your remote frontier. Being your subject, Taiwan is no different from the mainland. . . . Together we will push forward a constitutional draft, taking the good points of the American and French models; establish a legal system; inaugurate a parliament; establish an administration; use a banner of a golden tiger on a blue background as our national flag; and take the reign title "Yongqing" (Everlasting Qing). This will be Asia's first republic.[27]

In historical studies of modern China and Taiwan, this first republic has not received due attention. One main theory is that it was too ineffectual to be worth studying. The republic in Taipei collapsed only eleven days after its inception, with President Tang Jingsong fleeing back to the mainland, and never came close to realizing its original objective of protecting Taiwan against Japanese takeover. The Republic's second phase in Tainan did not last much longer. In the eyes of both Chinese and Western observers, therefore, the Taiwan Republic amounts to nothing but a "farce" and a "joke."[28]

What immediately upset observers of the inauguration of the Taiwan Republic was the suspicious juxtaposition of modern national institutions—a republic, a constitution, a legal system, a parliament, and a national flag—with notions of unyielding allegiance to the Qing Empire, which fit the traditional Chinese political framework. Symbolically, the reign title "Everlasting Qing" and the national flag bearing the image of a tiger indicated the republic's subjection to the absolute imperial authority, represented by the icon of dragon. As Lamley duly points out, "it must be noted that Ch'iu [Qiu] and his followers in their bid for self-rule wished to stop short of appearing to rebel against Ch'ing authority."[29] In enunciating loyalty to the Qing, the founders and supporters regarded the new republic more as an autonomous yet tributary state. Indeed, their notion of republic amounted to a self-ruled island-state rather than a form of sovereign nation-state, as conceptualized by modern Western political thought.

---

27. See Yang Bichuan, *Taiwan lishi cidian*, p. 265.

28. Davidson, *Island of Formosa*, esp. pp. 275–89; Liang Qichao, *Yinbingshi heji* 5: 205. Davidson (1872–1933), who was a journalist in Taipei during the advent of the republic, contributed one of the earliest observations on the Taiwan Republic.

29. Lamley, "1895 Taiwan Republic," p. 750.

Whereas the backers of the republic believed in their strategic device of tributary-republicanism, such inconsistency provoked the historians immensely.

More contradictions followed as the inauguration ceremony unfolded. Not only did the public perform the rite of "two kneelings and eight bows" (*lianggui bakou*) to President Tang Jingsong, but the president himself also surprised the world with his "dramatic kowtowing on his reception of the presidential seal."[30] As the former act of kowtow indicated the submission of the public to the ruler, the latter clearly signified the subordination of the presidency to the Qing court. Confused by the peculiar dual nature of Tang's behavior, Hosea B. Morse, who later helped Tang escape from Taiwan after the republic collapsed, mocked him as "governor-president."[31] He was not alone in his attitude of ridicule. In fact, in the accounts of the Taiwan Republic by historians who were either present at the inauguration or observed it from a contemporary perspective, the tone of derision or antipathy is clear. In his revisionist study of the 1895 Taiwan Republic, Harry J. Lamley endeavored to substantiate its historical significance. However, although he maintains that its rise notably foresaw the trends of radical reform and revolution that were about to come in late imperial China, he regards the republic itself as a "sham affair unworthy of its republican label,"[32] thus in turn reinforcing the Western trivialization of the Taiwan Republic. What upset the historians so that they hastily labeled the event a "hoax,"[33] which they initially believed launched "a new China in the nursery from whom great things may eventually be expected"?[34] How to account for their intolerance with the remnants of traditional Chinese

---

30. According to Chinese imperial rite, during the imperial audience, the subjects should perform three kneelings and nine bows (*sangui jiukou*) to the emperor. So two kneelings and eight bows probably indicates a ritual protocol for audiences with lesser lords; Morris, "Taiwan Republic of 1895," p. 15.

31. Morse, quoted in Lamley, "1895 Taiwan Republic," p. 753. Regarding Tang Jingsong's escape back to the mainland after the Taiwan Republic collapsed, see Huang Xiuzheng, *Taiwan gerang*, pp. 162–64.

32. Lamley, "1895 Taiwan Republic," p. 741.

33. Ibid., p. 740n2.

34. Ibid.

political rituals in the inception of a modern form of government? Although such aversion can be easily ascribed to the ambiguous implementation of modern Western political thought and institutions exemplified by the existence of traditional Chinese political notions and rituals, there is probably more at work in this case.

The emphasis on the act of kowtow in the account of the inception of the Taiwan Republic is worth noting. The issue is nothing new in the Euro-American imagery of China. The beginning of Sino-Western diplomatic relations is marked by a legendary kowtow story.[35] At the first formal encounter of Chinese and British empires in 1793, Lord Macartney refused to perform the "humiliating genuflexions and prostrations"[36] (later also known as kowtow) required by Chinese protocol when he was received by Emperor Qianlong, which allegedly led to China's rejection of the British request to establish trade relations and to the failure of the Macartney embassy. The standard explanation provided by Western historians considers it diplomatic conservatism on the part of the Qing court to insist on the sinocentric tributary protocols and therefore to decline British commercial demand. Historians such as John K. Fairbank argue that such traditionalist persistence exposed this ancient empire's inability to meet the challenge of modern Western diplomatic practice and foresaw a series of disasters it would confront in international relations over the century launched by the Opium War (1840–42).[37] In retelling the Macartney story, Lydia H. Liu, however, interprets the Qing court's insistence on Chinese traditional tributary protocols as its resistance to the European imperial expansion, concluding that "the dismissal of the contemporary resistance as 'traditional' lies at the heart of colonial historiography in the study of international relations and is by no means limited to Sino-Western relations."[38]

---

35. For a discussion of the mission of Lord Macartney, see Hevia, *Cherishing Men from Afar.*

36. Ibid., p. 1.

37. See, for instance, John K. Fairbank, *Trade and Diplomacy on the China Coast,* p. 31.

38. Lydia H. Liu, *Clash of Empires*, p. 111.

Evidently, just as the kowtow incident was described as "a distasteful and scandalous act typical of China's premodern sense of universal superiority"[39] in the account of the Macartney embassy, the kowtow at the inauguration of the Taiwan Republic was similarly regarded as an act of submission. If the kowtow story in the heyday of the Qing Empire could be attributed to the ignorance and arrogance of an oriental empire, the one at the critical moment of the declining empire seemed necessarily provocative to Western historians of the time. Regarded continuously as the token of Chinese tradition, the haunting fetish of kowtow invited further considerations of how historians conceived the antithesis of tradition versus modernity. Whereas the insistence on the tributary protocol by the Qianlong court was denounced as exposing a backward civilization, the kowtow at the advent of an improvised republic in the collapsing empire was ridiculed for its appearance in a situation that was supposed to be modern. Therefore, whereas the late eighteenth-century decision of the Qianlong court was dismissed for its traditionality, its stubborn refusal of modernity and progress, the creation of a modern form of representative government in the turmoil of the late nineteenth century was belittled for its inappropriate adaptation of modernity. When China finally employed Western ways to deal with the West, it was accused of not using them right. Although the 1793 diplomatic exclusion of the modern Western world performed in the name of tradition upset the historians, the 1895 "sham" adoption of Western modernity was even more provocative. Hence, in the scholarship of the Taiwan Republic, obsessed with the superficial or improper usage of Western political thought by late Qing Chinese, the historians were trapped in yet another dangerous and more evasive blind spot.

Embedded in such colonial historiography is first of all the unquestioned and uncriticized claim of the universality of Western modernity. In postcolonial studies, there has been a plethora of criticism on such pretensions. Suffice it to say that the universality of Western political discourse is itself something imagined and constructed. In

---

39. Hevia, *Cherishing Men from Afar,* p. 237. Thus Hevia briefly delineates this notion on Qing guest ritual and the Macartney embassy in Western historical studies.

her study of the translingual circulation of international law in the nineteenth century, Lyida Liu forcefully argues how efforts were made to establish international law's universality in the process of translation between different languages. What I would like to foreground in this discussion is the deep anxiety rooted in the apparent aversion to traditionality as evidenced in the scholarship of the Taiwan Republic. Tradition was viewed as opposed to progress and thus backward. Chinese tradition, or to be precise, late imperial Chinese tradition, was regarded as something particular, thus not universal and dispensable. This sensitivity amounts to the old yet resilient anxiety of modernity: its clear break from the past. Hence what is not modern is necessarily traditional; what is not progressive is necessarily backward. Therefore, the dismissal of the Taiwan Republic as a poor, inauthentic imitation of a Western archetype by historians such as Lamley exposes their own theoretical limits that insist on the predetermined conceptual models of tradition and modernity, backwardness and progress, particular and universal.

Constrained by such binary theoretical perspectives, the historians criticized the Chinese practitioners of Western political thought for using the Western ideas as "labels," and the first republicanism as "artificial," or at best, "premature." Accordingly, this temporary expedient that some desperate Chinese scholars improvised to ward off Japanese takeover was bound to fail. In fact, the ambiguities in the implementation of modern Western political notions and institutions exposed in the foundation of the Taiwan Republic are the main argument most Western historians and some of their Chinese colleagues have made over the years to explain the inevitable doom of the ephemeral 1895 republic. The logic is that had the Western political terms and practices been carried out "maturely" or "properly," or more "seriously," the Taiwan Republic would have been "genuine" and the course of its history would have been altered. The collapse of the republic was hence conveniently attributed to its inability to meet the challenge of utilizing Western political thought. Such a stance on an authentic version of republicanism obscures some significant matters at work: the Western countries' game of power balancing in their expansion in East Asia, for instance, played a crucial role in the cession of Taiwan, which has been curiously overlooked by most historians. After conducting an elaborate analysis of the power struggles among the central figures of the republic, Lamley trivializes the whole attempt to create a republic as a way of Tang Jingsong securing nominal power against his political rivals—in particular, Liu Yongfu and Qiu Fengjia. Lamley, however, totally overlooks another set of decisive geopolitical relationships, namely, the power games among the Western countries in this apparent intra-Asian political affair.

One of the key motives for scholars such as Qiu Fengjia to create an independent republic was to draw assistance from Western powers against Japanese imperialism. From their readings on international law and the information gathered from French politicians and merchants, Qiu Fengjia and Chen Jitong (1851–1907; also known as Tcheng Ki-tong, the French spelling of his Foochow-dialect name)[40] reached the conclusion that only as an independent state would Taiwan be able to solicit diplomatic intervention from Western countries. However, even after Taiwan claimed independence, such interventions did not occur—not because the republic was not true or authentic enough, but rather because diplomatic involvement of the related Western countries in the cession of Taiwan would not serve their political and economic interests in Asia. Therefore, although the Tripartite Intervention by Russia, Germany, and France in the terms of the Treaty of Shimonoseki successfully realized the retrocession of the Liaodong Peninsula to China, the same geopolitical concerns about maintaining the international balance of power in East Asia and achieving the greatest national interests also conditioned the cession of Taiwan to Japan, which was stipulated in the

---

40. One of the earliest Chinese scholars who studied in France, Chen Jitong was important in introducing and translating Chinese and French literature. Chen also translated several works on Napoleonic law into Chinese. He served as cultural counselor in the Chinese embassy in France in late Qing and played an important role as counselor for Tang Jingsong during the foundation of the Taiwan Republic. In chapters 31 and 32 of *Niehai hua* (A flower in the sinful sea, 1905), Zeng Pu, who regarded Chen as his mentor of French literature, provided a sympathetic depiction of Chen Jitong (under the pseudonym of Chen Jidong) and his heroic engagement in the Taiwan Republic. On the life of Chen Jitong, see Guo Yanli, "Chen Jitong." On Chen's role in the Taiwan Republic, see, for instance, Li Xiaofeng, *Taiwanshi yibaijian dashi*, pp. 97–102.

same treaty.[41] Evidentially, whether or not the "modern" or "Western" ideas had been used "appropriately" had nothing to do with whether Western powers would agree to intervene in the cession of Taiwan. Indeed, the advent of the Taiwan Republic was not just an isolated effort of self-defense but from the very beginning a strategic diplomatic practice following the rules of modern international law. Therefore, the emphasis by historians of Cold War area studies on an authentic or singular version of modernity easily overlooks the specific historical and political forces at stake in late imperial Taiwan.

The insistence on the antithesis of modernity and traditionality is by no means limited to Western Cold War historians. Liang Qichao, during his visit to Taiwan after the 1911 Revolution, which overthrew the last Chinese empire and led to the founding of a republic on mainland China, remarked, "I've heard of the (Taiwan) republic. It came suddenly from above into the world of men."[42] Even a century later, Taiwan historians still ridiculed it as a fake independence. Although contemporary historians in Taiwan accept Lamley's major thesis without much criticism and blame the failure of the republic on the late Qing intellectuals' superficial understandings of Western political thought, there is a tangible resentment among these historians about the founders' escape to the mainland shortly after the establishment of the republic. Li Xiaofeng, for instance, after asserting that the failure of the republic was due to its "fake independence, fake revolution," condemns the cowardly behavior of its founders: "Although Qiu was passionate in his petition, when it came to a real fight, he fled."[43] A deep sense of shame can be felt in such remarks.

41. While the Tripartite Intervention by Russia, Germany, and France into the terms of the Treaty of Shimonoseki has been a well-studied case in international politics, the nonintervention by these countries in the cession of Taiwan has attracted less attention. Regarding the international political tensions behind the cession of Taiwan, see Quo, "British Diplomacy and the Cession." Qian Chongshi, "Zhongri jiawu zhanzheng hou," analyzes the power struggles among Germany, France, Russia, England, and Japan, and how this power balancing eventually led to the cession of Taiwan to Japan.

42. Liang Qichao, "Letters from My Travel in Taiwan," in *Yinbingshi heji*, pp. 205–6.

43. Li Xiaofeng, "Buxiang duli de duli yundong."

These historians cannot get over the fact that two months after he submitted the famous petition to the Qing court declaring, "We will die with Taiwan," Qiu Fengjia crossed the Taiwan Strait and returned to the continent even before the Japanese army took over the whole island.

How dare these partisans so easily and readily abandon their endeavor to build a republic? Such apparent blame by contemporary Taiwan historians is far more complicated than it sounds. Rather than an immature republic split between modernity and traditionality, what they cared most about was the abandonment of the island of Taiwan. However, ironically, it is not clear what these predecessors of modern republicanism actually forsook: Taiwan as a modern republican state or Taiwan as island homeland, Taiwan as Qing territory or Taiwan as anti-Qing base in the genealogy of its pro-Ming loyalism? Given the complicated historical formation of modern Taiwan, there existed a plethora of modern Taiwan subjectivities that have never been unequivocal. At the advent of modernity in Taiwan by force of Western and Japanese imperial intimidation, what was the subjective position of these 1895 intellectuals? Were they loyal to the independent Taiwan Republic, to the anti-Manchu pro-Ming loyalism tradition, or to the Qing Empire? Considering that the Qing court regarded Taiwan as a savage island "beyond the pale of civilization" (*huawai zhidi*) and did not establish a province there until 1885, after Japan's colonial venture failed in the 1871 Ryukyu Incident,[44] *yimin* (loyalists) can also be regarded as *yimin* (barbarians). If contemporary Taiwan historians criticize the 1895 partisans for not sticking to their defense of the Taiwan Republic, then what "correct" standpoint do they believe these partisans should have taken? Was a clear stance possible? Such critical anxiety betrays only these historians' own constraints of remaining loyal to political orthodoxy and legitimacy. Given that the modern itself is constructed on the premise that a clear division exists between tradition and modernity, between the past and the future, the advent of the modern era in Taiwan was

---

44. On Japan's colonial attempt in Taiwan after the Ryukyu Incident between 1871 and 1874 and how the Qing court handled this incident in its foreign relations with Japan and other Western countries, see, for instance, Leonard Gordon, "Japan's Abortive Colonial Venture"; I. C. Y. Hsu, "Late Ch'ing Foreign Relations."

shot through with contradictions and ambiguities, with ambivalence and inauthenticity.

In effect, the expeditious use of international law by the Taiwan Republic speaks more of a syndrome of modernity. Never intended as an unreflective implantation of Western ideas, authentic or not, it bears an ambiguity that precisely reflects the historical reality of late Qing China. The republic was built as a modern state, yet also a constructive part of the Qing Empire. Indeed, it was designed as a modern entity that was not necessarily disavowing Chinese tradition. And intriguingly, it is precisely because of this political ambiguity that the contemporary pro-independence camp in Taiwan, which made every effort to grasp something with which to construct a history for Taiwan as a sovereign state, stopped short of referring to the 1895 republic as the first version of Taiwan as an independent state.

Ever since the beginning of its modern voyage, the Taiwan subjectivity has been situated in division and ambiguity, in controversial fractures of modernity and traditionality. The ethos of modernity is best described by Paul de Man: "Modernity exists in the form of a desire to wipe out whatever came earlier, in the hope of reaching at last a point that marks a new departure."[45] There is no way back after the advent of the modern. However, this does not mean that the past has to be killed, buried, or banished. On the contrary, the past always exists and helps form the perception of modernity. The case of the Taiwan Republic reveals that there has never been an utterly new departure and that no leap forward can occur without carrying along the shadow of the haunting past.

The ephemeral history of the Taiwan Republic and the beginning of the island's colonial era demonstrate that it is the result of contested and negotiated discourses of traditional Chinese civilization, the complicated course of Chinese modernization, Western imperialist and colonial expansion in the Far East, and finally, a Japanese endeavor at modernization aiming to step out of the long-term shadow of Chinese civilization and to emulate Western modernity. Ever since the 1860s, after W. A. P. Martin's Chinese translation of

---

45. Paul de Man, "Literary History and Literary Modernity," in *Blindness and Insight*, pp. 388–89.

Henry Wheaton's *Elements of International Law* was translated into Japanese, the Meiji government had used the new political and legal concepts and vocabularies as the terminology of power. In this way, as Alexis Dudden maintains, the newly introduced and translated lexicon effectively delegitimated the Chinese continent as the arbiter of diplomatic discourse and as the center of power. The Treaty of Shimonoseki is the first legal document in which both Japan and China used English as the legally sanctioned referent language in Asia. This tangibly enabled the rewriting of the practice of intranation exchange within the kanji world. And even before the notion of "shedding Asia," which Fukuzawa Yukichi (1835–1901) delineates in his most disputed short essay "Datsu-a-ron" (On shedding Asia, 1885),[46] gained currency, Japan had already set out to use Western power language to escape from the long-China-centered East Asian world. These changes resulted not only in a transformation of concepts and terminology but also in a new discourse of modernity. As Wang Hui argues, Japan's idea of "shedding Asia and joining Europe" meant "entering Asia and confronting Europe" by establishing a modern Japanese nation-state, rather than a simplified abandonment of China-centered Confucian ideology.[47] Indeed, the annexation of Ryukyu and the ensuing colonization of Taiwan were just the initial steps toward Japan's project of expansion and domination in Asia.[48]

Significantly, no clear-cut boundaries exist between tradition and modernity, between Japanese colonialism and Chinese nationalism. This situation is exactly that which every Taiwanese has to reckon with, and the main theme that modern Taiwan literature, including Wu Zhuoliu's *Orphan of Asia*, has to deal with. The subject no longer has a secure position. *"Hic Rhodus, hic salta!"* Marx's famous appeal to the maxim in *The Eighteenth Brumaire of Louis Bonaparte* ironically conveys the dilemma of modern Taiwan orphans. *Hic salta*, where to

---

46. The article was published in *Jiji-shimpo*, March 16, 1885. The translation by Sinh Vinh is given in *Fukuzawa Yukichi nenkan* (Annals), vol. 11, Mita (Tokyo, Fukuzawa Yukichi kyokai, 1984).

47. Wang Hui, "Politics of Imagining Asia," pp. 13–14.

48. For a detailed description of Japan's introduction of international law, see Alexis Dudden, "Japan's Engagement with International Terms." Dudden's article examines the crucial connection between words and power in modern Japanese history.

leap? Among the ancestral Chinese continent, metropolitan Japan, and home island Taiwan, between tradition and colonial modernity, the orphan has nowhere to land and winds up as a schizophrenic.

Wu Zhuoliu's Orphan of Asia: *Colonial Modernity in Taiwan Literature*

These significant complications between China, Japan, and various modernization discourses are best evidenced in Wu Zhuoliu's novel *Orphan of Asia*, which is celebrated as the cultural practice of resistance against Japanese colonialism. In the study of Taiwan literature, which emerged as a particular rubric of literary study during the debate on *xiangtu wenxue* (nativist literature) of the 1970s,[49] Wu was regarded as a writer who bridged the Japanese colonial period and the subsequent epoch of the Nationalist ROC in Taiwan. *Orphan of Asia*, though not the best achievement of Taiwan literature under Japanese colonial rule, was unanimously recognized as its representative work. Significantly introducing the notion of "orphanization" of Taiwan, the novel has often been utilized as an allegory to depict Taiwan's political, cultural, and social status during the Japanese colonial period and in the succeeding decades.[50] As fellow writers and literary critics emphasized, this work alone would bring immortal fame for Wu Zhuoliu.

Orphan of Asia, Wu's first full-length novel, was written in secrecy between 1943 and 1945 during the intensifying Pacific War. With the tightening of the *kominka* (*huangminhua*, or Japanization) policy by the Japanese colonial government in Taiwan, Wu wrote this novel not only with no immediate prospect for publication but also in severe danger of political persecution. With the declaration of martial law in Taiwan in 1949, when anti-Communist literature dominated the island, Wu Zhuoliu painstakingly sought to promote literary

49. For a study of the *xiangtu wenxue* debate between modernist and nativist writers of the 1970s, see S. Y. Chang, *Modernism and the Nativist Resistance.*

50. Even literary works by Taiwanese writers of the 1950s and 1960s were defined as "orphan literature." See Chen Fangming (Song Dongyang), "Chaoxiang xuyuanzhong de liming," p. 6, in which he asserted that this orphan literature preceded the "xiangtu wenxue" (nativist literature) of the 1970s.

creation by Taiwanese writers and cultivate a special Taiwanese consciousness. To that end, he founded a literary magazine *Taiwan wenyi* (Taiwanese literature) in 1964 and sold all his assets to establish the Wu Zhuoliu Literary Award. Although never as prominent as Lai He (1894–1943), Yang Kui (1906–85), or Long Yingzong (1911–99) during Japanese rule, Wu Zhuoliu was respected as a representative of the resistance literature and a fighter for Taiwan literature.

Orphan of Asia depicts Hu Taiming and his life through the fifty-year Japanese colonial rule. Born in Taiwan under the Japanese occupation and having received both Chinese and Japanese education, Hu is a representative Taiwan intellectual in the twentieth century. The contestations between Chinese and Japanese cultures, traditional and modern values, inscribed his cultural formation. Compelled by cultural anxiety and identity crisis, he travels in Taiwan, Japan, and mainland China vainly searching for a definite and unconstrained identity. However, neither the spatial nor the cultural displacement solves his problem. As a matter of fact, the dislocation only aggravates the travail and agony of the modern subjectivity amid cultural and political exigencies. When he finally arrives in China, his "motherland and ancestral home," in pursuit of his Chinese roots, Hu Taiming is confronted with the differences between a modernized Japanese culture and a seemingly backward yet far more complicated Chinese culture. Moreover, as a Taiwanese under the complicated historical and political circumstances during the Second Sino-Japanese War, his identity quest puts him in an awkward predicament: he is attacked as a "Chinese collaborator," a "Japanese collaborator," and a "Taiwan collaborator" successively. The novel winds up with the psychological collapse of Hu Taiming during the intensifying Pacific War.

As one of the very few books published in Japanese after the retrocession of Taiwan to Nationalist China, *Orphan of Asia* went through an intriguing course of title modifications. When first published in 1946, it bore the title *Hu Zhiming*, the original name of the male protagonist. By indicating literally "Why not hold the aspiration for the Ming dynasty (the last Han empire before the foundation of the Manchu Qing dynasty)?" this title exposes the determination to restore the political and cultural origin of Han Chinese in Taiwan, which had been looming large among Taiwan intellectuals under the

Japanese colonial rule. Shortly after its first edition, the book title was changed from *Hu Zhiming* to *Hu Taiming* to avoid possible Communist implications because Hu Zhiming happened to be the name of a Vietnam Communist leader (1890–1969). When the novel was published in Japan in 1956, the title was changed to *Ajia no koji* (Orphan of Asia), and to *Yugamerareta shima* (The distorted island) the next year. The first Chinese translation of the novel appeared two years later with the title *Gu fan* (The lonely sail, 1959), followed by a more popular Chinese rendition by Fu Enrong in 1962 with the prevailing title *Yaxiya de gu'er* (Orphan of Asia).[51] Originally written in Japanese, the novel gained its importance and popularity with the publication of the Chinese translation.

From the aspiration for Han China through the "distorted island" to the ultimate "orphan of Asia," the changing title of the novel suggests a large interpretative space, in which contested political and cultural implications were imposed upon the literary text. Two main opposite interpretations are represented by Chen Yingzhen and Chen Fangming. Chen Yingzhen is himself a prominent writer, editor, critic, and political activist. In his important 1976 article "Gu'er de lishi, lishi de gu'er: Shiping Yaxiya de gu'er" (The history of an orphan, the orphan of history: Interpreting *Orphan of Asia*), which was written during the nativist literary debate, he observes that Hu Taiming's agony and his sense of abandonment derived from his hesitation to participate in the anti-Japanese movement of Chinese people. Therefore, "the tragedy of Hu Taiming is, ultimately, that of those intellectuals who 'hesitated,' 'stood idle and refused to take action,' took the middle of the road, and escaped and folded their arms in the tremendous epoch-making age of revolution versus counter-revolution, invasion versus anti-invasion in the whole China."[52] Given that the "distorted history" of Taiwan is part of the grander history of modern China mutilated by Western and Japanese imperialism, Chen argues that Wu Zhuoliu's *Orphan of Asia* must be interpreted from a larger perspective, in terms of the experiences of all Chinese

---

51. It was first translated by Yang Zhaoxi and published by Huanghe Press in Gaoxiong in 1959. The second Chinese translation was rendered by Fu Enrong and published by Nanhua Press in Taipei in 1962.

52. Chen Yingzhen, "Gu'er de lishi," p. 48.

people who suffered under the Japanese imperialist oppression. Indeed, he concludes, only by overcoming its self-isolation from the overarching picture of China can the island and its people be reintegrated into the whole anti-imperialist history of modern China.

This notion has been fervently attacked by Chen Fangming, who favors an independent Taiwan identity. In his 1984 article "Chaoxiang xuyuan zhong de liming" (Facing the dawn with hope), written in the raging surge of Taiwan's independence movement, Chen Fangming claims that Chen Yingzhen's insistence on the totality of an anti-imperialist Chinese history would inevitably devour the uniqueness of historical exigencies in Taiwan.[53] Chen Fangming argues that the orphanhood portrayed in Wu's novel was the initial stage of an emergent Taiwan consciousness. No doubt, this idea reflected the specific political agenda of the Taiwan autonomy movement of the 1980s. He then concludes that the orphan mentality described in Wu's work, which he categorized as the masterpiece of "orphan literature," was Wu's major contribution to Taiwan literary history. Thus, the novel made an essential step in the construction of an autonomous Taiwan identity. Also highlighted by other important contemporary Taiwan critics such as Peng Ruijin, *Orphan of Asia* not only constituted the peak of literary anticolonial resistance during Japanese rule, but more important, it marked "the guidepost of postwar Taiwan new literature."[54]

Whether advocating eventual Chinese reunification or championing Taiwan independence, the central question that these two critics have posed boils down to the allusion of "Chinese" or "Taiwanese" consciousness the novel might point to. Such political interpretations have dominated Wu Zhuoliu scholarship. Even the postcolonial study of *Orphan of Asia* by Leo Ching, which sets out to deconstruct the dichotomy between Chinese reunification and Taiwan independence, falls into a similar trap in his theoretical triangulation between Japanese colonialism, Chinese nationalism, and local Taiwanese identity formation.[55]

---

53. Chen Fangming, "Chaoxiang xuyuanzhong de liming," pp. 5–33.
54. Peng Ruijin, "Zhanhou Taiwan xinwenxue yundong," p. 13.
55. Leo Ching, *Becoming "Japanese,"* esp. pp. 174–210.

However, such attempts to inscribe the novel within the binary or triangular political antagonism only level out the historical complexity and specificity of modern Taiwan and of mainland China. Thinking mainly in terms of political implications, the existing scholarship has left unasked historical and cultural questions that are crucial not only to the interpretation of the literary text but also to the understanding of the course of Chinese modernization around the mid-twentieth century. Chen Fangming is surely right in pointing out that the imperialist oppression inflicted on Chinese people is not enough to account for the clashes and disputes between those on the continent and their island compatriots. However, Chen Yingzhen also raises a significant point: one has to put the issue of Taiwan into the larger context of imperialist invasions of China since the Opium War in order to deal with the island's particular history. Indeed, any study of modern Taiwan cannot avoid a study of its colonial past, which, however, by no means implies a return to a mythical, timeless, authentic Taiwanese or Chinese origin.

In the following reading of *Orphan of Asia*, I seek to demonstrate that the uniqueness of modern Taiwan resides precisely in its being the battleground for various modernization discourses in China and Japan against the backdrop of Western imperial and colonial histories. I propose to read orphanhood not as symbolizing a deserted or victimized Taiwan or Taiwanese people between the motherland and metropolitan colonial Japan, but rather as an inability or uncertainty of a modern Taiwan subjectivity to establish a definite position between various historical and cultural identities. In this light, Hu Taiming is one of the intellectuals who sought self-knowledge under the heavy burden of tradition and modernity.

The historical convolution is best manifested in Hu Taiming's diverse and sometimes contested cultural formations. If the 1895 cession started Taiwan's modern history in the most anguished manner, it also ingrained in the mentality of modern Taiwan intellectuals an ineffaceable sense of abandonment. Although they were severed from the Chinese continent and under the colonial rule of Japan, Chinese cultural tradition remained their spiritual home. Hu receives his first education in a traditional Chinese private school (*sishu*), described as a "ladder to the clouds," "a secluded place with a picture of Confucius on the wall and incense smoke that trailed like a piece of string."[56] He is taught classical Chinese learning by Scholar Peng and his grandfather, who, after the cession of Taiwan, still live within their lost world of China, in full adulation of "春秋大義，孔孟遺教，漢唐文章，宋明理學 (the essences of the book Chunqiu, the teachings of Confucius and Mencius, the literature of Han and Tang dynasties, the philosophy of Song and Ming dynasties)."[57] They live as hermits or, to be more accurate, as *yimin* (loyalists), who remain loyal not necessarily to the Manchu Qing Empire, but definitely to Chinese culture, which they are determined to transmit to new generations. As Scholar Peng expresses in his New Year couplets, "The grand tree does not moisten with new rain dew, the 'ladder to the clouds' still upholds the old customs and values."[58]

Thus, they stand in the tradition of Chinese loyalism that can be traced back to "Boyi and Shuqi"[59] in the first important dynastic transition from Shang to Zhou and that emerged in virtually every change in dynasties in Chinese history. The history of Taiwan is marked by discourses of loyalism and migrations, which are both characterized by temporal and geographical displacements. After the Ming Empire fell to the Manchurians in 1644, Taiwan became the most important loyalist bastion from which to fight back and restore political legitimacy with heaven's mandate on the mainland China. To this end, Zheng Chenggong (Koxinga, 1624–62) defeated the Dutch army, ended the thirty-eight-year Dutch colonial rule, and established the first official Han Chinese political authority in Taiwan. However, like the foundation of the Taiwan Republic some two hundred years later, Zheng's rule in Taiwan was also controversial in that he did not make substantial efforts to confront the Manchu court and restore the mainland after establishing his political administration in Taiwan.[60] This was further complicated by the fact that Zheng Chenggong's birth mother was Japanese. Zheng's father, Zheng Zhilong (1600–61),

---

56. Wu Zhuoliu, *Yaxiya de gu'er*, p. 16.

57. Ibid., p. 25.

58. Ibid., p. 23.

59. Ibid.

60. This point is raised mainly by Ralph C. Croizier in his significant work *Koxinga and Chinese Nationalism*, which questions the deification of Zheng Chenggong in Chinese history.

was a maritime merchant and pirate in Quanzhou, Fujian, of the southeast coastal area of China. Zheng Chenggong was conceived with Zheng Zhilong's Japanese wife, Tamura Matsu, on one of his trips to Hirato in Japan to trade and was not brought to mainland China until he was seven. In Japanese folk literature, Zheng Chenggong is deified as a Japanese hero. Even at the time of signing the Treaty of Shimonoseki, the Japanese government claimed that Taiwan formerly belonged to Japan since Zheng Chenggong made the first colonial venture and founded a polity there.[61]

While Ming loyalists such as Zheng Chenggong still had a real geographical ground from which to confront the Manchu Empire across the Taiwan Strait, Taiwan people who fell under the colonial rule of Japan after the Shimonoseki Treaty could claim only their Chinese cultural heritage as a site of cultural resistance and political loyalty. Accordingly, the establishment or continuous existence of traditional-style schools after the cession conveyed this particular cultural and political implication. Owing to this form of cultural transmission, most modern Taiwan intellectuals received a classical Chinese education in their childhood. Hong Yueqiao (1867–1929), for instance, was one of these loyalists who chose to stay in Taiwan after the cession and dedicated himself to the transmission of Chinese culture. After Taiwan was ceded to Japan, he changed his name to Qisheng (literally, abandoning life), to indicate his determination that even though Taiwan had to be abandoned by China, he would rather abandon his life than sacrifice Chinese culture and become a colonized subject of a different nation. Even under the increasing pressure from the Japanese colonial administration to abolish private Chinese tutorials, Hong continued teaching classical Chinese learning. Among his students were Zhang Shenqie and his own son Hong Yanqiu, both of whom later went to the mainland for further education and became important cultural figures in modern Taiwan.[62] Scholars such as Hong Yueqiao who advocated Chinese culturalism constitute a significant character type in modern Taiwan literature.

61. On Zheng Chenggong's deification in China and Japan in various historical periods, see Chen Fangming, "Zheng Chenggong yu Shi Lang," pp. 293–314.

62. On Zhang Shenqie and Hong Yanqiu's cultural activities in mainland China, see Yeh, "Taiwanren zai Beijing."

For instance, Mr. Douwen in Zhu Dianren's short story "Qiuyi" (The sense of autumn) can be placed under this rubric.

Although Wu Zhuoliu did not formally attend a traditional-style Chinese school, he was deeply influenced by his Chinese teacher, Lin. Years later, in his reminiscent writings, Wu recollected how Mr. Lin gave him his calligraphy of a famous poem of the Tang dynasty.[63] After his short teaching career in Taiwan, Mr. Lin continued his diasporic dislocation and moved with his whole family to mainland China, where he finally died of disease. It was in Beijing, the ancient Chinese capital, that his own daughter, the renowned woman writer Lin Haiyin, spent her years of cultural formation and started her career as a journalist. Returning to Taiwan in 1948 after its retrocession, Lin Haiyin endeavored with fellow writers such as Wu Zhuoliu to open up a territory for pure literature in 1960s Taiwan: Lin Haiyin edited the literary supplement of *Lianhe bao* (United Daily News), and Wu Zhuoliu founded *Taiwan wenyi* in 1964. Their emphasis on "pure literature" marked Taiwan literature of the 1960s, which significantly challenged the anti-Communist literature that had dominated the 1950s with its slogan of an anticommunist restoration of the mainland. Hence, deeply intrinsic in the cultural transmission of Chinese heritage, these pungent temporal and geographical displacements of modern Taiwan intellectuals had already become ingrained.

However, the insistence on the Chinese cultural heritage took place under the urgent threat brought by the modernization process. In *Orphan of Asia*, modernity arrives mediated in the form of Japanese colonialism—in the scent of Japanese soap[64] and in the tune of Japanese melody[65]; the traditional society can hardly hold its ground. Soon, Hu Taiming, like the majority of children his age in Taiwan, attends Japanese schools where modern knowledge is disseminated. Later, he goes to Japan for further study in physics. But modern education cannot change the fact that he feels like a second-class citizen as a colonial subject, an attitude best evidenced in his frustrated romance with his Japanese colleague Naito Hisako. When he serves as

63. See Wu Zhuoliu, *Wuhua guo*, p. 22; also see Lin Haiyin's recollection on her father and Wu Zhuoliu in *Jianying hua wentan*, pp. 91–95.

64. Wu, *Yaxiya de gu'er*, p. 24.

65. Ibid., p. 29.

a teacher in the primary school, Hu Taiming is irritated by the obvious discriminations against Taiwanese teachers by Japanese colleagues under the sham principle of "Japano-Taiwanese harmony."[66] Taiwanese teachers are ridiculed for their accented Japanese. The order of name plates in the principal's office, which is supposed to reflect seniority and rank, puts Japanese names above Taiwanese ones. Despite all the prejudice of his Japanese colleagues, Hu Taiming is strongly attracted by the beautiful Hisako. However, when she responds to his proposal that "it is impossible, because you and I are different," Hu is finally forced to confront the irreducible colonial distinction that "he is Taiwanese and she is Japanese."[67] Tortured by his despair over the hopeless love and incapable of fighting the racial bias between the colonizer and the colonized upheld by Japanese colonial policies, Hu Taiming concludes that "my blood is muddy, and this sin must be washed away."[68] Yet, neither his classical Chinese essence nor his modern scientific education enables him to overcome the deep sense of frustration and inferiority.

If such a psychological crisis is substantiated by Hu's identity as a colonial subject, then the sense of alienation and uncertainty becomes even more bitter during his next dislocation, to the mainland. It strikes him all the more intensely because it comes from the most unexpected and vulnerable place, namely, his motherland and his spiritual grounding. Indeed, given its controversial and ambivalent depiction by the author, Hu Taiming's experience on mainland China has been the focal point of most interpretations of *Orphan of Asia*. Wu Zhuoliu himself traveled to Nanjing in 1941 and spent a year there. After returning to Taiwan, he wrote *Nanjing zagan* (Miscellaneous thoughts on Nanjing), a travelogue that provided the basis for the Nanjing chapter in the novel.[69]

Hu Taiming's travel across the Taiwan Strait to the mainland started with a scene of poetry composition. On the deck of the vessel to Shanghai, he writes a poem in classical Chinese:

---

66. Ibid., pp. 62–67.
67. Ibid., p. 77.
68. Ibid., p. 49.
69. Wu Zhuoliu, *Nanjing zagan*. For a discussion of this work, see Ping-hui Liao, "Yiguo jiyi yu linglei xiandaixing."

Hesitating for ten-odd years,
I looked at the covered sky above the East Sea,
Tied to the stable not because I possess no talent,
with great ambitions not being realized, I was so anguished;
Thinking that I spent half of my life in hardship, my tears drown my eyes,
like the waves in the vast ocean,
I travel to the mainland not for high official posts,
for the sake of literature, I dare to cast away money and power.[70]

It is interesting to note that some twenty years earlier, another Taiwan poet also finished a poem when crossing the Taiwan Strait in the opposite direction. In October 1924, Zhang Wojun (1902–55), the forefather of modern Taiwan literature and poetry, wrote "Luandu zhilian" (Love in a turbulent capital) on his way back from Beijing to Taiwan:

I didn't want to go back,
But I had to go back;
I could only leave my soul
To her in the turbulent capital.

The "capital" in the last line refers to "chaotic Beijing, still covered completely by dust,"[71] where Zhang Wojun was enlightened by the May Fourth New Culture Movement and met the love of his life, Luo Xinxiang. Published in 1925, his anthology *Love in a Turbulent Capital* was the first collection of poems in modern vernacular Chinese composed by a Taiwanese writer. Zhang came to Beijing in early 1924 as a young student. Deeply influenced by the May Fourth movement, he determined to strive for a new literature in his home island as well and contributed greatly to the construction of Taiwan new literature. Inspired by the cultural spirit of the time, Zhang's poetic representations are saturated with powerful yet lucid passions toward Beijing and toward his lover in this ancient city. In contrast, Wu Zhuoliu's verses, which were written in early 1940s during the height of the Second Sino-Japanese War, do not sound so unequivocal.

The ambiguity is to be found in the significant detail about word alteration that Wu emphasizes in this episode. While the first couple

---

70. Wu, *Yaxiya de gu'er*, p. 142.
71. Zhang Wojun, *Zhang Wojun shiwen ji*, p. 203.

of quatrains pop up in his mind with ease, Hu Taiming makes quite an effort to revise the last line, which originally read "*gui guguo*" (return to my motherland) instead of "*you dalu*" (travel to the mainland). In revising the line, Hu is doubtlessly aware of his dubious identity: After all, as his passport shows, he is a citizen of the Japanese Empire. Officially, he will enter the mainland as a foreigner. How can he then still claim that he is about to return to his motherland?

The seemingly trivial slip of the pen could thus result in suspicious political implications. The crucial moment of modification amounts to the author's awareness of his complicated identity, thus signifying the loss of innocence about being Chinese in colonial Taiwan, which has been so simple and unequivocal in his childhood. Whenever people asked him where his hometown was, he readily recited the exact location of the specific village, county, and province on mainland China ("*yuanxiang tangshan*").[72] As Zhong Lihe (1915–60) remarks in his ethnographical delineation of his native land "*yuanxiang*" in his short story "Yuanxiang ren" (People of the native land): "When I gradually grew up, I learned from my father that 'yuanxiang' (the native land) was originally called 'zhongguo' (China), 'yuanxiang ren' (people of the native land) was called 'zhongguo ren' (Chinese)."[73] Zhong Lihe, Wu's contemporary fellow Taiwanese writer also from a Hakka family, was among those who traveled across the strait to the mainland because, as his famous ending remarks in "People of the Native Land" assert, "I am not a nationalist, but the blood of people of the native land must flow back to the native land, in order to stop roaring."[74]

Hu Taiming's experiences on the mainland have received the most attention from critics. To be sure, Wu Zhuoliu's description of continental experiences is not unique in modern Taiwan literature, yet it definitely amounts to the most ambivalent one. Zhang Wojun's Beijing descriptions are surely more affectionate and sympathetic, which is, as mentioned previously, mostly to be attributed to his passionate engagement in the New Culture Movement and his similarly passionate romance with Luo Xinxiang. Zhong Lihe also produced

---

72. Wu, *Yaxiya de gu'er*, p. 17.
73. Zhong Lihe, "Yuanxiang ren," p. 7.
74. Ibid., p. 12.

an important piece of literature on continental experiences. Like Zhang, Zhong came to the continent because of a love affair. He fell in love with Zhong Taimei, a woman worker in his father's farm in Taiwan. However, according to the Hakka custom, people with the same surname are not allowed to get married. To overcome this barrier, Zhong Lihe fled to the Chinese continent where he finally married Zhong Taimei. During their sojourn in Beijing, Zhong published the novella "Jiazhutao" (Oleander, 1945). Written around the same time as Wu Zhuoliu's *Miscellaneous Thoughts on Nanjing*, this novella describes in a gloomy tone the poor and inhuman life in the urban slum in southern Beijing, Nanchizi. The immorality and cruelty of life represented in this work constitute a stark contrast with another novella, "Chengnan jiushi" (Memoirs of southern Beijing, 1960) that also depicts life experiences of Taiwan people in southern Beijing.[75] Written by Lin Haiyin after returning to Taiwan at the Chinese division, the latter is characterized by a bright and crisp tone with a delicate touch of nostalgia reminiscing her age of innocence in Beijing.

Among these narratives of Taiwan sojourners on the Chinese mainland, Wu Zhuoliu's Nanjing depiction stands out for its unique complexity and ambivalence at the core. Critics have primarily concentrated on Hu Taiming's mistreatment by his fellow Chinese, especially when he was mistaken as a Japanese collaborator and put in jail. Although he eventually fled back to Taiwan, his dream of the mainland was completely dispelled. The dilemma of being Taiwanese on the mainland during the Second Sino-Japanese War is best reflected in the following remarks. Mr. Zeng, Hu's colleague in the primary school, warns him that as Taiwanese,

> we are mistrusted wherever we go. We are like the predestined deformed children. We ourselves have committed no crime, so to warrant such treatment is unfair. However, there is nothing we can do. Without the ill nature of a stepchild, we must do our best to prove our worth through action and not words, because in our passion to sacrifice for the reconstruction of China, we do not fall behind anyone.[76]

---

75. Lin Haiyin, "Chengnan jiushi" (Memoirs of southern Beijing), in *Chengnan jiushi* (Memoirs of southern Beijing).

76. Wu, *Yaxiya de gu'er*, p. 145.

However, Mr. Zeng's forceful resolution to contribute to the modernization of China is more or less obscured by the ineradicable sense of despair and uncertainty in every line. Indeed, as the experiences of Hu Taiming and many other Taiwanese on the mainland show, straightforward patriotism cannot solve the dilemma of identity. Furthermore, Hu Taiming's ambivalence comes not only from such political humiliations but also, more importantly, from his confusion confronting the culture of *yuanxiang* (the native land), which has been his spiritual homeland and support. In this light, Hu's travel on the mainland is first and foremost a cultural voyage. Upon visiting various historical sites and landmarks such as the Yangtze River, Mountain Zijin, Lake Xuanwu, and the Beiji Pavilion that have hitherto only existed in his imaginations evoked by classical Chinese literature, he cannot help noticing that this classical China is being crushed and vanishing irreversibly confronted with the destructive force of modernization. In Shanghai, for instance,

> Europeans, Americans, Chinese, and Japanese coexisted in Shanghai in a disharmonious harmony. They also visited the International Settlement, where stood a forest of looming skyscrapers—those inhuman products of monstrous plutocracy. At their feet, crowds and automobiles flooded turbulently, so that the torrent was traversed at risk to one's life. When Taiming and Mr. Zeng thought they had gained the opposite shore and entered Xianshi department store, they were suddenly sucked into a veritable whirlpool of human desires, whose gaudy, artificial intensity gave them a headache in a matter of minutes.[77]

Such antimodernist reflections on modern urban life amid the mostly realistic tone of *Orphan of Asia* have not yet received due attention. I would argue that passages like this in the novel considerably complicate Hu's ambivalent sentiment toward the Chinese continent. Hu's confusion regarding China is conditioned not only by the gap in modern facilities or infrastructure between China and Taiwan or the colonial metropolitan Japan but also, more intriguingly, by the very arrival of the modern age that relentlessly destroys his dream imagery of classical Chinese civilization. The traditional, cultural China, with which the Taiwan intellectuals feel the strongest bond, no longer exists. Wu's disquiet results from his awareness

---

77. Ibid., p. 147.

of the destructiveness of modernization. It is worth noting that Hu Taiming's marital crisis in Nanjing is mainly caused by the conflicts between his areas of interest and those of his wife: whereas Hu soaked himself in Chinese classics such as *Chunqiu* (The chronicles of Lu) and *Zhuzi baijia* (Anthology of various philosophical schools), Shuchun, his wife who was "too much of a 'modern woman' " (*xinnüxing*), loves modern lifestyles and spends most nights in dance halls.[78] Therefore, Hu's sense of groundlessness is far more complicated than just, as most critics have claimed, the dichotomy between a war-ridden backward motherland and a modern colonial metropolitan state of Japan, or sometimes, in the triangular antagonism among China, Japan, and Taiwan with its colonial modernity. Such assertions of a binary or triple consciousness often miss the Janus face of modernization depicted in Wu Zhuoliu's writings.

Finally, with nowhere to locate his cultural identity, the protagonist breaks down: "Alas, Hu Taiming finally went mad. He who had conscience would not be mad?"[79] Thus appears in modern Chinese literature yet another madman. And intriguingly, this one goes missing. He might be somewhere in Taiwan, or on the mainland, as someone reports.[80] How to decode the implication of this missing hero has always been at the center of debate among critics with disparate political stances.[81] Especially with the rise of the Taiwan independence movement, it becomes essential to pin down this missing madman. As Lin Boyan sarcastically remarked, while the motherland was calling, "Come back! Come back! Hu Taiming, nobody will discriminate against you!," those Taiwanese writers favoring independent Taiwan consciousness also cried out, "Taiming, you fool! Don't wander around anymore! Let's fight together, no matter what

78. Ibid., pp. 177–84. Regarding Wu's harsh critique of Shuchun's enjoyment of dancing, Lin Boyan provided an explanation: he attributed Wu's negation of modern women to his Hakka heritage. See Lin Boyan, "Wu Zhuoliu de dalu jingyan," pp. 346–48.

79. Wu, *Yaxiya de gu'er*, p. 10.

80. Ibid., p. 329.

81. For a survey of Taiwanese and mainland Chinese critics' readings of the concept of "orphan," see Chen Wanyi, "Hu Taiming jiqi gu'er yishi."

we are—big yam or some lizard, you can't run around. Except for Taiwan, there is no place for you to survive!"[82]

In regard to Hu's madness, let us take another look at Chen Yingzhen's and Chen Fangming's interpretations of the novel. Chen Yingzhen asserts that Hu Taiming only pretends to be mad in order to deceive the Japanese police and get back to mainland China to participate in the revolution.[83] In this notion of contributing to the national revolution of China, one will hardly miss the echo of Mr. Zeng, quoted previously, in *Orphan of Asia*, who advocates sacrificing for the mission of China so as to confirm one's standpoint as Chinese. In fact, the history of Taiwan has never lacked such idealistic figures. Zhong Heming (better known as Zhong Haodong, 1915–50), the older brother of Zhong Lihe, makes the most illuminating example. Zhong went to the mainland in the 1930s and actively joined the Chinese revolution against the Japanese imperial invasion. In the years of his precarious revolutionary venture, he might not have had time to ponder the issue of identity or to expose the poverty in urban lower-class life or the humiliation of Taiwan people as "*baishu*" (yam) in Beijing after Taiwan's retrocession, as did his little brother Zhong Lihe.[84] However, his dedication to the greater mission of China could not spare him from being executed as a suspicious leftist during the White Terror.[85] Given such historical irony and anguish, Chen Yingzhen's claim that "those Taiwanese who courageously engaged in modern Chinese history, sought for national

---

82. Lin Boyan, "Wu Zhuoliu de dalu jingyan," pp. 348–49. Both yam and lizard are tropes for Taiwan.

83. Chen Yingzhen, "Gu'er de lishi," p. 58.

84. See Zhong Lihe, "Baishu de bei'ai" (The sadness of the yam), which describes the dilemma of Taiwan people on the mainland after the end of the Second Sino-Japanese War.

85. Zhong Haodong was arrested in 1949 for his editing an underground newspaper *Guangming bao* (Guangming daily) to disseminate leftist ideas and executed the next year. Lü Heruo was forced into exile for his involvement in this incident. Hou Hsiao-hsien's film *Haonan haonü* (Good men, good women, 1995), the last one in his Taiwan trilogy (the first two are *City of Sadness* [1989] and *Ximeng rensheng* [The puppet master, 1993]), provides a cinematic reflection of the life of Zhong Haodong and his wife Jiang Biyu.

freedom and independence don't have the difficulty of identification"[86] sounds more like a faith than a solution. Chen Yingzhen himself was not unaware of it given his own experiences in and out of prison for his socialist tendencies.

By contrast, Chen Fangming emphasizes that Hu Taiming's true intention is to fight for Taiwan's self-determination, just as Wu Zhuoliu hinted with the contemporary Korean independence movement. Chen Fangming's condemnation of Chen Yingzhen's large China vision as a "chauvinism of Han Chinese"[87] only betrays his own anxiety embedded in his preoccupation with an autonomous Taiwan identity. Chen Fangming's Taiwan autonomy constituted itself through an imperative of exclusion, a fear of contamination by any Chinese claim, be it Han Chinese as in Ming dynasty, Manchu Qing, Nationalist government, or even the latter's antagonistic Communist state across the Taiwan Strait. In his definition of Wu Zhuoliu's "spirit of orphanization," he vehemently attacks the inferior Chinese national character, which he believes to be the main reason for all kinds of abuse that Taiwan people suffer in their communication with mainland Chinese people. Thus, this Sinophobia appears in the guise of an intense resentment and mistrust toward Chinese cultural or historical traces in Taiwan. Chen Fangming's basic idea is that any acknowledgment of the history of Taiwan as part of Chinese history necessarily indicates disloyalty to Taiwan. Thus, he was actually not that different from those historians discussed earlier in this chapter who eagerly denounced Tang Jingsong and Qiu Fengjia for their political infidelity toward a modern Taiwan Republic or the island province of the Qing Empire. And paradoxically, such a conceptualization of Taiwan autonomy permeated with orphan sentiments has always already departed from an uncanny self-nativization, or to be more accurate, a self-orphanization. Therefore, Chen's efforts to challenge the ideology of abandonment are bound to remain trapped in a frustrating, tail-chasing loop. Such bitter insistence on an uncontaminated autonomous Taiwan con-

---

86. Chen Yingzhen, "Gu'er de lishi," p. 59.

87. Chen Fangming, "Chaoxiang xuyuanzhong de liming," p. 32.

sciousness excluded from any Chinese connections is exactly the flip side of a claim of an authentic eternal Chinese culture.

In mid-twentieth-century Taiwan narratives, the notions of division and schizophrenia characterize not only the lives of Taiwan intellectuals such as Hu Taiming but also a unique writing strategy to deal with issues of nation and culture. If schizophrenia as a cultural metaphor helps consider Shen Congwen's 1949 transition, then in Wu Zhuoliu's case, only schizophrenic writing is able to convey the split subjectivity between the native motherland and the colonial metropolitan state, between multiple layers of Chinese historical temporalities, between the modern and the traditional, and between the prosperity façade and the self-destructive dark side of the modern. Hence, schizophrenia in this instance is both psychological and narratorial: it is cultural and political as well as historical. In this sense, the orphan of Asia best illustrates the severed subjectivity abandoned in the interstices of history.

From "Orphan of Asia" to "Child of Taiwan"

A critical reflection on Wu Zhuoliu's Taiwan narrative at the retrocession and Taiwanese literature at large is possible only if we transcend the discursive limitation of colonialism or nationalism. A postnationalist reorientation helps expand the analytical scope to cover other crucial issues in mid-twentieth-century Taiwanese literature. The politics of language would be one of them. Wu Zhuoliu's continuous literary creation traverses the boundaries between Chinese and Japanese, between Mandarin Chinese, Hakka, and Fukienese dialects. In dealing with the body of literature written by the colonized using the colonizer's language, postcolonial critics formulated notions such as mimicry, hybridity, and (mis)appropriation to theorize colonial and postcolonial writing as resistance, as building a cultural empire that "writes back" to the imperial center.[88] Although such theories provide insightful perspectives on postwar Taiwanese literature, they cannot fully fathom the depth and the complexity of the linguistic and cultural landscape. For example, most of Wu

88. See, for instance, Ashcroft, Griffiths, and Tiffin, *Empire Writes Back*.

Zhouliu's fictional work was written in Japanese including his Taiwan trilogy, *Orphan of Asia*, *The Fig Tree*, and *Taiwan lianqiao* (Taiwan forsythia), which reflect on the formation of Taiwan's cultural consciousness in its modern history. Although Wu used Japanese to write fiction, his poems were all composed in Chinese—classical Chinese to be precise. Wu composed more than two thousand classical Chinese poems throughout his life and had always viewed himself as a poet rather than a fiction writer.[89] He even requested that his children inscribe on his tombstone, "The poet Wu Zhuoliu is buried in this beautiful city." For this sentiment, his friend Zhong Zhaozheng commended him as a "poet with iron blood."[90] His Japanese novels, *Orphan in Asia* in particular, are interwoven with classical Chinese verses, which generate intriguing linguistic and textual mélange and interruption, creating a space for cultural and historical contradictions and complicities.

The political implication inherent in such linguistic hybridity was pondered by the renowned scholar Qian Zhongshu during the height of the Second Sino-Japanese War, although in a different context.[91] In a satirical fiction entitled "Linggan" (The inspiration), Qian Zhongshu mapped out a linguistic cartography of semicolonial China, suggesting that Chinese dialects should include English spoken by Chinese people in Shanghai concessions and in the British colony of Hong Kong; Japanese spoken by Chinese people in Qingdao, the Japanese semicolony in Shandong province; Russian spoken by Chinese people in Manchuria; and so on. In recent years, scholars in North American academia have been trying to conceptualize the term "Sinophone literature," seeking to transcend the boundaries of strictly defined geopolitical and cultural entities and thus open up the field of Chinese-language literary study.[92] Then, in the geography of Sinophone literature, how should one position these Taiwanese writers, who used Fukienese or Hakka dialects as their main

89. Not much research has been done on Wu's poetry. One important analysis of Wu's poems is Huang Mei'e's "Tiexue yu tiexue zhiwai."

90. See Zhong Zhaozheng, "Tiexue shiren Wu Zhuoliu."

91. Qian Zhongshu, "Linggan."

92. For a conceptualization of "Sinophone," see Shih, *Visuality and Identity*, pp. 23–39, and "Concept of the Sinophone."

spoken language and Japanese as their written language? What kind of interrelations, if any, can be constructed among Taiwanese literature written in Japanese and Shanghai literature, Hong Kong literature, Chu (Hunan) literature? Are these bodies of literature to be considered in terms of regional, cultural, linguistic, or geopolitical categories? Reflections on questions like these will surely enrich and complicate our understanding of postwar Taiwanese literature and modern Chinese literature at large and reveal the complexity of history.

The forced prohibition of Japanese and propagation of Mandarin Chinese as the national language in 1946 intensified a sense of linguistic and cultural orphanization. As chapter 1 briefly outlined, after Japanese colonial rule ended, Taiwanese writers who used to write in Japanese had to wrestle with the language predicament. Some of these writers endeavored to grasp the modern Chinese vernacular within a short time in order to continue their literary career; others had to terminate literary creation. Whereas Wu took great efforts to learn to use Mandarin Chinese to write stories, he strongly questioned the Nationalist government's notion of eradicating "slave mentality" among Taiwanese by cleansing Japanese cultural poisons including the enslaving language. In "Yoakemae no Taiwan" (Liming qian de Taiwan, Taiwan before dawn, 1947), a piece written one year after the instigation of the language policy, Wu remarks,

> As for Japanese, why is Japanese a bad thing? It is because it was armored in the past. Now that the armor has been removed and it has restored its original state, Japanese is not bad at all. . . . In its disarmed condition, it has the important mission of cultural transmission, especially because most cultures in the world have already been translated into Japanese. If one knows Japanese, one is able to make contact with world cultures. . . . For the sake of culture, whether or not the preservation of Japanese would hinder the spread of Chinese culture, this has to be weighed up from a cultural perspective.[93]

In Wu's view, although Japanese colonialism and imperialism undoubtedly impaired cultural and sociopolitical developments in Taiwan, the Japanese language itself may well serve as a neutral carrier of culture, information, and ideas separated from power coercion. A

93. Wu Zhuoliu, *Liming qian de Taiwan*, pp. 120–121.

complete ban of Japanese would be like throwing the baby of access to new ideas out with the bathwater of Japanese imperialism.

With the increasing gap between mainlanders and Taiwanese after the retrocession amid deteriorating economic and political circumstances, the dilemma of orphanization was even aggravated. Xiao Qian's report of Taiwan in early 1947 is noteworthy. During World War II, Xiao Qian worked as a war journalist in England. After he returned to China, he visited Taiwan and wrote a report, entitled "Lengyan kan Taiwan" (Looking at Taiwan objectively), in January 1947, one month before the February 28 Massacre. In this article, Xiao emphasized that " 'constructing a new Taiwan' is only an unrealistic slogan; the essential task is to maintain its current good foundation."[94] Compared with Lieutenant General Albert C. Wedemeyer's report to the U.S. Department of State, Xiao Qian's analytic account is more realistic and on point, given his familiarity with the situation on the mainland, which provided him a better comparative scope. From his point of view, the most fundamental question after Taiwan's retrocession was "What can the motherland offer Taiwan?"[95] Concerned with the current socio-political situation of Nationalist China, Xiao questioned, "Whether Taiwan becomes China's Ireland or is integrated into the whole body of China, that depends on the political bearing of the mainland. Don't forget that Taiwan keeps comparing the present with the past. Don't forget what they need is not yet another fetter, but a warm and firm hand."[96]

However, the exacerbating corruption of economics and politics of the Nationalist regime soon engulfed the newly restored Taiwan. Dissatisfaction with the Nationalist government became the major theme of Taiwan literature of the time, if there was still any possibility for literary creation and publication.[97] In fact, a few months before Xiao Qian wrote his Taiwan report, Yang Kui, an important leftist Taiwanese writer, had already lamented the new restrictions imposed on Taiwan people by the new motherland government. In an article entitled

94. Xiao Qian, "Lengyan kan Taiwan," p. 315.

95. Ibid., p. 324.

96. Ibid., p. 328.

97. For a brief survey of writings conveying Taiwan people's resentment after the retrocession, see Chen Jianzhong, "Bei zuzhou de wenxue?" pp. 43–48.

"Wei ciyinian ku" (I cry for this year, 1946) on the first anniversary of Taiwan's retrocession,[98] Yang expresses his disappointment:

> Many young people are complaining about unemployment, many people are eating preserved vegetables, living on the edge of death; there are numerous corrupt officials, cunning businessmen exploiting people; right and wrong are reversed, evil is on the way, what a world is this? Those who speak out loud and write something honest are threatened; we cracked the old fetters, only to get the new chains. . . . Looking back at this year . . . I can't help crying. I cry over the fact that the Republic is not democratic, that freedom of speech and meeting is not protected. I cry over the precious year that has been spent in vain.[99]

The crisis found its most violent explosion in the February 28 Incident two years after Taiwan's return to the motherland, which was regarded as marking "a watershed between a Chinese and a Taiwanese identity in the development of the national consciousness in Taiwan."[100] Martial law was declared, and in the following months, thousands of people, mostly Taiwanese intellectuals and professionals, were arrested, jailed, and executed. Hou Hsiao-hsien's 1989 movie *Beiqing chengshi* (City of sadness) provides a cinematic representation of life during the intervening years between Taiwan's retrocession and the February 28 Incident. The film won the Golden Lion Award at the Venice Film Festival of 1989 and became the first Taiwanese film to achieve international recognition. It is worth noting that *City of Sadness* was released in the same year that the Cold War antagonism started to thaw worldwide and the Tiananmen Incident took place in Beijing on the mainland, which of course imposed certain dubious political implications on the artistic cinematic achievement. The speech by the governor of Taiwan, Chen Yi, during the February 28 Incident easily reminded people of that authoritative voice of mainland Chinese government vibrating through broadcasts and televisions in the spring months of 1989. It is probably for this reason that the film premiered exactly one hundred days after the Tiananmen crackdown on pro-democracy protests. Consequently,

98. For a study of Yang Kui's work, see, for instance, Chen Fangming, "Yang Kui de fanzhimin jingshen" (Yang Kui's anticolonial spirit).

99. Yang Kui, quoted in Chen Jianzhong, "Bei zuzhou de wenxue?" p. 44.

100. Liao Xianhao, "Zai jiegou yu jieti," p. 199.

even the most authentic filmic national allegory of Taiwan cannot escape from a presumed symbolization of Chinese politics on the mainland.

The movie presents a striking equivalent of Hu Taiming—the deaf and dumb photographer in the port city Keelung. Ping-hui Liao observes that "this cunning or even manipulative tactic of muteness allows various forms of interpretation while making no commitment to any one view."[101] Muteness becomes the most effective cinematographical strategy of Hou Hsiao-hsien's filmic construction. Hence, during the February 28 Incident of 1947, the schizoid orphan of Asia becomes deaf and mute.

With the ensuing implementation of the White Terror, the problems of Taiwan's colonial past were easily and eagerly marginalized, if not absolutely repressed, under the fundamental principle of "restoring the lost mainland" superimposed on this newly "restored" island. In the 1970s, when the restoration dream was becoming increasingly unreachable with the new international political dilemma confronting the Nationalist government—its replacement by the PRC in the United Nations, and the establishment of diplomatic relations between the United States and the PRC after Richard Nixon's China visits, the orphan of Asia was resurrected with the prevalence of a popular song. Bearing the same title, Luo Dayou's "Orphan of Asia" laments: "The orphan of Asia cries in the wind / People are still pursuing that unsolvable question / Dear mother, what kind of truth is this?"

Since the last decades of the twentieth century, with the gradual collapse of the KMT's political authoritarianism, the emergent rival party, the Democratic Progressive Party (DPP), has impatiently claimed an autonomous Taiwanese consciousness. In its anxiety about anything ambiguous, it even disavowed the 1895 Taiwan Republic as a valid model of nation building. In its eager search for an imagined transcendental Taiwan subjectivity, the orphan of Asia was hastily transformed into the child of Taiwan. Therefore, this conceptualization of Taiwan subjectivity embraced all Taiwanese writers with disparate political agendas—Wu Zhuoliu's "orphan of Asia," or

---

101. Ping-hui Liao, "Rewriting Taiwanese National History," p. 294.

Lai He's "Han loyalist," Zhou Jinbo's "volunteer soldier," or Yang Kui's "newspapermen," into the same genealogy of Taiwan state building and thus created a *déjà perdu* (already lost) prehistory of a nation that is yet to be founded. In this process, these writers were deprived of their historical and cultural complications and specificities, and reshaped into easily recognizable figures in an emergent canon of national literature. Such a mission of nation-building and literary canonization is what David Wang insightfully describes as both "a priori and a posteriori": these writers were conceived as "helpless yet expectant loyalists—they are left (in advance) by the future, not the past. When *a posteriori* becomes *a priori*, the post-*yimin* narrative effectively creates its pre-*yimin* double."[102] Thus, in the hasty leap from pre-*yimin* to post-*yimin*, the orphan of Asia in the uncanny guise of the child of Taiwan not only remains undetermined but also is deprived of any historical specificity.

102. David Der-wei Wang, "Hou yimin xiezuo," p. 51.

CHAPTER 5

Fashioning Socialist Affinity: Feng Zhi and the Legacy of European Humanism in Modern Chinese Poetry

The formation of modern Chinese literature has been from the very start entangled with the influences of Western literature and philosophy. The European intellectual heritage, in particular Enlightenment thought, has been introduced, embraced, and contested throughout China's search for modernity. How to reconcile the relationship between the individual and the social, art and the nation, as well as the aesthetic and the political remains a central question for modern Chinese intellectuals. Different modes of reconciliation determined different personal, aesthetic, and political choices at the Chinese Cold War division and validated and reinforced the demarcations among various cultural and political entities. In the age of division, when China was even more deeply involved in the international system, the Western impact appeared in its most unexpected form. During the White Terror period in Taiwan, European modernism and avant-garde literature and art were introduced on a large scale as depoliticized pure aesthetic, which nurtured the construction of modern Taiwan literature. On the mainland, when the obliteration of capitalist influences in every aspect of society constituted the essence of the socialist modernization movement, their debris lingered at unanticipated sites and thus was uncannily ingrained into the topography of socialist Chinese literature.

This chapter explores how the solitary, contemplative individual relates to the universe, the social, and the national through various aesthetic means, and overcomes its finitude by effacing the a-relational self and emplacing itself within a larger Whole of the national collectivity. To that end, I provide a case study of Feng Zhi (1905–93), the eminent Chinese poet and scholar of German literature who introduced and translated Novalis, Hölderlin, Goethe, and Rainer Maria Rilke (1875–1926), among others, and of the impact of the German aesthetic on his view of the relationship between the individual and society, which informed his mid-twentieth-century transition from poetry to politics in socialist China. Through an examination of Feng's ideas of poetic solitude, analogy, metamorphosis, and social engagement formed through his study of Rilke and Goethe, I consider his endeavor to forge an affirmative relationship between the aesthetic and the political across the Cold War divide in China. I will address mainly the following questions: How did Feng deal with the finitude of the poetic subject? In what ways was German modern aesthetics—as embodied in the key figures of Rilke and Goethe—incorporated into Feng Zhi's reflections? Whereas reading Rilke helped Feng form a unique concept of relational solitude in the unitary wholeness, it was through his study of Goethe that he effectively bridged the inward and outward life, the aesthetic and the social. How did that concept of aesthetics and politics enable him to assimilate the aesthetic subject into the ideology of socialist collectivism and eventually inform his 1949 embrace of Chinese socialism?

Feng Zhi studied German literature at Peking University between 1921 and 1927, and then went to Germany to pursue his doctoral research. From 1930 to 1935, he studied at Heidelberg University and the University of Berlin. In 1933, he returned from Berlin to Heidelberg to attend Karl Jaspers (1883–1969)'s lecture and to complete his dissertation, "Die Analogie von Natur und Geist als Stilprinzip in Novalis' Dichtung" (The analogy of nature and spirit as the principle of style in Novalis' work), under the guidance of Ewald A. Boucke. On June 26, 1935, he passed his dissertation defense, the committee for which included Jaspers. After returning to China, Feng worked as a Germanistik (German studies) professor at various universities while continuing his poetic creation.

The German intellectual dynamics of enlightenment, romanticism, and modernism have been one of the most significant resources in

China's quest for modernity. Feng Zhi followed a long line of Chinese intellectuals immersed in German culture and philosophy, which can be traced back to Cai Yuanpei (1868–1940), Wang Guowei (1877–1927), Lu Xun (1881–1936), Chen Yinke (1890–1969), Zong Baihua (1897–1986), Zhu Guangqian (1897–1986), and so forth. Reflections on the mission of intellectuals in modern society stand at the core of the Chinese reception of the German-language philosophical and cultural legacy. In the last years of imperial China in the late nineteenth century, Wang Guowei employed Arthur Schopenhauer (1788–1860)'s notions of life, desire, and suffering to interpret classical Chinese poetry and the novel *Honglou meng* (Dream of the red chamber). As he pondered the chaotic Chinese society in its transition from an old civilization to its ideal modernized form, he turned to German philosophy, particularly that of Kant, Schopenhauer, and Nietzsche, for intellectual illumination. How could the human intellect engage with the world, as subjective representation or as objective knowledge? Foreseeing even more profound historical and cultural crises entailed by China's quest for modernity in the decades to come, Wang Guowei finally committed suicide at the threshold of the old and the new. Cai Yuanpei, president of Peking University between 1917 and 1926, was deeply influenced by the intellectual legacy of German classicism. His central concept of *meiyu* in his thinking and practice of educational reform in modern China derived from Friedrich Schiller (1759–1805)'s *ästhetische Erziehung* (aesthetic education). Following Wilhelm von Humboldt (1767–1835)'s humanistic notion of modern education, Cai sought to implement the principle of *Bildung durch Wissenschaft* (education via scholarship) in undertaking to restructure Peking University into a modern humanistic institution, which not only directly nurtured the May Fourth New Culture Movement but also educated generations of new Chinese intellectuals. Chinese aesthetic philosopher Zong Baihua was educated at Frankfurt University in the 1920s. A passionate scholar of German idealism, he introduced and translated German philosophers, Kant and Hegel in particular, into Chinese.[1] Confronting the

1. For studies of Zong Baihua and his aesthetic thinking, see, for instance, Kubin, "Zong Baihua (1896–1996)."

historical crisis during the Second Sino-Japanese War, Zong enthusiastically proposed to establish a cultural nation-state and examined the mission of modern Chinese intellectuals in this endeavor.

On November 7, 1948, a group of professors and writers of the liberal camp held a gathering in the Cai Yuanpei Memorial Hall at Peking University. Their debate was later published as "Jinri wenxue de fangxiang" (The direction of today's literature).[2] The main topic of the debate was the relationship between literature and politics, between intellectuals and the political authority. There have been frequent discussions on politics and literature throughout China's search for modernity and modernization. Under the pivotal circumstances of 1948, when the Chinese civil war was about to end advantageously to the Communist side and the ultimate decisive moment of division was oppressing all Chinese people, such a debate inevitably revealed poignant ideas, foreshadowing disparate decisions that these intellectuals eventually made at the 1949 turning point. Both Shen Congwen and Feng Zhi were present. Employing the notion of traffic lights to symbolize political regimentation, Shen Congwen had his reservations about its manipulative power and negative impact on literature. Although Feng Zhi insisted on the independent stance of intellectuals in society, he held an intriguingly different attitude toward this necessity: "Since one has to walk on this road, one has to observe the traffic lights."[3] Although Feng and Shen expressed similar literary outlooks, the distinction in their opinions regarding political control was subtle yet meaningful. This difference appears all the more significant as both of them in effect stuck to their principles when confronted with the 1949 division and endured its disparate consequences in the post-1949 era. Whereas Shen Congwen terminated his literary career after a failed suicide attempt, Feng Zhi made an apparently smooth transition into the socialist People's Republic and became an eminent cultural celebrity.

Indeed, the 1949 divide pressed every Chinese writer with utmost urgency. During this transitional period, some faced the termination

---

2. Hong Zicheng, *Zhongguo dangdai wenxueshi shiliaoxuan*, pp. 143–49. The transcript of "The Direction of Today's Literature" was first published in *Dagong bao* 107, November 14, 1948.

3. Ibid., p. 145.

of their literary career; some were forced into exile, within or outside the mainland; and some sacrificed their lives to defend their ideals. Feng Zhi, the "greatest Chinese lyricist"[4] of the 1920s and the modernist poet par excellence of the 1940s, however, seemed to effortlessly assimilate into the new age of socialist collectivism and exchanged the aura of a modernist poet for the license and medallion of a Maoist literary worker. It often has been claimed that Feng's unexpected conversion reflected the schizophrenic mentality of Chinese intellectuals in the mid-twentieth century and resulted from external political contingencies.[5] Friedrich Engels observed in 1847 that Goethe had a double nature, "at one time colossal, at another petty; sometimes a defiant, scornful genius full of contempt for the world, other times a cautious, contented, narrow Philistine."[6] Citing Engels's comments on Goethe, Feng Zhi's critics pointed out that Feng's political and aesthetic transformations across the 1949 Chinese division revealed the same duality in his personality.[7] Feng was well aware of the split subjectivity in Goethe and in himself. During the Thought Reform movement in 1952, the only political campaign in which Feng ran into trouble before the Cultural Revolution, he confessed that he had two names—Feng Chengzhi, as recorded in his family genealogy record, and Feng Zhi, a pen name he created—each responsible for one section of his private and public life. He was then accused by the masses of possessing *shuangchong renge* (split

4. Lu Xun highly praised Feng Zhi's first poetry collection, *Zuori zhi ge* (Songs from Yesterday), and called the young poet "the greatest modern Chinese lyricist" in his preface to the second volume of *Zhongguo xin wenxue daxi* (Compendium of new Chinese literature) (Shanghai: Liangyou chuban gongsi, 1935). Feng Zhi, *Songs from Yesterday*, in *Feng Zhi quanji*, vol. 1, pp. 3–118. Feng Zhi's works are cited according to *Feng Zhi quanji* (Complete works of Feng Zhi, hereafter cited as *FZQJ*), 12 vols. References are in a format with volume number followed by page number. All translations from the Chinese are my own unless otherwise noted.

5. For a biographical study of Feng Zhi, see Jiang Qinguo, *Feng Zhi pingzhuan*; Zhou Liangpei, *Feng Zhi pingzhuan*; and Lu Yaodong, *Feng Zhi zhuan*; among others.

6. Engels, quoted in Demetz, *Marx, Engels and the Poets,* p. 169. Feng Zhi first read Engels's review of Karl Grün's *Über Goethe vom menschlichen Standpunkte* in 1948, but did not discuss it in length until the end of the Cultural Revolution, when he picked up Goethe study again, which he stopped after the foundation of socialist China in 1949.

7. See, for instance, He Guimei, *Zhuanzhe de shidai*, pp. 134–204.

personality).[8] Whether Feng was able to mold a complete and unequivocal self to suit the volatile political climate in post-1949 China remains moot. In 1990, shortly after the Tiananmen Incident, Feng composed his last poem to encapsulate various transitions in his life:

三十年代我否定過我二十年代的詩歌，
五十年代我否定過我四十年代的創作，
六十年代、七十年代把過去的一切都說成錯。
八十年代又悔恨否定的事物怎麼那麼多，
于是又否定了過去的那些否定。
我這一生都像是在"否定"裡生活，
縱使否定的否定裡也有肯定。
到底應該肯定什麼，否定什麼？
進入了九十年代，要有些清醒，
才明白，人生最難得到的是"自知之明"。[9]

In the 1930s, I negated my poetry of the 1920s;
In the 1950s, I negated my work of the 1940s;
In the 1960s and '70s, I declared that everything in the past was wrong.
In the 1980s, I regretted how many things I had ever negated,
And thus negated all my previous negations.
It is as if I spend my whole life in "negation";
Even in the negation of negation there exists affirmation.
What on earth should be affirmed, and what negated?
Now it is the 1990s, it takes some sobriety,
To realize that the most difficult thing to achieve is "Know yourself."

"What on earth should be affirmed, and what negated?" Feng's last poem is not yet another assertion or negation. Instead, it is a self-portrait of a life full of constant insistence and denial. As Feng remarked in his Heidelberg years in a letter to his best friend, Yang Hui, "The most severe calamity in life is a plethora of schizophrenia."[10]

The significance of Feng Zhi's case can be fully grasped only when viewed against the larger picture of the 1949 Chinese division. His lifelong search for an affirmative reconciliation between the self and the society, between the aesthetic and the political, then seems all the more poignant. Rather than accusing him of betraying his aesthetic ideals, I suggest that Feng's post-1949 conversion was in various ways a consequence of his poetic crisis amid the historical

---

8. This event was accounted by Feng Zhi's wife, Yao Kekun, in her memoir *Wo yu Feng Zhi*.

9. *FZQJ* 2: 291.

10. *FZQJ* 12: 111.

and political changes of mid-century China. Feng's ideas of the poetic subject, *entsagen* (disavowal), and metamorphosis, which were conceptualized through his reading and translation of Rilke and Goethe, significantly informed his mid-twentieth-century transition from poetry to politics in socialist China.

The Republic of Thousands of Solitude: Feng Zhi's Sonnets *and Rainer Maria Rilke*

> 他們要開花,
> 開花是燦爛的，可是我們要成熟，
> 這叫做居於幽暗而自己努力。
>
> —Rainer Maria Rilke, quoted and translated in Feng Zhi, "Gongzuo er dengdai"

> Sie wollten blühn,
> und blühn ist schön sein; doch wir wollen reifen,
> und das heißt dunkel sein und sich bemühn.
>
> —Rainer Maria Rilke, "Im Saal"

In the post-Mao era, Feng Zhi was honored with numerous international prizes for his *Shisihang ji* (Sonnets) and for his contribution to cultural exchanges between Germany and China. In his acceptance speech at the ceremony of the Inter-Nationes Kunstpreis (Inter-Nations Art Prize) in 1987, Feng delineated the influences he had drawn from Goethe and Rilke and discussed in detail how both poets dealt with solitude and managed to live in their respective times "connected with the society."[11] Feng noted that every time he read Rilke's *Duineser Elegien* (Duino elegies) and *Die Sonette an Orpheus* (Sonnets to Orpheus), what came to his mind were the last lines in Goethe's *Faust*, the "chorus mysticus":

> Alles Vergängliche / Ist nur ein Gleichnis;
> Das Unzulängliche / Hier wird's Ereignis;
> Das Unbeschreibliche, / Hier ist's getan;
> Das Ewig-Weibliche / Zieht uns hinan.[12]

---

11. Feng, *FZQJ* 5: 204.

12. Goethe, *Faust. Der Tragödie zweiter Theil in fünf Acten* (Faust. The tragedy's second part of five acts, 1831), verse 12104–11.

Feng translated the chorus into Chinese:

> 一切無常的/只是一個比喻;
> 不能企及的/這裡成為事跡;
> 不能描述的/這裡已經完成;
> 引渡我們的/是永恆的女性。[13]

Interestingly, he used the notion *yindu* to render *hinanziehen*. In the Chinese context, *yindu* carries Buddhist connotations of ferrying across the sea of mortal life to the other shore, to complete the process of transformation and thus to attain the supreme state of nirvana, rebirth, and enlightenment. For Feng Zhi, the compositions of these poems mark the moment of *Vollendung* (perfection) in both poets' lives. How to reconcile the relationship between the solitary poetic subject and the outside world and how to achieve spiritual transformation and self-fulfillment through aesthetic means are at the core of Feng Zhi's poetic world.

Critics have duly noted Rilke's influence on Feng. Without Feng's introduction of Rilke and his own poetic experimentation, the constellation of Chinese modernist poetry would have been quite different. Feng's reading of Rilke's writings, especially those between 1912 and 1922, helped him work through the poetic and psychological crisis of solitude dominating his early work. Feng often claimed that he turned to Rilke to learn how to cope with loneliness and to construct a complete, self-sufficient subjectivity. He conceptualized a notion of poetic solitude as an autonomous, complete status of the *selbständig* aesthetic self. Aesthetic autonomy is only complete in its ability to build an analogical relationship with others in the world, thus forming a Whole.

Poetic solitude is the central theme of Feng Zhi's early poetry. An intense and unbearable sentiment of loneliness permeates his first two poetry collections, *Zuori zhi ge* (Songs from yesterday, 1927) and *Beiyou ji qita* (Northern expedition and others, 1929), and dozens of essays published in various journals and newspapers.[14] These writings

---

13. Feng, *FZQJ* 5: 202.

14. Both of Feng Zhi's first two poetry collections were published by the Chenzhong Press (Die versunkene Glocke, the sunken bell), which he and his friends founded. The literature group and the affiliated press were named after Gerhart Hauptmann's play *Die versunkene Glocke*. This group lasted some eight years. Although it was once valued by Lu Xun as the most promising literary group of the time, it was small and its audience very limited. Therefore, although Lu Xun praised

are full of images such as the gloomy twilight, the lonely cloud, the leftover wine, the morbid shadow, the setting sun, and so on. "She" (Snake) in *Songs of Yesterday* provides a salient example:

我的寂寞是一條蛇，
靜靜地沒有言語。
你萬一夢到它時，
千萬啊，不要悚懼！

它是我忠誠的侶伴，
心裡害著熱烈的鄉思：
它想那茂密的草原——
你頭上的、濃郁的烏絲。

它月影一般輕輕地
從你那兒輕輕走過；
它把你的夢境銜了來，
象一隻緋紅的花朵。[15]

My loneliness is a snake,
Who is silent, doesn't speak a word.
If you happen to dream of him,
Please, don't be scared!

He is my loyal companion,
Suffering from a deep nostalgia:
Longing for the lavish meadow —
Your long, luxuriant hair.

He, as quiet as the moon shadow,
Walks quietly past you;
He plucks your dream with his mouth,
Like a rosy red flower.

The poet employs the metaphorical image of the snake to present the feeling of loneliness—quiet, elusive, yet pervasive. Feng later recalled that Aubrey Beardsley (1872–98)'s drawing of a snake holding a flower in its mouth gave him the inspiration.[16] In an essay dated June 10, 1924, the young Feng asserted that "all poets' lives are lonely, and all poets are confronted with solitude."[17] This loneliness anxiety permeates his early writings. In the 1980s, looking back at his pre-

---

Feng Zhi as "the most prominent modern Chinese lyricist" and selected several of Feng's poems for Volume II of *Compendium of New Chinese Literature* he edited, Feng Zhi's early work is much less known compared with *Sonnets*, published in 1943.

15. Feng, *FZQJ* 1:77.
16. Ibid., 5: 197–98.
17. Ibid., 3: 170.

1949 years, Feng Zhi observed that the mood expressed in his early poetry was shared by his generation, who grew up in the aftermath of the May Fourth New Culture Movement, and could be viewed as the zeitgeist of the post-May Fourth era. "Oh, desolate; oh, lonely, these are the two words that often come out of the mouths of young people."[18] Feng Zhi stated that this prevalence of desolation and woe partly justified the unprecedented popularity of the Chinese translation of Goethe's *Die Leiden des jungen Werthers* (Sorrows of Young Werther) among the youth. *Werther* was translated into Chinese by another important poet, Guo Moruo, and swept China soon after its publication in 1922. Among numerous Chinese translations of foreign literature of the time, *Werther* was by far the most influential and most enthusiastically embraced. As Feng further elucidated, "Those young people who were enlightened in the May Fourth movement yet couldn't find the future had lots to share with those during the *Sturm und Drang* in 1770s Germany, and for them, this novel that fully represented the spirit of the *Sturm und Drang* struck a sympathetic chord." It is thus no surprise that its popularity was "no less than that during the 'Werther craze' in Western Europe 150 years ago."[19]

However, the experiences of solitude as rendered in Feng Zhi's writings of the 1920s are not, as he himself claimed, just examples of the anxiety of the age.[20] While the dominance of loneliness among Chinese youth of the post-May Fourth epoch derived mainly from the oppressive political climate, in Feng Zhi's poetry it seems to have profound personal and psychological roots. Compared with that of his contemporary writers, Feng's work seldom touches upon principal themes such as nationalism, modernization, sexuality, and revolution, which evidently engendered anguish and loneliness among enlightened young people. Yu Dafu's *Chenlun* (Sinking, 1921), for in-

---

18. Ibid., 5: 196.

19. Ibid., 5: 195–96.

20. Feng emphasized at times that his early poetry had two major sources: Chinese poetry of the late Tang period and German poetry of the Romantic period, especially ballads and other poems by Hölderlin, Nikolaus Lenau (1802–50), and Heinrich Heine (1797–1856). (For instance, see his letters in the mid-1920s to Yang Hui, *FZQJ* 12: 57.) The dissertation Feng completed at Heidelberg University deals with the relationship between the human being and nature as reflected in Novalis' work. An examination of Feng's poetry must take note of both native and foreign traditions.

stance, which describes a Wertherian sentimental, romantic, and sexually frustrated expatriate Chinese student in Japan, is much closer in tone to *Werther*, albeit with a rather awkward nationalist twist.[21] The ending chapter takes place in a Japanese tavern. After another sexual humiliation and frustration facing the Japanese waitress, the protagonist walks into the sea, crying out the famous line in modern Chinese literature: "Oh, Motherland, when will you finally become strong!" Interestingly, Feng Zhi's long poem *Northern Expedition* also ends with the poetic subject in a Japanese wine shop, desperate and anxious about his lonely youth in the hostile foreign world.[22] The original last section of the poem, which was deleted in the 1955 version, reads,

> 夜半我走上了一家小樓，
> 我訪問一個日本的歌女—
> 只因我忽然想起一茶：
> "噯，這是我終老的住家嗎？—雪五尺！"
> 這時的月輪像是瓦斯將滅，
> 朦朦朧朧的仿佛在我的懷內消沉；
> 這時的瓦斯像是月輪將落，
> 懷裡，房裡，宇宙裡，陰沉，陰沉。

> At midnight I walked up to a small shop,
> To visit a Japanese courtesan—
> Only because I suddenly thought of Issa Kobayashi:
> "Oh, is this my final dwelling? — Buried now in five-foot snow!"
> At that moment, the moon was like the gas light that was burning out,
> So dim that it would vanish in my lap;
> At that moment, the gas light was like the moon that was falling,
> In my lap, in the room, in the universe, it was gloomy, gloomy.

Compared with Yu Dafu's entanglement of solitude, sexuality, and nationalism, the trenchant feeling of loneliness and the agonizing need for affection evidenced in Feng Zhi's poetry clearly come from elsewhere.

---

21. For a study of *Sinking* that focuses on the complicated entanglement of nationalist and masochistic psychology, see Tsu, *Failure, Nationalism, and Literature*, pp. 167–94.

22. The original last section of *Northern Expedition*, "Xue wuchi" (Five-foot snow), was completely deleted when Feng Zhi had the volume reprinted in 1955. In this section, Feng quoted from Japanese haiku poet Issa Kobayashi (1763–1827), who is also famous for his depiction of loneliness: "Oh, is this my final dwelling?—Buried now in five-foot snow!" The title "Five-Foot Snow" clearly refers to it.

The early loss of his mother needs particular consideration. It is evident that this loss was "the most distressing event" in Feng's childhood,[23] left an incurable trauma. A quick look at his early work between 1923 and 1930 demonstrates that most of his writings are variations on that central theme. Feng Zhi was born into an impoverished gentry family in north China. His father was away much of the time making a living. Feng spent most of his childhood alone with his mother, who died of tuberculosis when he was nine years old. Her death is depicted in a plethora of writings. "Zuihou zhige" (Swan song), the last poem collected in *Songs from Yesterday*, is a good example. The first two stanzas read,

記起母親臨終的禱告，
　　是一曲最后的"生命之歌"，
那正是暮春的一晚，
另樣的光輝漾著她的病臉；
　　蠟燭在台上花花地爆，
　　仿佛是宇宙啊，沒有明朝—
她把那時的情調深深地交給我，
　　還有我衣上的她的手澤！

箱子裡貯藏著兒時的衣裳，
　　心内隱埋著她最后的面龐；
偶然把灰塵裡的箱子打開，
那當時的情味也涌上心來。
　　蠟燭在台上花花地爆，
　　仿佛是宇宙啊，沒有明朝—
可是中間又度了許多的年月，
　　此刻啊，一個清新的秋夜！[24]

I remember Mother's prayer before her death.
It was the last "song of life."
That was an evening of late spring
An extraordinary glow lit her sickly face;
The candle burned vehemently in the holder,
As if in the universe, there would be no tomorrow—
She left me the atmosphere of that moment,
And on my clothes the warmth of her hands!

There store in the suitcase the clothes of my childhood,
There bury in my heart her last countenance;
When I happen to open the suitcase covered in dust,

---

23. Feng, *FZQJ* 3: 351.
24. Ibid., 1: 83–84.

> At once emerges the atmosphere of that moment.
> The candle burned vehemently in the holder,
> As if in the universe, there would be no tomorrow—
> Yet, how many years have passed since then,
> Now, a cool autumn night!

The verses rhyme with "ao," "an," and "ang," respectively. Although written in the form of modern free verse, this poem, like almost all Feng Zhi's poetry, rhymes beautifully. The lines "The candle burned vehemently in the holder / As if in the universe, there would be no tomorrow—;" are repeated in all eight stanzas and create thematically and vocally a lingering melancholic tone. Whereas the 1926 essay "Wuya" (Raven) most tangibly yet realistically portrays the death scene, the essay "Laowu" (The old house), published four years later and inspired by Baudelaire's prose poetry, conveys the mother's death with a modernist touch:

> Soon after twilight, it becomes quiet.
>
> As for the other rooms, there live a lot of "deaths": the "deaths" of gray-haired grandparents, the "deaths" of my cousin and aunt as young girls, and the "death" of my middle-aged mother. On windy mornings, in rainy dusks, they look after this house sunken in the sluggish time that slowly slips away. I believe that they may come out to enjoy the cool in the shade of the tree in the summer, and in the winter, they may sit around the charcoal brazier, whose remaining ashes have already gone cold, for some warmth. Some children are playing next to them. They are the "childhoods" of my brothers and sisters and me, which we couldn't bring away but had to leave here. . . .
>
> When I raise my head, the "death" of my mother has already walked into the hallway. It seems to know me. It is silent like a shadow, solemn like a shadow. I cry out, "What a lonely 'death' of my mother!"[25]

To a certain extent, Feng's emotional attachment to his mother explains why love poems make up such a small part of his poetic work, even though he was a main lyricist of his generation. Although the quest for love pervades early modern Chinese poetry, Feng Zhi's articulation of it pertains to maternal rather than romantic love. This psychological dependence cannot be accounted for by Freud's theory of the Oedipus complex. In Feng Zhi's work, the relationship to the mother is far more important than that to the father. In this regard,

---

25. Ibid., 3: 347–48.

post-Freudian psychoanalytic theories that examine the symbiotic unity of child and mother and the subsequent process of separation are more illuminating.[26] Focusing on the dyadic relationship between the child and the parent, Melanie Klein points out that the unsuccessful transition from symbiosis with the mother to object relations may disturb the process of subjectivity formation. In Feng's case, the dyadic relationship was cut short at the age of nine because of his mother's death, which resulted in a problematic transition from symbiosis to object relations. This theory well accounts for his psychological vulnerability and insecurity. Indeed, the psychic disturbance was manifested in his excessive susceptibility to loneliness and his excessive longing for affection. The early loss of his mother thus conditioned the lack of psychological stability. It not only stands at the core of his fear of loneliness but also produces it. The loss of the mother is repetitively revisited and addressed both psychologically and verbally, so much so that instead of working through it, the poet is perpetually caught up in the very idea of loss. In other words, her death is no more a distinct, localizable loss; it seems to gain a life of its own. As the void of solitude gradually grows out of bounds, the subjectivity of the poet is more and more paralyzed. Accordingly, the fear of loneliness takes a surprising turn into excessive indulgence in that very fear. It deviates into a fascination with the fear of the abyss, of indefinite emptiness, which entices the poet with evil yet seductive power.

Such a profound sense of loneliness predominated Feng's poetry until the early 1940s when he finally worked through it by reading and studying Rilke. Rilke is a key figure in the formation of modern Chinese aesthetic thought. In 1938, the British poet W. H. Auden came to Wuhan in its most critical moment, before it was taken over by the Japanese during the Second Sino-Japanese War. He wrote a series of sonnets, among which was "In Time of War":

> When all the apparatus of report
> Confirms the triumph of our enemy;
> Our bastion pierced, our army in retreat,
> Violence successful like a new decease,

---

26. Melanie Klein, *Das Seelenleben des Kleinkindes*; Margaret S. Mahler, *Psychological Birth of the Human Infant.*

And wrong a charmer everywhere invited;
When we regret that we were ever born:
Let us remember all who seemed deserted.
Tonight in China let me think of one,

Who through ten years of silence worked and waited,
Until in Muzot all his powers spoke,
And everything was given once for all:

And with the gratitude of the Completed
He went out in the winter night to stroke
That little tower like a great animal.[27]

The person Auden thought of in the night of war in China is evidently Rainer Maria Rilke. This sonnet was translated by the poet Bian Zhilin into Chinese and quoted by Feng Zhi in his article "Gongzuo er dengdai" ("Worked and waited") in 1943.[28] It is no coincidence that Feng talked about Rilke's silent years of work and endurance at that particular moment. Like Rilke, Feng experienced a decade of writer's block before he finally broke out with his most mature works in the early 1940s, including *Shisihang ji* (Sonnets, 1941) and *Wu Zixu* (Wu Zixu, 1943). The year 1943, when Feng quoted Auden's sonnet on China's calamity and Rilke's "work and endurance," witnessed the termination of Feng's own aesthetic crisis.

---

27. Auden, *Journey to a War*, p. 259. Bian Zhilin's Chinese translation of this sonnet is as follows:

當所有用以報告消息的工具
一齊証實了我們的敵人的勝利；
我們的棱堡被突破，軍隊在退卻，
“暴行”風靡像一種新的疫癘，

“邪惡”是一個妖精，到處受歡迎；
當我們悔不該生於此世的時份：
且記起一切似被遺棄的孤靈。
今夜在中國，讓我想起一個人，

他經過十年的沉默，工作而等待，
直到在繆佐他顯了全部的魄力，
一舉而叫什麼都有了個交代：

於是帶了完成者所懷的感激，
他在冬天的夜裡走出去撫摩
那座小古堡，當一個龐然的大物。

28. Feng, *FZQJ* 4: 94–100.

More important, this was a pivotal time when Feng Zhi the poet turned from his most prolific years of literary creation and his hitherto reclusive life to a new stage of active social participation. Indeed, it marked the birth of a socially engaged Feng Zhi, anticipating his post-1949 cultural celebrity in socialist China, rather than the emergence of a Chinese modernist poet par excellence.

Shortly after returning to Beijing from eight years of war exile in 1946, Feng Zhi took over as the new editor in chief for the "Weekly Literature and Art" *feuilleton* of *Dagong bao*, replacing Shen Congwen, who was at the time in charge of the art and literature supplements of three other leading newspapers. As 1948 approached, with China still trapped in civil war and human despair, Feng noted in his New Year's editorial message that the unremitting war situation would make the field of art and literature even bleaker: "People are all talking about it, and all worried about it; but since they talk about it and are worried about it, it proves that they don't want to die like this, they still want to struggle through it, even if the outside world doesn't make it any easier."[29] Feng continued, saying that the *feuilleton*, like everything in this hopeless condition, "from everyday meals to the loftiest ideal," attempted to put up a last struggle to survive. In this age, which "can't afford to ornament itself" and in which the "calamity of human beings is just like trees in the winter, standing bare in the wind and snow, without any covering or protection," endurance was the most significant determinant of a true survivor because "even if his voice is like midnight coughing, unpleasant, yet it touches people who hear it, strikes a chord in them, because this is the voice of survival."

In this passage, there is a subtle yet discernible hint of social responsibility that hardly appeared in Feng's early writings. The crucial notion is *shengcun*, which means literally "survive," yet generally indicates "endure." In Feng's writings of the time, *shengcun* points to similar connotations such as *rennai* (endure), *dandang* (take responsibility), and *fudan* (bear). This concept runs through his life and writings of the 1940s, informing his poetics, his philosophy, and his social and political outlook.

---

29. Ibid., 5: 339–40.

The crucial figure in Feng Zhi's transformation was evidently Rilke. What notions did Feng Zhi adopt from his reading of Rilke? How did they help him overcome the aesthetic crisis of the 1930s and shape his poetics and social attitude of the 1940s? What new problematic emerged that eventually informed his 1949 embrace of socialist collectivism? By examining his most important and acclaimed work of the 1940s, the thin collection of poems *Shisihang ji* (Sonnets), I suggest that while Rilke's notion of solitude helped Feng through his adolescent crisis, it paradoxically encouraged a dangerous tendency toward a mysterious and nihilistic attitude that could not effectively address the relationship between the poetic subject and the social reality. The recognition and contestation of this very dilemma characterize Feng Zhi's poetry in its most modernist form.

Let us first look at two "Venice" poems, written respectively in 1935 and in 1941. During this span of nearly a decade, what changed the poet's notion of loneliness?

無數寂寞的島嶼，
織就了一座美麗的城。
它是理想世界的縮影——
其中的人們，寂寞，孤零。

彼此通消息，這邊是
一架橋梁，那邊窗對著窗——
此外家家都關起門，緊抱著
幾百年的隆替興亡。

水街上是這般寧靜，
一任遠來的行人仔細傾聽；
傍晚穿過長怨橋下，只依稀
聽見了嘆息三兩聲。[30]

A myriad of lonely islands
Fabricate a beautiful city.
It's the epitome of the ideal world—
People in it are, lonely, desolate.

Here is a bridge, there are windows facing each other,
To exchange news—
Except for that, everyone closes his door, holding tightly
Hundreds of years of dynastic changes, rises and falls.

---

30. Ibid., 1: 327.

It's so quiet on the water streets,
So much so that travelers from afar can almost hear everything;
When they pass under the Bridge of Sighs, they seem to
Hear someone sighing.

The second one was collected as the fifth sonnet in his volume *Sonnets*:

我永遠不會忘記
西方的那座水城，
它是個人世的象征，
千百個寂寞的集體。

一個寂寞是一座島，
一座座都結成朋友。
當你向我拉一拉手，
便像一座水上的橋；

當你向我笑一笑，
便像是對面島上
忽然開了一扇樓窗。

只擔心夜深靜悄，
樓上的窗兒關閉，
橋上也斷了人跡。[31]

I shall never forget
That water city in the West,
It's a symbol of the human world,
A collection of thousands of lonelinesses.

One loneliness is one island,
All are connected as friends.
When you give me your hand,
It is as if a bridge has formed on the water;

When you smile at me,
It is as if on the island across the water
There has suddenly opened a window.

I'm only afraid that when it gets late at night,
The window will be closed,
And there will be nobody on the bridge.[32]

Both poems continue to ponder Feng's central subject: the state of loneliness. However, compared with his poetry from the 1920s, which

31. Ibid., 1: 220.

32. Dominic Cheung translated all twenty-seven sonnets in *Feng Chih*, app. 1, pp. 77–89. English translations of these sonnets are based on Cheung's renditions with minor revisions.

is saturated with an unendurable desolation, these two poems express a different sense. Both envision the myriad of separate islands in the city of Venice as a metaphor for individual human beings in the world. The ending lines of the first stanzas, "It's the epitome of the ideal world / People in it are, lonely, desolate" and "It's a symbol of the human world / A collection of thousands of lonelinesses," pronounce the central message that solitude is the essential nature of daily life.

However, as soon as we look at these poems closely, some significant differences emerge. Whereas the first poem dwells on a lingering subjective sentimentalism reminiscent of the 1920s verses, the second one, composed a decade later, is characterized by a detached tone. The strong, self-conscious voice of a poetic subject and his melancholic indulgence in the feeling of loneliness are obvious in the first poem, thematically, stylistically, rhythmically, even melodically. The constant pauses in the middle of the lines—for instance, "people in it are," "lonely," "desolate"—convey a sense of grief, isolation, and hesitation. Whereas the 1935 poem regards sporadic communications as exceptions in the larger picture of desolation, the 1941 sonnet portrays a much more positive vision of interpersonal interactions. Hence, the subjective adolescent perception of loneliness is transformed into a self-sufficient, complete state of solitude. Indeed, the sonnet seems to break out of the previous self-containment entailed by the prevalence of loneliness and foregrounds more or less a collectivity of solitude, on the basis of which interpersonal relationships become possible and can be constructed. Therefore, Feng remarked when reflecting on the Venice sonnet, "I thought that the self would not have existed without the feeling of solitude, the society would not have existed without intersubjective communications,"[33] a notion he obtained from Karl Jaspers at Heidelberg University.[34]

The passage from the incomplete subjectivity who feels like an "ignorant child toyed with in the hands of a giant"[35] to the poet in spiritual adulthood "capable of taking responsibility for the universe"[36]

---

33. Feng, *FZQJ* 5: 206.

34. Feng, "Zizhuan" (Autobiography), in *Zhongguo xiandai zuojia zhuanlüe* (Brief biographies of modern Chinese writers) (Chongqing: Sichuan renmin, 1981), 1: 143.

35. Feng, *Northern Expedition*, *FZQJ* 1: 123.

36. Feng, *FZQJ* 12: 123.

was a significant development. In this coming-of-age transition, the figure of Rilke certainly played the most crucial role, his work pointing the way out of those most confusing and incomplete years. Feng Zhi went to Germany in 1930 for his graduate studies in the Department of German Literature at Heidelberg University and found in the work of Rilke his new spiritual guide in this foreign college town. As Feng noted in a letter to his best friend, Yang Hui: "Now you are so far away from me, and can't advise me every day, I have to ask 'Rilke' to direct my stubborn mind."[37] Indeed, the name Rilke appears in almost every letter to Yang Hui from the entire year of 1931. In a letter dated April 10, 1931, Feng wrote, "In these six books, I saw my ideal poetry, ideal prose."[38]

Although Feng Zhi had encountered Rilke's work as early as 1924, it was not until 1931, when Feng read the first published volume of the author's correspondence, that Rilke truly struck him with force. In the next few years, in addition to his dissertation research on Rilke's fiction *Die Aufzeichnungen des Malte Laurids Brigge* (Notebooks of Malte Laurids Brigge, 1910),[39] he translated a number of Rilke's writings into Chinese, including a thin collection of poems,[40] *Briefe an einen jungen Dichter* (Letters to a young poet, Gei yige qingnian

---

37. Ibid., 12: 114.

38. Ibid., 12: 118. "These six books" refers to the six volumes of Rilke's first complete works, *Rainer Maria Rilke: Gesammelte Werke* (Leipzig: Insel, 1927).

39. Feng Zhi initially chose *Notebooks of Malte Laurids Brigge* as his dissertation topic and also planned to translate the entire novel into Chinese. However, the plan was soon interrupted because Feng's first advisor, Richard Alewyn, was expelled in 1933 from his professorship at Heidelberg University because of his Jewish origin. At the time, there were no other professors at Heidelberg University who were able to advise Feng on this topic. He thought of following Alewyn to Paris or finding professors from other universities in order to complete his dissertation. But he stayed at Heidelberg, changed to the study of Novalis under the guidance of Ewald A. Boucke, and obtained his PhD.

40. Feng Zhi's translations of Rilke's six poems were published in the special edition of *Xinshi* (New poetry) on Rilke's tenth anniversary in 1936: 豹 (Der Panther); Pietà (Pietà); 一個婦女的命運 (Ein Frauen-Schicksal); 啊，朋友們，這幷不是新鮮 (Du, mein Freund, bist einsam, weil); 奧爾弗斯 (Nur wer die Leier schon hob)；縱使這世界轉變 (Wandelt sich rasch auch die Welt), 9: 431–77. Feng's translation of *Letters to a Young Poet* was first serialized in the literary supplement of *Huangbei ribao* (North China daily) in 1931 later published as a monograph by Shangwu Press. His selected translation of *Notebooks of Malte Laurids Brigge* was first published together with "On

shiren de shifengxin, 1903), a small selection of *Notebooks*, and the article "Von der Landschaft" (On the landscape, 1902). The first two significant articles Feng Zhi published after returning to China were both on Rilke: "Li'erke: Wei shizhounian jiri zuo" (Rilke: On the tenth anniversary of his death), and a preface to his rendition of Rilke's "Ten Letters to a Young Poet."[41] A close reading of Feng's writings at this time reveals that his interest in Rilke lay more in his meditations on the existence of human beings and the status of the aesthetic subject than in his poetic style and innovations.

The major ideas in Rilke that resonated strongly with Feng were solitude and analogy, which are most fully represented in Feng's writings of the 1940s, in particular *Sonnets*. As the reading of the two "Venice" poems indicates, Feng sought to break out of his loneliness and anxiety and create a new notion of solitude, which is complete in its analogical relationship with all other beings. "Solitude and endurance"[42] are central themes in *Sonnets*. Rilke helped him reach this stage, as Feng admitted in a letter to Yang Hui: "Now that there exists such a great and beautiful soul as Rilke in the mundane life, I only feel a sense of loneliness like the ocean; I don't feel that sort of desolation like the desert."[43] What is the difference between oceanlike and desertlike solitude? If Feng sounds too passionate, thus inexplicit, in the letter to Yang Hui, his elucidation in the preface to his translation of *Letters to a Young Poet* is surely more distinct: "But he (Rilke) told us that the human being who was born into this world is lonely. Every human being in the world is like those trees standing side by side in the garden. There may be some connections among their branches and leaves, but their roots, which extend deep into the ground in order to obtain nutrition, are separated from each other. They are silent and solitary."[44] In this new concept of solitude, every individual is fundamentally lonely, yet complete. The state of

---

Landscape" in the journal *Chenzhong* (Die versunkene Glocke) and later collected in an appendix to the monograph of *Letters to a Young Poet*; *FZQJ* 11: 277–342.

41. These two articles are included in Feng, *FZQJ* 4: 83–88, and 11: 281–84.

42. Feng, *FZQJ* 12: 123.

43. Ibid., 12: 125.

44. Ibid., 11: 282.

solitude is essential, the prerequisite for the formation of a complete subjectivity. As Rilke observed in his letter to the young poet, Franz Xaver Krappus, which was translated by Feng into Chinese as early as 1931, "Your personality will gradually be formed, your solitude will gradually expand into a vague room, where the noises of other people will only pass by."[45] Instead of escaping, as he had in his early years, Feng learned to embrace the deepest solitude.

This autonomy of solitude not only leads to the inner self but also opens one's eyes to a new outer world. Indeed, it is both inward and outward. The embrace of a solitary yet complete subjectivity allows one to experience expansiveness that leads to overcoming one's finitude. Among Feng's translations of Rilke is an interesting small piece entitled "On Landscape," originally written by Rilke in 1902 as the preface to his book *Worpswede*, published the following year.[46] In this article, as he maps out the development of landscape painting in Western art history, Rilke in effect attempts to conceptualize the relationship between human beings and nature, or to be more precise, "the world of things." He remarks that

> Landschaft so zu schauen als ein Fernes und Fremdes, als ein Entlegenes und Liebloses, das sich ganz in sich vollzieht, war notwendig, wenn sie je einer selbständigen Kunst Mittel und Anlaß sein sollte; denn sie mußte fern sein und sehr anders als wir, um ein erlösendes Gleichnis werden zu können unserem Schicksal. Fast feindlich mußte sie sein in erhabener Gleichgültigkeit, um unserem Dasein eine neue Deutung zu geben mit ihren Dingen.[47]

> (if landscape is to become the medium and motive of an independent art, it has to be looked at as something distant and foreign, as something isolated and impassive, as something that progresses in itself; because it has to be distant and totally different from us, in order to become a redemptive equivalent of our fate. It has to be almost hostile in its lofty nonchalance, in order to provide, with its things, a new explanation for our existence.)

Although one has to look at the world of things as "distant and foreign" to grasp its true meaning and its implication for one's own

---

45. Ibid., 11: 289.

46. However, Rilke's preface was not included in the book but was eventually published posthumously in 1932. This article deeply struck Feng, so much so that he used the same title for his own prose collection, *Shanshui* (Landscape); *FZQJ* 3: 3–76.

47. Rilke, "Von der Landschaft," p. 520.

existence, Rilke emphasizes a *Gleichnis* (resemblance) between the self and others. This principle of analogy marks the foundation of a notion of *Weltinnerraum* (the inner space of the world).

In her seminal work *Flesh of My Flesh*, Kaja Silverman delineates a lineage of a different modernity that emphasizes resemblance, kinship, and analogies among various categories of things, among disparate times and spaces. Unlike Descartes, who claimed a unique, exclusive, and heterogeneous individual, this lineage, which included intellectuals such as Leonardo da Vinci, Darwin, Fourier, Baudelaire, Freud, Rilke, and Whitman, looked back at Ovid and asserted that all beings derive from the same flesh. Analogy is the principle of our world.[48] Rilke's *Die Sonette an Orpheus* speaks to this very connection: "Ohne unsern wahren Platz zu kennen, / handeln wir aus wirklichem Bezug. / Die Antennen fühlen die Antennen, / und die leere Ferne trug" (I, XII).[49] Feng Zhi's writings elucidate similar ideas of an analogical relationship between the poetic subject and other beings in the world. Sonnet No. 16 makes a good example in this context:

我們站立在高高的山巔
化身為一望無邊的遠景，
化成面前的廣漠的平原，
化成平原上交錯的蹊徑。

哪條路、哪道水，沒有關聯，
哪陣風、哪片雲，沒有呼應：
我們走過的城市、山川，
都化成了我們的生命。

我們的生長、我們的憂愁
是某某山坡的一棵鬆樹，
是某某城上的一片濃霧；

我們隨著風吹，隨著水流，
化成平原上交錯的蹊徑，
化成蹊徑上行人的生命。[50]

---

48. Silverman, *Flesh of My Flesh*.

49. Rilke, "Sonette an Orpheus," I, XII, in *Werke. Kommentierte Ausgabe in vier Bänden*, hrsg. von Manfred Engel und Ulrich Fülleborn (Frankfurt am Main, 1996), Band 2, p. 246.

50. Feng, *FZQJ* 1: 231.

We stand on the top of the mountain
And are transformed into the boundless panorama,
Into the vast plain in front of us,
Into the criss-crossing paths on the plain.

Which road, which river, doesn't have correlation,
Which wind, which cloud, doesn't have correspondence:
The cities, mountains, and rivers we have been through,
Have all been transformed into our lives.

Our growth, our sorrow
Are a pine tree on a certain hill,
A thick fog over a certain town;

We blow with the wind, flow with the water,
And are transformed into the criss-crossing roads on the plain,
Into the lives of the travelers on the paths.

This poem yields crucial insights regarding the shared experiences and memories of men and the world of things. Whereas objects and places we have experienced become part of our lives, we also leave our traces in animate and inanimate beings. This relationship echoes in lines in the same collection such as "Thousands of years ago / there seemed to exist everywhere / our lives" (Sonnet No. 24),[51] and "How many times have we been / projected onto a remote sky, / providing boatmen or travelers in the desert/with fresh nutrition for their dreams" (Sonnet No. 20).[52]

In addition to Rilke, the early German romanticist Novalis provided Feng Zhi with significant inspiration. In his 1935 dissertation at Heidelberg University entitled "Die Analogie von Natur und Geist als Stilprinzip in Novalis' Dichtung" (The analogy of nature and mind as the principle of style in Novalis's poetry), Feng contemplated the notion of kinship and affinity among all beings. He argued that in Novalis's work, "all boundaries disappeared, all distances were reduced, and all oppositions were eliminated."[53] He pointed out that the idea of relationality manifests itself, for instance, in Novalis's poem "Die Vermählung der Jahreszeiten" (The marriage of the seasons):

51. Ibid., 1: 239.
52. Ibid., 1: 235.
53. Ibid., 7: 4.

Wären die Zeiten nicht so ungesellig, verbände
Zukunft mit Gegenwart und mit Vergangenheit sich,
Schlösse Frühling sich an den Herbst, und Sommer an Winter,
Wäre zu spielenden Ernst Jugend mit Alter gepaart:
Dann mein süßer Gemahl versiegte die Quelle der Schmerzen,
Aller Empfindungen Wunsch wäre dem Herzen gewährt.[54]

(If time was not so unsociable,
future and present and past would connect with each other,
spring and autumn, summer and winter would interconnect,
youth and aged would couple together in a serious game:
If so, my sweet partner, the spring of pain would dry up,
And all wishes of the heart would come to true.)

In December 1936, the journal *Xinshi* (New poetry) published a special edition to mark the tenth anniversary of Rilke's death. For this occasion, Feng Zhi wrote "Li'erke: Wei shizhounian jiri zuo" (Rilke: On the tenth anniversary of his death), his first article after his return from Germany. A central theme is how Rilke configures the relationship between men and the world of things. As Feng encapsulates, "He (Rilke) realized that each object has its own world, and all of the objects together constitute a real, serious, and living republic."[55] This relational living republic is exactly what Feng describes in his Venice poems as "the ideal world," the "collection of thousands of lonelinesses." In it, every individual is solitary, yet complete, and connected with other members of the world. Together they constitute a collectivity with an immanent order. The notion "other members" refers not only to fellow human beings but also to plants and animals, all animate and inanimate beings. This living republic is what Feng Zhi prayed for in his Sonnet No. 22: "Gei wo xiazai de xin/yige dade yuzhou (Dilute my narrow heart / that it may comprise the great universe), alluding to one of Goethe's letters to Johann Gottfried Herder, dated July 10, 1772, in which he wrote, "Er sprach (Moses): O mein Herr mache mir Raum in meiner engen Brust."[56] In his study of Feng Zhi's *Sonnets*, Marian Galik calls this "an astral universe," "comprising all myriads of

54. Novalis, *Schriften* 1: 3.
55. Feng, *FZQJ* 4: 85.
56. Ibid., 5: 205.

things in our world and outside of it, a kind of pantheistic *Deus sive Natura*."[57]

Stirb und Werde: *Feng Zhi's* Wu Zixu *and Goethe Studies*

Und so lang du das nicht hast,
Dieses: *Stirb und Werde*!
Bist du nur ein trüber Gast
Auf der dunklen Erde.

—Johann Wolfgang Goethe, "Selige Sehnsucht"

Central in Feng Zhi's *Sonnets* is the relationship between man and the world outside. Although Feng agrees with Rilke that human beings and the world of things are interrelated and construct a *Gemeinschaft* (community) with a fundamental order "where the root of every growth is located,"[58] this relationship in Feng's poetics is characterized by a deep uncertainty about the configuration of this very "living republic." How to define or materialize it? How to avoid sliding into a void, a utopian empty space? This dilemma significantly informed Feng's creation of *Sonnets*, which was finished between October 1940 and November 1941, a time of massive Japanese air raids on the city of Kunming. With his war exile into the vast inner China, Feng's doubt became all the more intense.

Sonnets was written during the time when Feng Zhi served as a German literature professor at the exiled Peking University, at the time part of the National Southwest Associated University in Kunming, and taught courses on German literary history, German lyric tradition, Nietzsche, Goethe, and special topics on *Faust*.[59] This collection has often been regarded as his greatest contribution to modern

57. Galik, "Feng Zhi and His Goethean Sonnet," p. 131.

58. Rilke, "Von der Landschaft," p. 521.

59. *Guoli xinan lianhe daxue xiaoshi: 1937 zhi 1946 nian de beida, tsinghua, nankai* (The university history of the Southwestern United University: Beida, Tsinghua, Nankai Universities between 1937 and 1946) (Beijing: Peking University Press, 1996), pp. 134–36.

Chinese poetry. It is innovative both structurally and thematically, a successful combination of the essences of the Western sonnet and classical Chinese poetry.[60] Among Feng's contemporaries, the poetry critic Li Guangtian, in his article written one year after *Sonnets* was published, read the sonnets as poetic meditations on life and existence, permeated with Buddhist and Taoist illuminations.[61] He Lin, the renowned Hegel scholar, even included one paragraph on Feng Zhi's poetry into his monograph on Chinese philosophy and regarded *Sonnets* in particular as "having accurately preserved poetic metrics on the one hand, and brought to bear philosophical insights and contemplations on the other hand."[62] Kai-yu Hsu considered Feng Zhi as one of the "metaphysical poets."[63] Whereas the metaphysical and philosophical aspect is highlighted in the scholarship of the 1940s, the post-Mao rediscovery of this poetry collection lauds its individual voices against the "mainstream melody" (*zhuxuanlü*) characterized by the growing ideology of collectivity during the Second Sino-Japanese War, which obviously alludes to the post-1949 socialist collectivism.[64]

However, what is largely overlooked is the profound ambivalence inherent in these twenty-seven sonnets. Although the poetic subjectivity finds a secure position in a world where all solitary objects are interconnected according to an immanent order, it is accompanied by a deep skepticism toward this very ideal republic. Sonnet No. 15 sets out to present the mystical correspondences between lives and occurrences in myriad parts of the world; the poem takes an unex-

---

60. Zhu Ziqing, for instance, praised Feng's sonnet sequence as perfectly transplanting this classical Western poetry form into the Chinese context. See Zhu, *Xinshi zahua*, p. 27. It was originally published with the same title in 1947 in Shanghai.

61. Li Guangtian, "Chensi de shi: Lun Feng Zhi de 'Shisihang ji'" (Poetry of meditations: On Feng Zhi's *Sonnets*), in *Shi de yishu* (Hong Kong: Huiwenke shudian, 1972), first published in 1943 by Kaiming shudian in Shanghai.

62. He Lin, *Wushinianlai de zhongguo zhexue*, p. 60. Originally entitled *Dangdai zhongguo zhexue* (Contemporary Chinese philosophy), the book was published in 1947 in Chongqing.

63. Kai-yu Hsu, *Twentieth-century Chinese Poetry: An Anthology*, pp. 148–55.

64. For instance, see Wang Jiaxin in Feng Yaoping, *Feng Zhi he tade shijie*. Feng Zhi scholarship in North America and Europe mainly focuses on separate motives in his poems, in particular, on the Orpheus motive. See, for instance, Cheung, *Feng Chih*; Galik, "Feng Chih's *Sonnets*; Haft, "Some Rhythmic Structures."

pected turn in the middle of the second quatrain to contest the realness of such correspondences and foregrounds the ambivalence between "the fullness of the universe" and "the deepest void": "we have passed numerous landscapes, / now possessing them, now leaving them behind, / Like a bird, fluttering in the sky, / now ruling the fullness of the universe, / now feeling the deepest void." The last tercet winds up in the urgency of three successive questions: "What is our real existence? / What have we brought from afar? / What have we to deliver from here?"[65]

The fourteen-line sonnet form contains an inherent ambivalence within its very structure. Judith Ryan, in her study of Rilke's poetry, points out that the contrastive structure of the sonnet mediates the conflict between stasis and mobility, space and time.[66] In quoting his friend Li Guangtian, Feng Zhi elucidated that he employed the sonnet form for "its rising and falling layer upon layer, concentrating gradually and dissolving, and for its structural variation and conformity, and its interweaving rhythm schemes." Thanks to its structural and rhythmic fluidity, the form constitutes an extension of his thought: "it doesn't constrain my flowing ideas, instead, it provides them a suitable composition."[67] It often has been claimed that the last sonnet in this sequence is the most salient reflection on the very process of poetic creation, on the dialect of form and content. It reads,

從一片泛濫無形的水裡，
取水人取來橢圓的一瓶，
這點水就得到一個定形；
看，在秋風裡飄揚的風旗，

它把住些把不住的事體，
讓遠方的光、遠方的黑夜
和些遠方的草木的榮謝，
還有個奔向遠方的心意，

65. Feng, *FZQJ* 1: 230. Feng Zhi's sonnets do not precisely follow the metrics of either the Petrarchan or the Shakespearean sonnet form. Each of his sonnets is constructed of two quatrains and two tercets with various rhyme schemes. I will not go into detail about the sonnet metrics in Feng's collection. Zhang Kuan points to the similarity in poetic structure between Feng's sonnets and Rilke's Orpheus sonnets; see Zhang, "A Remarkable Cultural Encounter."

66. Ryan, *Umschlag und Verwandlung*, pp. 55–65.

67. Feng, *FZQJ* 1: 214.

都保留一些在這面旗上。
我們空空聽過一夜風聲,
空看了一天的草黃葉紅,

向何處安排我們的思、想?
但願這些詩象一面風旗,
把住一些把不住的事體。[68]

From a flow of shapeless water,
The water carrier fills his oval bottle.
Thus this water obtains a definite shape;
Look, the banner that waves in the autumn wind,

Holds things that can't be held,
And it grasps the distant light, the distant night,
The wax and wane of distant grasses and trees,
And that wish to run toward the infinite,

And preserves them on this banner.
We have listened to a whole night of winds
And watched a whole day of yellow grasses and red leaves,

All in vain: where shall we dispose of our ideas?
I hope that these poems hold like a banner
Certain things that cannot be held.

Critical interpretations often emphasize that this last poem bespeaks the nature of poetic creation: like the water bottle and the banner, poetry shapes random thoughts into verse form. Dominic Cheung has noted that like the banner that serves as "a means of indicating the direction taken by the wind," the sonnet form becomes "an indicator of the imagination's movements, a means whereby the poet's inner thoughts are formalized and made manifest."[69]

What I want to call attention to, however, is a sense of crisis regarding aesthetic creation in both the theme and the structure of this sonnet. I suggest that this poem reveals the ambivalence between the dynamic movement it features and the petrified form that contains it. Whereas the bottle gives a definite form to the originally amorphous fluid water, it also cuts off the flow of the water, thus confining the infinite in the constraints of a finite container. Similarly, the dynamic current of the wind is petrified into the limited materiality of the banner. Whereas the floating poetic structure conveys thoughts

68. Feng, *FZQJ* 1: 242.
69. Cheung, "Feng Zhi: *Shisihang ji*," p. 105.

and develops them into poetry, the extreme fixation with the form paradoxically confines productivity and imprisons language and imagination, eventually leading to a dangerous, barren state of aesthetic autonomy. Therefore, rather than providing a conclusion to the argument presented in the first two quatrains, the verses from the second line of the first tercet on actually challenge it and thus serve as a turning point (*volta*). Instead of proposing a certain answer to the question "All in vain, where shall we dispose of our ideas?" the last two lines, "I hope that these poems hold like a banner / Certain things that cannot be held," express hope, but not without a hint of hesitation.

Indeed, Feng's *Sonnets* is characterized by an intriguing ambivalence between the world of interconnected solitude and its paradoxical form of infertility and isolation, between autonomous artistic creation and a total separation between the poetic and the social. In this sense, *Sonnets* is rather a reflection on the crisis than its poetic overcoming. This partly explains why Feng felt as if he had experienced a severe illness upon completion of the sonnet collection and why he was never able to write such poetry again. Also, the external political calamity, particularly after 1949, made poetry writing extremely difficult.

It was exactly this spiritual impasse that prompted Feng's 1949 transition both aesthetically and politically. The change is first anticipated in his historical fiction *Wu Zixu* (1943), which brings up the concept of endurance as a way of social engagement and Goethe's *Naturdenken* (theory of nature) of metamorphosis, the notion of *Stirb und werde* in particular, as a way of spiritual renewal. He had read Goethe's *Die Leiden des jungen Werthers* in the early 1920s, but the German *Sturm und Drang* passion struck him only temporarily. It was during the Sino-Japanese War of the late 1930s and 1940s that he came to Goethe again. Interestingly, it was late Goethe, the author of *West-östlicher Divan* (1819), *Wilhelm Meisters Wanderjahre oder die Entsagenden* (1820s), and the last version of *Faust*, that fascinated Feng Zhi and helped him forge a viable intersection between the aesthetic and the political to overcome his poetic crisis.

The overcoming of finitude through aesthetic creation is not sufficient to build an effective relationship between the poetic subject and the society. The introspective cultivation of the subject is not fertile. Feng resorted to Goethe's notion of a life of fullness, a life inward and outward, in order to expand and enrich the aesthetic experience and develop a positive relationship between the aesthetic and the social. Like Gottfried Wilhelm Leibniz (1646–1716) and Friedrich Schelling (1775–1854), Goethe thought that inner and outer experiences were comparable and inseparable. The particular reflects the whole; what is inward is also outward: "Müsset im Naturbetrachten / Immer eins wie alles achten; / Nichts ist drinnen, nichts ist draußen: / Denn was innen, das ist außen. / So ergreifet ohne Säumnis/ Heilig öffentlich Geheimnis."[70] Feng often foregrounded Goethe's notion of a dynamic unity of inward and outward forces in one's life, following the natural rhythm of the living organism, that of the eternal breathing in and out (*Ein- und Ausatmen*). He saw Goethe as a full human being who was able to balance an outward life, in which he served as a privy councilor in Weimar and observed nature, and an inward life, which "required him to disavow external business and returned to an inner world." Feng then asserted, "an outward pursuit and an inward homecoming to the self—these two forces alternate and exert mutual impacts, which gradually uplifts and deepens Goethe's feelings and thoughts."[71] He quoted from *Wilhelm Meisters Wanderjahre* to further illustrate Goethe's efforts to fuse an inward and outward life: "Denken und Tun, Tun und Denken, das ist die Summe aller Weisheit, von jeher anerkannt, von jeher geübt, nicht eingesehen von einem jeden. Beides muss wie Aus- und Einatmen sich im Leben ewig fort hin und wider bewegen; wie Frage und Antwort sollte eins ohne das andere nicht stattfinden" (Thinking and Doing, Doing and Thinking, from all time admitted, from all time practised, but not discerned by every one. Like expiration and inhalation, the two must forever be pulsating backwards and forwards in life; like question and answer, the one cannot exist without the other).[72]

Feng often reflected that at the heart of his Goethe reception and interpretation were three notions: the affirmative spirit; *Metamorphosenlehre*, an everlasting process of transmutation and becoming

---

70. Goethe, "Epirrhema," in *Sämtliche Werke*. Münchner Ausgabe, Bd. 12: 92.

71. Feng, *FZQJ* 8: 7.

72. The English translation comes from *Wilhelm Meister's Travels*, book 2, p. 264. In *Goethe's works,* vol. 9, edited and translated by Edward Bell (London: George Bell and Sons, 1885).

through death and rebirth; and the unity of an outward and an inward life.[73] He regarded *Faust* as a work of contestation between the affirmative, positive and the passive, negative forces, which enabled him to resist the nihilistic and pessimistic atmosphere pervasive in wartime China. Feng Zhi was particularly fascinated by Goethe's idea of metamorphosis (*Gestaltung-Umgestaltung*) and by such images of transition as the chrysalis and the snake repeatedly shedding its skin. Similar images often appear in Feng's 1940s writings: for instance, in Sonnet No. 2, lines 7–9, "we arrange ourselves / In nature, as cicadas and moths / Cast all old skins into the mud."[74] The third stanza of Sonnet No. 3 starts with "You are shedding your shell all the time, / and grow in the moment of withering."[75] In life's enduring mutability, Feng saw its force of renewal and eternity. In his reading, the concept of metamorphosis is best illustrated in Goethe's poem "Selige Sehnsucht" (Spiritual yearning), which praises the dynamics of the life force and its perfection as it unfolds in an upward spiral of deaths and rebirths.[76]

Feng Zhi quoted Goethe's maxim *Stirb und werde* in the last line of his Sonnet No. 13, dedicated to Goethe:

你生長在平凡的市民的家庭，
你為過許多良家的女孩流淚，
在一代雄主的面前你也敬畏；
你八十年的歲月是那樣平靜，

好象宇宙在那兒寂寞地運行，
但是不曾有一分一秒的停息，
隨時隨處都演化出新的生機，
不管風風雨雨或是日朗天晴。

從沉重的病中換來新的健康，
從絕望的愛裡換來新的營養，
你知道飛蛾為什麼投向火焰，

73. See Feng, *FZQJ* 8: 72–80; 5: 219–21.

74. Ibid., 1: 217.

75. Ibid., 1: 218.

76. This poem has had a surprisingly powerful impact on modern Chinese poetry. The notion of *Stirb und werde* is elucidated several times in Feng Zhi's writings and especially in his Sonnet No. 13, "Goethe." Zheng Min, a poet who was later regarded as member of the Jiuye (Nine leaves) poetry group, also wrote a poem responding to Goethe's "Selige Sehnsucht."

蛇為什麼脫去舊皮才能生長；
萬物都在享用你的那句名言，
它道破一切生的意義："死和變。"[77]

You were born into a family of commoners,
shed tears for many ordinary girls,
You feared, revered the one who rules the realm,
and lived a life of eighty tranquil years.

Just as the globe turns silently,
without a minute or a second's rest,
new signs evolve, all the time, everywhere,
in wind and rain, fair weather and foul,

comes new health from heavy sickness
new strength out of desperate love;
you know why moths plunge into fire,

why snakes shed their skins in growth;
all things observe your creed
which reveals the meaning of life: Death and metamorphosis.

This English translation was done by Cheung.[78] In his Chinese rendition of the Goethean notion *Stirb und werde*, Feng chose the characters *si yu bian*, which Cheung translated into English as "death and metamorphosis." Later, in his 1947 essay "Gede de xidong heji" (Goethe's *West-Eastern Divan*), Feng translated the entire poem "Spiritual Yearning" into Chinese and further considered the significance of self-sacrifice and spiritual rebirth conveyed in it. Galik points out that Feng Zhi's translation and interpretation of *Stirb und werde* as "dying and transforming" were actually not accurate. *werden* here means *vollenden*, "make perfection," rather than "transform."[79] Feng himself was not unaware of the semantic deviation. When he resumed Goethe research after the Cultural Revolution, he clarified his decision to translate the German imperative *werde* as *bian* (metamorphosis or change) in a 1982 study of Goethe's poetry. He eluci-

77. This sonnet comes from the first edition of *Sonnets* published by the Mingri Press in Guilin in May 1942. After the Cultural Revolution, when *Sonnets* was republished in 1980 by the Renmin Press in Sichuan, Feng Zhi made some major revisions. In Sonnet No. 13, he changed the second and third lines into "你為過許多平凡的事物感嘆， / 你卻寫出許多不平凡的詩篇。"

78. Cheung, "Feng Zhi: *Shisihang ji* (Sonnets), 1942." In *A Selective Guide to Chinese Literature*, 1900–1949.

79. For Galik's discussion, see "Feng Zhi and His Goethean Sonnet," pp. 123–34.

dated that a faithful rendition of the original word *werde* is *wancheng* (self-fulfillment, perfection). However, he could not find a better monosyllablic word in Chinese than *bian* to render *werde*, and thus remained firm about his original choice.[80] Feng's linguistic considerations notwithstanding, the conspicuous semantic differences of *bian* (metamorphosis) and *wancheng* (self-fulfillment) and his preference of the former indicated that Feng interpreted *Stirb und werde* as representing Goethe's *Metamorphosenlehre.*

This principle applies to the development of not only plants and insects but also human beings and the society. Accordingly, Feng found in Goethe's *Entwicklungsroman* (development novel, or Bildungsroman) the best novelization of the theory of metamorphosis in the human world: "The growth of the protagonist of the novel *Wilhelm Meister* also goes through development from one stage to the next, until he eventually understands the meaning of life, which therefore contributes the notion of *Entwicklungsroman* to German literary history. However, the advance from one phase to the next is not easy. One has to experience an arduous death of the previous phase in order to fulfill a happy rebirth of the next one."[81] Feng Zhi stays close to scholars such as Konrad Burdach, who in his note "Anmerkungen" to the Cotta edition of *Goethes Sämtliche Werke* (Complete works of Goethe) understands the formula *Stirb und werde* to reflect Goethe's natural philosophy. What intrigues Feng is not the moth's surrender to the two primal forces, Eros and the death instinct, but rather its desire for light, a higher form of self-fulfillment through the mediation of enlightenment. In his reading, it is through self-annulment or self-absorption into the light that the moth is able to overcome the lower form of consummation of carnal love to accomplish the ultimate spiritual enlightenment and perfection. In this, Feng is a scholar of the Enlightenment par excellence, much like his spiritual mentor Goethe. In a 1980s elucidation of "Spiritual Yearning," Feng quoted two lines from a poem by King Wu of the Liang dynasty, which used the same image of a moth incinerating itself in a flame to illustrate the idea of obtaining artistic perfection

80. Feng, *FZQJ* 8: 149.
81. Ibid., 8: 7.

through self-sacrifice. In comparing King Wu's poem with Goethe's, he asserted that the latter's moth imagery contains a deeper dialectic meaning of "sacrifice and completion, death and rebirth."[82] For Feng, the earlier titles of "Spiritual Yearning," "Selbstopfer" (Self-sacrifice) or "Vollendung," are probably more incisive.

Feng Zhi's work *Wu Zixu* best illustrates his reflections on the Goethean concept of death and becoming. *Wu Zixu* is composed in the vein of Lu Xun's *Gushi xinbian* (Old tales retold); both works employ historical tales as sources of literary imagination, and they are both written in poetic prose. Wu Zixu (559? BC–484 BC) is a famous historical figure of the Spring-Autumn period. The junior son of an ex-Chu official, Zixu fled the state of Chu to seek revenge for his father's death. Exiled, he passed through a number of different states, finally sought asylum in the state of Wu, and helped it become one of the strongest states of the time. With the help of the Wu army, Zixu eventually conquered his home country, the state of Chu, and lynched the dead body of the former Chu king who was responsible for his father's death. Historical accounts of Wu Zixu can be found in *Shiji* (The records of the grand historian), *Chunqiu sanzhuan* (Three commentaries on *Spring and Autumn Annals*), and *Wuyue chunqiu* (The spring and autumn annals of Wu and Yue), among which the last contains the most thorough biographical records. Feng Zhi's novelization of Zixu's story largely follows that work's chronological line. Whereas other historical or fictional accounts mainly focus on the dramatic experiences of war, revenge, and betrayal, Feng takes only Zixu's exile as the subject, exploring his journey from the city Chengfu in the state of Chu to the state of Wu. Of the nine chapters, each devoted to one of the critical locations where Zixu's physical and psychological transitions occur, "Wanqiu" and "Yanling" are Feng's fictional additions.

As early as 1924, when he was an undergraduate student in the German department at Peking University and read Rilke's prose poem *Die Weise von Liebe und Tod des Cornets Christoph Rilke* (The lay of love and death of Cornet Christopher Rilke), Feng Zhi came up with the idea to write about Wu Zixu in a similar literary style. He

---

82. Ibid., 8: 149.

later recalled that he was immediately touched by "the rich color, fine tone, and haunting melancholic and mysterious atmosphere" of this piece.[83] Although *Cornet* was one of Rilke's few works that enjoyed popular success even during his lifetime, scholarship on it has been surprisingly sparse. Judith Ryan points to the tension between "neo-Romantic sensibilities and modernist understandings of the psyche" and regards this work as an important transitional piece in Rilke's literary trajectory.[84] The text's musicality, explorations of interiority, and highly stylish combination of aestheticism and historicism must be among the main features that prompted the young Feng Zhi to write about the legendary historical character Wu Zixu in the same manner: "The evening in Zhaoguan, the twilight over the Yangtze River, and the sunshine in Li River, all these scenes flash like pieces of melody through my mind. However, I couldn't catch them."[85]

Indeed, it was not until sixteen years later that Feng started to write *Wu Zixu*. The final version is totally different from the initial idea of a romantic retelling of a historical story. As Feng observes in the afterword, "comparing (it) with that prose poem by Rilke, there is nothing the same or even similar. It lacks musical elements, as well as a certain kind of innocence. There are many mundane events, which reflect the calamity experienced by modern men, especially by Chinese people in recent years."[86] The inclusion of these "mundane events" of personal and national calamity during the war is precisely what makes *Wu Zixu* not just an aesthetic success but a work with an incisive concern for social realities in a transitional historical time. The poetic subject does not indulge in the divine beauty of nature symbolized in the scene of "Linze" (The woods), "aware that there would come the day when there would be no innocent place left uncorrupted anymore."[87]

---

83. Ibid., 5: 83. Rilke's prose poem *The Lay of Love and Death of Cornet Christopher Rilke* has several Chinese renditions and is still very popular among Chinese readers today. The prevalent translations are 軍旗手的愛與死之歌 by Liang Zongdai (1903–83) and 旗手克裡斯托夫·里爾克的愛與死之歌 by Bian Zhilin (1910–2000); both translators were themselves prominent poets in the 1930s and 1940s.

84. Ryan, *Rilke, Modernism and Poetic Tradition*, pp. 32–41.

85. Feng, *FZQJ* 3: 426.

86. Ibid., 3: 427.

87. Ibid., 3: 375–82.

He "cherishes his own harsh destiny" and disavows the preservation of pure interiority and noble personality represented in the figure of Jizha in "Yanling" (The town of Yanling),[88] who refuses to accept the position of king to avoid contaminating his integrity with political and social engagements. Even the loss of the mother that pervades Feng's work from the very beginning of his literary career is transformed into the scene of the laundry woman who offers Zixu rice—an allegorical image of the mother of life and goddess of order, thus sublimated into the mythology of genesis:

> This is a timeless eternal picture: in the middle of the field, a female body, on her knees in front of a foreign man, as if burgeoning from the meadow, holds a basin of white rice. Who is this man? She doesn't know. Perhaps a soldier, perhaps a saint. Taken into his body, this basin of rice will grow into towering trees, like seeds planted into soils. This picture vanishes briefly—yet, it remains forever in the field of humanity, and turns into a significant chapter of human history." (Lishui)[89]

In this way, Zixu bids farewell to the innocent dreams and ideals of his past and marches arduously yet firmly toward the "ugly society," to confront the site "full of spider webs, which stick to the body with every step."[90] Some ten years earlier, unable to bear severe psychological anxieties, Feng had to quit his teaching position and run away from the foreign, ugly city Harbin, "which stands clearly in Chinese territory, but is full of exotic tones . . . like those colossal, gray cities often read about in Northern European literature."[91] His long poem "Northern Expedition" best delineates the immense feeling of frustration and alienation of the poetic subject. Feng quoted the last sentence of *Der kleine Johannes* (Little John), written by the Dutch writer and psychiatrist Frederik van Eeden (1860–1932), as the epigraph for his poem: "Und mit seinem Begleiter ging er den frostigen Nachtwinde entgegen, den schweren Weg nach der grossen, finstern Stadt, wo die Menschheit war und ihr Weh" (And with his companion, against the freezing evening wind, he embarked on the road to that

88. Ibid., 3: 413–17.
89. Ibid., 3: 411.
90. Ibid., 3: 401.
91. Ibid., 1: 123.

big, sinister city, where humanity and its calamity are located.).[92] The colossal, sinister place of human society, which once marked for the young poet the calamity of humanity, becomes the destination of Zixu, who resolutely embraces his dreadful yet heroic destiny.

In the critical chapter "Zhaoguan" (The pass of Zhao), Feng describes Zixu's ultimate disavowal of his physical and emotional attachment to his past and his hometown. The Pass of Zhao marks the last station in Zixu's home state of Chu, a point of no return. Through an excruciating sleepless night at this frontier station between Chu and Wu, Zixu completes the key phase of *Stirb und werde* in his life of exile and vengeance:

> He imagined that it would be a new and free world on the other side of the forest and the mountain. Once he was able to go across the forest and the mountain, he would feel as if he had shed a heavy layer of skin off his body. Zixu now fully appreciated the agony of a silkworm shedding its skin. The old skin is no longer connected to the body closely, yet it still latches on and won't be discarded; on the other hand, the new tender skin is constantly yearning for the contact with the external air. Zixu felt that the new skin was growing and maturing, but when could he completely cast off his old skin?[93]

The poetic subject, *der Entsagende*, eventually disavows the divine beauty of nature as well as introspective self-cultivation, in order to embrace the idea of social and political commitment as the highest form of self-fulfillment through a series of transformations and self-sacrifices, through the unification of the inward and outward aspects of life. Notably, Rilke's poetic musicality and form shape the poetic world of Wu Zixu, whereas Goethe's conception of metamorphosis—death and spiritual rebirth—informs its thematic structure.

The central theme of *Wu Zixu* is not revenge but "a parabolic trajectory" of transformation, which Feng regarded as the best manifestation of the Goethean notion of *Stirb und werde*. In the postscript, Feng elucidates that "a piece of beautiful life, be it for love or hatred,

---

92. Ibid., 1: 153. Van Eeden's 1887 book was translated by Lu Xun from German to Chinese in 1926. When Feng referred to it, the version he read must have been the Chinese, for the phrase "with his companion" was missing. For some reason, Lu Xun omitted it. Yet, had Feng Zhi known of this interesting slip, his journey to "that big, sinister city" without any companion would have been more dreadful.

93. Ibid., 3: 398–99.

for life or death, is like tracing a parabola: there is persistence in the standstill, overcoming in the descending."[94] For Zixu, *Stirb und werde* means the abandonment of freedom and the simultaneous confinement in moral perfection and self-preservation, and unreserved self-submergence in a higher unity, social responsibility as analogized by revenge. The trajectory of metamorphosis through phases of disavowal and selection marks Feng's idea of enlightenment, spiritual renewal, and self-fulfillment. In contemplating Goethe's notion of *entsagen* (disavow), Feng regarded it as the crucial and affirmative stage of one's spiritual rebirth (he rendered it as *duannian* in Chinese). The following passage in one of his Goethe studies, written in 1947, easily reminds us of Zixu at the Pass of Zhao:

> He (Goethe) imagines, after many restraints, once he is able to achieve that goal, he will see freedom of a higher form, desire of a more profound mode, waiting for him. Therefore, no matter how desolate these notions "disavow" and "renounce" may sound, one always feels positive connotations when reading them in Goethe's work: the richer one's emotions are, the stronger the power one needs to restrain oneself. Both sides are growing, stimulating, and containing each other simultaneously, and will eventually merge and form the classic Goethe.[95]

After completing *Wu Zixu*, Feng came out of his hitherto reclusive academic life and participated in various social and political gatherings and demonstrations. Accordingly, he turned to writing critical essays on cultural and social issues and published dozens of articles in leading newspapers.[96] In these social critiques, key words such as *jianchi* (persistence), *kefu* (overcoming), *chengdan* (sustentation), and *rennai* (endurance) anticipate that famous editor's note quoted at the beginning of this section. Like the protagonist in *Wu Zixu*, he turned his back on his past, marked by aesthetic beauty and the serenity of nature, and embarked on the road leading to the "big, sinister city," where humanity and its calamities are located, yet simultaneously,

---

94. Ibid., 3: 425.

95. Ibid., 8: 74.

96. Interestingly, these articles were later collected into the volume "Wentan bianyuan suibi" (Casual articles on the margin of literature), as part of the fifth volume of *Complete works of Feng Zhi*, which indicates that Feng Zhi was surely aware of the "unusual" nature of these essays and regarded them as something "on the margin."

there is a positive life of social commitment. He finally embraced the challenge he had failed to meet in Harbin and went toward the society and the crowds, with those beauties he had experienced embedded in his heart and incorporated into his life. With this determination, when confronted with the crucial 1949 division in China, Feng Zhi chose to stay on the mainland and embrace the socialist state. How did his journey to the social reality turn out?

Shakespeare as a Weapon for Rightists: A Modern China beyond Capitalist Humanism

In July 1949, Feng Zhi participated as the associate director of the Beijing delegation to the First All-China Congress of Literary and Art Representatives, from which his friend and colleague Shen Congwen was excluded, having been denied the honor of being a cultural worker in the People's Republic. In an article published on July 2, 1949, in the leading party newspaper *Renmin ribao* (People's daily), Feng described his feelings right before attending this inaugural conference of socialist literature:

> I as an individual, an attendee of this conference, feel at this moment a deep responsibility that I have never felt before: from now on, every word I write will take responsibility for this whole new society, just as every brick and tile must take responsibility for the whole building. This makes me realize a clear sincerity that I have never realized before: I have to wash off all the narrow characteristics of intellectuals in front of the people. At this moment I hear a forceful call that I have never heard before: "The need of the people!" If more fire is needed, make yourself a piece of wood and throw yourself into the fire; if more water is needed, make yourself a drop of water and throw yourself into the water.[97]

While the syntactic and semantic features of this paragraph, such as metaphorical images and parallel couplets, are strong reminders of the lyrical nature of Chinese classical literature, the critical idea of self-transformation for the sake of a larger totality reflects the core ideology of the new socialist republic. And one has to take Feng's enthusiasm and sincerity seriously. In 1949, Feng Zhi made a seemingly unproblematic merge into the new state, into the republic of

---

97. Feng, *FZQJ* 5: 341.

collectivity for which he had been yearning. He was appointed a member of the Chinese delegation to Hungary, Czechoslovakia, the German Democratic Republic, and the Soviet Union, while Ding Ling was busy flying around the Soviet Union and East European socialist countries representing liberated new Chinese women. In the 1950s, Feng was successively assigned as editor of the literary column of *People's Daily*, associate editor-in-chief of the People's Literature Publishing House, chair of the Department of Western European Languages and Literatures at Peking University, and member of the Chinese Academy of Social Sciences, among other positions.[98] In June 1956, he joined the Chinese Communist Party, which marked the ultimate acknowledgment of his successful assimilation into the socialist regime.

What appears perplexing is not just that Feng became an illustrious public figure in the post-1949 socialist regime, but more intriguingly, that he did it without a strenuous process of assimilation, something as contradictory as his previous history. However, it would be all too convenient to dismiss the case by charging that Feng was a political opportunist and his post-1949 career a total betrayal of his poetic ideal. I suggest that Feng's 1949 transition must be viewed in the larger context of his embrace of the notions of poetic affinity, metamorphosis, and a new collectivity formulated in his contemplations of the 1940s, in particular, with regard to his study and translation of Rilke and Goethe. The shock of the infinite solitude of aesthetic beauty forced him to seek a more dynamic and fruitful relationship with the external world. As discussed in the previous section, his determination to confront the social reality and engage in pursuits connected with the lofty entity of people had already started to take shape in *Wu Zixu*. It transformed the poet and professor in the ivory tower into a clumsy yet resolute figure amid political gatherings and protests as early as 1943. It is therefore not surprising that his research and writing of the 1940s favored Goethe of Weimar Classicism and Du Fu over all other poets, Chinese and foreign, classical and modern. All personal and political contingencies

---

98. For a complete list of official positions Feng Zhi took in the 1950s and 1960s, see Lu Yaodong, *Feng Zhi zhuan*, pp. 230–31.

notwithstanding,[99] Feng's 1949 transition was not that unforeseen after all.

In Chinese socialism, Feng envisioned a new collectivity, a living republic, and a higher stage of life force. In the socialist totality, he anticipated an opening to a capacious relationality and a possible emplacement of the aesthetic subject within a larger Whole. The redemption of the aesthetic subject can only be achieved through its total absorption into the national collectivity. The socialist totality would set the normative framework for, yet simultaneously free, the aesthetic and the political subject. Only in the socialist society would the bourgeois humanist ideal of the unity of "freedom and law, the individual and the collective" be realized, as manifested in the closing lines in Goethe's sonnet "Natur und Kunst" (Nature and art): "In der Beschränkung zeigt sich erst der Meister, / Und das Gesetz nur kann uns Freiheit geben."[100]

---

99. As some biographies and friends' recollections point out, one important family reason for Feng's embrace of the CCP regime is that his wife, Yao Kekun, was elected as representative to the First People's Congress of the Republic of China in 1948. This suspicious political affiliation rendered Feng's political choice at the time all the more urgent. Given the millions of purges during political campaigns in the first few decades of the Communist regime caused by suspicious family history, Feng's concern and determination at that transitional moment seem rather clever. Another political engagement that would have endangered Feng's post-1949 career was his membership in *Zhongguo shehui jingji yanjiu hui* (The association of Chinese social and economic studies), which gathered many liberal intellectuals including Xiao Qian and was later condemned by the leftists as promoting "a third road."

100. Feng, "Lüelun ouzhou zichan jieji wenxue li de rendao zhuyi he geren zhuyi" (On humanism and individualism in European bourgeois literature), in *Beijing daxue xuebao* (Journal of Peking University), 1 (1958): 19. This article was first published in *Journal of Peking University* in 1958 and later included in the collection *Shi yu yichan* (Poetry and legacy) in 1963. *Poetry and Legacy* is the only anthology of Feng's scholarly articles between the establishment of the People's Republic of China in 1949 and the outbreak of the Cultural Revolution in 1966, which revealed his ideological and cultural accommodations and his determination to acquire Marxist Maoist discourse in the fledgling socialist state. When *Poetry and Legacy* was republished in *Complete Works of Feng Zhi* in 1999, the editor noted that few changes had been made to the highly politicized terms and language used in the original articles, in order to remain faithful to the specific historical situation of high socialism. However, in the above-mentioned article included in *Complete Works of Feng Zhi* (*FZQJ* 6: 270–88), the passages on Goethe and Feng's socialist criticism of *Faust* and *Wilhelm Meister* were deleted.

When Feng decisively dedicated himself to "the need of the people" in the newly founded socialist republic, the notion *renmin* (people) was conspicuously distinct from his earlier conceptualization of *gongzhong* (the mass) in the 1940s. In "Yige duiyu shidai de piping" (A criticism on our time), written in 1941, he observes:

> *Gongzhong* (the mass) merges all "individuals" to become a totality. But this totality is most unreliable and irresponsible, because it is nothingness. An age, a nation, a group, an "individual," they are all substantial existences, thus able to have senses of responsibility, shame, and conscientiousness—of which the public doesn't possess a single one.
>
> However, whoever plunges into this sea of the public will indeed turn into nothingness. The concrete turns into the abstract. Those people on the shore are as disparate as ice and charcoal. Once thrust into this sea, the ice stops being cold and the charcoal hot. This is indeed the ideal state of "equalitarianism"! It is everything and nothing, it is as omnipotent as God, yet without any sense of responsibility any living being should possess.[101]

If Feng's poetics in the 1940s passed through a transformation defined by a Goethean *Stirb und werde*, this process of dying and becoming must be characterized by the leap from the concept of *gongzhong* (the mass), which is essentially a nothingness, to that of *renmin* (the people), which calls out with urgency and into which the poet plunges himself decisively. The idea of the people was so appealing to him at the 1949 division because it represented a totality with "senses of responsibility, shame, and conscientiousness," thus overcoming the illusory notion of *gongzhong*, which sucked all individuals into the void. In this new collectivity, a living republic, individuals would be interconnected to a common root or an immanent order. The need of the people, a "new collectivity as anticipated in Goethe's *Wilhelm Meisters Wanderjahre*," is the ultimate call for Feng Zhi across the Cold War division.[102] Although the 1949 transition marked the distinction between these two disparate notions of collectivity, whether or not the new People's Republic amounted to the living republic Feng had envisioned remains moot. Is this common root to be specified as the party, the immanent order as the new socialist ideology? The question remains unresolved and unexplored in Feng's post-1949 writings.

---

101. Feng, *FZQJ* 8: 246.
102. Ibid., 8: 85–86.

As an emergent high-cultural celebrity, Feng Zhi published *Xijiao ji* (The western suburb, 1958), his first and only poetry collection in the post-1949 epoch. Written as "a response to the evil cries of the Rightists," this volume includes nothing but political hymns. It suffices to look at the titles to predict their contents: "Gechang angang" (Glorifying Anshan steelworks), "Weida de shiye" (Great deeds), "Wo de ganxie" (My gratitude), "Gei meiguo qinlüezhe" (To American invaders), and "Women gaohu" (We shout out loudly).[103] In the epilogue, Feng noted that "these poems are poor in quality, however, comparing them with my preliberation (i.e., pre-1949) poems, I believe that I embarked upon a correct road, and this road is the one marked by 'Everything is for the people, not for myself.' "[104] To be sure, these works can hardly be defined as poetry, given Feng's "preliberation" achievement. However, even his most coarse political hymns are informed by his consideration of the ambiguous notion of collectivity. The opening poem of *The Western Suburb*, "Women de xijiao" (Our western suburb), is a salient example. Following a glorification of the western suburb of Beijing under the socialist construction, the last two stanzas read,

從前有過一個天真的詩人，
要從一朵野花裡看見天堂；
一朵野花的確很美好，
但是他的天堂未免太渺茫。

我們卻從這天天生長的西郊，
看見了祖國從首都到邊疆
在千千萬萬勞動者的手裡
轉變成幸福的地上的天堂。[105]

There was once a naïve poet,
He wanted to see heaven in a wild flower;
A wild flower is indeed very beautiful,
But his heaven was rather too vague.

We, however, from this growing western suburb,
See that our motherland, from the capital to the frontier,
In the hands of thousands of workers
Has become a blissful heaven on earth.

---

103. Ibid., 2: 13–134.
104. Ibid., 2: 133.
105. Ibid., 2: 14.

This "naïve poet" is without question the English poet William Blake, whose poem "Auguries of Innocence" was translated into Chinese by Liang Zongdai, the Chinese translator of Rilke's *Cornet*.[106] Blake is another major European poet who strongly influenced Feng Zhi's work. Cheung notes a resemblance between Feng's early poems and Blake's lyrics.[107] In fact, Feng's first poetry collection, published in 1927, *Songs of Yesterday*, uses a drawing by Blake on its cover. What motivated Feng Zhi to refer to the opening lines of Blake's poem in the post-1949 context was evidently considerations of the correlation between the poetic subjectivity and the outer world: "To see a world in a grain of sand, / And a heaven in a wild flower, / Hold infinity in the palm of your hand, / And eternity in an hour." Indeed, in the heyday of socialist modernization marked by the Great Leap Forward, the Blakean ideals of poetic subjectivity and disinterested eternal beauty, which are central to Western humanistic thought, had to be obliterated.

How to deal with the Western intellectual heritage, which has been an indispensible part of the formation of Chinese modernity, remains a volatile yet resilient question within the official cultural discourse of the CCP. One of the key debates that emerged in the early years of the young socialist republic was concerned with the "abstract concept of human being and humanity that the eighteenth-century European humanism advocated."[108] The notion of a human being free of any class and political attributes was the core issue of the *renxing lun* (on the nature of humanity) versus *jieji lun* (on the nature of class identity) controversy. The debates on the European intellectual legacy and humanism remained unresolved and repressed during the politically radical decades of the Mao era; they would burst out right after the end of the Cultural Revolution and occupy the center of intellectual attention in the Deng Xiaoping era. The first significant post-Mao theoretic debate would again focus on

---

106. This poem has several Chinese renditions, among which Liang Zongdai's and Zong Baihua's are the most popular. Zong Baihua (1897–1986) was a renowned scholar of German philosophy and aesthetic theory who studied at Universität Berlin in the mid-1920s.

107. Cheung, "Feng Zhi: *Zuori zhi ge*," p. 98.

108. Wang Hui, "Humanism as the Theme."

Marxist humanism and the issue of alienation that Marx discussed in his *Economic and Philosophical Manuscripts of 1844*.[109]

In the 1956 Hundred Flowers Campaign (*baihua qifang, baijia zhengming*; let a hundred flowers bloom and a hundred schools of thought contend), in which the CCP encouraged its critics to speak out, a few key articles contributed to the promotion of universal humanity that transcended class consciousness: Qian Gurong, "Lun 'wenxue shi renxue'" (On "Literature is the study of humanity," *Literature & Arts Monthly*, no. 9 [1956]); Ba Ren, "Lun renqing" (On human feelings, *New Port*, no. 1 [1957]); and Wang Shuming, "Lun renqing he renxing" (On human feelings and human nature, *New Port*, no. 7 [1957]); among others.[110] In the subsequent Anti-Rightist Campaign with accelerating radical ideological control by the party, Feng Zhi, now an intellectual authority whose conference presentations and articles "were often interpretations of party policies,"[111] fiercely reproached the advocacy of bourgeois humanistic ideals. Although it might go too far to accuse him of being a party accomplice purging his fellow writers, Feng was without doubt high up in the very power structure that produced and surveilled literary and cultural discourses in the fledgling socialist state. In addition to his literary criticism and editing of key official newspapers and periodicals, he was on the supervision committee of national textbook compilation and composition for the humanities at higher educational institutions. In articles such as "Lüelun ouzhou zichan jieji wenxue li de rendao zhuyi he geren zhuyi" (On humanism and individualism in European bourgeois literature) and "Cong youpai fenzi qiequ de yizhong 'wuqi' tanqi" (On a "weapon" stolen by the rightists), Feng set out to reevaluate European humanistic and individualist ideas

---

109. For a discussion of the humanism debates in the 1980s and 1990s, see Wang Hui, "Humanism as the Theme"; Xudong Zhang, *Postsocialism and Cultural Politics*, pp. 25–101; He Guimei, *"Xin qimeng" zhishi dang'an*, pp. 51–114.

110. Hong Zicheng, *History of Contemporary Chinese Literature*, p. 45. Accordingly to the study of He Guimei, this wave of advocacy of humanism was also triggered by the intellectual transformation in the Thaw period in the Soviet Union; see He Guimei, *"Xin qimeng" zhishi dang'an*.

111. Hong Zicheng, *Wenti yu fangfa*, p. 234. In the article, Hong Zicheng points out that Feng's cultural criticism amounted to political intervention in art and literature.

and warned young socialist readers that oeuvres of great Western minds such as Shakespeare, Voltaire, and Goethe could be easily "stolen" by rightists as reactionary weapons against socialism. By coining "an abstract supraclass and suprareal notion of the human being," Feng wrote, the antagonist rightists intended to overthrow the party and the socialist system.[112] Accusing his former colleagues in the republic of letters of stealing bourgeois humanistic weapons for antiparty purposes, Feng's authoritative voice amounted to what He Guimei called the "embodiment of power, exerting judgments of historical violence."[113]

In "On Humanism and Individualism in European Bourgeois Literature," Feng utilized a newly adopted aesthetic discourse of "Marxist historical materialism," which highlighted a heroic sublime figure of the people as a collective subject of history in a teleological trajectory of progress, to reinterpret Faust's verses before his death as envisioning a socialist utopia: "Solch ein Gewimmel möcht ich sehn, / Auf freiem Grund mit freiem Volke stehn!" (Such a throng I would like to see, / stand on a free soil with a people free!)[114] Feng contended that in Goethe's time, "when the proletariat had just begun to form a class," it was never possible to actualize such a utopian vision. In the twentieth century, however, this ultimate goal had been "achieved in socialist countries led by the party of the working class."[115] Therefore, in Goethe's time, the final scene could be nothing more than a Catholic transcendental illusion.

In proposing this statement, Feng Zhi went even further than did Georg Lukács in his speech, "Unser Goethe," at the celebration of Goethe's 200th birthday in the German Democratic Republic (GDR)

---

112. Feng, "On Humanism and Individualism in European Bourgeois Literature," *Journal of Peking University* 1 (1958): 21.

113. He Guimei, *Zhuanzhe de shidai*, p. 202. Feng's articles written during the Anti-Rightist Campaign indeed served as "weapons" in the purge of some of his fellow writers. A case in point is his 1958 article, "Bo Ai Qing de 'Liaojie zuojia, zunzhong zuojia'" (Critique on Ai Qing's "To understand writers, to respect writers"), which was included in the now notorious collection *Zai pipan* (Re-critique) published in *Wenyi bao* (Literary gazette) on January 26, 1958, with an editorial introduction revised by Mao Zedong himself. This collection was a key document that sealed the fate of a group of eminent writers, including Ding Ling and Ai Qing.

114. Goethe, *Faust. Der Tragödie zweiter Theil in fünf Acten*, verse 11579–11580.

115. He Guimei, *Zhuanzhe de shidai*, pp. 19–20.

in 1949.[116] Lukács asserts that Faust's final vision of "a free people on free land" could only be composed by Goethe when he saw "contemporary capitalism penetrating into the corrupt world of the Holy Roman Empire."[117] In Lukács's view, Goethe's work, in a realistic manner, reflected the emergence of capitalism in splintered Germany. In *Goethe und seine Zeit*, which laid the cornerstone for the East German interpretation of the classical Goethe, Lukács discusses Goethe and his work against the backdrop of the political and cultural history of his time, in particular, the desperate combat of the growing bourgeoisie against the oppressive feudal conditions in Germany.[118] In the 1950s, when he had to reevaluate Goethe according to the dominant socialist ideology in the PRC, Feng may or may not have been aware of Lukács's Goethe studies. After all, Lukács was also denounced in socialist China after the 1956 Hungarian Revolution, and in other socialist countries including the GDR.[119] However, Feng was well acquainted with the official cultural policy in the GDR, especially that regarding Goethe. According to his later recollections, when he taught Goethe at Peking University during the 1950s, he followed the major thesis of Goethe assessment advocated in the GDR: Goethe held a positive attitude toward the French Revolution; Goethe maintained a socialist vision for the human being as evidenced in Faust's final lines; and Goethe was a classical realist, as he expressed in one of his conversations with Eckermann that "Klassisch ist das Gesunde, romantisch das Kranke."[120]

---

116. Lukács, *Goethe und seine Zeit*, pp. 330–65.

117. Ibid.

118. Since Lukács tended to stay remote from the actual literary texts, Herbert Marcuse in his review of *Goethe und seine Zeit* in 1950 criticized that Lukács's methods failed to connect the social analysis with that of the literary style and content of Goethe's work. See Marcuse, "Review of Georg Lukács, *Goethe und Seine Zeit.*"

119. In the 1960s, after the Soviet Union started to reevaluate Lukács and his work, socialist China paid more attention to Lukács and began to introduce his work systematically. Feng Zhi was a member of the group that worked on a selection and translation of Lukács's writings from German into Chinese in the 1960s, shortly before the outbreak of the Cultural Revolution. However, these weren't published until 1980.

120. Feng , *FZQJ* 8: 9–10. For a study of Goethe's reception in East Germany, see, for instance, Daniel J. Farrelly, *Goethe in East Germany, 1949–1989;* for a discussion of the reception of Weimarer Klassik in the GDR with regard to the Bauerbach case, see Ingeborg Cleve, "Subverted Heritage and Subversive Memory."

Although Feng knew all too well the party policy behind these partial or distorted opinions, he remained convinced that a re-(mis)interpretation of Goethe was necessary to help forge a national culture and collectivity in socialist Germany as well as socialist China.

Despite all his sincere efforts to accommodate the new relation between the individual and the national, the poetic subject and the political being, ironically, Feng Zhi would eventually came to realize that "naïve poet" referred not just to William Blake but also himself. When he began in the socialist state with his resolution of embracing the collectivity, Feng might not have expected that his idea about fulfilling the mission of the poetic subject through social engagement could only be realized by the total annihilation of that very subject. In the Maoist era of radical collectivism, the monstrous, nameless totality could only be materialized through the obliteration of any individual voices. Therefore, it is no wonder that Feng was not capable of continuing to create poetry with "good quality,"[121] or to be precise, with an original voice. Moreover, he had to forcefully condemn this type of "preliberation" poetry, in particular, his *Sonnets*, as "deeply influenced by capitalist literature and depraved in both content and form."[122] When the first German literary history was composed "collectively" in socialist China, Feng Zhi, the director of the writing collective, had to categorize his spiritual guide Rilke into the "decadent group of imperialism" and criticize his mysticism.[123] Decadent modernist works were nothing but irrational and formalist, composed by a group of timid and wavering bourgeois intellectuals, "mice in a burning house," "who were stuck in the cleft of increasingly vehement class struggles"—as Mao Dun's 1958 article "Yedu ouji" (Random notes on night readings) rendered, which resolutely

---

121. Feng, *FZQJ* 2: 133.

122. Feng, *FZQJ* 2: 3–4.

123. See "Di si bian: Diguo zhuyi shiqi de wenxue" (Pt. 4: Literature of the imperialist period), in *Deguo wenxue jianshi* (A brief history of German literature) (Beijing: Renmin wenxue chubanshe, 1958), pp. 331–35. The first Chinese work on the history of German literature was written by Feng Zhi and a group of his students at Peking University, including Tian Dewang, Zhang Yushu, Sun Fengcheng, Li Shu, and Du Wentang, who later all became professors in the German department. This book was based primarily on Feng's manuscript prepared for German literary history lectures at Peking University.

defended socialist realism and condemned Western modernism.[124] Feng, who firmly embraced Rilke's idea that poetry was based not on emotion but on experiences and disavowed his early romantic sentimentalism, now plunged himself into the fanatical flames of Maoist revolutionary romanticism.

In that there are no human beings, or humanity, or literature transcending the bondage of class consciousness, what would have become of the poet? Feng's persistent study of Du Fu (712–770) from the 1940s to the early 1960s provides a case in point. Although this chapter will not go into details of Feng's Du Fu research, it suffices to consider the choice of Du Fu as subject matter. Feng Zhi started his Du Fu study in the 1940s, around the same time when he devoted himself to Goethe studies. Goethe and Du Fu are among the few historical figures to whom Feng dedicated his sonnets. Within the Chinese tradition, two figures are often invoked by modern writers as their moral and aesthetic role models on which to project their own Weltanschauung: Qu Yuan (343? BC–278 BC) and Li Bo (701–762). Both are perceived as poets alienated, misunderstood, and banished from the mundane and insensitive society, yet still in unyielding pursuit of aesthetic beauty.[125] Feng Zhi was one of the very few poets who did not seek inspiration in Qu Yuan or Li Bo, who are, using Michelle Yeh's term, "tragic heroes."[126] The role model he chose instead was Du Fu. A contemporary of Li Bo, Du is characterized by his realistic poetics and deep concern with ordinary people. Feng's figure of Wu Zixu bids farewell to nature and the pure aesthetic world and walks toward the crowds, whereas Feng's figure of Du Fu is more forceful in that he takes responsibility for the totality of the people and the mundane society in turbulent historical times. In this, Feng saw a great affinity between Du Fu and Goethe, who were both able to combine an inward and an outward life. In his later

---

124. Mao Dun, quoted in Hong Zicheng, *Wenti yu fangfa*, p. 247. "Yedu ouji" was originally serialized in *Wenyi bao* (Literary gazette), nos. 1, 2, 8, 10 (1958). Selected portions are collected in Hong Zicheng, *Zhongguo dangdai wenxueshi shiliaoxuan,* pp. 398–414.

125. For the influences of Qu Yuan and Li Bo on modern Chinese poets, see Michelle Yeh, *Modern Chinese Poetry*, pp. 29–55.

126. Ibid., p. 30.

years, he even wrote an article entitled "Gede he Du Fu" (Goethe and Du Fu) comparing these two poets.[127]

The irony of history is that Feng's *Du Fu zhuan* (Biography of Du Fu), a biographical study portraying a "people's poet," was condemned for extolling "capitulationism" during the Cultural Revolution. In his article "Li Bo and Du Fu," Guo Moruo, a Goethe devotee himself whose early poetry deeply inspired Feng and who became the official Maoist poet, harshly criticized Feng Zhi and denounced Du Fu as a reactionary who subjected himself to the emperor and the feudal court. Li Bo, who had been regarded as against authority, was hailed as the archetypal revolutionary fighting the restraints of feudalist dominion. Evidently, Guo's condemnation of Du and deification of Li can be attributed to the praise of Li Bo by Mao Zedong himself. Who are "the people"? With his naïve conviction of writing for the people about the "people's poet," Feng Zhi did not realize that he had gone too far in defining which lines were written for the people and who were the people's poets. After all, except for Chairman Mao himself, who could have the authority or revolutionary passion to determine these issues? Although Feng was the one who suggested publishing Mao's classic Chinese poetry in the inaugural issue of *Shikan* (Poetry), which officially launched the Mao poetry craze in the People's Republic, he did not realize that no one but Chairman Mao could be worshipped as *the poet of the people*.[128]

What could better characterize the transformation of Feng Zhi from a modernist poet into a Maoist celebrator than the notion of the death of a poet? The frenetic Maoist era was marked by millions of deaths, from the famine in the countryside and the suicides and murders of numerous intellectuals. Among them was Li Guangtian (1906–68), a prominent writer and critic who once highly appreciated Feng Zhi's *Sonnets*. Shortly after the outbreak of the Cultural Revolution, Li drowned himself in the famous Lianhua chi (Lotus pond) in suburban Kunming, where, ironically, the legendary beauty Chen Yuanyuan, who was reproached in unofficial history as the

---

127. Feng, *FZQJ* 8: 174–89.

128. See Lu Yaodong, *Feng Zhi zhuan*, p. 234. For a study of Mao Zedong's poetic work against the backdrop of the socialist zeal, see, for instance, Ban Wang, *Sublime Figure of History*, pp. 108–14, 188–92.

main cause of the eventual defeat of the Ming dynasty, committed suicide during the chaotic Ming-Qing dynastic transition.

The irony of Feng Zhi's negation of his poetry and the disappearance of a modernist poet appears all the stronger in comparison to another suicide earlier in the twentieth century. Wang Guowei, a preeminent scholar, poet, literary critic, and also a scholar of German philosophy, drowned himself in a pond at the Summer Palace in 1927. There has been a plethora of critical reflections on Wang's suicide in his disillusionment with sociopolitical and cultural chaos.[129] In a tragic way, Wang's death testifies to the dilemma of a modern Chinese subjectivity in the era of Chinese enlightenment and modernization. A fine Chinese literatus and an advocate of Western knowledge, Wang employed Western aesthetics and philosophy to explore issues of pain, desire, and the sublime in the Qing dynasty classic novel, *Dream of the Red Chamber.* At the beginning of the Chinese modern age, he keenly discerned the radical incompatibilities between disparate historical epochs, between the Enlightenment's boundless optimism about reason and progress and the bleak vision of disjunction and uncertainty that entails the death of the modern subjectivity. Therefore, Wang's suicide points not only to the demise of the traditional culture but also to the predicament of the modernization project and the pernicious force of self-destruction it carries.

Whereas Wang Guowei asserted his notion of modernity through a corporeal annihilation of subjectivity, interestingly, Feng Zhi, who also dedicated his life to the reconciliation of the individual and the social, the aesthetic and the political, went the other way. His assertion of the newly founded socialist totality worked because it entirely destroyed the modernist sensibilities that informed his previous poetic creations. As it turned out, the Maoist collectivity further complicated the ambivalence between the barren aesthetic utopia and Feng's ideal republic based on an affirmative relationship between the individual and the societal. Inasmuch as the socialist collectivity is predicated on the negation of humanistic individuality, it is no less void and precarious than the one entailed by aesthetic autonomy. In

129. For discussions of Wang Guowei's scholarly contributions and his suicide, see, for instance, Ye Jiaying, *Wang Guowei jiqi wenxue piping*; B. Wang, *Sublime Figure of History*, pp. 17–54; David Der-wei Wang, *Monster That Is History*, pp. 224–61.

order to stay on the road he chose to follow, Feng Zhi had to bury his premature notions of socialist affinity and unity under the cloak of the Maoist vision of totalitarian collectivism. In this way, the modernist poet par excellence became a vociferous celebrant of the totalitarianism he originally set out to avoid.

CHAPTER 6

Eileen Chang, Hong Kong, and the Cold War

Hong Kong held an important geopolitical position during the Cold War years in relations between the two competing Chinese states across the Taiwan Strait and the United Kingdom, staunchly anti-Communist yet the first Western power to recognize the PRC. Since the 1950s, it had provided a haven for immigrants, exiles, and refugees from mainland China and Taiwan, becoming an East Asian "showcase of democracy" in the global Cold War constellation and a base from which the opposing Chinese regimes could maneuver against each other. Both the CCP and the KMT governments had their cultural agencies established in Hong Kong. As long as they did not violate local law and order publicly, they were both tolerated by the colonial government to further British interests in Hong Kong and East Asia. The basic policy of the colonial government was "to maintain 'complete impartiality' toward the two Chinese regimes."[1] Whereas on the Chinese mainland and Taiwan, the ideological and cultural war was waged against the Cold War Other safely separated on the other shore, in the Crown Colony of Hong Kong, the left and the right were fighting in daily life on the same street. Ma Lang's

1. Tsang, *Cold War's Odd Couple*, p. 47. Tsang examines how the UK developed its political relationships with the PRC and the ROC in Taiwan in the formative years of the Cold War.

1956 short story, "Taiyang xia de jie" (Streets under the sun), describes such a street-level riot breaking out in Kowloon on the Double Tenth National Day of 1956. Published in *Wenyi xinchao* (New literary trends), a modernist literary magazine founded by the author himself, it depicts the political enthusiasm and disillusionment experienced by a young participant in the riot and takes up issues of the performative nature of political agitation and the fragile boundary between the left and the right.[2]

This ideological division was the essential nature of the Cold War polarization. However, the distinction between these two camps was never absolute. They were mutually dependent and informed by the same political discourses and cultural imaginations of nationalism, progress, and modernization.[3] In Cold War Hong Kong, where the left and the right operated in the same territory, traffic between apparently antagonist sides was easier than was commonly claimed. As this chapter will reveal, on the highly contested cultural terrain of the British colony, the ideological borders were as fluid and permeable as the boundary between Hong Kong and mainland China along the Sham Chun River. There were not just people going to the other side as defectors or double agents; as critics like Leung Ping-Kwan points out, some writers and artists worked for both camps and were good friends in their personal lives.[4] In reflecting on the nebulous relationship between political loyalty and betrayal, Eileen Chang (Zhang Ailing) observed in closing her short story, "The Spyring or Ch'ing K'e! Ch'ing K'e!" the English version of the 1977 story, "Se, jie" (Lust, caution): "Since the war began there has been this saying, 'T'eh wu pu fung chia, special agents are all one family,' because they could switch sides with ease."[5] When Chang wrote this

---

2. Ma Lang, "Taiyang xia de jie." For a brief discussion of the special cultural position this modernist magazine took in 1950s Hong Kong, see Leung Ping-Kwan, "1957 Hong Kong," pp. 199–200.

3. On the ideological and cultural competitions between the United States and the Soviet Union during the Cold War based on the same Enlightenment intellectual legacy, see Caute, *Dancer Defects*.

4. Leung, "1957 Hong Kong," pp. 199–211. See also Tsang, "Strategy for Survival."

5. Eileen Chang, "The Spyring or Ch'ing K'e! Ch'ing K'e!," p. 72. The manuscript for this English version of "Se, jie" was discovered by Stephen Soong in 2008

during her second sojourn in Hong Kong in 1953, the condition of political ambiguity that she addressed surely applied not just to Shanghai during the Second Sino-Japanese War, the immediate setting of the story, but also to Cold War Hong Kong. Cultural activities and productions in Hong Kong made the binary ideological confrontation problematic rather than reinforced it.

Chinese literature across the 1949 divide better represents the capricious nature of the Cold War experiences than any political or historical narratives. At no other time in the course of the twentieth century was modern Chinese literature more intricately intertwined with politics than during the Cold War. As previous chapters in this book have discussed, both the PRC and the KMT regimes stipulated a concept of literature as a political instrument, though both failed to produce the ideal work despite all their thoroughly premeditated and meticulously implemented literary policies and investments. Hong Kong's cultural scene during the Cold War era is another compelling case attesting to the convoluted relationship between literature and politics. When political propaganda shared the same newspaper page with horse-race gambling guides, the theatricality in politics found its most glaring manifestation. I have discussed in the first chapter of this book how various politico-cultural forces endeavored and competed to envision a modern Chinese identity and a national culture in Hong Kong, a geographical, cultural, and linguistic periphery that was in every sense a product of colonialism, nationalism, and imperialism. The intricate relationship between culture and polity, nation and narration, was played out in intriguing ways in Cold War Hong Kong.

To consider these issues, I will focus on Eileen Chang's post-1949 diasporic, translingual, and cross-media literary and cultural practices, which were deeply embedded in the Cold War history of the East Asian front, including Hong Kong and Taiwan, and of the United States. With the release of Ang Lee's film *Lust, Caution* (2007), adapted from Chang's short story of the same name, and the posthumous publication of *Xiao tuanyuan* (Little reunion, 2009) and of *The Fall of the Pagoda* (2010) and *The Book of Change* (2010) in English

---

and published in the Hong Kong journal *Muse* in March 2008, after the release of Ang Lee's film *Lust, Caution,* which was adapted from Chang's Chinese short story of the same title.

(a series of autobiographical works she was still revising at the time of her death), Eileen Chang experienced a great resurgence of popularity. Although provoking instant controversy for their bold sex scenes and moral indecisiveness, these works, set primarily in Shanghai during the Japanese occupation, stirred intense popular interest in this historical period. Often overlooked, however, is the deep connection of these works with Hong Kong and their complicated embeddedness in Cold War cultural history. Chang was very productive during her second Hong Kong stay between 1952 and 1955. Some of her most significant later works, including "Lust, caution" and the autobiographical series, started to take shape and later underwent a long process of writing and revision that lasted from the 1950s through the 1990s.

Eileen Chang spent the first few years after the Chinese Communist takeover of mainland China in Shanghai. During this period, she wrote *Shiba chun* (Eighteen springs, 1951) and *Xiao'ai* (Xiao'ai, 1952), which carry the leftist message of the time. In 1952, Chang decided to leave her native city for Hong Kong. During her time there, from 1952 to 1955, she finished *Yang ge* (The rice-sprout song) and *Chidi zhilian* (Naked earth), sponsored by the United States Information Agency (USIA). Whereas these two Cold War novels focus on human frailty and thus to a certain extent dwell on Chang's unique notion of history, which is marked by temporal discrepancies and ruins as against any grand narrative of historical monumentality, they nevertheless bear the clear imprint of the propagandistic anti-Communist novel and belong to the genre of *roman à these*. In 1955, Chang left for the United States, where she attempted to restart her literary career as a writer of English-language fiction. Except for a brief visit to Taiwan and Hong Kong in the early 1960s, she never again revisited China.[6]

The volatile yet poignant vacillation between antagonistic ideologies in Eileen Chang's 1950s fiction, as well as her diasporic experi-

6. For this trip, Chang wrote a long article, "A Return to the Frontier," published in *The Reporter* in 1963. In 2008, the Hungguan Press published Chang's Chinese rewriting of the English travelogue, titled *Chongfang biancheng* (A revisit of the frontier cities), a much richer depiction of her trip to Taiwan and Hong Kong than the English original one.

ences across the Cold War division, offers a best case in point through which to examine the cultural landscape of Cold War Hong Kong. To better understand Chang's post-1949 writing career as it spanned the mainland, Hong Kong, and the United States, this chapter first examines *The Rice-Sprout Song* and *Naked Earth* in the context of both 1950s anti-Communist fiction and the confrontation between the left and the right in the Hong Kong cultural field during the early Cold War years. The second and third section of the chapter considers Chang's two endeavors to rework the Qing dynasty classic novel *Honglou meng* (Dream of the red chamber, also translated as *The Story of the Stone*, from one of its earliest Chinese titles, *Shitou ji*; abbreviated hereafter as *Dream*) in the 1960s and 1970s. In 1961 and 1962, Chang spent five months in Hong Kong writing a screenplay based on *Dream* for the film company Motion Picture & General Investment Co. (MP&GI). Shortly after her return to the United States, she embarked on an extensive study of *Dream* and wrote a series of research articles in Redology, which were published in 1976 by the Huangguan Press of Taipei, a book that Chang playfully named *Honglou mengyan* (The nightmare in the red chamber; hereafter simply *Nightmare*). The second section reads Chang's *Dream* screenwriting experience at the intersection of Hong Kong filmmaking history and Chinese Cold War cultural diplomatic tactics that pertain to *Dream*'s adaptation to opera forms. The third section ventures a textual and contextual analysis of Chang's *Dream* research to reflect on her distinctive aesthetics of desolation and poetics of the quotidian. Through an exploration of Chang's *Dream*-related endeavors, which consumed a substantial portion of her later years, I address how her diasporic writing career bespeaks Cold War cultural and political restraints and how in turn these affected her poetics and politics of writing. The concluding section of the chapter discusses the cultural significance of Chang's seemingly compulsive practice of rewriting across disparate languages, genres, and media.

The Making of the Right and the Left: When Anti-Communism Meets New School Martial Arts

Eileen Chang's literary significance is based primarily on a body of work she produced in Shanghai between 1943 and 1945. Her post-1949 creative activities have been considered less important, and therefore received less attention. She stayed in Shanghai when the PRC was founded, and in 1950, at the invitation of Xia Yan, the vice director of the Shanghai Committee of Literature and Art, she even attended the First Shanghai Congress of Literary and Art Representatives (*Shanghai shi wenxue yishu gongzuozhe daibiao dahui*). In spite of her efforts to fit into the new political environment, her skepticism of Communist ideology deepened with the increasingly tightening control of the socialist regime, which propelled her decision to leave the mainland for Hong Kong. In "Fuhua langrui" (Flowers in the floating waves), a story bearing some autobiographical traces that she started to write after arriving in Hong Kong but did not have published until some thirty years later, Chang described the postliberation uncertainty looming large in the daily lives of ordinary Shanghai residents: "When the Communists first came, those petty urbanites didn't know how serious it was. After two or three years, they started to feel it. It was like surrendering one's future into the hands of others, and being strangled from behind."[7] Chang reported to Hong Kong University in September 1952 and withdrew two months later. She left Hong Kong for Tokyo to visit her best friend, Yanying (Fatima), with the hope of finding a job there. Realizing that Hong Kong was not a safe harbor in a time of international political confrontation, "she only wanted to go as far away as she could, and she couldn't afford to miss the timing."[8] Chang failed to land a job in Japan and started to work as a translator for the USIA in Hong Kong in February 1953.[9] Meanwhile, she set out to write *The Rice-Sprout Song* and *Naked Earth*.

---

7. Eileen Chang, *Wangran ji*, p. 43. In the preface to this collection, Chang describes that there were three stories that had haunted her life since the 1950s: "Se, jie" (Lust, caution), "Fuhua langrui" (Flowers in the floating waves), and "Xiangjian huan" (Joy over the reunion). They were all initially written in the 1950s in Hong Kong and revised many times after. All three stories were later recollected in this anthology.

8. Chang portrayed a similar travel route for her protagonist Luozhen in "Fuhua langrui," an autobiographical piece; *Wangran ji*, p. 61. Regarding Chang's experiences at the University of Hong Kong, see Huang Kangxian, "Linggan yuanquan? Qinggan bingyuan?"

9. For Eileen Chang's life in Hong Kong, see Lin Yiliang, "Siyu Zhang Ailing"; Su Weizhen, *Gudao Zhang Ailing*; Leung Ping-Kwan, "Zhang Ailing yu Xianggang." During this period, Chang translated a few American literary works, including *The Portable Emerson* and Ernest Hemingway's *The Old Man and the Sea*.

To assess the position of these two fictions in the immediate context of the cultural Cold War in Hong Kong and East Asia, it is worth tracing their publication and reception history. *The Rice-Sprout Song* was first written in English in 1954,[10] followed by a Chinese version entitled *Yang ge*, which was serialized in 1954 in the weekly *Jinri shijie* (The world today), a USIA magazine in Hong Kong. The Chinese edition was published as a monograph by the USIA-sponsored Tianfeng Publishing House in Hong Kong in July 1954, and the English edition by Charles Scribner's Sons in the United States a year later. *Chidi zhilian* was first written in Chinese in 1954 and rewritten in English, titled *Naked Earth,* in 1956 and 1957 in America. The Chinese edition was published in October 1954 by the Tianfeng Publishing House, whereas the English one failed to find a publisher in America and was published in 1956 by Youlian (Union) Press of Hong Kong, a publishing house that was formed by a group of "third force" (*disan shili*) refugee Chinese intellectuals and received covert financial support from the CIA-funded Committee for Free Asia (later renamed Asia Foundation).[11] All the institutions involved in the expeditious publication and distribution of these two novels were either American Cold War cultural propaganda agencies or their direct or indirect affiliates. The USIA played a crucial role. As U.S. Cold War headquarters in Hong Kong, its main mission was to collect information about Communist China and disseminate anticommunist propaganda. According to Chi-kwan Mark, one of its major programs was to engage Chinese writers and publishers through financial support to produce anticommunist materials designed for the overseas Chinese in Southeast Asia. A complete picture of the operation of the USIA in Hong Kong is yet to be constructed. Whether *The Rice-Sprout Song* and *Naked Earth* were directly

---

10. Quotations from the English version comes from the edition published by University of California Press in 1998, which is a reprint of the original edition by Charles Scribner's Sons, 1955. Quotations from the Chinese edition are based on the Huangguan edition, 1991.

11. Chang's USIA supervisor Richard M. McCarthy, in an interview by Gao Quanzhi, *Zhang Ailing xue*, pp. 242–43. For a discussion of the political and cultural position the Union Press held during the Cold War era, see Tay, "Colonialism, the Cold War," pp. 36–37. For the financial support the CIA granted Hong Kong, see Mark, "The 'Problem of People.'"

commissioned by the USIA remains debatable.[12] Nevertheless, the novels were firmly entrenched in the cultural Cold War against Chinese communism.

Despite all the meticulous endorsement by the cultural propaganda machinery, these two novels were never successful political or commercial anticommunist works. Although *The Rice-Sprout Song* was published in America and received favorable reviews in major media such as the *New York Times*, the *New York Herald Tribune*, the *Saturday Review of Literature*, and *Time* magazine,[13] it only had one print run and did not sell as well as contemporary fiction about China, "which has more sentimental appeal: Han Suyin's *A Many-splendored Thing* and Pearl S. Buck's *Imperial Woman*."[14] *Naked Earth* was unable to land a publisher. The books were not popular in free China either. Despite its anticommunist theme, *Naked Earth* even failed to pass the KMT censorship during the martial law period, let alone compete with prevalent tendentious works such as Chen Jiying's *Dicun zhuan* (1951), which, ironically, was translated into English in 1959, titled *Fool in the Reeds*, by no other but Eileen Chang. How to account for their failure as political fiction, despite the fact that these two works ostensibly conform to the dominant Cold War ideology? Chang's critical reflections on her lack of popularity as a political writer as compared with Chen Ruoxi (Chen Jo-Hsi)'s success in the 1970s opens up an interesting perspective. Chen Ruoxi, one of the major writers of the Taiwan modernist group surrounding *Wenxue zazhi* (Literary magazine), made her way to mainland China in the 1960s to pursue her socialist ideals. Having experienced the Cultural Revolution and being completely disillusioned with socialist politics, she left the PRC via Hong Kong in 1973. Her stories of these firsthand experiences in the fiction collection *Yin xianzhang* (Mayor Yin), which was followed two years later by an English translation entitled *The Execution of Mayor Yin and Other Stories*, became an

12. General scholarship on Chang has regarded both *The Rice-Sprout Song* and *Naked Earth* as works commissioned by the USIA; for instance, Nicole Huang, *Women, War, Domesticity*, pp. 213–14. Gao Quanzhi's interview with Richard M. McCarthy clarifies it.

13. Lin Yiliang, "Siyu Zhang Ailing."

14. Hsia, *History of Modern Chinese Fiction*, p. 389.

instant success among both Chinese and English readers. In such a context, Chang made an intriguing observation:

> Only a dedicated patriotic socialist who then became disillusioned with the Chinese brand of socialism anyway—has credibility. If I'd stayed as long on the mainland I'd still be heeded no more than any other refugee. Perhaps it takes Chen Jo-Hsi's kind of Plaintalk to penetrate the vast ignorance about China, but it's her ideological fervor that carries weight. There is this double standard, for a long-suffering poor country like China.[15]

In this instance, the notion "plaintalk" refers to the monthly magazine *Plain Talk*, edited by Isaac Don Levine from 1946 to 1950, a Cold War publication known for its reports on the socialist bloc based on substantial data and refugee interviews. Chang's observation touches upon at least two respects of such publishing. First, not just any refugee was qualified to offer trustworthy testimony. A regular refugee needed to be tested. Political credibility could only be granted to those who underwent ideological transformations. Second, there was a double standard imposed by Western powers on industrially undeveloped nations like China, which were deemed good at providing only primary materials, data, and testimonies, not artistic creations or imagination. Therefore, as Chang keenly observed, even at the most fervent moment of political antagonism, what was actually at stake was not just ideology, but ironically, literary and artistic qualifications of writers of a culturally minor nation. Through the efforts of postcolonial theorists, this notion is by now not unfamiliar. Can the subaltern speak? Or can they only be represented? In *The Flight of the Innocents* (1964), an anticommunist romantic thriller depicting the escape of a group of refugees fleeing the mainland into Hong Kong on the verge of the Great Leap Forward in 1959, Lin Yutang employed a melodramatic scheme of an Englishman James Thayer rescuing his Chinese fiancée out of Communist China to reach Hong Kong, the blissful capitalist "city of liberty."[16] Although it fits well with the dominant political, racial, gender, and sexual

---

15. See Eileen Chang's letter in Hsia, "Zhang Ailing gei wo de xinjian," pp. 52–53.

16. Lin Yutang, *Flight of the Innocents*. A Chinese translation came out the following year, titled *Taoxiang ziyou cheng*, which literally means "an escape to the liberty city," published by the Central News Agency in Taipei.

discourse of the time, the novel is nevertheless artistically disappointing with predictable plots and a lack of psychological depth and subtlety.

Eileen Chang's political writings of the 1950s, however, never compromised artistically, as she implied in the quoted passage. Although political issues such as nation, politics, and revolution, which she had been accused of sidelining in her early career, are given center stage in *The Rice-Sprout Song* and *Naked Earth*, they were never formulaic propaganda. To illustrate this, I will take *The Rice-Sprout Song* as a point of departure. Set in a southern village near Shanghai during the 1950s land-reform movement, *The Rice-Sprout Song* tells how peasants in newly liberated China struggle with food shortages and are forced to riot. After the violent intervention of the local militia, the surviving villagers are ordered to perform the rice-sprout song in a ghastly New Year's celebration.

Hu Shi offers the earliest comments on *The Rice-Sprout Song* and highly praises its "fine, modest, and sincere" depiction of hunger in Communist China.[17] In his groundbreaking work *A History of Modern Chinese Fiction*, C. T. Hsia places Chang for the first time in the canon of modern Chinese literature and regards *The Rice-Sprout Song* as an instant classic. Hsia's analysis focuses on how the fiction conveyed communism's impingement upon traditional Chinese values and manners. The success of this work is in its ability to go beyond "mere contemporaneity." Hsia concludes that "Whereas other novelists, in writing about Communist China, will be solely engrossed in the atrocities perpetrated by the regime, she sees steadily before her eyes the culture of a whole nation."[18] David Wang furthers Hu Shi's reading and positions the hunger theme in the Chinese Communist revolutionary discourse since the 1920s that incorporates both bio-

---

17. See Hu Shi's letter to Eileen Chang, reprinted as the epigraph in the Huangguan Press edition of *The Rice-Sprout Song*.

18. Hsia, *History of Modern Chinese Fiction*, p. 426. Hsia's book had crucial influence not only on Eileen Chang studies but also on the entire trajectory of modern Chinese literary study in the United States, Taiwan, Hong Kong, and later the PRC. A Chinese version of his chapter on Eileen Chang was published as early as 1957 as two separate articles, "Zhang Ailing de duanpian xiaoshuo" (Eileen Chang's short stories) and "Ping *Yang ge*" (A review of *The Rice-Sprout Song*) in *Literary Magazine*, which kindled great interest in Chang in Taiwan.

logical and ideological hunger. He considers how hunger in *The Rice-Sprout Song* entails "a tension between digestive and diegetic imagination, and metabolic and metaphoric action."[19]

Playing on the same themes of women, family, famine, and land as its Communist counterpart, Ding Ling's "Du Wanxiang," Chang's fiction presented an absurd drama of ideological hyperbole, material scarcity, and the spectral human/woman subject in the authoritarian, collectivist socialist republic. Instituted in the 1940s, the CCP's land-reform movement aimed at the transformation of both the land and the people on it. The mission to harness the land was to be accomplished not merely through agricultural mechanization and modernization, but through an antitechnocratic mental transformation of the people, a process marked by a faith in human will, endurance, and moral purity that would surpass any technological advantage. Therefore, the ideological and cultural edifice is of utmost significance, which is interestingly in line with both the Confucian educational-moral tradition and the Cold War rationale of attaining ideological superiority.

As discussed in chapter 3, Ding Ling's "Du Wanxiang" registers precisely such socialist mores. In Wanxiang's socialist Bildung, ideological dissipation obscures or cures food scarcity. The socialist citizen feeds off political ideology and communist morality and by growing spiritually, he/she gains a livelihood. Wanxiang "labored with intense joy absolved from fatigue and hunger."[20] The physical nutritional deficiency does not hinder the socialist new person in his/her pursuit of communist moral self-cultivation and perfection. On the contrary, it becomes a prerequisite for the communist Bildung, functioning as a form of penance to worship ideological purity and invincibility. Such communist morality is evidenced in the "lofty, solemn, and virginal glow radiating from Wanxiang's ordinary face."[21]

In Eileen Chang's *The Rice-Sprout Song*, however, food and the human instinct of survival surpass everything, including the ideological bubble everyone seems to maintain cautiously in the newly founded socialist state. In Chang's reckoning with everyday life in the early

---

19. David Der-wei Wang, *Monster That Is History*, p. 119.
20. Ding Ling, "Du Wanxiang," in Barlow, *I Myself am a Woman*, p. 347.
21. Ibid.

1950s PRC, the myth of Maoist spiritual gastronomy was rewritten: the scarcity of food occurs in conjunction with the ideological hyperbole and tight political surveillance. After returning to her hometown from Shanghai, Tan Yuexiang, the female protagonist, soon realizes the harsh situation of food shortage. To survive hunger, she cheats cadres, refuses her sister-in-law's request for a loan, and serves her family increasingly diluted rice porridge. Rather than feeding on ideology at the cost of having her family go hungry, as Du Wanxiang does in North China, Yuexiang, an equally resilient woman in South China, fights a selfish, desperate war to secure food and protect her family from the intensive political surveillance in her village. Ideological dissipation accompanies dietary dilution and deprivation at the daily dinner table. The oversupply of political propaganda only aggravates the shortage of material provisions.

When food becomes a problem, politics does not matter. With the hunger strike looming large, the primitive instinct of physical survival becomes the dominant impulse. Aunt Tan drops her communist theatrics when it is impossible for her to bring food to the table. Jin'gen, Yuexiang's Model Labor husband, openly resists Comrade Wang's order to provide food for the troops serving in the anti-imperialist Korean War, which eventually leads to the food riot in the village. Yuexiang, who carefully guards her family through the political control of the time, sets the village barn on fire as a final means of revenge. In this light, Chang's political novel is not so much about politics as it is about the most essential parts of humanity: the land and human life, food, illness, and death. Her reckoning with feminine subjectivity, as embodied by the selfish, earthy, and pragmatic Yuexiang, reveals her distinctive notion of the human subject, which is marked by frailty rather than rationality, strength, and moral virtue as defined by the Enlightenment idea of the universal subject. Therefore, Chang's project goes beyond what C. T. Hsia describes as the novel's great humanitarian contribution to human compassion. It is instead based on what David Wang calls Chang's "lack of confidence in humanity."[22] This partly explains the unpopularity of *The*

---

22. Hsia, *History of Modern Chinese Fiction;* David Der-wei Wang, *Monster That Is History*, p. 134.

Rice-Sprout Song as an anti-Communist novel in the "free world." Such a focus on human frailty and resilience, no matter what political ideology the state adheres to, contributes to its failure as propagandist political fiction, which requires an unequivocal political commitment.

Compared with *The Rice-Sprout Song*, *Naked Earth* was less favorably regarded by literary scholars.[23] It has a more ambitious scope: to novelize the period of land reform through the Three-Anti Campaign (anti-corruption, anti-waste, and anti-bureaucracy) to the Korean War in the young socialist state. According to Hsia, the novel "falls short of the formal perfection of *The Rice-Sprout Song*" and contains "an unwarrantably large amount of exposition."[24] Although Chang allegedly received a synopsis from the USIA,[25] the ideological themes in this fiction were clandestinely underpinned yet simultaneously undermined by the private themes of love, individualism, and betrayal. Like Chang's pro-Communist novel *Eighteen Springs*, *Naked Earth* portrays a love story of a young couple, Liu Quan and Huang Juan, to illustrate political and emotional disillusionment during a time of dramatic historical turmoil. As recent college graduates, they witness the brutality of the land-reform movement. After Liu Quan is reassigned to Shanghai, he gets involved in a political conspiracy and is sent to jail. Huang Juan consents to become the mistress of a Communist cadre in exchange for Liu's release. Devastated and disillusioned, Liu volunteers to fight in the Korean War. Although the first part of the novel is set in a rural area during the land reform,

---

23. On the history of publication of *Chidi zhilian* and its English version *Naked Earth*, see Gao Quanzhi, *Zhang Ailing xue*, pp. 221–23. *Naked Earth* is not a direct English translation of *Chidi zhilian*. There are some major revisions and rewritings. On the main differences between the two versions, see Gao Quanzhi, *Zhang Ailing xue*, pp. 219–36. One main change of plot is that Huang Juan (named Su Nan in *Naked Earth*) is impregnated by the Communist cadre and dies of abortion. According to Sima Xin, this revision is related to Chang's having an abortion in 1956. See Sima Xin, *Zhang Ailing yu Laiya*, pp. 101–8. "Se, jie" also differed substantially from its early version in English, written in 1953 Hong Kong, which goes by the title of "Spyring or Ch'ing K'e." My discussion of *Chidi zhilian* here is based on the Chinese edition published by Huangguan in 1991.

24. Hsia, *History of Modern Chinese Fiction*, p. 427.

25. See Shui Jing, *Zhang Ailing xiaoshuo de yishu*, p. 27.

urban life in Shanghai in the initial years of socialist China takes center stage for the remainder of the novel. This capitalist and Westernized city par excellence appears far more ghostly than the *danse macabre* wrapping up *The Rice-Sprout Song*'s socialist rural story. Rather than villagers performing the festival folk dance on a gloomy land of famine, the lurking specters of Shanghai petty urbanites in Chang's early fiction collection *Chuanqi* (Romances, 1944) all come out into the socialist limelight and join an uncanny labor-day parade on Shanghai's former commercial and cosmopolitan streets. Familiar themes and plots from her early writings are resurrected for a last farewell, a memorial for a vanishing city. As Liu, a socialist newcomer to Shanghai, an invader of this former bourgeois city, observes from within the parade:

> These people here strove to survive in between the wheels of this age . . . at present, life is a bit harder for them; still they are able to carry on much as before and find a bit of comfort in the texture of life itself. No turbulence as overpowering as the Land Reform had swept over them yet. Although it will be their turn sooner or later, right now, they are just living a borrowed life. But even if their lives are borrowed, that does not make them any less real.[26]

In the protagonists Liu Quan and Huang Juan, we can easily locate the haunting images of Fan Liuyuan and Bai Liusu in the fallen city of Hong Kong, leaning against a gray brick wall and lamenting: "The wall is cold and coarse, and has the color of death. . . . One day, when our whole civilization has been destroyed, when everything is burnt, burst, utterly collapsed and ruined, this wall might still be here."[27] Only this time, it is not the fall of Hong Kong, but that of all China.

The most anticommunist charged moment comes at the end of the story. During the Korean War, when Liu Quan is captured by the Americans and given the choice to be repatriated in free China—Taiwan—he rejects and opts to return to the mainland to subvert communism from within as a secret agent. Personal distress winds up in a political commitment, as if ideological infatuation could serve as a panacea for psychological malaise. In this instance, the dialectics of physical and metaphysical narratives of any political im-

---

26. Eileen Chang, *Chidi zhilian*, p. 125.
27. Chang, *Qingcheng zhilian* (Love in a fallen city), p. 226.

peratives, communist and anticommunist, has its most conspicuous yet sarcastic manifestation. How seriously can such a commitment be taken? Given Liu's suspicious political *résumé*, his secret anticommunist operation would hardly foresee a bright future. Such an enmeshment of personal and public life had already occurred in Chang's procommunist *Eighteen Springs*, written before she left for Hong Kong. When the two couples, Manzhen and Shijun, Cuizhi and Shuhui, are not able to find a solution for their emotional entanglements, the author sends them all to the frontier of socialist reconstruction in Manchurian China. Exhausted in their political and romantic striving, they make a selfish, most personal leap for ideological sublimation in the national cause—be it a CCP or a KMT model of new China. This is not far from the action of Chang'an, the abused daughter in Ch'i-ch'iao's suffocating house of no light: "A clean break—she felt this sacrifice was a beautiful desolate gesture."[28]

C. T. Hsia contends that *Naked Earth* is about betrayal, consisting of a series of betrayals, personal and political.[29] In a recent article on Chang's late career, Shuang Shen argues that the theme of betrayal takes a central position in Chang's post-1949 work: "Writing about betrayal allows her to describe the complex contextualization of the diasporic subject vis-à-vis multiple nation-states in the context of the Cold War."[30] Although betrayal bespeaks the ethical and political dilemma of Chinese intellectuals caught between capricious political imperatives across the 1949 divide, the notion suggests a convenient, clear-cut boundary between two opponents. Ideas such as betrayal and loyalty reveal precisely the anxieties inherent in the dichotomous discourse of the Cold War. At their best, Chang's writings about betrayal lay bare the arbitrary nature of polarization, severance, and ideological antagonism that marked the Cold War rhetoric. In that sense, her writings, political or not, are about ambiguity and compromise rather than betrayal. Ambiguity was the essential feature of Chang's life and work: her rise to fame in the politically suspicious, occupied Shanghai; her flirtations with both the Mandarin Duck and Butterfly type of popular culture and the May Fourth new

---

28. Ibid., p. 209.
29. Hsia, *History of Modern Chinese Fiction*, pp. 427–31.
30. Shen Shuang, "Betrayal, Impersonation, and Bilingualism," pp. 92–93.

literature; her marriage to Hu Lancheng, an intellectual who collaborated with the puppet regime headed by Wang Jingwei during the Second Sino-Japanese War; her volatile sway between procommunist and anticommunist writings in the 1950s—all attest to her ambiguous political stance and cultural strategy.

Indeed, such ambiguity best captures the capricious nature of Cold War experiences of the time. Hong Kong provides a significant case in point, where propagandist, subversive, and espionage operatives of the PRC, the ROC, and the USA competed and coexisted as the colonial government finessed the neutrality of Hong Kong during the high Cold War. It is not surprising that the leftist and rightist rivals fought in the daylight, then sat together at the dinner table. The most treacherous combat was in the republic of letters. Whereas both the Communist and the Nationalist regimes were preoccupied with the politicization of literature inscribed by the opposite ideology, Hong Kong was a unique locale where nationalism and colonialism, politics and entertainment, left and right converged. Hong Kong literature has been sustained by newspaper literary supplements, magazines, and publishing houses. In his mapping of Hong Kong's literary scene during the Cold War era, William Tay delineates major leftist, rightist, and commercial presses and notes that serialized fiction was a crucial form during this period.[31]

However, the political orientation of the press did not necessarily restrain the political propensity of a work accepted for publication. Eileen Chang's case is a notable example. In 1954, in addition to the Chinese editions of *The Rice-Sprout Song* and *Naked Earth*, Chang's first fiction collection, *Romances*, was reprinted in Hong Kong by the Tianfeng Publishing House with the title *Zhang Ailing duanpian xiaoshuo ji* (Short stories of Eileen Chang). In 1966, Chang's Chinese novels, *Yuannü* (Embittered woman) and *Bansheng yuan*, a rewriting of *Eighteen Springs*, were serialized in *Xingdao wanbao* (Sing Tao evening news), an essential commercial newspaper that leaned toward Taiwan politically. Although all the newspapers and publishing houses that handled her writings belonged to the rightist camp, Chang's work hardly succeeded in disseminating anticommunist messages, as examined earlier in this chapter.

---

31. Tay, "Colonialism, the Cold War," p. 34.

The leftist media testified to the intricate relationship between art and politics to the same degree. The most intriguing case is the rise of New School martial arts fiction in the leading leftist newspaper *Xin wanbao* in high Cold War Hong Kong.[32] *Xin wanbao* was the evening paper of *Dagong bao*, which, together with *Wenhui bao*, constituted the mainstay of the left. In 1954, when the rightist *World Today* serialized Eileen Chang's land-reform novel *The Rice-Sprout Song*, *Xin wanbao* began to serialize a martial arts story, *Longhu dou jinghua* (Dragon and tiger vie in the capital), by Chen Wentong, under the pen name Liang Yusheng. A year later, Liang's friend, Zha Liangyong, later known by his pen name Jin Yong, joined in with his tour de force *Shujian enchou lu* (The book and the sword), which would be followed by fourteen other novels. This was the formation of the New School martial arts fiction, and Liang Yusheng and Jin Yong have ever since been regarded as two great masters. These works soon captured the passion and imagination of readers in Hong Kong, Singapore, and Southeast Asia, and in the years that followed, Taiwan and ultimately mainland China.

In the rigorous self-legitimation of Beijing and Taipei, martial arts fiction did not have a chance to survive either the PRC's socialist realism or the KMT's *zhandou wenyi* (combat literature and art) and *fangong wenyi* (anticommunist literature and art). That martial arts fiction found its ideal site of rebirth in Hong Kong, with promotion by a leftist press, requires further consideration. When Liang Yusheng was approached by his friend Luo Fu, the editor-in-chief of *Xin wanbao* and an underground Communist engaged in the PRC's united front undertaking in Hong Kong, to rush out a chivalric story, it was certainly not meant to be direct political propaganda via the medium of martial arts adventures.[33] The tremendous enthusiasm triggered by the boxing match in Macau early that month must have

32. For a thorough discussion of the emergence of the New School martial arts fiction in postwar Hong Kong, see Hamm, *Paper Swordsmen*, pp. 1–31.

33. In the late 1980s, Luo Fu was accused by the CCP of being a traitor and an "American agent" for his interactions with the Americans during the high Cold War era and put under a secret house arrest in Beijing for ten years—yet another case of loyalty and betrayal and the unpredictable nature of party politics. His son has recently published a book about this suspicious case. See Luo Hailei, *Wo de fuqin Luo Fu*.

given Luo Fu the idea that the martial arts world would appeal to readers. Indeed, the immediate success of Liang's *Dragon and Tiger Vie in the Capital* boosted the sales of *Xin wanbao* dramatically: it almost overtook its main rightist rival, *Xingdao wanbao,* overnight.

In the fierce ideological confrontation across 1949, the leftists resorted to martial arts fiction to appeal to the masses so as to sell its political doctrine of a socialist China. What could more incisively demonstrate the treacherous relationship between politics and art? Modern Chinese literature and politics have been inextricably tied together since Liang Qichao (1873–1929)'s advocacy of *xin xiaoshuo* (new fiction) in the late Qing dynasty. In his seminal thesis "Lun xiaoshuo yu qunzhi de guanxi" (On the relationship between fiction and the government of the people),[34] Liang attributed the decline of the Chinese nation to the adverse impact of traditional popular literature that propagated violence and sex, which included *Dream of the Red Chamber* and *Shuihu zhuan* (The water margin), the archetypal chivalric fiction.[35] Seeing the great influence fiction exerted on people, he proposed to create a new type of fiction that would modernize the Chinese nation. This proposition was forcefully carried out by intellectuals of the May Fourth New Culture Movement. Ironically, half a century later, in yet another war of letters to project a modern nation, the Chinese leftists, who claimed to be the genuine successors of the May Fourth movement, spared no effort to resuscitate that banished literary genre with its ostracized knights-errant to fight ideological antagonists across the Taiwan Strait.

What makes the tension between traditional and modern literature, fiction and history, even more complicated is that since Mao Zedong's "On New Democracy" and "Talks at the Yan'an Forum," which called for a creative application of traditional Chinese literary and artistic forms to enlighten the people, leftist writers and artists have never ceased to remodel traditional folk narrative forms to

34. An English translation of the article is collected in Denton, *Modern Chinese Literary Thought*, pp. 74–81.

35. For studies of the tradition of Chinese chivalric fiction, see J. J. Y. Liu, *The Chinese Knight-errant*; Chen Pingyuan, *Qiangu wenren xiake meng*. For research on late-Qing chivalric and court-case novels, see David Der-wei Wang, *Fin-de-siècle Splendor*, pp. 117–82.

propagate revolutionary and nationalist ideas. The 1940s works of "dazhong wenyi" (mass literature and arts) of the Yan'an style employed traditional plots of bandits, outlaws, and rebels to produce a narrative that was no less serious than a "revolutionary nationalist literature."[36] In late 1940s leftist war novels such as *Lüliang yingxiong zhuan* (Heroes of the Lüliang mountain, 1948) and *Xin ernü yingxiong zhuan* (New tale of heroes and lovers, 1949) and 1950s revolutionary historical fiction such as *Baowei Yan'an* (Guarding Yan'an, 1954), it is not difficult to locate the classical form of chivalry and heroism of *The Water Margin* and the late Qing *Ernü yingxiong zhuan* (Tale of heroes and lovers, 1878) in Communist disguise.

Although emerging through the leftist *Xin wanbao*, the New School martial arts fiction presented a fantastic literary world marked by unique artistic creativity and far more complicated national and historical imaginations than any rigorous leftist ideology could ever contain.[37] Styled in the traditional *zhanghui* (episodic-chaptered) form like the Old School martial arts fiction of the 1920s and 1930s, Liang Yusheng's and Jin Yong's novels are characterized by fine usage of modern narratorial skills and realistic historical anchoring. In addition to redefining central notions of heroism, masculinity, fraternity, and loyalty, they sought to refashion the Chinese national imagination in intricate geopolitical and historical frameworks. The stories are often set at the geographical, cultural, or ethnic margins of the Chinese empire. Issues including ethnic conflicts, political ambiguity, cultural authenticity, and individual and national identities are explored against the backdrop of dynastic transitions.[38] These

---

36. Song, *Cong yule xingwei*, p. 210.

37. Although both Liang Yusheng and Jin Yong were *Xin wanbao* employees, they were never uncompromising leftists. Jin Yong leaned toward the left in his early *Xin wanbao* days, but changed his political views as the radical leftist political campaigns in the PRC proceeded, especially after 1959, when he left *Xin wanbao* and founded *Ming bao*. See, for instance, Zhang Guiyang, *Jin Yong yu* Ming bao *chuanqi*.

38. For a thorough study of cultural and historical implications of Jin Yong's fiction, see Song, "Nation-State, Individual Identity, and Historical Memory"; "Space, Swordsmen, and Utopia." For a discussion on the historical and cultural contexts of Jin Yong's fiction in Cold War Asia, see P. Liu, *Stateless Subjects*, pp. 107–52.

individual, ethnic, and national discourses created in the special cultural and geopolitical environment of Cold War Hong Kong implied the New School martial arts' own embeddedness at the national periphery, a borrowed time and space of the British colony and a Chinese territory outside of Chinese sovereignty. The efforts of these writers to address the convergence of fiction and history, of nation and narration, and of ethnos and topos recall their contemporary New Confucianists' conceptualization of cultural nationalism in exile, as discussed in chapter 1. Under British sovereignty, by means of literary imaginations, New School martial arts fiction provides yet another incisive vision of cultural nationalism outside China.

The ideologues, right or left, could not have expected that years later, when the two regimes across the Taiwan Strait initiated communications with each other, the New School martial arts fiction and Eileen Chang's work would both make a dazzling appearance in mainland China. Since the 1980s, the era of the "second Chinese Enlightenment," Eileen Chang and Jin Yong, writers housed oppositely in Hong Kong's newspapers, right and left, joined forces to sweep the cultural ruins of the Cultural Revolution and conquered a readership larger than their former editors could have dared to anticipate. And in recent years, in the Sinophone world, their writings have circulated across conventional borders—national, political, and cultural—and become a shared source to initiate people into the world of Chinese culture. The junction of art and politics, popular culture and serious literature, as well as entertainment and enlightenment, appears all the more intriguing.

Cold War Adaptations of Dream of the Red Chamber

In November 1961, Eileen Chang arrived in Hong Kong to adapt the classical novel *Dream of the Red Chamber* into a film commissioned by MP&GI. This was not Chang's first collaboration with MP&GI. In 1955, during an earlier stay in Hong Kong, Chang had joined the script committee of MP&GI,[39] which comprised a group of exiled

39. K. K. K. Ng, "Romantic Comedies of Cathay."

writers, including Sun Jinsan, Qin Yu, and Stephen Soong (Song Qi).[40] After she settled in the United States, Chang completed a number of film scripts for MP&GI, and screenwriting actually became her major source of income during her first few years in the United States. Most of the films Chang wrote are sophisticated comedies and urban romances that combined elements taken from what some critics called American screwball comedy and Chinese family drama with an ethical dimension.[41] She had already begun to experiment with this cinematic model in the late 1940s when she wrote two screenplays for Shanghai's Wenhua film studio, *Buliao qing* (Neverending love, 1947) and *Taitai wansui* (Viva the wife, 1947).

However, the assignment to adapt *Dream* differs considerably from Chang's earlier screenwriting projects. Rather than making yet another sleek, witty romantic comedy, Chang faced the challenge of adapting to a film script an epic work that she often claimed was the essential source of her literary inspiration.[42] Chang's *Dream*-related undertakings began much earlier. In her early teens, she was so captivated by *Dream* that she was unable to resist the temptation to write her own modern version. Composing five chapters under the title *Modeng Honglou meng* (Modern Dream of the Red Chamber, 1934), at the age of thirteen Chang fabricated her own *Dream* of a twentieth-century Prospect Garden much along the lines of late Qing-dynasty *Dream* fantasy, particularly Wu Jianren's innovative utopian science fiction novel *Xin Shitouji* (New story of the stone, 1908). Wu reincarnated Jia Bao-yu as an adventurer floating on air in an "aerial car" on a trip to central Africa, whereas Chang sent Bao-yu abroad to obtain a college degree.

After three months of hard work and numerous revisions, Chang's screenplay was rejected by MP&GI and the plan to make the film was shelved. As Chang's original screenplay for *Dream* has not

---

40. Stephen Soong later became Eileen Chang's lifetime friend. It was actually with Soong's support that she was able to obtain the opportunity to write screenplays for MP&GI during the 1950s and 1960s. For further discussion on the MP&GI screen committee, see P. Fu, "Modernity, Diasporic Capital"; Law, "A Glimpse of MP&GI's"; Shu, "Notes on MP&GI."

41. For a study of Eileen Chang's film scripts, see Lee, *Shanghai Modern*, pp. 276–80; Tay, "Zhang Ailing yu liangge pianzhong."

42. Eileen Chang, *Honglou mengyan*, p. 10.

survived, a textual analysis is not possible. Instead, I will venture a contextual and historical analysis to explore the poignant cultural and political implications of cross-generic and cross-media *Dream* adaptations in mainland China and Hong Kong in the 1950s and 1960s.

It was not mere chance that MP&GI decided to shoot a *Dream* film in 1961. What prompted the decision was no doubt the tremendous success of the recent Yue opera performance *Dream of the Red Chamber* by the visiting Shanghai Yue Opera Company, starring Xu Yulan and Wang Wenjuan. The play was then filmed in a joint project by the Shanghai Haiyan film studio and the Hong Kong Phoenix studio in 1962. In the heyday of the Cold War standoff, the visit of the leading Shanghai Yue Opera Company from a fledgling socialist state to Hong Kong, a frontier of the capitalist world, was by no means devoid of political implications. As Chairman Liu Shaoqi stated at a meeting with the Yue opera troupe, they were charged with the political mission of building a cultural united front. To dispel the "rumor" that the country was facing famine as a consequence of the so-called Great Leap Forward, the troupe was even "ghettoed" for two weeks in a resort hotel in Guangzhou, where they were offered nutritious food to put them in the best physical condition before their departure for Hong Kong.[43] The *Dream* opera ran for eighteen consecutive performances and became an instant sensation in Hong Kong in 1960. Given its romantic plot, artistic sophistication, and poetic lyricism, the Yue opera may have seemed the best form of cultural promotion to allow the young government to demonstrate its spiritual superiority, claim the high ground of culture and tradition, and win public endorsement among the Chinese diaspora.

In the mainland historical context, the production of the Yue opera *Dream* involved political and cultural complications on a different level. The first decade of the PRC is often regarded as a golden age of Yue opera.[44] The Shanghai Yue Opera Company's performance of

---

43. Wang Kai, "Yueju *Honglou meng* de dansheng."

44. Adaptations of *Dream* on the big screen continued in the 1970s. The production with the greatest circulation was the Shaw Brothers' *Jinyu liangyuan Honglou meng* (*Dream of the Red Chamber*, 1977), which starred Brigette Lin Qingxia and Sylvia Zhang Aijia and was directed by Li Hanxiang.

the Yue opera *Dream* premiered in mainland China in 1958 and became an instant classic in the Yue theater repertoire. Xu Jin served as its playwright. The play gained such popularity that the troupe was summoned the following year to perform in Beijing to celebrate the tenth anniversary of the Chinese socialist state. Given the time of its production, we may well wonder how such a drama of "feudal" *caizi jiaren* (scholar and beauty) could possibly have survived the volatile political and cultural climate, let alone become such an enormous success.

Indeed, during the mid-twentieth-century socialist modernization, this Qing-dynasty classic was, in an uncanny way, thrust into the cultural and political limelight. At the peak of the socialist construction in mainland China, *Dream of the Red Chamber*, a fiction that could not be more detached from the socialist reality, unexpectedly became the catalyst for the first wave of political campaigns against intellectuals. In September 1952, Yu Pingbo (1900–90), a prestigious essayist, poet, historian, and literary critic, published a Redology anthology, *Honglou meng yanjiu* (Studies on *Dream of the Red Chamber*, 1952), which includes revised parts of his old book *Honglou meng bian* (Explicating *Dream of the Red Chamber*, 1923) and some additional articles.[45] In May of the following year, *Wenyi bao* (Literary gazette) published a series of review articles highly lauding Yu's book and his *Dream* research. In the first few years of the young socialist state, *Dream* study seemed to occupy a safe niche far from the political and social reality.

However, things took a dramatic turn in 1954. Li Xifan and Lan Ling, two recent graduates of Shandong University, wrote an article critical of Yu Pingbo's recent Redology anthology. They first submitted their article to *Literary Gazette*, which did not show any interest in publishing it, in early 1954. Nine months later, this article finally appeared in *Wenshizhe* (Philosophy, History, and Literature), a journal of Shandong University. It is not difficult to understand why an article written by two young college graduates attempting to challenge a prominent scholar in the field of classical literature did not

45. Yu Pingbo, *Honglou meng yanjiu* (Studies on *Dream of the Red Chamber*) (Shanghai: Tangdi, 1952); *Honglou meng bian* (Explicating *Dream of the Red Chamber*) (Shanghai: Yadong, 1923).

get much attention from principal literary periodicals. Unexpectedly, however, this seemingly esoteric academic event caught the attention of Chairman Mao Zedong. With his sharp political sensibility, Mao saw it as a perfect chance to start a battle of thought criticism against "bourgeois intellectual authorities."

On October 16, 1954, Mao Zedong issued a letter to the members of the Central Political Bureau, entitled "Guanyu *Honglou meng* yanjiu wenti de xin" (My letter on the study of *Dream of the Red Chamber*). In it he extolled the article by Li and Lan as initiating "the first serious bombardment against the erroneous views of a so-called authoritative writer in the field of study of *Dream of the Red Chamber*"[46] and harshly reprimanded *Literary Gazette* for ignoring and obstructing this revolutionary effort. With Mao's imperative, every academic and cultural institution in mainland China was stipulated to criticize capitalistic idealism as represented by Yu Pingbo's *Dream* studies.

One may wonder why Mao Zedong, in the intense time of actualizing his socialist modernization project, took a personal interest in one piece of literary criticism. For Mao, however, literature or literary criticism was never just a site expressing individual opinions. Instead of occupying an autonomy of the aesthetic, literature was considered a battleground of no less importance than politics. This notion of literature can be traced back at least to the early 1940s. In his "Talks at the Yan'an Forum on Literature and Art," Mao explicitly stated that literature and art should serve the purpose of politics and revolution and asserted the party's control over all cultural activities. In what first appeared to be a difference of opinion concerning how to interpret a piece of classical literature, Mao Zedong seized the ideal opportunity to establish the appropriation of Marxist dialectical materialism and historical materialism in academic research. Mao envisioned it as combat to take over the field of literature and art from "intellectual authorities" like Yu Pingbo who were informed by capitalist "subjective idealism." Rather than residing in the secluded ivory tower of academia, the interpretation of classical literature became an essential part of the socialist transformation and

---

46. Mao Zedong, "Guanyu *Honglou meng* yanjiu wenti," p. 134.

construction. Therefore, the 1954 *Dream* controversy was a serious political confrontation between the Marxist and the capitalist ideologies, which shaped all the subsequent campaigns in Chinese academia, culminating in the Cultural Revolution.

By the spring of 1955, the Criticize Yu Pingbo Campaign, which had flared up so dramatically the previous year, had shifted its target to Hu Shi, the archetypical Chinese bourgeois intellectual and father of the New Redology,[47] and then to leaders of cultural and propagandist departments of the Communist Party, Hu Feng in particular. Ultimately, the *Dream* controversy expanded to the nationwide Anti-Rightist Campaign in 1957, aimed at the entire Chinese intelligentsia. At the peak of anti–Hu Shi criticism, Yu Pingbo had to write a confessional article to denounce Hu Shi's thought. Entitled "Jianjue yu fandong de Hu Shi sixiang huaqing jiexian" (To break with the reactionary thought of Hu Shi), it was published in *Literary Gazette*, the same journal that had promoted his *Dream* study just a couple of years earlier. Although hundreds of thousands were suffering because of the "pernicious impacts" of Hu Shi's thought, Hu Shi himself could only satisfy his intellectual ambition by reading reports in his Manhattan apartment about his own purge, soaring in the iron cage of the socialist state. The former leader of the May Fourth iconoclastic literary and cultural revolution half a century earlier was now engaged in socialist political radicalism vicariously through *Dream*, an eighteenth-century literary classic. As hundreds of thousands of people were accused and prosecuted, the irony of history is that the series of political movements triggered by the anti–Yu Pingbo campaign resulted in *Dream* being widely read in post-1949 socialist China. Between 1958 and 1962, printed copies numbered 140,000, and *Dream* became one of the highest-selling books apart from *Selected Works of Mao Zedong*.

Amidst the nationwide passion for *Dream*, the 1958 Yue opera by Xu Jin was the first drama to adapt the entire book rather than just excerpts. Distilling the intricacies of *Dream*'s epic dimensions was in

---

47. For a detailed examination of the 1955 Criticize Hu Shi Campaign, see, for instance, Grieder, "The Communist Critique of *Hung-lou meng*." For a discussion of the "New Redology" (New *Hongxue*) of the early twentieth century, see Edwards, "New *Hongxue*."

itself a herculean task. However, fitting the drama into the political ethos of the time was even more challenging. During the *Dream* debates of the 1950s, how the work could be interpreted in line with the Marxist political and cultural discourse espoused by the newly founded socialist state remained a focal point. While Hu Shi and Yu Pingbo were rebuked for their approach that was informed by subjective bourgeois idealism, Mao Zedong, himself an enthusiastic reader of *Dream*, asserted that only from the viewpoint of class struggle could one truly appreciate both *Dream* and Chinese history as a whole. Accordingly, he considered antifeudalist class struggles to be the leitmotif of the work: "severe class struggle, with the (sacrifice) of dozens of lives."[48]

An earlier attempt to rework *Dream* into a Yue opera within the thematic framework defined by the new political discourse had been made by none other than Su Qing, Eileen Chang's good friend who, much like Chang, achieved literary fame in occupied Shanghai for her work focusing on female space and subjectivity.[49] And much like Chang, Su Qing was also castigated by fellow writers after the end of the war for her suspicious political conformism during the Shanghai occupation. In the early years of the PRC, she had to switch from fiction writing to screenwriting for opera companies to make a living. In order to meet the dominant political criteria for the interpretation of *Dream*, Su Qing, in her play "Bao-yu and Dai-yu" written for Fanghua Yue Opera Company, created the maid Hui-xiang, who overcame brutal oppression to expose serious class struggles in the Jia family.[50]

However, when Xu Jin set out to adapt *Dream* for the Shanghai Yue Opera Company, he sought to do so in a more ambitious but refined way. Xu treated the work as a love tragedy brought about by the suffocating patriarchal family system, and Bao-yu and Dai-yu as

---

48. Mao Zedong, "Guanyu zhexue wenti de jianghua," p. 549.

49. Su Qing was implicated in the ensuing Anti–Hu Feng Campaign in 1955 and was imprisoned in the same year as a member of the Hu Feng cohort, which precipitated the virtual disappearance of the opera excerpt from the theater repertoire. The play "Bao-yu and Dai-yu" originally starred the opera diva Yin Guifang.

50. For a brief discussion of Su Qing's Yue opera reworking of *Dream*, see Wang Yixin, *Tamensan*, pp. 130–41.

victims of feudal marriage arrangements encapsulated in the adage "jinyu liangyuan" (the goodly affinity of gold and jade). In this light, this work is not just another outdated beauty-scholar story, but one that disavows feudal ethical and social codes and promotes the key values adopted by the May Fourth New Culture Movement, including the courage to fight against familial oppression and pursue individual freedom. Opening with Dai-yu's arrival in the Jia mansion, the play highlights episodes such as Bao-yu being beaten by his father, Dai-yu burying fallen flowers, Bao-yu and Dai-yu reading *Xixiang ji* (Romance of the west chamber) together, Bao-yu's wedding, and Dai-yu burning her manuscripts and her subsequent death. It ends with Bao-yu mourning Dai-yu's death and escaping from home, with the chorus singing the famous line "discarding the 'never lose, never forget' jade tablet, breaking the 'never leave, never abandon' golden locket; leaving the filthy place infested with flies, escaping the wealthy nest swarming with ants."[51] The finale stresses the main theme of the play, cursing the traditional marriage system and the corruption of the feudal household. In adopting the main plot of Gao E's 40-chapter sequel, whereby Bao-yu is tricked into marrying Bao-chai by the scheming of Xi-feng on the same evening that Dai-yu dies a dreadful, lonely death, the play has effectively reduced *Dream* to a tragic romance and successfully packaged it for popular consumption. In foregrounding the anti-feudalist theme, the play has managed to remain within the ambit of the prevailing political ideology and at the same time has preserved the poetic sophistication of the original work in its exquisite, lyrical arias, ensembles, and choruses.

It was under precisely such entangled political and cultural circumstances that Chang was invited by MP&GI to write a *Dream* film script for the Hong Kong market, which saw a surge of enthusiasm for *Dream* touched off by the performances of the Shanghai Yue Opera Company. Although it was political restraints that tethered playwrights such as Su Qing and Xu Jin on the mainland, Eileen Chang in Hong Kong was confronted by a dilemma of a different dimension. Certainly, both Su Qing's and Xu Jin's plays were censored

51. The original lyrics composed by Xu Jin reads: "抛卻了莫失莫忘通靈玉，掙脫了不離不棄黃金鎖。離開了蒼蠅競血骯髒地，撇開了黑蟻爭穴富貴窠。"

because of political violations. However, Chang's *Dream* adaptation did not even manage to pass the scrutiny of the film company. The letters Chang wrote during this time to Ferdinand Reyher, an American screenwriter she married in 1956, suggested two reasons for the rejection of her film script: The managers of MP&GI, who had never read the original work, were not able to appreciate her adaptation of *Dream*; and Shaw Brothers studio, MP&GI's primary competitor in Hong Kong, had also launched a plan to make a *Dream* film.[52]

MP&GI's managers may have not read *Dream*, and the Shaw Brothers Studio may have acted more quickly and thus seized the market opportunity, but it was not because Chang was unaware of how to appeal to a mass audience that her screenplay was rejected. After all, from the beginning of her literary career, Chang was well known for her constant flirtation with popular culture. I would like to suggest a different explanation for her dilemma. Chang once noted that all of the drama in *Dream* is to be found in the last forty chapters. She writes, "in the original 80 chapters of *Dream*, there is no single important event . . . All the important events occur in the last 40 chapters . . . What the first 80 chapters provide is the vivid and close texture of life."[53] How to deal with the outcome of *Dream*'s plot, or how to deal with the relationships between Bao-yu, Dai-yu, and Bao-chai at the end of the story, must have been the crucial concern for Chang in her reworking of *Dream*. It may well be that Chang's strategy for treating the ending of the story did not satisfy MP&GI's managers. Although there is no copy of Chang's *Dream* screenplay available for examination, a close reading of her research work on *Dream*, *Nightmare in the Red Chamber*, pertaining to her speculation about the authenticity of the last forty chapters, which she started shortly after the failed screenwriting project, provides important clues to her vision of *Dream*. I will pursue this issue further in the next section.

Indeed, as Chang was making countless revisions to the screenplay in order to garner MP&GI's approval, Shaw Brothers studio

---

52. See Chang's letters in Zhou Fenling, *Kongque landiao*, pp. 179–206.
53. Eileen Chang, *Haishang huakai, haishang hualuo*, p. 639.

produced a Huangmei (Yellow Plum) opera film version of *Dream*, which largely adopted the line of development of Xu Jin's opera version that ended with Dai-yu's death on Bao-yu and Bao-chai's wedding night, and with Bao-yu's subsequent escape from home. Released in 1962 and starring Betty Le Di, Shaw Brothers' *Dream of the Red Chamber* ultimately forced MP&GI to abort its plan. With Huangmei opera films being a mainstay of Hong Kong's Mandarin cinema in the 1950s and 1960s, this blockbuster film achieved huge box-office success.[54] By the time Shaw Brothers' Huangmei opera film *Dream* was enjoying wide circulation in the Chinese diaspora, the Shanghai Yue opera film *Dream*, which had been completed in the same year, had been censored in mainland China with the onset of yet another cultural movement on a grand scale, the Great Proletarian Cultural Revolution.

A Missed Moment of Modernity: Nightmare in the Red Chamber

In 1963, shortly after she returned to the United States from the aborted *Dream* filmmaking project, Eileen Chang started her research on *Dream*, a project on which she worked for the next ten years. The result is a series of articles that can be found in a monograph entitled *Nightmare in the Red Chamber.* In her diasporic life in the United States, especially in her secluded later years after the death of her second husband, why did Chang choose to delve into the world of *Dream*? And in what ways do *Dream* and Chang's reading of *Dream* relate to her own literary work and aesthetics? Little attention has been paid to Chang's only scholarly work. By addressing these questions, my exploration of Chang's *Nightmare* suggests a new perspective for reflecting on Chang's post-1949 writing career as well as providing a deeper look at her aesthetic world.

Chang's *Dream* study stands in a long and rich tradition of *Dream* scholarship, which started almost at the same time as the novel was written in the mid-eighteen century. In addition to the early *Dream*

54. For related research on this genre in Hong Kong film history, see, for instance, Chen Weizhi, *Wo ai Huangmei diao*; Ng Ho, *Guzhuang, xiayi, Huangmei diao.*

commentaries, Red Inkstone annotations being the most important of them, there have been two main schools of Redology: the *suoyin* (exploring obscurities) school, which interpreted the entire novel as a narrative about the palace intrigues during early reigns of the Qing dynasty or as a veiled ethnic criticism of the Manchu regime; and the *kaozheng* (textual analysis) mode of criticism, the so-called modern study of *Dream of the Red Chamber* initiated by Hu Shi, which sought to shift the focus onto the author of the novel and suggested that the novel was an autobiographical work of Cao Xueqin. However, in spite of their disparate focuses on political allegories or authorial history, both *suoyin* and *kaozheng* schools of interpretation treated *Dream* as a historical document rather than as a fictional work. As Haun Saussy points out, "both *suoyin* and *kaozheng* are modes of historical reading, only the assumptions about what constitutes history, or what is important in history, differ."[55]

In her preface to *Nightmare*, Chang notes that her study of *Dream* scrutinizes between the lines and between different hand-copied manuscripts and printed editions, a practice that she compares with experiences such as walking through a "labyrinth," assembling a "jigsaw puzzle," reading "a detective story," or following multiple possibilities as in "Rashomon."[56] Such a meticulous study, as I have argued in a recent article on *Dream*'s afterlife in modern China, combines both hermeneutic and philological approaches that characterize the *suoyin* and *kaozheng* schools.[57] *Nightmare* ploughs through layers of editions, marginalia, annotations, and commentaries, and brings these texts into complementary or contrastive dialogues. In her preface, Chang attributes her study of *Dream* to her thorough familiarity with the novel: "When I read different editions, even the slightest different usage of words would jump out at me instantly."[58] In her rigorous textual analysis, Chang draws heavily on previous scholarship, particularly on research done by *kaozheng* scholars including Hu Shi, Yu Pingbo, Zhou Ruchang, Wu Shichang, and Zhao Gang.

---

55. Saussy, "Age of Attribution," p. 129. In this article, Saussy provides an important perspective on the theory of *Dream*'s authorship.

56. Chang, *Honglou mengyan*, p. 10.

57. Xiaojue Wang, "*Stone* in Modern China."

58. Chang, *Honglou mengyan*, p. 6.

However, Chang's palimpsestic study of *Dream* deviates significantly from both leading schools. She never endeavors to propose yet another speculation about political allegories, dynastic secrets, or the family history and life of Cao Xueqin. Her research rather attempts to uncover how Cao's literary styles and techniques and aesthetic ideas gradually matured over the span of more than twenty years of writing and numerous revisions until his death, and to ponder major permutations of character creations and plot arrangements, as well as the central concepts of love and lust, desire and disillusionment. In discussing Chang's *Nightmare*, Guo Yuwen maintains that Chang's study treats *Dream* as a fictional creation rather than an autobiography or a mere social or historical source. It is thus inherently literary, whereas both the *suoyin* and *kaozheng* schools are historical.[59] Indeed, Chang's redological pursuit is permeated by her female authorial voice and uniquely marked by her refined perspective as a woman writer. It comes as no surprise that in the field of *Dream* study, Chang is often regarded as a quasi-Redologist for her eccentric approaches.[60] As much as he appreciates Chang's talent and her devotion to *Dream*, Zhou Ruchang, the noted Redologist, regards Chang as an "eccentric talent" (*guaijie*) in the tradition of *Dream* study and observes that *Nightmare* regretfully does not contribute much to Redology as an objective, scientific field.[61]

Questions about the authorship and authenticity of various editions of *Dream* have been the focus of different stages of *Dream* scholarship, particularly the *kaozheng* school.[62] One of the main concerns of Chang's research is how to assess Gao E's contribution to *Dream*. Recollecting her reading experiences in her early teens, Chang

---

59. Guo Yuwen, Honglou meng *xue*, pp. 341–68.

60. There have been a few studies of Eileen Chang's *Nightmare in the Red Chamber*, including Guo Yuwen, Honglou meng *xue*; Kang Laixin, "Duizhao ji: Zhang Ailing"; Zhao Gang, "Zhang Ailing yu hongxue."

61. Zhou Ruchang, *Dingshi Honglou meng li ren*, p. 5.

62. In his 1921 treatise "*Honglou meng* kaozheng" (Textual research on *Dream*), Hu Shi first identified Cao Xueqin as *Dream*'s author. More important, he utilized historical pragmatism as a critical method, providing a new point of departure for the study of *Dream*, and launched a new school of Redological studies—the *kaozheng* school. See Hu Shi, "*Honglou meng* kaozheng," pp. 575–620. Among recent *Dream* research, A. C. Yu's *Rereading the Stone* is particularly noteworthy.

writes, "When I reached the eighty-first chapter, everything suddenly felt unbearably stale and flat. The book stepped into an utterly different world thereafter . . . Many years later, I learned that the last forty chapters were actually a sequel."[63] Could it be possible that the last forty chapters might have contained some fragments from Cao Xueqin's original work? Could the composition of the last forty chapters be credited solely to Gao E, or might there have been multiple authors for them?

Chang attempts to respond to these questions by conducting a critical examination of the uneven literary quality of the last forty chapters and seeking to account for major changes made to *Dream*'s early editions.[64] Rather than focusing on mere textual comparisons between different editions, she explores inconsistencies in writing styles, character portrayals, and literary themes. One salient example would be Chang's analysis of the discrepancies in characterizing Dai-yu's outward appearance. Chang observes that throughout the first eighty chapters, there are virtually no material depictions of Dai-yu's countenance or clothes. The image of Dai-yu is conveyed as timeless, celestial, never corporeal: "There is no single physical detail (about her), merely a posture, a voice."[65] In this way, Cao Xueqin configures Dai-yu as transcending the earthy world, whereas Baochai, confined by the Confucian morality, is represented as a refined yet worldly character. Chang feels strongly upset when she reads an explicit illustration of Dai-yu's clothes in chapter 89: Dai-yu is described as dressed in a rose-colored embroidered coat, with a golden pin in her hair, which notably sabotages the image of Dai-yu as an intangible beauty. She thus comes to the conclusion that this must have been composed by someone other than Cao Xueqin.

Consequently, Eileen Chang argues that one has to take the eighty-chapter edition of *Dream* as an incomplete work in order to appreciate its genuine literary excellence. The last forty chapters penned by

---

63. Eileen Chang, *Zhang kan,* p. 152.

64. A main hypothesis Eileen Chang proposes in this regard is about the character Xi-ren. She maintains that Gao E has deliberately distorted the image of Xi-ren and projected his own failed relationship with his maid-cum-concubine Wanjun onto the persona of Xi-ren. See Eileen Chang, *Honglou mengyan*, pp. 57–68.

65. Ibid., p. 22.

Gao E are nothing but "a dog's tail replacing a sable" (*gouwei xudiao*), "an ulcer deeply rooted in bone" (*fugu zhiju*).[66] Gao E's edition has only turned *Dream* into the mawkish story of a love triangle with a dramatic ending and has therefore seriously corrupted Chinese reading tastes as well as literary criteria. Chang has noted elsewhere that the dramatization of life is not healthy.[67] In her *Dream* research, she is particularly concerned with one instance of controversy—the eventual outcome of the plot regarding the protagonist Bao-yu. She strongly reproaches Gao E for his "vulgar" addition, in which Bao-yu marries Bao-chai while Dai-yu dies a gloomy death and Bao-yu ultimately chooses a life of renunciation away from home. Rather, she is inclined to adopt the theory that in one of the early lost editions, Bao-yu eventually marries Xiang-yun, the cousin with whom he grows up before Dai-yu arrives, after the decline of the Jia family, and the novel ends with the couple living an impoverished life. According to Chang's reading, such an ending attests to one of couplets in the title of chapter 31, "Yin qilin fu baishou shuangxing" (The unicorn predicts that the twin stars will grow old together).

Chang spares no effort in extrapolating on this conclusion, which strikes her with such a tremendous impact as if "the stone broke and the sky thundered, the clouds tumbled down and the ocean soared up" (*shipo tianjing, yunchui haili*).[68] Evidently, she favors an ending that features the destitute couple Bao-yu and Xiang-yun to the melodramatic one Gao E embraced. Chang observes that the former gives the work a "realistic and modern" feel.[69] At the same time, she admits that such a mundane, undramatic solution would not have satisfied the popular tastes of the reading public of the time. For this reason, she argues, the author was obliged to revise it later to include a more dramatic closure when Bao-yu cuts off all human attachments and becomes a monk, an ultimate gesture that would appeal to the majority of readers. In this light, the revision of the work follows a trajectory "from modern to conventional" with regard to narrative strategies.[70]

---

66. Ibid., p. 9.
67. Eileen Chang, *Liuyan*, p. 12.
68. Chang, *Honglou mengyan*, p. 333.
69. Ibid.
70. Ibid.

Chang regrets that Chinese literature has thereby missed a moment of modernity.

Given Chang's preference for the early version of the story's ending, there is reason to assume that Chang may well have proposed the Bao-yu/Xiang-yun model in the screenplay she completed for MP&GI. When discussing the significance of the original ending in literary history, Chang speculates that "Even if such an ending was composed for a novel of a modern time, it wouldn't be any easier for modern readers to accept it."[71] If this is true of literature, it would be even more so for the new medium of moving pictures. Like Cao Xueqin, Eileen Chang was forced to trim her script extensively to meet the public taste. But this time, the public taste had been shaped for two centuries by the Gao E version of the story.

In the preface to *Nightmare*, Chang notes, "These two works (i.e., *Plum in the golden vase* and *Dream*) mean every source for me, especially *Dream*."[72] In modern Chinese literature, Chang is indeed the quintessential practitioner of *Dream*'s artistic sophistication and the finest interpreter of *Dream*'s idea about illusion and disillusionment, which is deeply rooted in the essential texture of the quotidian life. In reflecting on her own writing, Chang states, "So my fiction, with the exception of Cao Qiqiao in 'The Golden Cangue,' is populated with equivocal characters—They are not heroes, but they are of the majority who actually bear the weight of the times. As equivocal as they may be, they are also in earnest about their lives. They lack tragedy; all they have is desolation. Tragedy is a kind of closure, while desolation is a form of revelation."[73] The lack in tragedy and the emphasis on ambivalent yet true to life characters, which constitute the essence of humanity and life, is exactly what Chang appreciates in Cao Xueqin's *Dream*. From her point of view, this marks *Dream*'s literary modernity and renders this novel ahead of its time. According to Chang's study, the early version conceives the misfortune of the main heroes as triggered by their character flaws (*ziwu*), an idea close to

---

71. Ibid.

72. Ibid., p. 10. *Plum in the Golden Vase* is also translated as *The Golden Lotus*.

73. Eileen Chang, "Writings of One's Own," in *Written on Water*, p. 19. English translations are done by Andrew F. Jones.

hamartia in Greek dramaturgy. Only in later versions did the author add some overriding external force of fate such as the Imperial Concubine Yuan-chun's order that Bao-yu and Bao-chai shall marry. In analyzing Dai-yu and Bao-chai's personalities, Chang acknowledges one of the Red Inkstone comments and further elucidates, "Dai-yu is too bright and sensitive, which harms her health; and Bao-chai knows all and is erudite. Marrying a Ms. Know-all would inevitably harm the emotion between the couple."[74] The flaws and ambiguities in characters render them true. On this point, Chang shares a similar opinion with Lu Xun. As early as 1924, in his article "On the Historical Evolution of Chinese Fiction" (Zhongguo xiaoshuo de lishi bianqian), Lu Xun acclaimed *Dream* as contributing significantly to the school of fiction on "human sentiments" and asserted that *Dream*'s value lies particularly in "its depiction of characters in a true-to-life manner, without unnecessary trimmings, which distinguishes it from previous fictions, which describe good people as perfect, bad people as pure evil. Therefore, the characters in *Dream* are real."[75]

In her observations of the religious sentiment of the Chinese people, Eileen Chang remarks: "The fact that Chinese literature is full of sadness is due to lack of belief in anything. It takes pleasure only in material details (hence *The Golden Lotus* and *Dream of the Red Chamber* set out the menus of whole banquets in exact particular and with unflagging interest for no other reason than fondness), because the details are normally pleasant, satisfying and absorbing, while the main theme is always gloomy. All general observation of human life points to emptiness."[76] Chang's own literary writings are precisely characterized by a fascination with superfluous, sensuous, "feminine details" of everyday life and simultaneously by a deep penetration into human frailty and historical pathos.[77] Such a philoso-

---

74. Chang, *Honglou mengyan*, p. 329. The English word "Ms. Know-all" is from Chang's original text.

75. Lu Xun, *LXQJ* 9: 338.

76. Eileen Chang, *Yuyun*, p. 17. The English translation is from *The Chinese Essay*, ed. and trans. David Pollard (New York: Columbia University Press, 2000), p. 284.

77. For instance, see Lee, *Shanghai Modern*; Chow, *Woman and Chinese Modernity*, pp. 84–120.

phy, or "religious sentiment," is best conveyed in her favorite notion of "aesthetics of desolation." In her literary world, an impending catastrophe looms large in human civilizations. In "Ziji de wenzhang" (Writings of one's own), she notes, "In this era, the old things are being swept away and the new things are still being born. But until this historical era reaches its culmination, all certainty will remain an exception. People sense that everything about their everyday lives is a little out of order, out of order to a terrifying degree. All of us must live within a certain historical era, but this era sinks away from us like a shadow, and we feel we have been abandoned."[78] Permeated with a profound sense of loss and grief, Chang's aesthetics of desolation attests to the dialectic of worldly desire and its renunciation, which, according to Wang Guowei's philosophical reading of *Dream*, is the central theme of this classic novel.[79]

Ever since its publication in 1976, Chang's *Nightmare* has never been popular among *Dream* scholars or the large population of Chang fans in the Sinophone world. It is a fragmentary work composed of quotations, gleanings, extensive textual and edition comparisons, literary criticism, as well as recollections of her own reading and writing experiences. And, as Qian Min duly points out, there are no coherent connections between "rigorous and careful textual analysis and imaginative and daring fictional writings,"[80] which makes the book extremely hard to follow. In her study of *Nightmare*, Huang Xincun suggests that one read *Nightmare* as a work of literature rather than a scholarly monograph. Accordingly, she regards it as Chang's ruminations on her own life filtered through examinations of her *Dream* reading practices at different stages of her life. Viewed from this angle, *Nightmare* provides yet another reflection on Chang's central themes in her early fictions and essays such as temporal and spatial displacements.[81] I would argue that inasmuch as it continues to explore topics in Chang's work during the Shanghai Occupation, *Nightmare* marks a clear deviation from her early writings, fiction or

---

78. Eileen Chang, "Writings of One's Own," in *Written on Water,* p. 19.
79. Wang Guowei, "*Honglou meng* pinglun."
80. Qian Min, "Zhang Ailing he ta."
81. Huang Xincun (Huang, Nicole), "Mengzai honglou, xiezai geshi."

essay, with regard to her literary styles. The renowned Redologist Zhou Ruchang may not agree with many speculations Chang proposed in her *Dream* study, however, he is definitely right in describing Chang's writing style in this work as "unadorned, plain, and simple."[82] The embellished writing style infiltrated with elaborate vocabularies and exquisite imageries, which characterized her early writings and made her a literary star in occupied Shanghai, has completely vanished, which without doubt contributed to its unfavorable reception by the readers. Yu Bin suggests that such a change in style can be traced back to Chang's postwar writings before she ultimately left mainland China for Hong Kong. From my point of view, Chang's pursuit of a simple yet mature narrative and aesthetic style is best manifested in her 1950s novel *The Rice-Sprout Song*. In his comments on this novel, Hu Shi observes that *The Rice-Sprout Song* evokes a "realistic or natural artistic quality," the same remark he used thirty years earlier in his appreciation of Han Bangqing's late-Qing courtesan novel *Haishanghua liezhuan* (Sing-song girls of Shanghai, 1892).[83] Interestingly, Eileen Chang herself quoted this notion in her initial letter to Hu Shi sent together with a copy of *The Rice-Sprout Song*, hoping that the style of this novel could be characterized by a "realistic or natural artistic quality."[84] Not coincidentally, Chang praised *Sing-Song Girls* as the true follower of *Dream*, and spent years in translating this novel in Wu dialect first into English and then into Mandarin Chinese. *Nightmare* marks another effort by Chang to create a "realistic or natural" style in probing her favorite novel. Chang's endeavor to appreciate Cao Xueqin's incomplete work results in an incomplete work of her own. In defying a definite closure, a conventional narrative structure, and a distinct literary genre, *Nightmare* attests to a form of literary modernity initiated by *Dream*.

---

82. Zhou Ruchang, *Dingshi Honglou meng li ren*, p. 30.

83. For Hu Shi's letter to Eileen Chang, see Chang, *Zhang kan*, pp. 141–54. For Hu Shi's article on *Sing-song Girls of Shanghai*, see Hu Shi, preface to Han Bangqing, *Haishanghua liezhuan* (Sing-song Girls of Shanghai) (Taipei: Guangya, 1984), p. 8. This remark was originally proposed by Lu Xun.

84. See Su Weizhen, *Gudao Zhang Ailing*, pp. 79–80.

The Politics of Rewriting: Eileen Chang at the Cold War Frontier

Since the mid-1980s, works by writers such as Qian Zhongshu, Shen Congwen, and Eileen Chang who literally vanished from post-1949 versions of modern Chinese literary history, have been resurrected in mainland China. In the introduction, I discussed Ye Zhaoyan's reflection on the political and cultural predicament facing these writers in the post-1949 era. In that quoted passage, he observes that the distinctive post-1949 environment did not allow writers in the PRC such as Qian Zhongshu and Ba Jin to continue writing as they had previously. He then maintained: "However, Eileen Chang escaped the mainland and had way too much free time to write, yet still she did not produce any good works."[85] By "environment," he clearly refers to the political constraints imposed on intellectuals in the newly founded socialist state. However, in commenting that Eileen Chang, who left Communist China, did not produce any good works either, Ye fails to mention that writers on the opposite side of the Cold War divide also suffered intense political pressure.

In this regard, Eileen Chang's strenuous attempts to get published in the United States provide an intriguing case in point. In 1956, Chang completed her English novel *Pink Tears*, which was an English expansion and rewriting of her earlier novella "Jinsuo ji" (The Golden Cangue), but it was rejected by major publishing houses including Scribner's, Knopf, and Norton.[86] Given the strident Red Scare in the era of Joseph McCarthy, it comes as no surprise that a work such as *Pink Tears* would not have met political expectations. Focusing on revealing human frailty, *Pink Tears* by no means belongs to the rubric of anticommunist novels such as Chen Jiying's *Fool in the Reeds* and Jiang Wen's *Langtaosha* (To the tune of "waves scour the sands"), which appeared high on publishers' lists at the time. Ironically, both works were translated into English by none other than Eileen Chang. With her own literary efforts rejected, Chang was

---

85. Ye Zhaoyan, "Weicheng li de xiaosheng," p. 149.

86. For an exploration of how the McCarthyistic anti-Communist campaign affected cultural production in the United States in the Cold War era, see Saunders, *The Cultural Cold War.*

forced to rely on translation to make a living. The irony does not stop there. As apolitical as it is, *Pink Tears* was considered to carry dubious political implications. The Knopf review says of the manuscript that "all characters are loathsome. If the old China was like this, wouldn't it make the Communist Party the savior?"[87]

Furthermore, Knopf's review contains an underlying message that points to a different issue. The editor is obviously disappointed with or, to be more precise, provoked by the China represented by Eileen Chang. The image of China conveyed in *Pink Tears* does not meet the Orientalist expectations of Western readers. In responding to such Orientalist anxiety, Chang remarks, "I always have a hunch, for those who love China, the China they love is exactly the China I intend to disavow."[88] She is well aware of the constructedness of China and Chineseness in the eyes of the West. Her fiction never lacks moments satirizing characters who fall in love with a China fabricated by their own imaginations. Fan Liuyuan in "Qingcheng zhilian" (Love in a fallen city) and Tong Shifang in "The Golden Cangue" are two conspicuous examples. In this light, Chang's China differs significantly from that depicted in popular novels such as *A Many-Splendoured Thing* by Han Suyin (Elisabeth Comber).[89] According to Chang's reading, Han's China is not only a world "ornamented with classical poetry," but one that features sentimental love stories between a Chinese girl and a Caucasian. It is a vision of China with which Western readers can easily identify.[90] Therefore, Cold War cultural policy certainly imposed severe constraints on diasporic writers of the time, but the negative outpouring of Orientalism was equally precarious.

As noted earlier, Ye Zhaoyan opined that Chang did not produce any good works after 1949, but he is certainly not the first to point out that her later works do not measure up to her earlier literary achievements. Yet, when he attributes this literary degeneration to

87. See Chang's letter in Hsia, "Zhang Ailing gei wo de xinjian," pp. 69–71.

88. Ibid., pp. 70–71.

89. For an examination of the construction of China imageries in Chinese American literature, theater, and film, see, for instance, S. C. Wong, *Reading Asian American Literature*; Shan Dexing, *Mingke yu zaixian*.

90. See Chang's letter in Hsia, "Zhang Ailing gei wo de xinjian," pp. 52–53.

the lack of inner drive among post-1949 Chinese writers, he seems to be unaware of Chang's almost compulsive writing output in the second half of the twentieth century. It is noteworthy to mention just the novels she completed during the 1950s: *Eighteen Springs*, *The Rice-Sprout Song*, *Naked Earth*, and *Pink Tears*, which she then revised as *Rouge of the North*. Her output was remarkable, even more so for a writer who had never before written in the form of the novel. Her research on *Dream* and the project to translate *Dream*'s late Qing follower *Sing-Song Girls of Shanghai* are just as remarkable. Indeed, whether in Chinese or in English, Chang never stopped writing.

Furthermore, Chang's post-1949 literary career is characterized by an intriguing degree of compulsive rewriting. "Lust, Caution" was written as early as 1953, and then went through numerous revisions over a period of thirty years, and was not actually published until 1983. *Little Reunion*, which Chang began to write in the 1970s, took another twenty years to write and rewrite, and Chang still did not consider it ready for publication. The writing and revising of *Little Reunion* proceeded simultaneously with an English variation, which was discovered in 2009 and published in 2010 in two books, *The Fall of the Pagoda* and *The Book of Change*. These two English novels provide yet another piece in the "jigsaw puzzle" of a life story Chang never stopped fabricating, an autobiographical tapestry. The revision and reworking of "The Golden Cangue" serve as another conspicuous case. As noted earlier, the first novel Chang finished after arriving in the United States, *Pink Tears*, was an English reworking of her early novella "The Golden Cangue," which also has an English version translated by Chang. After it was rejected by a number of mainstream publishers, Chang rewrote it as *Rouge of the North*, which was eventually published by Cassell in England in 1967. At the same time, she translated it into Chinese under the title *Yuannü* (Embittered woman), and had it serialized in Hong Kong and Taiwan. Indeed, Chang's literary life in the United States was marked by constant rewriting and translation across languages and literary genres, and across a variety of media including literature, photo album, theater, film, and radio production. Her projects on *Dream* and *Sing-Song Girls of Shanghai* can also be considered in this framework.

Such literary and cultural practice needs to be examined in the larger context of the Cold War period. David Wang suggests that using English provided a way for Eileen Chang to flee modern Chinese literature dominated by literary realism. He observes that "A foreign language was no more alien a medium than Chinese to transmit, or translate, her already alienated existence in the Chinese environment."[91] I would take this argument even further to suggest that Chang's translingual practices not only question the restraints of modern Chinese literary and political discourse but also bespeak the equally manipulative ideological and cultural control of the Cold War United States. Chang migrated from Communist mainland China, only to find herself trapped by McCarthyism on the other side of the Iron Curtain. Knowing all too well the political and cultural rationale that prevented her work from being accepted by major American publishers, she nevertheless maintained her literary and aesthetic stance. Her deep suspicion of ideological hegemony of any kind is not only revealed in her arbitrary vacillation between pro- and anti-Communist novels between 1949 and 1953, but more importantly, is brought to the foreground by her prolific repetitions, or to be more precise, her trans-lingual and trans-generic fission of works devoted to the portrayal of epochal transitions. In this way, rewriting, or a kind of literary schizogenesis, became her strategy of deterritorialization, a way of avoiding any political dominion over literary creation by either side of the Cold War antagonism—Communist or anti-Communist.

In Chang's case, literary schizogenesis provided a way to confound the apparently relentless Cold War dichotomy. Indeed, her post-1949 literary practice asserts its standpoint by inducing the proliferation of the same yet differentiated subjectivity, a capricious subjectivity not only of the poetic characters but also of the poet herself. Such a strategy seems all the more trenchant in Chang's last work, *Duizhao ji: kan laozhaoxiangbu* (Mutual reflections: Reading old photographs, 1994), which is more a self-presentation in photographs than a representation in the conventional form of written words.[92] In 1994,

---

91. David Der-wei Wang, in Chang, *Rouge of the North*, pp. xi–xii.

92. Eileen Chang, *Duizhao ji* (Mutual reflections). For a detailed discussion of Chang's *Mutual Reflections*, see Wang Xiaojue, "Individual Memory, Photographic Seduction."

Chang produced this family photo album for Chinese audiences across mainland China, Taiwan, Hong Kong, and overseas communities. Using dozens of photos taken over the course of a century, she presented her life image as a multiply split self and subjectivity. Comprising fifty-four family photos paired with text of different lengths, *Mutual Reflections* constructs a visual and textual autobiographical narrative. Some of the captions consist of just one short sentence, noting when and where the picture was taken, whereas others are miniature essays, reminiscent of her other autobiographical writings such as "Tongyan wuji" (The guileless words of a child) or passages in *Little Reunion*. To collect pictures, no matter how blurred or grainy they may look, in an autobiography appears to serve a straightforward purpose: to illustrate and supplement the verbal narrative. However, the relationship between pictures and texts functions in a much more complicated manner in this book. W. G. Sebald, the contemporary German writer who was also fond of using photographs in his work, once remarked that both photography and fiction writing seem to act as tokens of authenticity. Yet, since they can be deduced, forged, and constructed, they "arrive at the truth on a crooked route."[93] As *Mutual Reflections* demonstrates, the interactions between texts and images often intensify the ambiguity of both modes of representation. Indeed, Eileen Chang's late career across cultural, linguistic, ideological, and national boundaries powerfully attests to the volatile circulation and negotiation between politics and literature, nation and narration, in the cultural Cold War.

---

93. Toby Green, quoted in T. D. Adams, "Photographs on the Walls of the House of Fiction Poetics," *Poetics Today* 29, no. 1 (2008): 188.

Epilogue: Toward a De-Cold War Criticism

This book has explored the competing modes of imagining nation, culture, and ways of human life across generic, gender, disciplinary, linguistic, and ideological boundaries in Cold War Chinese literature. In the strongest of their works, these Chinese writers created ways of connection, communication, and articulation to uncover and undermine the grid of Cold War dichotomous antagonism that positioned East against West, communism against capitalism, and totalitarianism against democracy. These instances of discrepancies and convergence, contestations and negotiations, testified to the intellectual agencies that rendered the totality of the Cold War world a porous space.

The international Cold War confrontation came to an end with the collapse of Eastern European socialism in 1989. However, it did not bring about the end of global conflicts and divisions even as globalization seemed to sweep across geopolitical borders with ease. In a time when the Cold War phase seems passé, Cold War ways of thinking remain obstinately with us today. A Cold War discursive specter uncannily emerges in Chinese neoleftists' invocation of an irreconcilable antagonism between revolutionary statism and capitalist globalization, as well as in the binary categorization of overseas Chinese and mainland Chinese in recent scholarly efforts to map out a Sinophone literature.

How can we form a new way of thinking, a viable praxis of de–Cold War criticism to address the changing global realities and exigencies of the post–Cold War era, seek new forms of knowledge to break the Cold War binary discourse, reach out to other cultures and other histories, and reconfigure the dialectic between history and literature? How will literature and literary criticism as loci of expression, representation, and transmission still be possible, valid, and meaningful? Bearing these questions in mind, this epilogue highlights a few poignant moments of narrative lapse, concealment, and silence during the last years of the Cold War. Discussions of these instances of discursive contestation around notions of literature, humanism, and internationalism probe potentials of a de–Cold War criticism, which carves out a new network of transnational exchange among people, cultures, and ideas and creates a new form of intellectual internationalism, a notion of *Weltliteratur*, so to speak, that is closer to Goethe's original idea suggesting new modes of transmission, communication, and articulation of human experiences.

In 1981, after her political rehabilitation, Ding Ling came to the United States to attend the International Writing Program (IWP) at the University of Iowa. During her visit to the PRC's archenemy across the Iron Curtain, Ding was asked repeatedly about her ordeal in the Mao time. For her American audience, Ding's experiences of raising chickens during her banishment in the Great Northern Wasteland, in particular, testified to Communist political persecution and state violence. Ding, however, offered a favorable account of her farm life, which aroused perplexity, disappointment, and anger among her audience and was often used as an evidence to expose her radical leftist stance in the post-Mao era.

At one evening gathering in Washington, D.C., Ding Ling was once again approached to speak by Chinese American expatriates about her chicken-raising days. Astonished by Ding's response that "raising chickens is beneficial," they asked a related question and suggested that she write an autobiography to enlighten the next generation. Facing all eager gazes, Ding replied calmly that she would not care for a personal testimony, "a book about a single individual, it's not worth the trouble."[1] The conversation stopped in an uneasy silence. Ding later recalled that she wanted to talk some sense to those people, yet failed to find the right words. So she beat a quick retreat.

---

1. Ding Ling, "Yangji yu yanggou," p. 149.

In this typical Cold War encounter, lack of communication occurs between a Communist notion of human collectivity and a liberal democratic one of humanism. For Ding, communism was the paramount ideal for all human societies despite its recent erroneous course in China. For her U.S. audience, to banish a (wo)man of letters to life as a tender of animals was undoubtedly a violation of basic humanity, which exposed the inhuman nature of communist authoritarianism. The compulsion to use liberal capitalist notions of humanism or individualism to bear on Ding Ling's experiences in Mao China prefigured Ding as a victim, a witness, and a survivor of communism. Such an identity is precisely what Ding Ling tenaciously rejected, within post-Mao China as well as beyond, as discussed in chapter 3.

The notion of humanism or individualism was surely not unfamiliar to Ding Ling, who made her literary debut in the 1920s by exposing its constraints. Tackling the predicaments facing Chinese women with newly acquired individuality in a time of semicolonial capitalist modernization, her early writings, including "Miss Sophie's Diary," question the idea of individualism with its claim of universal validity, which only obscures historical and contextual specificities such as issues of imperialism and colonialism, not to mention race and gender. The notions of humanism and humanity are key components of the Cold War binary discourse that positions communism against liberal democracy. In his seminal work *Orientalism*, written a decade before the Cold War dénouement, Edward W. Said criticized liberal humanism as a dominant mode of knowledge and warned of the imperial legacy in this apparently universal concept: "Liberal humanism, of which Orientalism has historically been one department, retards the process of enlarged and enlarging meaning through which true understanding can be attained."[2]

What upsets Ding Ling in such a Cold War nuisance of miscommunication or noncommunication, however, is not merely a suspicious classical, liberal humanist coding of problems that are of a more complicated international sociopolitical order. More significantly, it is a moment when a different type of humanism, Marxist

---

2. Said, *Orientalism*, p. 254.

humanism, was on the rise in the early 1980s PRC. From Wang Ruoshui's "Ren shi makesi zhuyi de chufadian" (The human being is the starting point of Marxism, 1980) to Zhou Yang's "Guanyu makesi zhuyi de jige lilun wenti de tantao" (An exploration of several theoretical problems in Marxism, 1983), from Bai Hua's film script "Ku Lian" (Bitter love, 1979) to scar literature (*shanghen wenxue*), from Li Zehou's Kantian aesthetics to Liu Zaifu's "literary subjectivity," the resurgence of humanism, humanity, and humanitarianism occurred on official, popular, and critical levels.[3] The 1980s Marxist humanist debate and the critique of alienation sought to work through the socialist crisis that culminated in the Cultural Revolution. However, the conceptualization of a socialist humanism was grounded on the very epistemological basis of European Enlightenment values. In this way, it is a post-Maoist continuation of the ill-fated mid-1950s brief return to European humanism, an intellectual tendency that people such as Feng Zhi avidly condemned, and a belated assertion and rehabilitation of European Enlightenment ideals. The late Ding Ling was well known for her harsh criticism of scar literature and the idea of humanity it foregrounded. Although I do not share her literary stance, I think that Ding is keen in discerning the subsiding revolutionary passion inherent in socialist humanist works that would eventually anticipate the post-Tiananmen era of depoliticization and derevolutionization.[4] Given its concealed affinity with liberal humanism, the model of Marxist humanism also failed to attain a true understanding of the recent Chinese socialist past. As Wang Hui points out, "in this explanatory model, socialism was never an anticapitalist modernization formation; on the contrary, the socialist historical experience was a complete affirmation of the values of the European modernity."[5]

Ding confronted in a time of Cold War détente both a capitalist and a Marxist notion of humanism, neither of which presented an effective way of understanding China's socialist experiences. Inasmuch

---

3. One part of Zhou Yang's report was written by the literary theorist Wang Yuanhua.

4. For Ding Ling's critique on scar literature, see, for instance, Ding Ling, "Zai zhongxuanbu yici wenyi."

5. Wang Hui, "Contemporary Chinese Thought," p. 39.

as these two types of humanism are bound by the Cold War discursive dichotomy of totalitarianism versus democracy, oppression versus freedom, they are more exclusionary than their inclusionary, universalist claims seem to be in understanding human histories. At the dawn of the Cold War, Erich Auerbach (1892–1957) observed that the Cold War cultural crisis resulted from a tendency in which "All human activity is being concentrated either into European-American or into Russian-Bolshevist patterns."[6] The leveling and polarizing forces of the Cold War severely endangered a human world with cultural multiplicity. If the Cold War is a way of knowing, "a style of thought through which power worked to create divisions, distinctions, and discriminations,"[7] it simultaneously creates a way of not-knowing and thus circumscribes the production of knowledge.

If humanism, concerned with human condition and human history, has not yet exhausted its steam of criticism in the post–Cold War time, then what type of humanism is still viable? How can humanism maintain its validity as a praxis of criticism that is still relevant to the exigencies of our contemporary life? What "new" concept of humanism can help formulate a de–Cold War critical consciousness that will efficiently deal with the Cold War legacy and eliminate the discursive specter that is still very much alive in our post–Cold War age?

In "Philology and *Weltliteratur*" (1952), Auerbach departed from a German romantic tradition of philology and advocated for a notion of humanistic philology, in which he saw a mode of cultural criticism that investigated the connection between history and literature, an interpretive practice that traced man's "advance to consciousness of his human condition and to the realization of his given potential."[8] Although discerning in the Cold War age a "mighty and rapid process" of leveling and homogenization that imposed uniformity upon the diverse repertoire of human cultures, Auerbach nevertheless entertained hope for a humanistic practice. His concept of a secular

---

6. Auerbach, "Philology and *Weltliteratur*."

7. Rubin, *Archives of Authority*, p. 103. In this work, Rubin studies how the CIA-sponsored Congress for Cultural Freedom (CCF) attempted to manipulate global Cold War cultural life through canonization of a group of world-class literary masters.

8. Auerbach, "Philology and *Weltliteratur*," p. 5.

humanism aimed at fostering mutual understanding and cultural exchanges among different cultural traditions and at producing a mode of knowledge that saw humanity "unified in its multiplicities."[9]

In a set of lectures first delivered at Columbia University and later at Cambridge University, Edward W. Said made a final appeal to humanism and proposed that a notion of critical, worldly humanism may help address a post–September 11 world marked by globalization and terrorism. Building upon Auerbach's secular humanism, Said suggested that the task of a worldly humanist is to employ his power of interpretation to resist against any dominant, hegemonic culture. A cosmopolitan, worldly, and mobile humanism, Said asserted, "must excavate the silences, the world of memory, of itinerant, barely surviving groups, the places of exclusion and invisibility."[10] Therefore, the critical agency of humanistic philology lies in its capacity of interpretation to disclose what is concealed, hidden, and distorted in language. Said concluded,

> Humanism, I think, is the means, perhaps the consciousness we have for providing that kind of finally antinomian or oppositional analysis between the space of words and their various origins and deployments in physical and social place, from text to actualized site of either appropriation or resistance, to transmission, to reading and interpretation, from private to public, from silence to explication and utterance, and back again, as we encounter our own silence and mortality—all of it occurring in the world, on the ground of daily life and history and hopes, and the search for knowledge and justice, and then perhaps also for liberation.[11]

Such a humanistic practice that provides an "antinomian or oppositional analysis" between the text and the social reality in which it is situated can be taken as a point of departure for a de–Cold War criticism. Throughout this book, potentials of intellectual resistance and agency have been investigated, even under the deepest Cold War restrictions, to traverse the boundaries imposed by ideology or any forms of dominative knowledge. A de–Cold War cultural criticism contests the containment of Cold War separations, distinctions, and discriminations and resists "the ideological forms of closure, synthesis,

9. Ibid., p. 7.
10. Said, *Humanism and Democratic Criticism*, p. 81.
11. Ibid., p. 83.

and resolution."[12] If humanism can still lend any vigor to today's intellectual criticism, a de–Cold War humanist approach must fight against the leveling force of modernization and globalization and challenge the constraints of partition and distinction while respecting historical and contextual specificities of all human traditions. Only then is any intellectual critical consciousness possible and able to hold political agency in the post–Cold War era.

On this point, it is worth recalling an insightful notion of culture expressed by Shen Congwen in the early 1980s. In a lecture delivered at Columbia University during his U.S. visit, Shen reassessed his life's work and reflected on how the imperial capital, Beijing, served as a museum of Chinese arts, culture, and humanities, which significantly informed his two interrelated passions: writing and researching historical cultural artifacts.[13] In his narrative representations of West Hunan life as well as in his art historical research, Shen does not merely catalogue, delineate, and archive diverse human activities and cultural artifacts. More important, he treats them as texts, to locate their positions within the social, historical reality of human life and thus present the connection between the past, the present, and the future in a way that was lived and articulated in what his contemporary Auerbach called the "inner history" of "mankind achieving self-expression."[14] In this light, Shen's cultural practice stands close to a humanistic philologist criticism. In an age of cultural crisis with growing ideological homogenization in Mao China, Shen sees in such textual and contextual study of cultural artifacts—be those made of words, threads, numbers, bronze, or music notes—a possible way of preserving the humanities and attaining consciousness of ourselves within history. The human being and humanity are the foundation and faith of his life's work, as his grave epitaph testifies: "One can understand me on the basis of 'me,' one can know human beings on the basis of me" (*Zhao wo sisuo, neng lijie "wo," zhao wo sisuo, ke renshi ren*). Although he remained reticent about specific political concerns in Mao China, his cultural practice

---

12. Rubin, *Archives of Authority*, p. 107.

13. Shen Congwen, "Ershi niandai de zhongguo xin wenxue" (new Chinese literature in the 1920s), *SCWQJ* 12: 374–82.

14. Auerbach, "Philology and *Weltliteratur*," p. 6.

during this time period can be read as an engaged response to the crisis of Chinese civilization that culminated in the Cultural Revolution. Shen's cultural reflection provides an important clue for critical intellectuals in the post–Cold War era. A de–Cold War criticism must be one that is able to read texts outside of any ideological manipulation and coercion, to discern and preserve differences and specificities among texts, cultures, and histories.

After the collapse of communism, when state socialism seemed to have exhausted its innovation and experimentation, a de–Cold War criticism also means the courage to hope for the alternative—an alternative way of life, of self-expression, and of international cultural exchange—to challenge the process of standardization and homogenization set off by a neoliberal globalization. Whereas Francis Fukuyama's notion of the "end of history" suggests a liberal democracy as the ultimate form of human society, it is marked by an ineffable anxiety about the absence of an "attractive alternative way of life or way of organising human collectives that could rival liberal democracy."[15] Is a form of internationalism still possible as an alternative to the neoliberal globalization? How would this internationalism help restore the vigor of Goethe's *Weltliteratur* that anticipates fruitful connections and interactions among cultural traditions? The following case provides us with further reflections on these questions.

In 2003, Chen Yingzhen was awarded the top Malaysian Chinese-language literary award, "Huazong shijie huawen wenxue jiang" (Flower Trail World Chinese Language Literature Prize), in Kuala Lumpur. At the presentation ceremony, Wang Anyi, the first recipient of this award, spoke about her intellectual debt to Chen since their first encounter at the IWP in 1982 and lamented that Chen was a solitary intellectual "abandoned by his time, like the ideal society of utopia, which we've never seen yet are all too familiar with."[16] This neverland is perhaps best represented by what Wang Anyi later named her article published in *Sin Chew Daily*, "the 'Internationale,'" an ideal of internationalism that has never been realized before being tragically deserted.

15. Müller, "The Cold War and the Intellectual," p. 21.
16. Wang Anyi, "Yingte naixiong nai'er."

Two years later, Chen Yingzhen also reflected on a moment of the "Internationale," a moment of linguistic and conceptual lapse and miscommunication between socialists and internationalists at the IWP during the last few years of the Cold War. Chen was first invited by the IWP's cofounder and director, Nieh Hualing, to join the program in 1968, shortly before he was imprisoned by the KMT government because of his leftist tendencies. He did not obtain permission to depart for Iowa City until 1982, one year after Ding Ling finished her IWP term. Nieh conceived the idea of an international forum for writers out of her own diasporic Cold War experiences. Nieh started her writing career during the Chinese civil war and served as an editor of the literary supplement of *Free China Fortnightly* (1949–60), which maintained a significant literary terrain beyond the dominant anti-Communist literature of 1950s Taiwan. After this liberal periodical was censored by the KMT, she fled the White Terror in Taiwan and continued her literary career in the United States.

One afternoon, Chen and Aquino, a leftist writer from the Philippines, visited their Eastern European comrades to weigh ideas of socialism and socialist literature. The conversation, however, was unexpectedly stranded in a fierce dispute over American movies. Whereas the Eastern European writers admired them for their depiction of human nature, Chen and Aquino condemned them as imparting American imperialism among people in American Cold War protectorates. At this intense moment of failed communication—because of the application of an awkward English, a foreign tongue, as well as of incommensurable notions of humanity and socialism, someone suddenly started to hum a song—the "Internationale"—and everyone followed suit in different languages. That afternoon ended in the melody of the "Internationale," in tears and hugs.

Years later, in his reflections on third-worldism and internationalism, Chen was still wondering about that particular evocation of the "Internationale": Was it "for a bygone revolution? For a zealous faith that we once shared? For an awakened nostalgia for the red banner and internationalism?"[17] This apparently irreconcilable confrontation, which burst out at the IWP, allegedly conceived to provide a

17. Chen Yingzhen, "Dui wo eryan de 'disan shijie.' "

meeting place for international writers, where "the mainland Chinese will meet the East Europeans and find out how very different their Socialisms are from rigid Marxism," seemed to be solved or displaced in the "Internationale" performed in diverse national languages.[18] In effect, this stranded international union revealed significant layers of conflict: between disparate socialist imaginaries; between American imperialism and neocolonialism in the guise of Cold War anticommunism, and the decolonial and independence movements in countries and regions of Asia, Africa, and Latin America; between East and West, two concepts that are intersecting—East in this case means both Asia and the Communist bloc of Eastern Europe, while West means both Europe and the capitalist bloc, including Taiwan and the Philippians. More importantly, it illuminated the predicament, therefore the urgency, of the need to find an alternative to capitalist domination—a third world that differentiated from what was defined by Western or Maoist "Three Worlds" theories. Therefore, in recalling this moment two decades later, when neoliberal globalization seemed to seal the end of history, Chen took it as illuminating a different form of internationalism rather than as anticipating requiem for communism.

In such resilient faith and commitment must a de–Cold War intellectual criticism be grounded: a critical consciousness that resists any leveling force, be it in the name of communism, universal humanism, globalization, or antiterrorism; that makes connections between cultures and traditions deeply concerned with the human condition; that sees humanity unified in its multiplicity. Only with such a critical stance can we exorcise the lingering Cold War specter and avoid slipping into a sentimental discursive and moral position on the individual as someone who stands against the state machine, against any hegemonic entity, against which I cautioned in the introduction and throughout the entire book. Only such a de–Cold War critical consciousness can allow us to see beyond the Cold War face and restore some of the nuance and complexity to the history of Chinese modernities.

18. Mitgang, "Publishing: Chinese Weekend in Iowa."

Character List

Ai Siqi 艾思奇
Ba Jin 巴金
Ba Ren 巴人
Bai Hua 白樺
Bai Liusu 白流蘇
baihua wenxue 白話文學
baishu 白薯
Beidahuang 北大荒
Beixin qiao 北新橋
Bian Zhilin 卞之琳
Biantai xinli xue 變態心理學
Biantai xinli xue paibie 變態心理學派別
bingli xue 病理學
boluan fanzheng 撥亂反正
Cai Yi 蔡儀
Cai Yuanpei 蔡元培
Cao Juren 曹聚仁
Cao Qiqiao 曹七巧
Cao Xueqin 曹雪芹
Cao Zhi 曹植
Chan Kwok Kou 陳國球
Chen Fangming 陳芳明
Chen Jitong 陳季同
Chen Jiying 陳紀瀅
Chen Ming 陳明
Chen Pingyuan 陳平原
Chen Quan 陳銓
Chen Quzhen 陳渠珍
Chen Ruoxi 陳若曦
Chen Tushou 陳徒手
Chen Yi 陳儀
Chen Yingzhen 陳映真
Chen Yinke 陳寅恪
Cheng Ren 程仁
chengdan 承擔
Chi fandong wenyi 斥反動文藝
Chiang Kai-shek 蔣介石
Chidi zhilian 赤地之戀
chouxiang de shuqing 抽象的抒情
Cong xianshi xuexi 從現實學習
Dagong bao 大公報
dandang 擔當
danwei 單位
dangdai 當代
dangdai wenxue 當代文學
datong 大同
Dazhong wenyi 大眾文藝
Dazhong wenyi congkan 大眾文藝叢刊
Deng Yingchao 鄧穎超
disan shili 第三勢力
Ding Ling 丁玲
Dong Guihua 董桂花

Du Fu 杜甫
Du Wanxiang 杜晚香
duanmen 端門
duannian 斷念
dunwu 頓悟
Fan Liuyuan 范柳原
Fan Wenlan 范文瀾
Fang Xiangqian 方祥謙
fangong kang'e 反共抗俄
fangong wenyi 反共文藝
fanshen 翻身
Feng Da 馮達
Feng Naichao 馮乃超
Feng Xuefeng 馮雪峰
Feng Youlan 馮友蘭
Feng Zhi 馮至
Fenghuang 鳳凰
Fu Enrong 傅恩榮
fudan 負擔
fugu zhiju 附骨之疽
Gan Lu 甘露
ganqing 感情
ganying chaomei 趕英超美
Gao E 高鶚
Gao Xuhui 高旭輝
geming jianguo 革命建國
Gongfa huitong 公法會通
gongshe shitang 公社食堂
gongzhong 公眾
gouwei xudiao 狗尾續貂
gu 蠱
Gu Zhun 顧准
Guangming bao 光明報
guoyu wenxue 國語文學
Guo Moruo 郭沫若
guocui 國粹
Han Bangqing 韓邦慶
Han Shouxuan 韓壽萱
Han Suyin 韓素音
He Guimei 賀桂梅
He Lin 賀麟
Heini 黑妮
heishu ducao 黑書毒草
Hong Yanqiu 洪炎秋
Hong Yueqiao 洪月樵
Hong Zicheng 洪子誠
Honglou meng 紅樓夢
Hou Hsiao-hsien 侯孝賢
Hu Feng 胡風
Hu Lancheng 胡蘭成
Hu Taiming 胡太明
Hu Yepin 胡也頻
Huazong shijie huawen wenxue jiang 花蹤世界華文文學獎
Huang Juan 黃娟
Huang Yongyu 黃永玉
Huang Ziping 黃子平
Huanghun he wuye 黃昏和午夜
huawai zhidi 化外之地
jianchi 堅持
Jiang Gui 姜貴
Jiang Wen 江文
jieji lun 階級論
Jin Yong 金庸
jingshen fenlie zheng 精神分裂症
jingshen shichang 精神失常
Jinri shijie 今日世界
jinyu liangyuan 金玉良緣
jiu wenxue 舊文學
jixing de yanzhi 即興的言志
Jizha 季扎
Kan hong lu 看虹錄
kaozheng 考證
kefu 克服
Kuangren riji 狂人日記
Kumen de xiangzheng 苦悶的象徵
Lai He 賴和
Lan Ling 藍翎
Lao She 老舍
Lei Haizong 雷海宗
Leifang ta 雷峰塔
Leung Ping-Kwan 梁秉鈞（也斯）

Li Bo 李白
Li Guangtian 李廣田
Li Helin 李何林
Li Huiying 李輝英
Li Tuo 李陀
Li Xifan 李希凡
Li Yu 李漁
Li Zehou 李澤厚
lianggui bakou 兩跪八叩
Liang Qichao 梁啓超
Liang Sicheng 梁思成
Liang Yusheng 梁羽生
Liang Zongdai 梁宗岱
Lianhe bao 聯合報
Lin Boyan 林柏燕
Lin Haiyin 林海音
Lin Huiyin 林徽因
Lin Tongji 林同濟
Lin Yutang 林語堂
Ling Shuhua 凌叔華
liqun 離群
Liu Quan 劉荃
Liu Yichang 劉以鬯
Liu Yongfu 劉永福
Liu Zaifu 劉再復
Liulichang 琉璃廠
Long Zongying 龍宗瑛
Lü Heruo 呂赫若
Lu Ling 路翎
Lu Xun 魯迅
lunli 倫理
Luo Dayou 羅大佑
Luo Fu 羅孚
Luo Xinxiang 羅心鄉
Ma Lang 馬朗
Mao Dun 茅盾
Mao wenti 毛文體
Mao Zedong 毛澤東
mei 美
meiyu 美育
Mengzi 孟子
Minsheng zhuyi yule liangpian bushu 民生主義育樂兩篇補述
Mou Zongsan 牟宗三
Mu Dan 穆旦
mudi 目的
Mujie wen 墓碣文
nanlai zuojia 南來作家
Nieh Hualing 聶華苓
Pan Guangdan 潘光旦
Pan Renmu 潘人木
paobu jinru gongchan zhuyi 跑步進入共產主義
Peng Ruijin 彭瑞金
pingdan jinzhen 平淡近真
pingmin de wenxue 平民的文學
Qian Gurong 錢谷融
Qian Liqun 錢理群
Qian Wengui 錢文貴
Qian Zhongshu 錢鐘書
qilin'er 麒麟兒
Qin Yu 秦羽
qing 情
qinghua ci 青花瓷
Qiu Fengjia 丘逢甲
Qiyue 七月
Qu Yuan 屈原
rende wenxue 人的文學
renge fenlie 人格分裂
Renmin ribao 人民日報
rennai 忍耐
renxing lun 人性論
Shanghai shi wenxue yishu gongzuozhe daibiao dahui上海市文學藝術工作者代表大會
shanghen wenxue 傷痕文學
Shao Quanlin 邵荃麟
shaonü luodong 少女落洞
shen 神
Shen Congwen 沈從文
shengcun 生存
shenghuo 生活

shengming 生命
shenxing 神性
Shi Tuo 師陀
Shikan 詩刊
Shisihang ji 十四行集
shizi ban 識字班
shouxing 獸性
shuangchong renge 雙重人格
si 思
si yu bian 死與變
Sima Changfeng 司馬長風
sishu 私塾
Song cuntong naoxue tu 宋村童鬧學圖
Song Qi 宋淇（林以亮）
Su Qing 蘇青
Sun Jinsan 孫晉三
suoyin 索隱
Taiwan minzhuguo 台灣民主國
Taiwan wenyi 台灣文藝
Taiwan xinwenxue 台灣新文學
Tan Yuexiang 譚月香
Tang Jingsong 唐景崧
Tang Junyi 唐君毅
tangshan 唐山
tian xia yi jia 天下一家
Tong Shifang 童世舫
tongdian 童癲
wancheng 完成
Wang Anyi 王安憶
Wang Guowei 王國維
Wang Hui 汪暉
Wang Jingwei 汪精衛
Wang Lan 王藍
Wang Meng 王蒙
Wang Ruoshui 王若水
Wang Shilang 王詩琅
Wang Shuming 王淑明
Wang Wenjuan 王文娟
Wang Xun 王遜
Wang Yao 王瑤
Wang Zengqi 汪曾祺
Wei Zhongguo wenhua jinggao shijie renshi xuanyan 為中國文化敬告世界人士宣言
Wen Yiduo 聞一多
Wenhua qingjie yundong 文化清潔運動
Wenhui bao 文匯報
Wenshizhe 文史哲
wenwu 文物
Wenxing 文星
Wenxue zazhi 文學雜誌
Wenyi bao 文藝報
Wenyi dao junzhong qu 文藝到軍中去
Wenyi xinchao 文藝新潮
wu 巫
Wu Jianren 吳趼人
Wu Shichang 吳世昌
Wu Zhuoliu 吳濁流
Wu Zixu 伍子胥
Wumen 午門
Xia Yan 夏衍
xiandai 現代
xiandai wenxue 現代文學
Xiang Da 向達
xiangtu wenxue 鄉土文學
Xiangxi 湘西
Xiao Qian 蕭乾
xin 信
Xin minzhu zhuyi lun 新民主主義論
xin nüxing 新女性
Xin shenghuo yundong 新生活運動
Xin wanbao 新晚報
xin wenxue 新文學
xin xiaoshuo 新小說
Xingdao wanbao 星島晚報
Xinlu 新路
Xinshi 新詩
xinxing 心性
Xu Dishan 許地山

Xu Fuguan 徐復觀
Xu Jin 徐進
Xu Nanying 許南英
Xu Xu 徐訏
Xu Yulan 徐玉蘭
Xu Zhimo 徐志摩
yanzhi 言志
Yang Hui 楊晦
Yang Kui 楊逵
Yang Qianhe 楊千鶴
Yang Yunping 楊雲萍
Ye Zhaoyan 葉兆言
yimin 遺民
Yingzao she 營造社
Yongqing 永清
Yu Dafu 郁達夫
Yu Pingbo 俞平伯
Yuan kejia 袁可嘉
yuanxi tiaozheng 院系調整
yuanxiang ren 原鄉人
zaidao 載道
Zai pipan 再批判
zaowu 造物
zhandou wenyi 戰鬥文藝
Zhang Ailing 張愛玲
Zhang Daofan 張道藩
Zhang Dongsun 張東蓀
Zhang Junmai 張君勱
Zhang Shenqie 張深切
Zhang Wenhuan 張文環
Zhang Wojun 張我軍
Zhang Zhaohe 張兆和
zhanghui 章回
Zhanguo ce 戰國策
Zhao Gang 趙岡
Zhao Jiabi 趙家璧
Zhao Shuli 趙樹理
Zhao wo sisuo, neng lijie "wo," zhao wo sisuo, ke renshi ren 照我思索，能理解"我"，照我思索，可認識人
Zheng Chenggong 鄭成功
Zheng Min 鄭敏
Zheng Zhenduo 鄭振鐸
Zhenzhen 貞貞
Zhong Haodong 鐘浩東
Zhong Lihe 鐘理和
Zhong Taimei 鐘台妹
Zhong Zhaozheng 鐘肇政
Zhongguo gudai fushi yanjiu 中國古代服飾研究
Zhongguo wenyi xiehui 中國文藝協會
Zhonghua quanguo wenxue gongzuozhe xiehui 中華全國文學工作者協會
Zhonghua quanguo wenxue yishu gongzuozhe daibiao dahui 中華全國文學藝術工作者代表大會
Zhonghua quanguo wenxue yishujie lianhehui 中華全國文學藝術界聯合會
Zhonghua wenhua fuxing yundong 中華文化復興運動
Zhonghua wenyi jiangjin weiyuanhui 中華文藝獎金委員會
zhongnong 中農
Zhou Jinbo 周金波
Zhou Liangpei 周良沛
Zhou Ruchang 周汝昌
Zhou Yang 周揚
Zhou Zuoren 周作人
Zhu Dianren 朱點人
Zhu Guangqian 朱光潛
Zhu Keyu 竹可羽
Zhu Shunshui 朱舜水
Zhu Ziqing 朱自清
zihui 自毀
zishou bianjie 自首變節
ziwu 自誤
Ziyou Zhongguo 自由中國
Zong Baihua 宗白華
zuopai 左派

Bibliography

Adorno, Theodor W. "Valéry Proust Museum." In *Prisms*, translated by Samuel Weber and Shierry Weber, 173–86. London: Neville Spearman, 1967.

Alber, Charles J. *Embracing the Lie: Ding Ling and the Politics of Literature in the People's Republic of China*. Westport, CT: Praeger, 2004.

Anderson, Benedict. *Imagined Communities: Reflections on the Origin and Spread of Nationalism*. London: Verso, 1991.

Anderson, Mark M. *Kafka's Clothes: Ornament and Aestheticism in the Habsburg Fin de Siècle*. Oxford: Clarendon Press, 1992.

Artaud, Antonin. "Van Gogh: The Man Suicided by Society." In *Antonin Artaud Anthology*, edited by Jack Hirschman, 135–63. San Francisco: City Lights Books, 1965.

Ashcroft, Bill, Gareth Griffiths, and Helen Tiffin. *The Empire Writes Back: Theory and Practice in Post-Colonial Literatures*, 2nd ed. London: Routledge, 2002.

Auden, W. H. *Journey to a War*. New York: Random House, 1939.

Auerbach, Erich. "Philology and *Weltliteratur*." *Centennial Review* 13 (Winter 1969): 1–17.

Ba Jin 巴金. *Suixiang lu* 隨想錄 (Random thoughts). Beijing: Beijing renmin chubanshe, 1980.

Barghoorn, Frederick C. *Soviet Foreign Propaganda*. Princeton, NJ: Princeton University Press, 1964.

Barlow, Tani E., with Gary J. Bjorge, eds. *I Myself Am a Woman: Selected Writings of Ding Ling*. Boston: Beacon Press, 1989.

———. "Woman under Maoist Nationalism in the Thought of Ding Ling." In *The Question of Women in Chinese Feminism*, 190–252. Durham, NC: Duke University Press, 2004.

Becker, Jasper. *Hungry Ghosts: Mao's Secret Famine*. New York: Free Press, 1996.

Benjamin, Walter. "The Author as Producer," in Benjamin, *Reflections*, 220–38.

———. *Charles Baudelaire: A Lyric Poet in the Era of High Capitalism*, translated by Harry Zohn. London: Verso, 1983.

———. "Eduard Fuchs: Collector and Historian." In *The Essential Frankfurt School Reader,* edited by Andrew Arato and Eike Gebhardt, 225–53. New York: Continuum, 1998.

———. *Illuminations: Essays and Reflections,* edited by Hannah Arendt, translated by Harry Zohn. New York: Schocken Books, 1969.

———. "Politisierung der Intelligenz: Zu S. Kracauer 'Die Angestellten'" (The politicization of the intellectuals: On S. Kracauer's "The employees"). In *Angelus Novus, Ausgewählte Schriften,* Vol. 2. Frankfurt am Main: Suhrkamp, 1966.

———. *Reflections: Essays, Aphorisms, Autobiographical Writings*, edited by Peter Demetz. New York: Schocken Books, 1986.

———. "Surrealism: The Last Snapshot of the European Intelligentsia." In Benjamin, *Reflections,* 177–92.

———. "Theses on the Philosophy of History." In Benjamin, *Illuminations*, 253–64.

Bleuler, Eugen. *Dementia Praecox or the Group of Schizophrenias*, translated by Joseph Zinkin. New York: International Universities Press, 1950.

Brown, Jeremy, and Paul G. Pickowicz, eds. *Dilemmas of Victory: The Early Years of the People's Republic of China*. Cambridge, MA: Harvard University Press, 2007.

Bürger, Peter. *Theory of the Avant-garde*, translated by Michael Shaw. Minneapolis: University of Minnesota Press, 1984.

Cao Juren 曹聚仁. *Wentan wushi nian* 文壇五十年 (Fifty years in the cultural realm). Hong Kong: Xin wenhua chubanshe, 1955.

Carmichael, Virginia. *Framing History: The Rosenberg Story and the Cold War.* Minneapolis: University of Minnesota Press, 1993.

Caute, David. *The Dancer Defects: The Struggle for Cultural Supremacy during the Cold War.* New York: Oxford University Press, 2003.

Chan, Kwok Kou Leonard 陳國球. *Wenxueshi shuxie xingtai yu wenhua zhengzhi* 文學史書寫形態與文化政治 (Historiography of literary history and cultural politics). Beijing: Beijing daxue, 2004.

Chang, Carsun. "A Manifesto for a Re-appraisal of Sinology and Reconstruction of Chinese Culture." In *The Development of Neo-Confucian Thought*, vol. 2, app., 455–83. New York: Bookman, 1962.

Chang, Eileen (Zhang Ailing 張愛玲). *The Book of Change*. Hong Kong: Hong Kong University Press, 2010.

———. *Chidi zhilian* 赤地之戀 (Naked earth). Taipei: Huangguan, 1991.

———. *Chongfang biancheng* 重訪邊城 (A revisit of the frontier cities). Taipei: Huangguan, 2008.

———. *Duizhao ji: kan laozhaoxiangbu* 對照記：看老照相簿 (Mutual reflections: Reading old photographs). Taipei: Huangguan, 1994.

———. *The Fall of the Pagoda*. Hong Kong: Hong Kong University Press, 2010.

———. *Haishang huakai, haishang hualuo* 海上花開，海上花落 (Mandarin translation of Han Bangqing's *Sing-song Girls of Shanghai*). Taipei: Huangguan, 1983.

———. *Honglou mengyan* 紅樓夢魘 (Nightmare in the Red Chamber). Taipei: Huangguan, 1976.

———. *Liuyan* 流言 (Written on water). Taipei: Huangguan, 1991.

———. *Love in a Fallen City*, translated by Karen S. Kingsbury. New York: New York Review of Books, 2007.
———. *Qingcheng zhilian* 傾城之戀 (Love in a fallen city). Taipei: Huangguan, 1991.
———. *The Rice-Sprout Song.* Berkeley: University of California Press, 1998.
———. *Rouge of the North*. Berkeley: University of California Press, 1998.
———. "The Spyring or Ch'ing K'e! Ch'ing K'e!" *Muse* (Hong Kong) (March 2008): 64–72.
———. *Wangran ji* 惘然集 (Regrets). Taipei: Huangguan, 1983.
———. *Written on Water,* translated by Andrew F. Jones, co-edited by Nicole Huang. New York: Columbia University Press, 2005.
———. *Xiao tuanyuan* 小團圓 (Little reunion). Taipei: Huangguan, 2009.
———. *Yang ge* 秧歌 (The rice-sprout song). Taipei: Huangguan, 1991.
———. *Yuyun* 餘韻 (The lingering cadence). Taipei: Huangguan, 1991.
———. *Zhang kan* 張看 (Chang's view). Taipei: Huangguan, 1996.
Chang, Gordon H. *Friends and Enemies: The United States, China, and the Soviet Union, 1948–1972*. Stanford, CA: Stanford University Press, 1990.
Chang, Hao. "New Confucianism and the Intellectual Crisis of Modern China." In *The Limits of Change*, edited by Charlotte Furth, 276–302. Cambridge, MA: Harvard University Press, 1976.
Chang, Sung-sheng Yvonne. *Modernism and the Nativist Resistance: Contemporary Chinese Fiction from Taiwan.* Durham, NC: Duke University Press, 1993.
Chatterjee, Partha. *The Nation and Its Fragments: Colonial and Postcolonial Histories.* Princeton, NJ: Princeton University Press, 1993.
Chen Fangming 陳芳明 (Song Dongyang 宋冬陽). "Chaoxiang xuyuanzhong de liming: Shilun Wu Zhuoliu zuopin zhong de Zhongguo jingyan" 朝向許願中的黎明：試論吳濁流作品中的中國經驗 (Facing the dawn with hope: On Chinese experiences in Wu Zhuoliu's work). In *Fangdan wenzhang pinming jiu* 放膽文章拼命酒 (Courageous writing and drinking). Taipei: Linbai chubanshe, 1988.
———. "Yang Kui de fanzhimin jingshen" 楊逵的反殖民精神 (Yang Kui's anticolonial spirit). In Chen, *Zuoyi Taiwan: Zhimindi wenxue yundong shilun* 左翼台灣：殖民地文學運動史論 (Leftist Taiwan: A history of literary movements in the colony), 75–98. Taipei: Maitian, 1998.
———. "Zheng Chenggong yu Shi Lang: Taiwan lishi renwu pingjia de fansi" 鄭成功與施琅：台灣歷史人物評價的反思 (Zheng Chenggong and Shi Lang: A reflection on the evaluation of historical figures in Taiwan). In *Zhimindi modeng: Xiandaixing yu Taiwan shiguan* 殖民地摩登：現代性與台灣史觀 (Colonial modernity: Historical and literary perspectives on Taiwan), 293–314. Taipei: Maitian, 2004.
Chen Jian. *China's Road to the Korean War: The Making of the Sino-American Confrontation*. New York: Columbia University Press, 1997.
Chen Jianzhong 陳建忠. "Bei zuzhou de wenxue? Zhanhou chuqi (1945–1949) Taiwan xiaoshuo de lishi kaocha" 被詛咒的文學？ 戰後初期（1945–1949）台灣小說的歷史考察 (The cursed literature? A historical reflection on Taiwan fiction of early postwar years 1945–1949). In *Taiwan xiandai xiaoshuoshi zonglun* 台灣現代小說史綜論 (An anthology on history of modern Taiwan fiction), edited by Chen Yizhi 陳義芝, 31–82. Taipei: Lianjing, 1998.

Chen Pingyuan 陳平原. *Dangnian youxia ren* 當年游俠人 (Wandering knight-errants of the past). Taipei: Eryu, 2003.

———. *Ershi shiji Zhongguo xiaoshuo lilun ziliao* 二十世紀中國小說理論資料 (Critical materials on the Chinese novel by twentieth-century Chinese scholars), edited by Chen Pingyuan and Xia Xiaohong 夏曉虹, vol. 1, 1897–1916. Beijing: Beijing daxue chubanshe, 1989.

———. *Qiangu wenren xiake meng: Wuxia xiaoshuo leixing yanjiu* 千古文人俠客夢：武俠小說類型研究 (Chivalric dreams of the literati: A generic study of martial arts fiction). Beijing: Renmin wenxue, 1992.

———. *Zuowei xueke de wenxueshi* 作為學科的文學史 (Literary history as a discipline). Beijing: Beijing daxue chubanshe, 2011.

Chen Shunxin 陳順馨. *Shehui zhuyi xianshi zhuyi lilun zai zhongguo de jieshou yu zhuanhuan* 社會主義現實主義理論在中國的接受與轉換 (The reception and modification of the theory of socialist realism in China). Hefei: Anhui jiaoyu chubanshe, 2000.

Chen, Tina Mai. "Sulian dianying de yinjin jiqi dui suzao Mao Zedong shidai zhongguo de yiyi" 蘇聯電影的引進對塑造毛澤東時代中國的意義 (The importance of Sino-Soviet film exchange in the making of Maoist China). In Shen and Stiffler, *Cuiruo de lianmeng*, 142–67.

Chen Tushou 陳徒手. "Ding Ling de beidahuang rizi" 丁玲的北大荒日子 (Ding Ling in the Great Northern Wasteland). In Chen Tushou, *Renyoubing, tianzhifou*, 113–54.

———. *Renyoubing, tianzhifou: 1949 nianhou de zhongguo wentan jishi* 人有病 天知否——一九四九年後的中國文壇紀實 (People are sick, is heaven aware? Chronicles of the Chinese literary world after 1949). Beijing: Renmin wenxue, 2000.

———. "Wumen chengxia de Shen Congwen" 午門城下的沈從文 (Shen Congwen under the Wumen Gate). In Chen Tushou, *Renyoubing, tianzhifou,* 13–42.

Chen Wanyi 陳萬益. "Hu Taiming jiqi gu'er de yishi: *Yaxiya de gu'er* liang'an ping de butongdian" 胡太明及其孤兒的歷史：亞細亞的孤兒兩岸評的不同點 (The orphan consciousness of Hu Taiming: The differences on interpreting *Yaxiya de gu'er* by critics across the Taiwan Strait). In Chen, *Yu wushengchu ting jinglei* 於無聲處聽驚雷 (Listening to thunder in a soundless location), 71–89. Tainan: Tainan shili wenhua zhongxin, 1996.

Chen Weizhi 陳煒智. *Wo ai Huangmei diao: Sizhu zhongguo, gudian yinxiang—Gangtai Huangmei diao dianying chutan* 我愛黃梅調：絲竹中國，古典印象——港臺黃梅調電影初探 (I love Huangmei tune: Classic impressions of traditional China: A preliminary study of Hong Kong and Taiwan's Huangmei opera films). Taipei: Muchun, 2005.

Chen Yingzhen 陳映真. "Dui wo eryan de 'disan shijie'" 對我而言的"第三世界" (What the Third World means to me). *Dushu* (Reading), no. 10 (2005): 17–24.

———. "Gu'er de lishi, lishi de gu'er: Shiping Yaxiya de gu'er" 孤兒的歷史，歷史的孤兒：試評亞細亞的孤兒 (The history of an orphan, the orphan of history: Interpreting *Orphan of Asia*). In *Chen Yingzhen zuopin ji* 陳映真作品集 (Selected works of Chen Yingzhen). Vol. 9, *Bianzi yu tideng* 鞭子與提燈 (Lash and lamp). Taipei: Renjian chubanshe, 1988.

Cheung, Dominic. *Feng Chih*. Boston: Twayne, 1979.

———. "Feng Zhi: *Shisihang ji* (Sonnets), 1942." In *A Selective Guide to Chinese Literature, 1900–1949*. Vol. 3, *The Poem*, edited by Lloyd Haft, 103–105. Leiden: Brill, 1989.

———. "Feng Zhi: *Zuori zhi ge* (Songs of yesterday)." In *A Selective Guide to Chinese Literature, 1900–1949*, 98–100. Leiden: Brill, 1989.

Chi Pang-yuan, edited with David Der-wei Wang, *Chinese Literature in the Second Half of a Modern Century: A Critical Survey*. Bloomington: Indiana University Press, 2000.

Chiang Kai-shek 蔣介石. "Dangqian jige zhongyao wenti de da'an" 當前幾個重要問題的答案 (Answers to some important questions of our time). In *Wusi aiguo yundong sishi zhounian jinian tekan* 五四愛國運動四十周年紀念特刊 (A special issue on the fortieth anniversary of the May Fourth movement). Taiwan: Guoli Beijing daxue Taiwan tongxuehui, 1959.

———. "Minsheng zhuyi yule liangpian bushu" 民生主義育樂兩篇補述 (Supplementary treatises on education and recreation to the "Principle of Livelihood"). In Sun Yat-sen 孫中山, *Sanmin zhuyi: Zenglu minsheng zhuyi yule liangpian bushu* 三民主義：增錄民生主義育樂兩篇補述 (The three principles of the people: With supplementary treatises on education and recreation to the "Principle of Livelihood"), 1–86. Taipei: Zhongyang wenwu gongying she, 1985.

———. *Xin shenghuo yundong yaoyi* 新生活運動要義 (Essentials of the New Life Movement), n.p. Zhongguo guomindang zhongyang zhixing weiyuanhui xunlian weiyuanhui 中國國民黨中央執行委員會訓練委員會, 1939. Selected English translation is included in *Sources of Chinese Tradition: From 1600 through the Twentieth Century*, compiled by Wm. Theodore de Bary and Richard Lufrano, 2nd ed., vol. 2, 341–44. New York: Columbia University Press, 2000.

———. *Zhongguo zhi mingyun* (China's destiny). Taipei: Zhengzhong shuju, 1953.

Ching, Leo T. S. *Becoming "Japanese": Colonial Taiwan and the Politics of Identity Formation*. Berkeley: University of California Press, 2001.

Chow, Rey. "Fateful Attachments: On Collecting, Fidelity, and Lao She." *Critical Inquiry* 28, no.1 (Autumn 2001): 286–304.

———. *Woman and Chinese Modernity: The Politics of Reading between West and East*. Minneapolis: University of Minnesota Press, 1991.

Chu, S. C. "China's Attitudes toward Japan at the Time of the Sino-Japanese War." In Iriye, *The Chinese and the Japanese*, 74–95.

Cleve, Ingeborg. "Subverted Heritage and Subversive Memory: Weimarer Klassik in the GDR and the Bauerbach Case." In *German Literature, History and the Nation: Papers from the Conference "The Fragile Tradition," Cambridge 2002*, edited by Christian Emden and David Midgley. Vol. 2, 355–80. New York: Peter Lang, 2004.

Clunas, Craig. *Superfluous Things: Material Culture and Social Status in Early Modern China*. Urbana: University of Illinois Press, 1991.

Cohen, Paul A. "Ambiguities of a Watershed Date: The 1949 Divide in Chinese History." In Cohen, *China Unbound: Evolving Perspectives on the Chinese Past*, 131–47. London: Routledge, 2003.

Crimp, Douglas. *On the Museum's Ruins*, with photographs by Louise Lawler. Cambridge, MA: MIT Press, 1997.

Croizier, Ralph C. *Koxinga and Chinese Nationalism: History, Myth, and the Hero*. Cambridge, MA: Harvard University Press, 1977.

Cull, Nicholas J. *The Cold War and the United States Information Agency: American Propaganda and Public Diplomacy, 1945–1989*. Cambridge: Cambridge University Press, 2008.

Daruvala, Susan. *Zhou Zuoren and an Alternative Chinese Response to Modernity.* Cambridge, MA: Harvard University Asia Center, 2000.

Davidson, James W. *The Island of Formosa, Past and Present: History, People, Resources, and Commercial Prospects. Tea, Camphor, Sugar, Gold, Coal, Sulphur, Economical Plants, and Other Productions.* Taipei: Southern Materials Center Publishing, 1988.

Deleuze, Gilles, and Felix Guattari. *Anti-Oedipus.* Vol. 1, *Capitalism and Schizophrenia.* Minneapolis: University of Minnesota Press, 1983.

De Man, Paul. *Blindness and Insight: Essays in the Rhetoric of Contemporary Criticism.* Minneapolis: University of Minnesota Press, 1983.

Demetz, Peter. *Marx, Engels and the Poets: Origins of Marxist Literary Criticism.* Chicago: University of Chicago Press, 1967.

Deng Yingchao 鄧穎超. "Kangri minzu tongyi zhanxian zhong de funü yundong" 抗日民族統一戰線中的婦女運動 (The women's movement in the United Front of the Anti-Japanese war). In *Cai Chang, Deng Yingchao, Kang Keqing funü jiefang wenti wenxuan: 1938–1987* 蔡暢，鄧穎超，康克清婦女解放問題文選，1938–1987 (Selected writings of Cai Chang, Deng Yingchao, and Kang Keqing on women's emancipation, 1938–1987), 26–37. Beijing: Renmin chubanshe, 1988.

Denton, Kirk A., ed. *Modern Chinese Literary Thought: Writings on Literature, 1893–1945.* Stanford, CA: Stanford University Press, 1996.

———. "Museums, Memorials, and Exhibitionary Culture in the People's Republic of China." *China Quarterly* 183 (Fall 2005): 565–86.

———. "Visual Memory and the Construction of a Revolutionary Past: Paintings from the Museum of the Chinese Revolution." *Modern Chinese Literature and Culture*, no. 2 (Fall 2000): 203–35.

Dikötter, Frank. *The Discourse of Race in Modern China.* Stanford, CA: Stanford University Press, 1992.

Ding Ling 丁玲. "Chudao Mishan" 初到密山 (When I first arrived in Mishan). In *DLWJ* 5: 336.

———. *Ding Ling quanji* 丁玲全集 (Complete works of Ding Ling). 12 vol. Shijiazhuang: Hebei renmin chubanshe, 2001, abbreviated in the notes as *DLQJ.*

———. *Ding Ling wenji* 丁玲文集 (Selected works of Ding Ling). 10 vols. Changsha: Hunan renmin chubanshe, vols. 1–7, 1983, 1984; Changsha: Hunan wenyi chubanshe, vols. 8–10, 1995, abbreviated in the notes as *DLWJ.*

———. "Du Wanxiang" 杜晚香 (Du Wanxiang). *Renmin wenxue* 人民文學 (People's literature) 7 (1979): 45–58; *DLWJ* 3: 280–307. English translation in *I Myself Am a Woman*, 131–354.

———. "Fengyu zhong yi Xiao Hong" 風雨中憶蕭紅 (Memories of Xiao Hong). In *DLWJ* 5: 40–44.

———. "Gaizao" 改造 (Transformation). In *DLWJ* 6: 21.

———. *I Myself Am a Woman: Selected Writings of Ding Ling*, edited by Tani E. Barlow and Gary J. Bjorge. Boston: Beacon Press, 1989.

———. "1947–1954 nian shenghuo pianduan" 1947–1954年生活片段 (Fragments from my life between 1947 and 1954). In *DLWJ* 10: 259–73.

———. *Ouxing sanji* 歐行散記 (Sketches of the travels to Europe). Beijing: Renmin wenxue chubanshe, 1953.

———. "Sanbajie yougan" 三八節有感 (Thoughts on March 8, the international women's day, 1942). In *DLWJ* 4: 388–92.

———. "Shafei nüshi de riji" 莎菲女士的日記 (Miss Sophie's diary). In *DLWJ* 2: 45–86.

———. *The Sun Shines over the Sangkan River*, translated by Yang Hsien-yi and Gladys Yang. Beijing: Foreign Languages Press, 1954.

———. *Taiyang zhaozai Sangganhe shang* 太阳照在桑乾河上 (*The sun shines over the Sanggan River*). Beijing: Renmin wenxue chubanshe, 1997.

———. "Wangliang shijie (Nanjing yuju huiyi)" 魍魎世界（南京獄居回憶）(Ghostly world: Memories of my prison life in Nanjing). In *Ding Ling zizhuan* 丁玲自傳 (Autobiography of Ding Ling), edited by Xu Yangqing 許楊清 and Zong Cheng 宗誠, 98–215. Nanjing: Jiangsu wenyi chubanshe, 1996.

———. "Wo zai xiacun de shihou" 我在霞村的時候 (When I was in Xia village). In *DLWJ* 3: 221–42.

———. "Women xuyao zawen" 我們需要雜文 (We need essays). In *DLWJ* 4: 382–84.

———. "Yangji yu yanggou: Fangmei sanji" 養雞與養狗：訪美散記 (Raising chickens and raising dogs: Sketches of my U.S. visit). In *DLQJ* 6: 148–51.

———. "Yepin yu geming" 也頻與革命 (Yepin and the revolution). In *DLWJ* 5: 165–68.

———. "Zai zhongxuanbu yici wenyi zuotanhui shang de fayan" 在中宣部一次文藝座談會上的發言 (Speech at a meeting of the Central Propaganda Department on literature and art). In *DLQJ* 8: 441–42.

Ding Shu 丁抒. *Renhuo: Dayuejin yu dajihuang* 人禍："大躍進"與大飢荒 (Man-made disaster: The Great Leap Forward and the Great Famine). Hong Kong: Shiji niandai zazhishe, 1991.

Ding Yanzhao 丁言昭. *Zai nanren de shijie li: Ding Ling zhuan* 在男人的世界裡：丁玲傳 (In the world of men: Biography of Ding Ling). Shanghai: Shanghai wenyi chubanshe, 1998.

Dirlik, Arif. "Confucius in the Borderlands: Global Capitalism and the Reinvention of Confucianism." *boundary 2* 22 (Fall 1995): 229–73.

———. "The Predicament of Marxist Revolutionary Consciousness: Mao Zedong, Antonio Gramsci, and the Reformulation of Marxist Revolutionary Theory." *Modern China* 9, no. 2 (April 1983): 182–211.

Dudden, Alexis. "Japan's Engagement with International Terms." In *Tokens of Exchange,* edited by Lydia H. Liu, 165–91. Durham, NC: Duke University Press, 1999.

Edwards, Louise. "New *Hongxue* and the 'Birth of the Author': Yu Pingbo's 'On Qin Keqing's Death.'" *Chinese Literature: Essays, Articles, Reviews (CLEAR)* 23 (December 2001): 31–54.

Fairbank, John K. *Trade and Diplomacy on the China Coast.* Stanford, CA: Stanford University Press, 1953.

Fairbank, Wilma. *Liang and Lin: Partners in Exploring China's Architectural Past.* Philadelphia: University of Pennsylvania Press, 1994.

Fan, K. Sizheng. "A Classicist Architecture for Utopia: The Soviet Contacts." In *Chinese Architecture and the Beaux-Arts*, edited by Jeffrey W. Cody, Nancy S. Steinhardt, and Tony Atkin, 91–126. Honolulu: University of Hawaii Press / Hong Kong: Hong Kong University Press, 2011.

Farrelly, Daniel J. *Goethe in East Germany, 1949–1989: Toward a History of Goethe Reception in the GDR*. Rochester, NY: Camden House, 1998.

Feng Xuefeng 馮雪峰. "*Taiyang zhaozai Sangganhe shang* zai women wenxue fazhanshang de yiyi" 《太阳照在桑乾河上》在我們文學發展上的意義 (The significance of *The Sun Shines over the Sanggan River* in the development of our literature). In Yuan Liangjun, *Ding Ling yanjiu ziliao,* 340.

Feng Yaoping 馮姚平 ed. *Feng Zhi he tade shijie* 馮至和他的世界 (Feng Zhi and his world). Shijiazhuang: Hebei jiaoyu chubanshe, 2001.

Feng Zhi 馮至. *Feng Zhi quanji* 馮至全集 (Complete works of Feng Zhi). 12 vols. Shijiazhuang: Hebei jiaoyu chubanshe, 1999, abbreviated in the notes as *FZQJ*.

Feuerwerker, Yi-tsi Mei. *Ding Ling's Fiction: Ideology and Narrative in Modern Chinese Literature*. Cambridge, MA: Harvard University Press, 1982.

———. "Ting Ling's 'When I Was in Sha Chuan (Cloud Village),' with a Discussion by Yi-tsi Feuerwerker." *Signs: Journal of Women in Culture and Society* 2, no. 1 (Autumn 1976): 255–79.

Fichte, Johann Gottlieb. *Addresses to the German Nation*, translated by R. F. Jones and G. H. Turnbull. Westport, CT: Greenwood Press, 1979.

Foucault, Michel. *The Order of Things: An Archaeology of the Human Sciences*. New York: Vintage, 1973.

Franco, Jean. *The Decline and Fall of the Lettered City: Latin America in the Cold War*. Cambridge, MA: Harvard University Press, 2002.

Freud, Sigmund. "Psychoanalytic Notes upon an Autobiographical Account of a Case of Paranoia (Dementia Paranoides)." In *Three Case Histories*, 83–160. New York: Simon & Schuster, 1996.

Fu, Poshek. "Modernity, Diasporic Capital, and 1950's Hong Kong Mandarin Cinema." *Jump Cut: A Review of Contemporary Media* 49 (Spring 2007), www.ejumpcut.org/archive/jc49.2007/text.html.

Gaddis, John Lewis. *The Long Peace: Inquiries into the History of the Cold War*. New York: Oxford University Press, 1987.

———. *We Now Know: Rethinking Cold War History*. New York: Oxford University Press, 1997.

Galik, Marian. "Feng Chih's *Sonnets*: The Interliterary Relations with German Romanticism, Rilke and van Gogh." In *Milestones in Sino-Western Literary Confrontation (1898–1979)*, 177–200. Weisbaden: Otto Harrassowitz, 1986.

———. "Feng Zhi and His Goethean Sonnet." In *Crosscurrents in the Literatures of Asia and the West: Essays in Honor of A. Owen Aldridge*, edited by Masayuki Akiyama and Yiu-nam Leung, 123–34. Newark: University of Delaware Press / London: Associated University Presses, 1997.

Gan Lu 甘露. "Ding Ling yu Mao zhuxi ersan shi" 丁玲與毛主席二三事 (A few things about Ding Ling and Chairman Mao). *Xinwenxue shiliao* 新文學史料, no. 4 (1986): 87–90.

Gao Hua 高華. "Zhonggong cong wusi jiaoyu yichan zhong xuanze le shenme: Yan'an jiaoyu de jiazhi ji juxian" 中共從五四教育遺產中選擇了甚麼：延安教育的價值及局限 (What has the CCP selected from the May Fourth legacy on education: The values and limits of education in Yan'an). In Gao Hua, *Zai lishi de fengling dukou* 在歷史的風陵渡口 (From history's Fengling Ferry). Hong Kong: Shidai guoji chuban youxian gongsi, 2008), 70–78.

Gao Quanzhi (Chuan-chih Kao) 高全之. *Zhang Ailing xue: piping, kaozheng, gouchen* 張愛玲學：批評, 考證, 鉤沉 (Studies on Eileen Chang: Criticism, textual analysis, and exploration of lost materials). Taipei: Yifang, 2003.

Gao Xuhui 高旭輝. "Fayang 'wusi' de minzu sixiang yu aiguo jingshen" 發揚五四的民族思想與愛國精神 (To disseminate nationalism and patriotism of the May Fourth). *Guo hun* 國魂 192 (May 1961).

Gilman, Sander L. *Difference and Pathology: Stereotypes of Sexuality, Race, and Madness.* Ithaca: Cornell University Press, 1985.

Goethe, Johann Wolfgang. *Faust. Der Tragödie zweiter Theil in fünf Acten* (Faust. The tragedy's second part of five acts, 1831). In *Johann Wolfgang Goethe: Sämtliche Werke nach Epochen seines Schaffens* (Complete works of Goethe arranged by periods). Münchner Ausgabe. Bd. 18.1: Letzte Jahre. 1827–1832, hrsg. Gisela Henckmann und Dorothea Hölscher-Lohmeyer. München: Hanser Verlag, 1997, 103–351.

Goldman, Merle. *Literary Dissent in Communist China.* Cambridge, MA: Harvard University Press, 1967.

Gordon, Leonard. "Japan's Abortive Colonial Venture in Taiwan, 1874." *Journal of Modern History* 37, no. 1 (March 1965): 171–85.

Gramsci, Antonio. *Selections from the Prison Notebooks.* New York: International, 1971.

Grieder, Jerome. "The Communist Critique of *Hung-lou meng.*" *Papers on China* (Harvard University, East Asian Research Center) 10 (October 1956): 142–68.

Guo Moruo 郭沫若. "Chi fandong wenyi" 斥反動文藝 (A denunciation of reactionary literature and art). In Quanlin et al., *Wenyi de xin fangxiang*, 19–22.

Guo Yanli 郭延禮. "Chen Jitong: Zhongfa wenhua shizhe de qianqu" 陳季同：中法文化使者的前驅 (Chen Jitong: The predecessor of envoy between Chinese and French culture). *Zhonghua dushu bao*, March 22, 2000.

Guo Yuwen 郭玉雯. Honglou meng *xue: Cong Zhiyanzhai dao Zhang Ailing* 紅樓夢學：從脂硯齋到張愛玲 (Studies on *Dream of the Red Chamber*: From Red Inkstone to Eileen Chang). Taipei: Liren, 2004.

Habermas, Jürgen. "Citizenship and National Identity," *Praxis International* 12, no. 1 (April 1992): 1–19.

Haft, Lloyd. "Some Rhythmic Structures in Feng Zhi's *Sonnets.*" *Modern Chinese Literature* 9, no. 2 (1996): 297–326.

Hamm, John Christopher. *Paper Swordsmen: Jin Yong and the Modern Chinese Martial Arts Novel.* Honolulu: University of Hawaii Press, 2005.

Hardt, Michael. *Gilles Deleuze: An Apprenticeship in Philosophy.* Minneapolis: University of Minnesota Press, 1993.

Hardt, Michael, and Antonio Negri. *Empire.* Cambridge, MA: Harvard University Press, 2000.

Harootunian, Harry D. *The Empire's New Clothes: Paradigm Lost, and Regained.* Chicago: Prickly Paradigm Press, 2004.

———. *Learning Places: The Afterlives of Area Studies*, edited by Masao Miyoshi and H. D. Harootunian. Durham, NC: Duke University Press, 2002.

Hartmann, Heidi. "The Unhappy Marriage of Marxism and Feminism: Towards a More Progressive Union." In *Women and Revolution: A Discussion of the Unhappy Marriage of Marxism and Feminism*, edited by Lydia Sargent, 1–42. Boston: South End Press, 1981.

Harvey, David. *The Condition of Postmodernity.* Cambridge, MA: Blackwell, 1990.

———. *Paris, Capital of Modernity.* New York: Routledge, 2003.

Hayhoe, Ruth. *China's Universities, 1895–1995: A Century of Cultural Conflict.* New York: Garland, 1996.

Hayhoe, Ruth, and Ningsha Zhong. "University Autonomy and Civil Society." In *Civil Society in China*, edited by Timothy Brook and B. Michael Frolic, 99–123. Armonk, NY: M. E. Sharpe, 1997.

He Donghui. "'Gangtie shi zenyang liancheng de:' Sulian jiaoyu xiaoshuo yu liangdai zhongguo duzhe" 《鋼鐵是怎樣練成的》：蘇聯教育小說與兩代中國讀者 (How the steel was tempered: Soviet bildungsroman and two generations of Chinese readers). In Shen and Stiffler, *Cuiruo de lianmeng*, 114–41.

He Guimei 賀桂梅. "Xiandai, dangdai, wusi: Xin wenxue shi xiezuo fanshi de bianqian" 現代，當代，五四：新文學史寫作範式的變遷 (Modern, contemporary, May Fourth: The paradigmatic transformations in writings of literary history). In *Xiandai Zhongguo* 現代中國 (Modern China), ed. Chen Pingyuan, 57–71. Wuhan: Hubei jiaoyu, 2001.

———. "'Xiandai wenxue' de queli yu 1950 dao 1960 niandai de daxue jiaoyu tizhi" "現代文學"的確立與1950到1960年代的大學教育體制 (The establishment of "modern literature" and the system of higher education in the 1950s–60s). *Jiaoyu xuebao* 教育學報 (Journal of Education), no. 3 (2005): 83–91.

———. *"Xin qimeng" zhishi dang'an: Bashi niandai zhongguo wenhua yanjiu* 新啓蒙知識檔案：八十年代中國文化研究 (The knowledge archive of "Neo-enlightenment": A study of Chinese cultures of the 1980s). Beijing: Beijing daxue, 2010.

———. *Zhuanzhe de shidai: siwushi niandai zuojia yanjiu* 轉折的時代：四五十年代作家研究 (A time of transition: Studies of writers of the 1940s and 1950s). Jinan: Shandong jiaoyu chubanshe, 2003.

He Lin 賀麟. *Wushinianlai de zhongguo zhexue* 五十年來的中國哲學 (Chinese philosophy in the past fifty years). Shenyang: Liaoning jiaoyu chubanshe, 1989.

Herder, Johann Gottfried. *Outlines of a Philosophy of the History of Man*, translated by T. Churchill. New York: Bergman, 1966.

Hershatter, Gail. *Dangerous Pleasures: Prostitution and Modernity in Twentieth-Century Shanghai.* Berkeley: University of California Press, 1997.

Hevia, James. *Cherishing Men from Afar: Qing Guest Ritual and the Macartney Embassy of 1793.* Durham, NC: Duke University Press, 1995.

Hinton, William. *Fanshen: A Documentary of Revolution in a Chinese Village.* New York: Monthly Review Press, 1966.

Ho, Elaine Yee Lin. "China Abroad: Nation and Diaspora in a Chinese Frame." In *China Abroad: Travels, Subjects, Spaces*, edited by Elaine Yee Lin Ho and Julia Kuehn, 3–22. Hong Kong: Hong Kong University Press, 2009.

Hohendahl, Peter Uwe. *Building a National Literature: The Case of Germany, 1830–1870*. Ithaca: Cornell University Press, 1989.

Holland, Eugene W. *Deleuze and Guattari's Anti-Oedipus: Introduction to Schizoanalysis*. London: Routledge, 1999.

Hong Zicheng 洪子誠. "'Dangdai wenxue' de gainian" "當代文學"的概念 (The concept of "contemporary literature"). *Wenxue pinglun* 文學評論 (Literary Review), no. 1 (1998): 38–48.

———. *A History of Contemporary Chinese Literature*. Leiden: Brill, 2007.

———. *Wenti yu fangfa: Zhongguo dangdai wenxueshi yanjiu jianggao* 問題與方法：中國當代文學史研究講稿 (Problems and methods: Manuscripts of study on contemporary Chinese literary history). Beijing: Beijing daxue, 2010.

———. *Zhongguo dangdai wenxueshi* 中國當代文學史 (History of Chinese contemporary literature). Beijing: Beijing daxue chubanshe, 1999.

———. *Zhongguo dangdai wenxueshi shiliaoxuan 1945–1999* 中國當代文學史史料選 1945–1999 (Selections of historical materials for contemporary Chinese literary history). Wuhan: Changjiang wenyi, 2002.

Hsia, C. T. *C. T. Hsia on Chinese Literature*. New York: Columbia University Press, 2004.

———. *A History of Modern Chinese Fiction*. Bloomington: Indiana University Press, 1999.

———. "Xiandai zhongguo wenxueshi sizhong heping" 現代中國文學史四種合評 (A review of four works of modern Chinese literary history). *Xiandai wenxue* 現代文學 (Contemporary literature) 1 (July 1977): 41–61.

———. "Zhang Ailing gei wo de xinjian" 張愛玲給我的信件 (Eileen Chang's letters to me). *Unitas* 聯合文學 13, no. 6 (April 1997): 52–53.

———. "Zhang Ailing gei wo de xinjian" 張愛玲給我的信件 (Eileen Chang's letters to me). *Unitas* 13, no. 11 (September 1997): 69–71.

———. "Zhang Ailing gei wo de xinjian" 張愛玲給我的信件 (Eileen Chang's letters to me). *Unitas* 14, no. 9 (July 1998): 144–45.

Hsia, T. A. *The Gate of Darkness: Studies on the Leftist Literary Movement in China*. Seattle: University of Washington Press, 1968.

Hsu, Immanuel C. Y. "Late Ch'ing Foreign Relations, 1866–1905." In *The Cambridge History of China*. Vol. 11, *Late Ch'ing, 1800–1911*, pt. 2, edited by John K. Fairbank and Kwang-Ch'ing Liu, 86–87. Cambridge: Cambridge University Press, 1980.

Hsu, Kai-yu. *Twentieth-century Chinese Poetry: An Anthology*. Ithaca: Cornell University Press, 1970.

Hu Shi 胡適. "*Honglou meng* kaozheng" 紅樓夢考證 (Textual research on *Dream of the Red Chamber*). In *Hu Shi wencun* 胡適文存 (Selected Writings of Hu Shi), 575–620. Taipei: Yuandong tushu gongsi, 1953.

Huang Kangxian 黃康顯. "Linggan yuanquan? Qinggan bingyuan?: Zhang Ailing de xianggang daxue yinyuan" 靈感源泉？情感冰原？——張愛玲的香港大學因緣 (Sources of inspiration? Iceland of emotion? Eileen Chang and The University of Hong Kong). *Xianggang wenxue* 香港文學 (Hong Kong literary monthly) 136 (April 1996): 4–12.

Huang Mei'e 黃美娥. "Tiexue yu tiexue zhiwai: Yuedu 'shiren Wu Zhuoliu'" 鐵血與鐵血之外：閱讀"詩人吳濁流" (Iron blood and beyond: Reading "poet Wu Zhuoliu").

In *Wu Zhuoliu bainian danchen jinian zhuankan* 吳濁流百年誕辰紀念專刊 (Memorial special edition on the 100th anniversary of Wu Zhuoliu's birthday), edited by Lin Boyan 林柏燕, 26–43. Xinzhu: Zhuxian wenhuaju, 2000.

Huang, Nicole. "Mengzai honglou, xiezai geshi" 夢在紅樓，寫在隔世 (Dreaming in the red chamber, writing in a different age). In Shen Shuang, *Lingdu kanzhang*, 99–118.

———. *Women, War, Domesticity: Shanghai Literature and Popular Culture of the 1940s*. Leiden: Brill, 2005.

Huang, Philip C. C. "Rethinking the Chinese Revolution: An Introduction." *Modern China* 21, no. 1 (January 1995): 3–7.

Huang Xiuji 黃修己. *Zhongguo xin wenxueshi bianzhuanshi* 中國新文學史編撰史 (The historiography of new Chinese literature). Beijing: Beijing daxue, 2006. First published 1993.

Huang Xiuzheng 黃秀政. *Taiwan gerang yu yiwei kangri yundong* 臺灣割讓與乙未抗日運動 (The cession of Taiwan and the 1895 anti-Japanese resistance). Taipei: Taiwan shangwu yinshuguan, 1992.

Huang Yongyu 黃永玉, ed. *Changhe bujinliu: Huainian Shen Congwen xiansheng* 長河不盡流——懷念沈從文先生 (Long river flows endlessly: Memories of Mr. Shen Congwen). Changsha: Hunan wenyi, 1989.

———. "Zheyixie youyu de suoxie" 這一些憂鬱的瑣屑 (These gloomy fragments). In Huang Yongyu, *Changhe bujinliu,* 450–89.

Huang Ziping 黃子平. *Geming, lishi, xiaoshuo* 革命・歷史・小說 (Revolution, history, and fiction). Hong Kong: Oxford University Press, 1996.

Huangfu, Jenny. "Roads to Salvation: Shen Congwen, Xiao Qian, and the Problem of Non-Communist Celebrity Writers, 1948–1957." *Modern Chinese Literature and Culture* 22, no. 2 (Fall 2010): 39–87.

Hunt, Michael, and Steven Levine. "The Revolutionary Challenge to Early U.S. Cold War Policy in Asia." In *The Great Powers in East Asia, 1953–1960*, edited by Warren I. Cohen and Akira Iriye, 13–34. New York: Columbia University Press, 1990.

Huss, Ann, and Jianmei Liu, eds. *The Jin Yong Phenomenon: Chinese Martial Arts Fiction and Modern Chinese Literary History*. Youngstown, NY: Cambria Press, 2007.

Huyssen, Andreas. *After the Great Divide: Modernism, Mass Culture, Postmodernism*. Bloomington: Indiana University Press, 1986.

———. *Twilight Memories: Marking Time in a Culture of Amnesia*. New York: Routledge, 1995.

Iriye, Akira, ed. *The Chinese and the Japanese: Essays in Political and Cultural Interactions*. Princeton, NJ: Princeton University Press, 1980.

———. *The Cold War in Asia: A Historical Introduction*. Englewood Cliffs, NJ: Prentice Hall, 1974.

James, M. R. *The Apocryphal New Testament*. Oxford, UK: Clarendon Press, 1924.

Jameson, Fredric. "Postmodernism and Consumer Society." In *The Anti-Aesthetic: Essays on Postmodern Culture,* edited by Hal Foster, 111–25. Port Townsend, WA: Bay Press, 1983.

Jay, Martin. *Marxism and Totality: The Adventures of a Concept from Lukács to Habermas.* Berkeley: University of California Press, 1984.

Ji Xianlin 季羡林. *Niupeng zayi* 牛棚雜憶 (Memoirs in the cattle shed). Beijing: Zhonggong zhongyang dangxiao chubanshe, 1998.

Jiang Gui 姜貴. *Xuanfeng* 旋風 (Whirlwind). Taipei: Minghua shuju, 1959.

Jiang Qinguo 蔣勤國. *Feng Zhi pingzhuan* 馮至評傳 (A critical biography of Feng Zhi). Beijing: Renmin chubanshe, 2000.

Jusdanis, Gregory. *The Necessary Nation*. Princeton, NJ: Princeton University Press, 2001.

Kang Laixin 康來新. "Duizhao ji: Zhang Ailing yu *Honglou meng*" 對照記：張愛玲與《紅樓夢》 (Mutual Reflections: Eileen Chang and *Dream of the Red Chamber*). In Yang Ze, *Yuedu Zhang Ailing*, 29–58.

Kerr, George H. *Formosa Betrayed*. Boston: Houghton Mifflin, 1965.

Kinkley, Jeffrey C. *The Odyssey of Shen Congwen*. Stanford, CA: Stanford University Press, 1987.

Kirby, William C. "Continuity and Change in Modern China: Economic Planning on the Mainland and on Taiwan, 1943–1953." *Australian Journal of Chinese Affairs* 24 (July 1990): 121–41.

———. "Lessons of Modern Chinese History, To the US Congress, April 1998." *Chinese Historical Review* (Spring 2004): 15–22.

Klein, Melanie. *Das Seelenleben des Kleinkindes und andere Beiträge zur Psychoanalyse* (The mental life of children and other thesis on psychoanalysis). Stuttgart: Klett-Cotta, 1983.

Koeppen, Wolfgang. *Tauben im Gras* (Pigeons on the grass). Stuttgart: Scherz & Goverts, 1951.

Kraepelin, Emil. *Dementia praecox and Paraphrenia*, translated by R. M. Barclay. Huntington, NY: Robert E. Krieger, 1971. First published 1919.

Kubin, Wolfgang. "Zong Baihua (1896–1996) und sein ästhetisches Werk" (Zong Baihua and his aesthetic work). In *120 Jahre Chinesische Studierende an deutschen Hochschulen* (120 years of chinese students in German institutes of higher education), edited by Christoph Kaderas and Meng Hong, 139–46. Bonn: DAAD-Forum, Band 22, 2000.

Lai Zehan 賴澤涵. *Ererba shijian yanjiu baogao* 二二八事件研究報告 (February Twenty-eighth Incident Research Report). Taipei: Shibao, 1994.

Laing, R. D. *The Politics of Experience*. New York: Pantheon, 1967.

Lamley, Harry J. "The 1895 Taiwan Republic: A Significant Episode in Modern Chinese History." *Journal of Asian Studies* 27, no. 4 (August 1968): 739–54.

Landes, Joan B. "Marxism and the 'Woman Question.'" In *Promissory Notes: Women in the Transition to Socialism*, edited by Sonia Kruks, Rayna Rapp, and Marilyn B. Young, 15–28. New York: Monthly Review Press, 1989.

Lao She 老舍, Cai Yi 蔡儀, Wang Yao 王瑤, and Li Helin 李何林. "*Zhongguo xin wenxueshi jiaoxue dagang (chugao)*" [Pedagogical Outline for the History of New Chinese Literature (draft)]. In Li Helin et al. *Zhongguo xin wenxueshi yanjiu* 中國新文學史研究 (Studies on the History of New Chinese Literature), 1–18. Beijing: Xin jianshe, 1951.

Law Kar. "A Glimpse of MP&GI's Creative/Production Situation: Some Speculations and Doubts." In Wong, *The Cathay Story*, 58–65.

Lee, Leo Ou-fan. *Shanghai Modern: The Flowering of a New Urban Culture in China, 1930–1945*. Cambridge, MA: Harvard University Press, 1999.

———. *Voices from the Iron House: A Study of Lu Xun*. Bloomington: Indiana University Press, 1987.

Lei Mengshui 雷夢水. "Zhu Ziqing xiansheng maishu ji" 朱自清先生買書記 (Zhu Ziqing's book shopping story). *Dushu* 讀書 25, no. 4 (1981): 128–29.

Leung Ping-Kwan 梁秉鈞. "1957nian, Xianggang" 1957年，香港 (1957 Hong Kong). In Wang, Chen, and Xu, *1949 yihou*, 199–211.

———. "Zhang Ailing yu Xianggang" 張愛玲與香港 (Eileen Chang and Hong Kong). In *Zaidu Zhang Ailing* 再讀張愛玲 (Re-reading Eileen Chang), edited by Joseph S. M. Lau, Leung Ping-Kwan, and Xu Zidong, 197–206. Jinan: Shandong huabao, 2004.

Li Guangtian 李廣田. *Shi de yishu* 詩的藝術 (The art of poetry). Hong Kong: Huiwenke shudian, 1972.

Li Hui 李輝. "Linghun zai feixiang" 靈魂在飛翔 (His soul is flying). In *Lu Ling yinxiang* 路翎印象 (The impressions of Lu Ling), edited by Zhang Yesong 張業松, 288–95. Shanghai: Xuelin chubanshe, 1997.

Li Tuo 李陀. "Ding Ling bu jiandan: Mao tizhixia zhishifenzi zai huayu shengchanzhong de fuza juese" 丁玲不簡單：毛體制下知識份子在話語生產中的複雜角色 (Ding Ling is not simple: The complicated role of intellectuals in the production of discourse under the Maoist apparatus). *Jintian* 今天 (Today), no. 3 (1993): 236–40.

Li Wei 李偉. *Cao Juren zhuan* 曹聚仁傳 (The biography of Cao Juren). Nanjing: Nanjing daxue chubanshe, 1993.

Li Xiaofeng 李筱峰. "Buxiang duli de duli yundong: 1895nian Taiwan minzhuguo de benzhi" 不像獨立的獨立運動：1895年台灣民主國的本質 (A false independent movement: The nature of the 1895 Taiwan Republic). *Zili zaobao*, April 16, 1995.

———. *Taiwanshi yibaijian dashi* 台灣史一百件大事 (One hundred important events in Taiwan history). Taipei: Yushanshe chuban shiye gufen youxian gongsi, 1999.

Liang Qichao 梁啓超. *Yinbingshi heji* 飲冰室合集 (Collected works of Yinbing Chamber). Shanghai: Zhonghua shuju, 1961.

Liang Sicheng 梁思成. "Beiping de wenwu bixu zhengli yu baocun" 北平的文物必須整理與保存 (The cultural relics in Beijing must be preserved). In *Liang Sicheng wenji* 梁思成文集 (Selected writings of Liang Sicheng). 4 vols. Vol. 2: 365–71. Beijing: Zhongguo jianzhu chubanshe, 1982.

———. "Wo weishenme zheyang ai women de dang?" 我為甚麼這樣愛我們的黨 (Why I love our party so much). In *Renmin ribao* 人民日報 (People's daily), July 14, 1957.

Liao, Ping-hui. "Rewriting Taiwanese National History: The February 28 Incident as Spectacle." *Public Culture* 5 (1993): 281–96.

———. "Yiguo jiyi yu linglei xiandaixing: shitan Wu Zhuoliu de *Nanjing zagan*" 異國記憶與另類現代性：試探吳濁流的《南京雜感》 (Foreign memories and alternative modernity: A tentative interpretation of Wu Zhuoliu's *Nanjing zagan*). In *Linglei xiandaiqing* 現代情 (Alternative Modernity), 9–42. Taipei: Yunchen, 2000.

Liao Xianhao 廖咸浩. "Zai jiegou yu jieti zhijian paihuai: Taiwan xiandai xiaoshuo zhong zhongguo shenfen de zhuanbian" 在解構與解體之間徘徊：台灣現代小說中中

國身份的轉變 (Wandering between deconstruction and destruction: The transformation of "Chinese identity" in modern fiction in Taiwan). In *Houzhimin lilun yu wenhua rentong* 後殖民理論與文化認同 (Postcolonial Criticism and Cultural Identity), edited by Zhang Jingyuan 張京媛, 193–212. Taipei: Maitian, 1995.

Lin Boyan 林柏燕. "Wu Zhuoliu de dalu jingyan" 吳濁流的大陸經驗 (Wu Zhuoliu's experiences on the continent). In *Xiangtu yu wenxue* 鄉土與文學 (The native land and the literature), edited by Feng Deping 封德屏, 334–56. Taipei: Wenxun zazhishe, 1994.

Lin Haiyin 林海音. "Chengnan jiushi" 城南舊事 (Memoirs of southern Beijing). In *Chengnan jiushi* 城南舊事 (Memoirs of southern Beijing), 31–229. Taipei: Erya chubanshe, 1960.

———. *Jianying hua wentan* 剪影話文壇 (Profiles in the literary arena). Taipei: Chunwenxue, 1984.

Lin Shan 林杉. *Yidai cainü Lin Huiyin* 一代才女林徽因 (Lin Huiyin the talented lady). Beijing: Zuojia chubanshe, 2005.

Lin Yiliang 林以亮. "Siyu Zhang Ailing" 私語張愛玲 (Whispered words on Eileen Chang). In *Huali yu cangliang: Zhang Ailing jinian wenji* 華麗與蒼涼：張愛玲紀念文集 (Splendor and desolation: A collection of essays in memory of Eileen Chang), 105–24. Taipei: Huangguan, 1996.

Lin, Yutang. *The Flight of the Innocents*. New York: Putnam, 1964.

Lin Zhu 林洙. *Kunhuo de dajiang: Liang Sicheng* 困惑的大匠：梁思成 (The confused master Liang Sicheng). Jinan: Shangdong huabao chubanshe, 1997.

Ling Yu 凌宇. *Shen Congwen zhuan* 沈從文傳 (Biography of Shen Congwen). Beijing: Shiyue wenyi, 1988.

Liu, James J. Y. *The Chinese Knight-errant*. Chicago: University of Chicago Press, 1967.

Liu, Lydia H. *The Clash of Empires: The Invention of China in Modern World Making*. Cambridge, MA: Harvard University Press, 2004.

———. *Tokens of Exchange: The Problem of Translation in Global Circulation*. Durham, NC: Duke University Press, 1999.

———. *Translingual Practice: Literature, National Culture, and Translated Modernity—China, 1900–1937*. Stanford, CA: Stanford University Press, 1995.

Liu, Petrus. *Stateless Subjects: Chinese Martial Arts Literature and Postcolonial History*. Ithaca: Cornell East Asian Series, 2011.

Liu Zaifu 劉再復 and Lin Gang 林崗. "Zhongguo xiandai xiaoshuo de zhengzhishi xiezuo: Cong *Chuncan* dao *Taiyang zhaozai sangganhe shang*" 中國現代小說的政治式寫作：從《春蠶》到《太阳照在桑乾河上》 (The political writing of modern Chinese novels: From *Chuncan* [Spring silkworm] to *Taiyang zhaozai sangganhe shang* [The sun shines over the Sanggan River]). In Tang Xiaobing, *Zaijiedu*, 90–107.

Louie, Kam, ed. *Eileen Chang: Romancing Languages, Cultures, and Genres*. Hong Kong: Hong Kong University Press, 2011.

Lu Jiandong 陸鍵東. *Chen Yinke de zuihou ershi nian* 陳寅恪的最後二十年 (The last twenty years of Chen Yinke). Beijing: Sanlian shudian, 1995.

Lü Xinchang 呂新昌. *Tiexue shiren Wu Zhuoliu* 鐵血詩人吳濁流 (Wu Zhuoliu the iron blood poet). Taipei: Qianwei, 1996.

Lu Xun 魯迅. *Lu Xun quanji* 魯迅全集 (Complete works of Lu Xun). 16 vols. Beijing: Renmin wenxue, 1981, abbreviated in the notes as *LXQJ*.

———. *Selected Stories of Lu Hsun,* translated by Yang Hsien-yi and Gladys Yang. New York: Norton, 1977.

Lu Yaodong 陸耀東. *Feng Zhi zhuan* 馮至傳 (A biography of Feng Zhi). Beijing: Beijing shiyue, 2003.

Lü Zhenghui 呂正惠. *Zhanhou Taiwan wenxue jingyan* 戰後台灣文學經驗 (Literary experiences in postwar Taiwan). Taipei: Xindi wenxue, 1992.

Luk, Hung-kay Bernard. "Chinese Culture in the Hong Kong Curriculum: Heritage and Colonialism." *Comparative Education Review* 35, no. 4 (November 1991): 659–60.

Lukács, Georg. *Goethe und seine Zeit*. Berlin: Aufbau, 1950.

———. *History and Class Consciousness: Studies in Marxist Dialectics*, translated by Rodney Livingstone. Cambridge, MA: MIT Press, 1971.

Luo Hailei 羅海雷. *Wo de fuqin Luo Fu: Yige baoren, "jiandie," he zuojia de gushi* 我的父親羅孚——一個報人、「間諜」和作家的故事 (My father Luo Fu: Stories of a journalist, "a secret agent," and a writer). Hong Kong: Tiandi tushu, 2011.

Ma Lang 馬朗. "Taiyang xia de jie" 太阳下的街 (Streets under the sun). *Wenyi xinchao* 文藝新潮 (New literary trends), no. 7 (November 1956): 8.

Mahler, Margaret S. *The Psychological Birth of the Human Infant: Symbiosis and Individuation*. New York: Basic Books, 1975.

Mao Dun 茅盾. "Nüzuojia Ding Ling" 女作家丁玲 (Ding Ling the woman writer). In *Guancha Ding Ling* 觀察丁玲 (Observing Ding Ling), edited by Yang Guixin 楊桂欣, 204–8. Beijing: Dazhong wenyi chubanshe, 2001.

———. "Yedu ouji" 夜讀偶記 (Random notes on night readings). Selected portions collected in Hong Zicheng, *Zhongguo dangdai wenxueshi shiliaoxuan*, 398–414.

Mao Zedong 毛澤東. "Guanyu *Honglou meng* yanjiu wenti de xin" 關於《紅樓夢》研究問題的信 (My letter on the study of *Dream of the Red Chamber*). In *Mao Zedong wenji*, 6: 352–53. Beijing: Renmin chubanshe, 1999.

———. "Guanyu zhexue de jianghua" 關於哲學的講話 (Speech on Philosophical Issues). In *Mao Zedong sixiang wansui* 毛澤東思想萬歲 (Long live Mao Zedong thought), 549. n.p., 1969.

———. "Hunan nongmin yundong kaocha baogao" 湖南農民運動考察報告 (Report on an investigation into the peasant movement in Hunan). In *Mao Zedong xuanji*, 1: 12–44.

———. "Jiang geming jinxing daodi" 將革命進行到底 (Propel the revolution to its very end), In *Mao Zedong xuanji*, 4: 1372–80.

———. *Mao Zedong wenji* 毛澤東文集 (Writings of Mao Zedong), 8 vols. Beijing: Renmin chubanshe, 1993–99.

———. *Mao Zedong xuanji* 毛澤東選集 (Selected works of Mao Zedong), 4 vols. Beijing: Renmin chubanshe, 1991.

———. *On Art and Literature*. Beijing: Foreign Language Press, 1960.

———. *Selected Works of Mao Tse-tung*. 5 vols. Beijing: Foreign Language Press, 1965–67.

———. "Xin minzhu zhuyi lun" 新民主主義論 (On new democracy). In *Mao Zedong xuanji*, 2: 662–711.

———. "Zai Yan'an wenyi zuotanhui shang de jianghua" 在延安文藝座談會上的講話 (Talks at the Yan'an forum on literature and art). In *Mao Zedong xuanji*, 3: 847–79.

Marcuse, Herbert. "Review of Georg Lukács, *Goethe und Seine Zeit*." In *Philosophy and Phenomenological Research* 11, no. 1 (September 1950): 142–44.

Mark, Chi-kwan. "The 'Problem of People': British Colonials, Cold War Powers, and the Chinese Refugees in Hong Kong, 1949–62." *Modern Asian Studies* (November 2007): 1145–81.

Mei Jialing 梅家玲. *Xingbie, haishi jiaguo? Wushi yu bajiushi niandai Taiwan xiaoshuo lun* 性別，還是家國？五十與八九十年代台灣小說論 (Gender or nation? Criticism on contemporary Taiwan fiction). Taipei: Maitian, 2004.

Meinecke, Friedrich. *Cosmopolitanism and the National State*, translated by Robert B. Kimber. Princeton, NJ: Princeton University Press, 1970.

Meisner, Maurice. *Mao's China and After: A History of the People's Republic.* New York: Free Press, 1986.

Mitgang, Herbert. "Publishing: Chinese Weekend in Iowa." *New York Times*, August 17, 1979, C24.

Morris, Andrew. "The Taiwan Republic of 1895 and the Failure of the Qing Modernizing Project." In *Memories of the Future: National Identity Issues and the Search for a New Taiwan*, edited by Stephane Corcuff, 3–24. Armonk, NY: M. E. Sharpe, 2002.

Müller, Jan-Werner. "The Cold War and the Intellectual History of the Late Twentieth Century." In *The Cambridge History of the Cold War*, edited by Melvyn P. Leffler and Odd Arne Westad, vol. 3, 1–22. Cambridge: Cambridge University Press, 2010.

Ng Ho 吳昊. *Guzhuang, xiayi, Huangmei diao* 古裝，俠義，黃梅調 (Period drama, Huangmei opera). Hong Kong: Joint, 2004.

Ng, Kenny K. K. "Romantic Comedies of Cathay—MP&GI in the 1950s and 60s: Language, Locality, and Urban Character." *Jump Cut: A Review of Contemporary Media* 49 (Spring 2007), www.ejumpcut.org/archive/jc49.2007/text.html.

Novalis. *Schriften: Die Werke Friedrich von Hardenbergs*, edited by Paul Kluckhohn und Richard Samuel. Vol. 1. Stuttgart: Kohlhammer, 1960.

Ong, Aihwa. "Chinese Modernities: Narratives of Nation and of Capitalism." In *Ungrounded Empires: The Cultural Politics of Modern Chinese Transnationalism*, edited by Aihwa Ong and Donald M. Nonini, 171–202. New York: Routledge, 1997.

———. *Flexible Citizenship: The Cultural Logics of Transnationality.* Durham, NC: Duke University Press, 1999.

Owen, Stephen. *Remembrances: The Experience of the Past in Classical Chinese Literature.* Cambridge, MA: Harvard University Press, 1986.

Peng Ruijin 彭瑞金. *Taiwan xinwenxue yundong sishi nian* 台灣新文學運動四十年 (Forty years of new literature movement in Taiwan). Taipei: Zili wanbao, 1991.

———. "Zhanhou Taiwan xinwenxue yundong de lubiao: *Yaxiya de gu'er*" 戰後台灣新文學運動的路標：《亞細亞的孤兒》 (The guidepost of the postwar Taiwan new literary movement: *Orphan of Asia*). In *Miaozhun Taiwan zuojia: Peng Ruijin wenxue pinglun* 瞄準台灣作家：彭瑞金文學評論 (Aiming at Taiwan writers: Literary critiques by Peng Ruijin), 13–22. Gaoxiong: Paise wenhua, 1992.

Perry, Elizabeth J. *Shanghai on Strike: The Politics of Chinese Labor.* Stanford, CA: Stanford University Press, 1993.

Pollard, David. *A Chinese Look at Literature: The Literary Values of Zhou Zuoren in Relation to the Tradition*. London: Hurst, 1973.

Qi Qizhang 戚其章. "Qiu Fengjia litai neidu kao" 丘逢甲離台內渡考 (A study on Qiu Fengjia's leaving Taiwan and returning to the mainland). *Xueshu yanjiu* 學術研究 (Academic research), no. 191 (October 2000): 77–85.

Qian Chongshi 錢崇實. "Zhongri jiawu zhanzheng hou de geguo an'dou" 中日甲午戰爭後的各國暗鬥 (The secret battles among foreign countries behind the first Sino-Japanese War). *Dongfang zazhi* 5, no. 5 (November 1971): 63–83.

Qian Liqun 錢理群. *Duihua yu manyou: Sishi niandai xiaoshuo yandu* 對話與漫遊：四十年代小說研讀 (Dialogues and rambles: Studies of fiction of the 1940s). Shanghai: Shanghai wenyi chubanshe, 1999.

———. *1948 Tiandi xuanhuang* 1948 天地玄黃 (1948: World in-between). Jinan: Shandong jiaoyu chubanshe, 1998.

———. "Tan zuomeng" 談做夢 (On dreaming). In *Jujue yiwang: Qian Liqun wenxuan* 拒絕遺忘：錢理群文選 (Rejecting to forget: Selected writings of Qian Liqun), 71–82. Shantou: Shantou daxue chubanshe, 1999.

Qian Min 錢敏. "Zhang Ailing he ta de *Honglou mengyan*" 張愛玲和她的《紅樓夢魘》 (Eileen Chang and her *Nightmare in the Red Chamber*). *Dushu* 讀書 11 (2000): 110–11.

Qian Zhongshu 錢鍾書. "Linggan" 靈感 (The inspiration). In *Ren, Shou, Gui* 人，獸，鬼 (Human beings, animals, and ghosts), 89–119. Shanghai: Kaiming, 1946.

Qiu Fengjia 丘逢甲. "Chunchou" 春愁 (Grief in the spring). In *Lingyun hairi lou shichao* 嶺雲海日樓詩抄 (Anthology of poems of Tower Lingyun hairi), 29. Shanghai: Shanghai guji chubanshe, 1982.

Quanlin 荃麟, Naichao 乃超, et al. *Wenyi de xin fangxiang* 文藝的新方向 (New direction of literature and art). Hong Kong: Shenghuo shudian, 1948.

Quo, F. Q. "British Diplomacy and the Cession of Formosa, 1894–95." *Modern Asian Studies*, no. 2 (April 1968): 141–54.

Rickett, Allyn, and Adele Rickett. *Prisoners of Liberation*. New York: Cameron Associates, 1957.

Rilke, Rainer Maria. "Von der Landschaft." In *Rainer Maria Rilke: Sämtliche Werke.* 6 vols. Vol. 5, 516–23. Wiesbaden und Frankfurt am Main: Insel Verlag, 1955–66.

Rojas, Carlos, ed., with Eileen Chow. *Rethinking Modern Chinese Popular Culture: Cannibalizations of the Canon*. London: Routledge, 2009.

Rubin, Andrew N. *Archives of Authority: Empire, Culture, and the Cold War.* Princeton, NJ: Princeton University Press, 2012.

Ryan, Judith. *Rilke, Modernism and Poetic Tradition*. Cambridge: Cambridge University Press, 1999.

———. *Umschlag und Verwandlung. Poetische Struktur und Dichtungstheorie in R. M. Rilkes Lyrik der Mittleren Periode (1907–1914)*. Munich: Winkler, 1972.

Sadovnik, Alan R. *Knowledge and Pedagogy: The Sociology of Basil Bernstein*. Norwood, NJ: Ablex, 1995.

Said, Edward W. *Culture and Imperialism*. New York: Vintage, 1993.

———. *Humanism and Democratic Criticism*. New York: Columbia University Press, 2004.

———. *Orientalism*. New York: Vintage, 1978.

———. *The World, the Text, and the Critic*. Cambridge, MA: Harvard University Press, 1983.

Saunders, Frances Stonor. *The Cultural Cold War: The CIA and the World of Arts and Letters*. New York: New Press, 1999.

Saussy, Haun. "The Age of Attribution: Or, How the 'Honglou meng' Finally Acquired an Author." *Chinese Literature: Essays, Articles, Reviews (CLEAR)* 25 (December 2003): 119–32.

Schaeffer, Robert K. *Severed States: Dilemmas of Democracy in a Divided World*. Lanham, MD: Rowman & Littlefield, 1999.

Shan Dexing 單德興. *Mingke yu zaixian: Huayi meiguo wenxue yu wenhua lunji* 銘刻與再現：華裔美國文學與文化論集 (Inscriptions and representations: Chinese American literary and cultural studies). Taipei: Maitian, 2000.

Shen Congwen 沈從文. *Shen Congwen quanji* 沈從文全集 (Complete works of Shen Congwen), edited by Zhang Zhaohe 張兆和. 32 vols. Taiyuan: Beiyue wenyi chubanshe, 2002, abbreviated in the notes as *SCWQJ*.

Shen Huchu 沈虎雛. "Tuanju" 團聚 (Reunion). In Huang Yongyu, *Changhe bujinliu*, 490–520.

Shen Shuang 沈雙. "Betrayal, Impersonation, and Bilingualism: Eileen Chang's Self-Translation." In *Eileen Chang: Romancing Languages, Cultures, and Genres*, edited by Kam Louie, 91–112. Hong Kong: Hong Kong University Press, 2011.

———, ed. *Lingdu kanzhang: Chonggou Zhang Ailing* 零度看張：重構張愛玲 (Eileen Chang degree zero). Hong Kong: Chinese University Press, 2010.

Shen Zhihua 沈志華 and Douglas A. Stiffler, eds., *Cuiruo de lianmeng: Lengzhan yu Zhong-Su guanxi* 脆弱的聯盟：冷戰與中蘇關係 (Frail alliance: The cold war and Sino-Soviet relations). Beijing: Shehui kexue wenxian chubanshe, 2010.

Shih, Shu-mei. "The Concept of the Sinophone." *PMLA* 126, no. 3 (May 2011): 709–18.

———. *Visuality and Identity: Sinophone Articulations across the Pacific*. Berkeley: University of California Press, 2007.

Shiyi 適夷. "1948 nian xiaoshuo chuangzuo niaokan" 1948年小說創作鳥瞰 (A survey of literary writings in 1948). *Xiaoshuo yuekan* 小說月刊 2, no. 2 (February 1949).

Shu, Kei. "Notes on MP&GI." In Wong, *The Cathay Story*, 66–81.

Shui Jing 水晶. *Zhang Ailing xiaoshuo de yishu* 張愛玲小說的藝術 (The art of Eileen Chang's fiction). Taipei: Dadi, 1985.

Silverman, Kaja. *Flesh of My Flesh*. Stanford, CA: Stanford University Press, 2009.

Sima Changfeng 司馬長風. *Zhongguo xin wenxue shi* 中國新文學史 (History of new Chinese literature). 2 vols. Taipei: Zhuanji wenxue chubanshe, 1991.

Sima Xin 司馬新. *Zhang Ailing yu Laiya* 張愛玲與賴雅 (Eileen Chang and Reyher). Taipei: Dadi, 1996.

Sitong zi 思痛子. *Taihai sitong lu* 臺海思痛錄 (The sorrows of the Taiwan Strait). Taipei: Taiwan yinhang jingji yanjiushi, 1959.

Song, Weijie. *Cong yule xingwei dao wutuobang chongdong: Jin Yong xiaoshuo zai jiedu* 從娛樂行為到烏托邦衝動：金庸小說再解讀 (From entertainment activity to utopian impulse: Rereading Jin Yong's martial arts fiction). Nanjing: Jiangsu renming, 1999.

———. "Nation-State, Individual Identity, and Historical Memory: Conflicts between Han and Non-Han Peoples in Jin Yong's Novels." In Ann Huss and Jianmei Liu, eds., *The Jin Yong Phenomenon: Chinese Martial Arts Fiction and Modern Chinese Literary History*, 121–54. Youngstown, NY: Cambria Press, 2007.

———. "Space, Swordsmen, and Utopia: The Dualistic Imagination in Jin Yong's Narratives." In Ann Huss and Jianmei Liu, eds., *The Jin Yong Phenomenon: Chinese Martial Arts Fiction and Modern Chinese Literary History*, 155–78. Youngstown, NY: Cambria Press, 2007.

Su Weizhen 蘇偉貞. *Gudao Zhang Ailing: Zhuizong Zhang Ailing Xianggang shiqi xiaoshuo (1952–1955)* 孤島張愛玲：追蹤張愛玲香港時期小說（1952–1955）(Eileen Chang in the lonely island: Tracing Eileen Chang's fiction of the Hong Kong period, 1952–1955). Taipei: Sanmin shuju, 2002.

Su Xuelin 蘇雪林. "Shen Congwen lun" 沈從文論 (On Shen Congwen). In *Su Xuelin xuanji* 蘇雪林選集 (Selected works of Su Xuelin), 126–40. Taipei: Xinlu shuju, 1961. First published 1934.

Szasz, Thomas. *Schizophrenia: The Sacred Symbol of Psychiatry*. New York: Basic Books, 1976.

Tang Junyi 唐君毅, Carsun Chang 張君勱, Mou Zongsan 牟宗三, and Xu Fuguan 徐復觀. "Wei Zhongguo wenhua jinggao shijie renshi xuanyan" 為中國文化敬告世界人士宣言 (A manifesto to the world on behalf of Chinese culture). In *Tang Junyi quanji* 唐君毅全集 (Complete works of Tang Junyi), vol. 4, pt. 2. Taipei: Taiwan Student Bookstore, 1991.

Tang Xiaobing, ed. *Zaijiedu: Dazhong wenyi yu yishi xingtai* 再解讀：大眾文藝與意識形態 (Rereading: Popular culture and ideology). Hong Kong: Oxford University Press, 1993.

Tay, William. "Colonialism, the Cold War, and Marginal Space: The Existential Condition of Five Decades of Hong Kong Literature." In Chi Pang-yuan and Wang, *Chinese Literature,* 31–38.

———. 鄭樹森. "Zhang Ailing yu liangge pianzhong" 張愛玲與兩個片種 (Eileen Chang and Two Film Genres), *INK* (印刻文學生活誌) 2, no. 1 (September 2005), 154–55.

Tsang, Steve. *Cold War's Odd Couple: The Unintended Partnership between the Republic of China and the UK, 1950–1958*. London: I. B. Tauris, 2006.

———. "Strategy for Survival: The Cold War and Hong Kong's Policy towards Kuomintang and Chinese Communist Activities in the 1950s." *Journal of Imperial and Commonwealth History* 25, no. 2 (May 1997): 294–317.

Tsu, Jing. *Failure, Nationalism, and Literature: The Making of Modern Chinese Identity, 1895–1937*. Stanford, CA: Stanford University Press, 2005.

Tu, Wei-ming. "Cultural China: The Periphery as the Center." *Daedalus* 120, no. 2 (Spring 1991): 1–32.

Virno, Paolo, and Michael Hardt, eds. *Radical Thought in Italy: A Potential Politics*. Minneapolis: University of Minnesota Press, 1996.

Viswanathan, Gauri. *Masks of Conquest: Literary Study and British Rule in India*. New York: Columbia University Press, 1989.

Volland, Nicolai. "Zhengzhi rentong: 1950 niandai Zhongguo yu Sulian, dong ou de wenhua jiaoliu" 政治認同：1950年代中國與蘇聯，東歐的文化交流 (Political Identification: China's Cultural Exchange with the Soviet Union and Eastern Europe in the 1950s). In Shen and Stiffler, *Cuiruo de lianmeng*, 93–113.

Wagner, Rudolf G. *Inside a Service Trade: Studies in Contemporary Chinese Prose*. Cambridge, MA: Harvard University Asia Center, 1992.

Wang Anyi 王安憶. "Yingte naixiong nai'er" 英特奈雄乃爾 (The Internationale). *Shanghai wenxue* 上海文學 (Shanghai literature), vol. 315, no. 1 (2004): 75–77.

Wang, Ban. *The Sublime Figure of History: Aesthetics and Politics in Twentieth-Century China*. Stanford, CA: Stanford University Press, 1997.

Wang, David Der-wei. *Fictional Realism in 20th Century China: Mao Dun, Lao She, Shen Congwen*. New York: Columbia University Press, 1992.

———. *Fin-de-siècle Splendor: Repressed Modernities of Late Qing Fiction, 1849–1911*. Stanford, CA: Stanford University Press, 1997.

———. "Hou yimin xiezuo" 後遺民寫作 (Post-*yimin* writing). In Wang, *Hou yimin xiezuo: Shijian yu jiyi de zhengzhi xue* 後遺民寫作：時間與記憶的政治學 (Post-loyalist writing: The politics of time and memory), 23–70. Taipei: Maitian, 2007.

———. *The Monster That Is History: History, Violence, and Fictional Writing in Twentieth-Century China*. Berkeley: University of California Press, 2004.

———. "Reinventing National History: Communist and Anti-Communist Fiction of the Mid-Twentieth Century." In Chi Pang-yuan and Wang, *Chinese Literature*, 39–64.

———. *Writing Taiwan: A New Literary History*, edited by David Der-wei Wang and C. Rojas. Durham, NC: Duke University Press, 2007.

Wang, David Der-wei, Chen Sihe, and Xu Zidong, eds. *1949 yihou: dangdai wenxue liushi nian* 1949 以後：當代文學六十年 (After 1949: Sixty years of contemporary literature). Shanghai: Shanghai wenyi, 2011.

Wang Guowei 王國維. "*Honglou meng* pinglun" 紅樓夢評論 (A critique of *Dream of the Red Chamber*). In Chen Pingyuan, *Ershi shiji Zhongguo xiaoshuo lilun ziliao*, 96–115.

Wang Hong 汪洪, ed. *Zuoyou shuo Ding Ling* 左右說丁玲 (Ding Ling from left and right perspectives). Beijing: Zhongguo gongren chubanshe, 2002.

Wang Hui. "Contemporary Chinese Thought and the Question of Modernity," translated by Rebecca E. Karl, *Social Text* 55 (Summer 1998): 9–44.

———. "Humanism as the Theme of Chinese Modernity." *Surfaces* 5, no. 202 (1995).

———. "The Politics of Imagining Asia," translated by Matthew A. Hale. In Wang Hui, *The Politics of Imagining Asia*, edited by Theodore Huters, 10–62. Cambridge, MA: Harvard University Press, 2011.

Wang Jiancong 王劍叢. "Ping Sima Changfeng de *Zhongguo xin wenxue shi*" 評司馬長風的《中國新文學史》 (Review of Sima Changfeng's *History of New Chinese Literature*). *Xianggang wenxue* 香港文學 (Hong Kong literature), no. 22 (1986): 34–40.

Wang Jun 王軍. *Chengji* 城記 (On Beijing). Beijing: Sanlian shudian, 2002.

Wang Kai 王愷. "Yueju *Honglou meng* de dansheng" 越劇《紅樓夢》的誕生 (The birth of the Yue Opera *Dream of the Red Chamber*). *Sanlian Weekly* 三聯週刊 (July 9, 2009), 56–65.

Wang Meng 王蒙. "Wo xinmuzhong de Ding Ling" 我心目中的丁玲 (Ding Ling in My Mind). In Wang Hong, *Zuoyou shuo Ding Ling*, 201–14.

Wang Xiaojue. "Individual Memory, Photographic Seduction and Allegorical Correspondence: Zhang Ailing and Her *Mutual Reflections: Reading Old Photographs*." In Rojas, *Rethinking Modern Chinese Popular Culture*, 190–206.

———. "*Stone* in Modern China: Literature, Politics, and Culture." In *Approaches to Teaching* The Story of the Stone (Dream of the Red Chamber), edited by Andrew Schonebaum and Tina Lu, 662–91. Modern Language Association, 2013.

Wang Yao 王瑤. *Zhongguo xin wenxue shigao* 中國新文學史稿 (A draft history of new Chinese literature). Vol. 1: Beijing: Kaiming, 1951; Vol. 2: Beijing: Xin wenyi, 1958.

Wang Yixin 王一心. *Tamensan: Zhang Ailing, Suqing, Hu Lancheng* 他們仨：張愛玲，蘇青，胡蘭成 (They Three: Zhang Ailing, Su Qing, Hu Lancheng). Shanghai: Dongfang chuban zhongxin, 2008.

Wang Zengqi 汪曾祺. "Shen Congwen zhuanye zhimi" 沈從文轉業之謎 (The myth of Shen Congwen's professional change). In Huang Yongyu, *Changhe bujinliu*, 139–44.

Wang Zengru 王增如. *Wunai de niepan: Ding Ling zuihou de rizi* 無奈的涅磐：丁玲最後的日子 (An uneasy nirvana: The last days of Ding Ling). Shanghai: Shanghai shudian, 2003.

Wasserstrom, Jeffrey N. *Student Protest in Twentieth-Century China: The View from Shanghai*. Stanford, CA: Stanford University Press, 1991.

Westad, Odd Arne, ed. *Brothers in Arms: The Rise and Fall of the Sino-Soviet Alliance, 1945–1963*. Washington, DC: Woodrow Wilson Center Press, 1998.

———. *Cold War and Revolution: Soviet-American Rivalry and the Origins of the Chinese Civil War, 1944–1946*. New York: Columbia University Press, 1992.

———. "Rethinking Revolution: The Cold War in the Third World." *Journal of Peace Research* 29, no. 4 (November 1992): 455–64.

Williams, Raymond. *Marxism and Literature*. Oxford: Oxford University Press, 1977.

Wong, Ailing, ed. *The Cathay Story*. Hong Kong: Hong Kong Film Archive, 2002.

Wong, Sau-ling Cynthia. *Reading Asian American Literature: From Necessity to Extravagance*. Princeton, NJ: Princeton University Press, 1993.

Wong Wang-chi 王宏志. *Lishi de ouran: Cong Xianggang kan zhongguo xiandai wenxueshi* 歷史的偶然：從香港看中國現代文學史 (Historical coincidences: Reflections on history of modern Chinese literature from Hong Kong). Hong Kong: Oxford University Press, 1997.

Wu, Hung. *Remaking Beijing: Tiananmen Square and the Creation of a Political Space*. Chicago: University of Chicago Press, 2005.

Wu Micha 吳密察. "1895nian 'Taiwan minzhuguo' de chengli jingguo" 1895年台灣民主國的成立經過 (The course of the foundation of the 1895 Taiwan Republic). In *Taiwanshi lunwen jingxuan* 台灣史論文精選 (Selected theses on Taiwan history), edited by Zhang Yanxian 張炎憲, Li Xiaofeng 李筱峰, and Dai Baocun 戴寶村. Vol. 2, 11–54. Taipei: Yushan chubanshe, 1996.

Wu Shiyong 吳世勇. "Wei wenxue yundong de chongzao xunzhao yige zhendi: Shen Congwen canyu *Zhanguo ce* bianji jingli kaobian" 為文學運動的重造尋找一個陣地：沈從文參與《戰國策》編輯經歷考辯 (In search of a ground for the reconstruction of literary movements: Shen Congwen's involvement in the editorial activities of *Annals of the Warring States*). *Huainan shifan xueyuan xuebao* 淮南師範學院學報, no. 1 (2005): 18–21.

Wu Zhuoliu 吳濁流. "Bocitan kezhang" 波茨坦科長 (Director Potsdam). In *Bocitan kezhang* 波茨坦科長 (Director Potsdam), edited by Zhang Liangze 張良澤. Taipei: Yuanjing, 1993, 1–72.

———. *Gonggou* 功狗 (A distinguished dog). In Zhang Liangze, ed. *Wu Zhuoliu zuopinji* 吳濁流作品集 (Selected works of Wu Zhuoliu), vol. 2. Taipei: Yuanxing, 1977.

———. *Liming qian de Taiwan* 黎明前的台灣 (Taiwan before dawn). In Zhang Liangze, ed. *Wu Zhuoliu zuopinji*, vol. 5. Taipei: Yuanxing, 1977.

———. *Nanjing zagan* 南京雜感 (Miscellaneous thoughts on Nanjing). In Zhang Liangze, ed. *Wu Zhuoliu zuopinji*, vol. 4. Taipei: Yuanxing, 1977.

———. *Wuhua guo* 無花果 (The fig tree). Taipei: Caogen, 1995.

———. *Yaxiya de gu'er* 亞細亞的孤兒 (Orphan of Asia). Taipei: Caogen, 1995.

Xiao Qian 蕭乾. "Lengyan kan Taiwan" 冷眼看台灣 (Looking at Taiwan objectively). In Xiao, *Rensheng caifang* 人生採訪 (Reports on life). Shanghai: Wenhua shenghuo chubanshe, 1947.

Xie Yong 謝泳. "*Xinlu* yu *Guancha*" 《新路》與《觀察》 (*New road* and *Observation*). In *Shiqu de niandai: Zhongguo ziyou zhishi fenzi de mingyun* 逝去的年代：中國自由知識份子的命運 (Years gone by: The fate of Chinese liberal intellectuals), 358–68. Beijing: Wenhua yishu, 1999.

Xu Junya 許俊雅. *Riju shiqi Taiwan xiaoshuo yanjiu* 日據時期台灣小說研究 (Studies on Taiwan fiction during Japanese rule). Taipei: Wenshizhe chubanshe, 1995.

Yang Bichuan 楊碧川. *Taiwan lishi cidian* 台灣歷史詞典 (Dictionary of Taiwan history). Taipei: Qianwei, 1997.

Yang, Dali L. *Calamity and Reform in China: State, Rural Society, and Institutional Change Since the Great Leap Famine*. Stanford, CA: Stanford University Press, 1996.

———. "Cong dayuejin jihuang dao nongcun gaige" 從大躍進飢荒到農村改革 (From the famine of the Great Leap Forward to the reform of the countryside). *Twenty-first Century* 二十一世紀, no. 48 (August 1998): 4–13.

Yang Qianhe 楊千鶴. *Rensheng de sanleng jing* 人生的三棱鏡 (Life's prism), translated by Zhang Liangze and Lin Zhimei. Taipei: Nantian, 1999.

Yang Xiaomin 楊曉民 and Zhou Yihu 周翼虎. *Zhongguo danwei zhidu* 中國單位制度 (The system of work units in China). Beijing: Zhongguo jingji chubanshe, 1999.

Yang Zao 楊早. "Jiushi niandai wenhua yingxiong de fuhao yu xiangzheng" 九十年代文化英雄的符號與象徵 (The sign and symbol of cultural heroes of the 1990s). In *Shuxie wenhua yingxiong: Shiji zhijiao de wenhua yanjiu* 書寫文化英雄：世紀之交的文化研究 (Writing cultural heroes: Cultural studies in the twentieth-century fin-de-siecle), edited by Dai Jinhua 戴錦華, 18–45. Nanjing: Jiangsu renmin chubanshe, 2000.

Yang Ze 楊澤, ed. *Yuedu Zhang Ailing: Zhang Ailing guoji yantaohui lunwen ji* 閱讀張愛玲：張愛玲國際研討會論文集 (Reading Eileen Chang: Collected Essays from the International Conference on Eileen Chang Research). Taipei: Maitian, 1999.

Yao Kekun 姚可崑. *Wo yu Feng Zhi* 我與馮至 (Me and Feng Zhi). Guizhou: Guangxi jiaoyu, 1994.

Ye Jiaying 葉嘉瑩. *Wang Guowei jiqi wenxue piping* 王國維及其文學批評 (Wang Guowei and his literary criticism). Taipei: Yuanliu, 1982.

Ye Jibin 葉紀彬. *Zhongxi dianxing lilun shuping* 中西典型理論述評 (A survey of Chinese and Western theories on typical characters and typical environments). Shanghai: Huadong shifan daxue chubanshe, 1993.

Ye Shengtao 葉聖陶. *Ye Shengtao xuanji* 葉聖陶選集 (Selected works of Ye Shengtao). In *Xin wenxue xuanji* 新文學選集 (The anthology of new literature), edited by Mao Dun 茅盾. Beijing: Kaiming shudian, 1951.

Ye Shitao 葉石濤. *Taiwan wenxue shigang* 台灣文學史綱 (An outline of the history of Taiwanese literature). Gaoxiong: Wenxuejie, 1987.

Ye Zhaoyan 葉兆言. "Weicheng li de xiaosheng" 圍城里的笑聲 (Laughter in a besieged city). *Shouhuo* 收穫 (Harvest), no. 4 (2000): 141–50.

Yeh, Michelle. *Modern Chinese Poetry: Theory and Practice Since 1917*. New Haven, CT: Yale University Press, 1991.

———. " 'On Our Destitute Dinner Table': Modern Poetry Quarterly in the 1950s." In *Writing Taiwan: A New Literary History*, edited by David Der-wei Wang and C. Rojas, 113–39. Durham, NC: Duke University Press, 2007.

———. "Taiwanren zai Beijing" 台灣人在北京 (The Taiwanese in Beijing). In *Beijing: Dushi xiangxiang yu wenhua jiyi* 北京：都市想像與文化記憶 (Beijing: Urban imaginations and cultural memories), edited by Chen Pingyuan and David Wang, 371–89. Beijing: Beijing daxue chubanshe, 2005.

Ying Fenghuang 應鳳凰. "Fangong+xiandai: youyi ziyou zhuyi sichao wenxue ban" 反共＋現代：右翼自由主義思潮文學版 (Anticommunism and modernity: The literary version of the Rightist liberalism). In *Taiwan xiaoshuo shilun* 台灣小說史論 (Essays on Taiwan literary history), edited by Chen Jianzhong 陳建忠, Ying Fenghuang 應鳳凰, Qiu Guifen 邱貴芬, Zhang Songsheng 張誦聖, and Liu Liangya 劉亮雅, 111–96. Taipei: Maitian, 2007.

Yu, Anthony C. *Rereading the Stone: Desire and the Making of Fiction in* Dream of the Red Chamber. Princeton, NJ: Princeton University Press, 1997.

Yu Fengzheng 于風政. *Gaizao* 改造 (Rectifications). Zhengzhou: Henan renmin chubanshe, 2001.

Yuan Liangjun 袁良駿, ed. *Ding Ling yanjiu ziliao* 丁玲研究資料 (Research materials on Ding Ling). Tianjin: Tianjin renmin chubanshe, 1982.

Zahavi, Dan. "Schizophrenia and Self-Awareness." *Philosophy, Psychiatry and Psychology* 4 (2001): 339–41.

Zeng Lingcun 曾令存. "1948–1949: *Dazhong wenyi congkan*" 1948–1949: 大眾文藝叢刊 (1948–1949: Mass literature and arts collection). *Zhongguo xiandai wenxue yanjiu congkan,* no. 2 (2002): 45–69.

Zhang Ailing 張愛玲, *see* Chang, Eileen.

Zhang Dongsun 張東蓀. *Jingshen fenxi xue ABC* 精神分析學ABC (The ABCs of Psychoanalysis). Shanghai: Shijie shuju, 1929.

Zhang Guiyang 張圭陽. *Jin Yong yu* Ming bao *chuanqi* 金庸與明報傳奇 (Jin Yong and *Ming bao*). Taipei: Yunchen wenhua, 2005.

Zhang Jing. "Wilderness to Reclaim Farmland." *Asian Times*, May 15, 2000, http://www.atimes.com/china/BE16Ad01.html.

Zhang, Jingyuan. *Psychoanalysis in China: Literary Transformations, 1919–1949.* Ithaca, NY: Cornell East Asia Program, 1992.

Zhang, Kuan. "A Remarkable Cultural Encounter: The Reception of German Romanticism, Rilke, and Modernism in Feng Zhi's Poetry." PhD diss., Stanford University, 1999.

Zhang Qingping 張清平. *Lin Huiyin* 林徽因. Tianjin: Baihua wenyi chubanshe, 2002.

Zhang, Shu Guang. *Deterrence and Strategic Culture: Chinese-American Confrontations, 1949–1958.* Ithaca, NY: Cornell University Press, 1992.

Zhang Wojun 張我軍. *Zhang Wojun shiwen ji* 張我軍詩文集 (Collected poems and essays of Zhang Wojun), edited by Zhang Guangzhi 張光直. Taipei: Chunwenxue, 1989.

Zhang Xinying 張新穎. "Cong 'chouxiang de shuqing' dao 'yiyu kuangyan': Shen Congwen de sishi niandai" 從抽象的抒情到囈語狂言：沈從文的四十年代 (From "abstract lyricism" to "delirium remarks and wild talks": Shen Congwen in the 1940s). In *Ershi shiji shangbanqi zhongguo wenxue de xiandai yishi* 20世紀上半期中國文學的現代意識 (Modern consciousness of Chinese literature in the first half of the twentieth century), 225–48. Beijing: Sanlian shudian, 2001.

Zhang, Xudong. *Postsocialism and Cultural Politics: China in the Last Decade of the Twentieth Century.* Durham, NC: Duke University Press, 2008.

Zhang Yingjin. "Institutionalization of Modern Literary History in China." *Modern China* 20, no. 3 (July 1994): 347–77.

Zhang Yongquan 張永泉. "Zoubuchu de guaiquan: Ding Ling wannian xintai tanxi" 走不出的怪圈：丁玲晚年心態探析 (The uncanny circle: An exploration of the mentality of Ding Ling in her later years). In Wang Hong, *Zuoyou shuo Ding Ling,* 231–51.

Zhang Zige 張紫葛. *Xinxiang leiyu ji Wu Mi* 心香淚雨祭吳宓 (Providing sacrifice to Wu Mi with tears). Guangzhou: Guangzhou chubanshe, 1997.

Zhao Gang 趙岡. "Zhang Ailing yu hongxue" 張愛玲與紅學 (Eileen Chang and Redology). *United Daily News* 聯合報, November 21, 1995.

Zheng Hongsheng 鄭鴻生. "Taiwan de dalu xiangxiang" 台灣的大陸想像 (Taiwan's imagination of the mainland). *Dushu* 讀書 310, no. 1 (2005): 34–46.

Zheng Mingli 鄭明娳. "Dangdai Taiwan wenyi zhengce de fazhan, yingxiang, yu jiantao" 當代臺灣文藝政策的發展、影響與檢討 (The evolvement, impacts, and reconsideration of contemporary Taiwan literary policies). In *Dangdai Taiwan zhengzhi wenxue lun* 當代台灣政治文學論 (On contemporary Taiwan politics and literature), edited by Zheng Mingli, 13–68. Taipei: Shibao wenhua, 1994.

Zhong Lihe 鐘理和. "Baishu de bei'ai" 白薯的悲哀 (The sadness of the yam). In *Zhong Lihe ji* 鐘理和集 (Selected writings of Zhong Lihe), 93–102. Taipei: Qianwei chubanshe, 1991.

———. "Jiazhutao" 夾竹桃 (Oleander). In *Zhong Lihe daibiaozuo* 鐘理和代表作 (Representative writings of Zhong Lihe), 145–85. Beijing: Huaxia chubanshe, 1999.

———. "Yuanxiang ren" 原鄉人 (People of the native land). In *Zhong Lihe daibiaozuo*, 3–13.

Zhong Zhaozheng 鐘肇政. "Tiexue shiren Wu Zhuoliu" 鐵血詩人吳濁流 (Poet Wu Zhuoliu with iron blood). In *Zhong Zhaozheng huiyi lu* 鐘肇政回憶錄 (Memoirs of Zhong Zhaozheng), vol. 2, 69–118. Taipei: Qianwei, 1998.

Zhou Fenling 周芬伶. *Kongque landiao: Zhang Ailing pingzhuan* 孔雀藍調：張愛玲評傳 (Turquoise Blues: A Biography of Eileen Chang). Taipei: Maitian, 2005.

Zhou Liangpei 周良沛. *Ding Ling zhuan* 丁玲傳 (The biography of Ding Ling). Beijing: Beijing shiyue wenyi chubanshe, 1993.

———. *Feng Zhi pingzhuan* 馮至評傳 (A critical biography of Feng Zhi). Chongqing: Chongqing chubanshe, 2001.

Zhou Ruchang 周汝昌. *Dingshi Honglou meng li ren: Zhang Ailing yu* Honglou meng 定是紅樓夢裡人：張愛玲與紅樓夢 (She must have been a character in *Dream of the Red Chamber*: Eileen Chang and *Dream of the Red Chamber*). Beijing: Tuanjie chubanshe, 2005.

Zhou Yang 周揚. "Wenyi zhanxianshang de yichang da bianlun" 文藝戰線上的一場大辯論 (A big polemic on the frontier of literature and art). In Hong Zicheng, *Zhongguo dangdai wenxueshi shiliaoxuan*, 432–58.

Zhou Yiliang 周一良. *Bijing shi shusheng* 畢竟是書生 (I am a scholar after all). Beijing: Beijing shiyue chubanshe, 1998.

Zhou Zuoren 周作人. *Zhongguo xin wenxue de yuanliu* 中國新文學的源流 (The origins of new Chinese literature). Shijiazhuang: Hebei jiaoyu chubanshe, 2002.

Zhu Guangqian 朱光潛. *Biantai xinli xue paibie* 變態心理學派別 (Schools of abnormal psychology). In *Zhu Guangqian quanji* 朱光潛全集 (Complete works of Zhu Guangqian). Vol. 1, 85–194. Hefei: Anhui jiaoyu, 1987. First published 1930.

Zhu Keyu 竹可羽. "Lun 'Taiyang zhaozai sangganhe shang'" 論《太阳照在桑幹河上》 (On *The sun shines over the Sanggan River*). In Yuan Liangjun, *Ding Ling yanjiu ziliao*, 361–98.

Zhu Xiaodong 朱曉東. "Tongguo hunyin de zhili: 1930nian dao 1950nian gongchandang de hunyin he funü jiefang faling zhong de celüe yu shenti" 通過婚姻的治理：1930年到1950年共產黨的婚姻和婦女解放法令中的策略與身體 (Through regulation of marriage: The strategy and the body in the CCP's decrees of marriage and women's liberation from 1930 to 1950). In *Shenti de wenhua zhengzhi xue* 身體的文化政治學 (The cultural politics of body), edited by Wang Min'an 汪民安, 51–74. Zhengzhou: Henan daxue chubanshe, 2003.

Zhu Ziqing. 朱自清. "Lun buman xianzhuang" 論不滿現狀 (On being discontent with the status quo). In *Zhu Ziqing sanwen quanji* 3: 506–509.

———. "Wenwu, jiushu, maobi" 文物，舊書，毛筆 (Cultural relics, ancient books, writing brush). In *Zhu Ziqing sanwen quanji* 3: 517–21.

———. *Xinshi zahua* 新詩雜話 (On modern poetry). Beijing: Sanlian shudian, 1984.

———. *Zhu Ziqing sanwen quanji* 朱自清散文全集 (Complete prose of Zhu Ziqing), 3 vols., edited by Zhu Qiaosen 朱喬森. Nanjing: Jiangsu jiaoyu chubanshe, 1998.

Index

Harvard East Asian Monographs
(*out-of-print)

*1. Liang Fang-chung, *The Single-Whip Method of Taxation in China*
*2. Harold C. Hinton, *The Grain Tribute System of China, 1845–1911*
3. Ellsworth C. Carlson, *The Kaiping Mines, 1877–1912*
*4. Chao Kuo-chün, *Agrarian Policies of Mainland China: A Documentary Study, 1949–1956*
*5. Edgar Snow, *Random Notes on Red China, 1936–1945*
*6. Edwin George Beal, Jr., *The Origin of Likin, 1835–1864*
7. Chao Kuo-chün, *Economic Planning and Organization in Mainland China: A Documentary Study, 1949–1957*
*8. John K. Fairbank, *Ching Documents: An Introductory Syllabus*
*9. Helen Yin and Yi-chang Yin, *Economic Statistics of Mainland China, 1949–1957*
10. Wolfgang Franke, *The Reform and Abolition of the Traditional Chinese Examination System*
11. Albert Feuerwerker and S. Cheng, *Chinese Communist Studies of Modern Chinese History*
12. C. John Stanley, *Late Ching Finance: Hu Kuang-yung as an Innovator*
13. S. M. Meng, *The Tsungli Yamen: Its Organization and Functions*
*14. Ssu-yü Teng, *Historiography of the Taiping Rebellion*
15. Chun-Jo Liu, *Controversies in Modern Chinese Intellectual History: An Analytic Bibliography of Periodical Articles, Mainly of the May Fourth and Post-May Fourth Era*
*16. Edward J. M. Rhoads, *The Chinese Red Army, 1927–1963: An Annotated Bibliography*
*17. Andrew J. Nathan, *A History of the China International Famine Relief Commission*
*18. Frank H. H. King (ed.) and Prescott Clarke, *A Research Guide to China-Coast Newspapers, 1822–1911*
*19. Ellis Joffe, *Party and Army: Professionalism and Political Control in the Chinese Officer Corps, 1949–1964*
*20. Toshio G. Tsukahira, *Feudal Control in Tokugawa Japan: The Sankin Kōtai System*
*21. Kwang-Ching Liu, ed., *American Missionaries in China: Papers from Harvard Seminars*
*22. George Moseley, *A Sino-Soviet Cultural Frontier: The Ili Kazakh Autonomous Chou*

23. Carl F. Nathan, *Plague Prevention and Politics in Manchuria, 1910–1931*
*24. Adrian Arthur Bennett, *John Fryer: The Introduction of Western Science and Technology into Nineteenth-Century China*
*25. Donald J. Friedman, *The Road from Isolation: The Campaign of the American Committee for Non-Participation in Japanese Aggression, 1938–1941*
*26. Edward LeFevour, *Western Enterprise in Late Ching China: A Selective Survey of Jardine, Matheson and Company's Operations, 1842–1895*
27. Charles Neuhauser, *Third World Politics: China and the Afro-Asian People's Solidarity Organization, 1957–1967*
*28. Kungtu C. Sun, assisted by Ralph W. Huenemann, *The Economic Development of Manchuria in the First Half of the Twentieth Century*
*29. Shahid Javed Burki, *A Study of Chinese Communes, 1965*
30. John Carter Vincent, *The Extraterritorial System in China: Final Phase*
31. Madeleine Chi, *China Diplomacy, 1914–1918*
*32. Clifton Jackson Phillips, *Protestant America and the Pagan World: The First Half Century of the American Board of Commissioners for Foreign Missions, 1810–1860*
*33. James Pusey, *Wu Han: Attacking the Present Through the Past*
*34. Ying-wan Cheng, *Postal Communication in China and Its Modernization, 1860–1896*
35. Tuvia Blumenthal, *Saving in Postwar Japan*
36. Peter Frost, *The Bakumatsu Currency Crisis*
37. Stephen C. Lockwood, *Augustine Heard and Company, 1858–1862*
38. Robert R. Campbell, *James Duncan Campbell: A Memoir by His Son*
39. Jerome Alan Cohen, ed., *The Dynamics of China's Foreign Relations*
40. V. V. Vishnyakova-Akimova, *Two Years in Revolutionary China, 1925–1927*, trans. Steven L. Levine
41. Meron Medzini, *French Policy in Japan During the Closing Years of the Tokugawa Regime*
42. Ezra Vogel, Margie Sargent, Vivienne B. Shue, Thomas Jay Mathews, and Deborah S. Davis, *The Cultural Revolution in the Provinces*
43. Sidney A. Forsythe, *An American Missionary Community in China, 1895–1905*
*44. Benjamin I. Schwartz, ed., *Reflections on the May Fourth Movement.: A Symposium*
*45. Ching Young Choe, *The Rule of the Taewŏngun, 1864–1873: Restoration in Yi Korea*
46. W. P. J. Hall, *A Bibliographical Guide to Japanese Research on the Chinese Economy, 1958–1970*
47. Jack J. Gerson, *Horatio Nelson Lay and Sino-British Relations, 1854–1864*
48. Paul Richard Bohr, *Famine and the Missionary: Timothy Richard as Relief Administrator and Advocate of National Reform*
49. Endymion Wilkinson, *The History of Imperial China: A Research Guide*
50. Britten Dean, *China and Great Britain: The Diplomacy of Commercial Relations, 1860–1864*
51. Ellsworth C. Carlson, *The Foochow Missionaries, 1847–1880*
52. Yeh-chien Wang, *An Estimate of the Land-Tax Collection in China, 1753 and 1908*
53. Richard M. Pfeffer, *Understanding Business Contracts in China, 1949–1963*

*54. Han-sheng Chuan and Richard Kraus, *Mid-Ching Rice Markets and Trade: An Essay in Price History*
55. Ranbir Vohra, *Lao She and the Chinese Revolution*
56. Liang-lin Hsiao, *China's Foreign Trade Statistics, 1864–1949*
*57. Lee-hsia Hsu Ting, *Government Control of the Press in Modern China, 1900–1949*
*58. Edward W. Wagner, *The Literati Purges: Political Conflict in Early Yi Korea*
*59. Joungwon A. Kim, *Divided Korea: The Politics of Development, 1945–1972*
60. Noriko Kamachi, John K. Fairbank, and Chūzō Ichiko, *Japanese Studies of Modern China Since 1953: A Bibliographical Guide to Historical and Social-Science Research on the Nineteenth and Twentieth Centuries, Supplementary Volume for 1953–1969*
61. Donald A. Gibbs and Yun-chen Li, *A Bibliography of Studies and Translations of Modern Chinese Literature, 1918–1942*
62. Robert H. Silin, *Leadership and Values: The Organization of Large-Scale Taiwanese Enterprises*
63. David Pong, *A Critical Guide to the Kwangtung Provincial Archives Deposited at the Public Record Office of London*
*64. Fred W. Drake, *China Charts the World: Hsu Chi-yü and His Geography of 1848*
*65. William A. Brown and Urgrunge Onon, translators and annotators, *History of the Mongolian People's Republic*
66. Edward L. Farmer, *Early Ming Government: The Evolution of Dual Capitals*
*67. Ralph C. Croizier, *Koxinga and Chinese Nationalism: History, Myth, and the Hero*
*68. William J. Tyler, tr., *The Psychological World of Natsume Sōseki,* by Doi Takeo
69. Eric Widmer, *The Russian Ecclesiastical Mission in Peking During the Eighteenth Century*
*70. Charlton M. Lewis, *Prologue to the Chinese Revolution: The Transformation of Ideas and Institutions in Hunan Province, 1891–1907*
71. Preston Torbert, *The Ching Imperial Household Department: A Study of Its Organization and Principal Functions, 1662–1796*
72. Paul A. Cohen and John E. Schrecker, eds., *Reform in Nineteenth-Century China*
73. Jon Sigurdson, *Rural Industrialism in China*
74. Kang Chao, *The Development of Cotton Textile Production in China*
75. Valentin Rabe, *The Home Base of American China Missions, 1880–1920*
*76. Sarasin Viraphol, *Tribute and Profit: Sino-Siamese Trade, 1652–1853*
77. Ch'i-ch'ing Hsiao, *The Military Establishment of the Yuan Dynasty*
78. Meishi Tsai, *Contemporary Chinese Novels and Short Stories, 1949–1974: An Annotated Bibliography*
*79. Wellington K. K. Chan, *Merchants, Mandarins and Modern Enterprise in Late Ching China*
80. Endymion Wilkinson, *Landlord and Labor in Late Imperial China: Case Studies from Shandong by Jing Su and Luo Lun*
*81. Barry Keenan, *The Dewey Experiment in China: Educational Reform and Political Power in the Early Republic*
*82. George A. Hayden, *Crime and Punishment in Medieval Chinese Drama: Three Judge Pao Plays*

*83. Sang-Chul Suh, *Growth and Structural Changes in the Korean Economy, 1910–1940*
84. J. W. Dower, *Empire and Aftermath: Yoshida Shigeru and the Japanese Experience, 1878–1954*
85. Martin Collcutt, *Five Mountains: The Rinzai Zen Monastic Institution in Medieval Japan*
86. Kwang Suk Kim and Michael Roemer, *Growth and Structural Transformation*
87. Anne O. Krueger, *The Developmental Role of the Foreign Sector and Aid*
*88. Edwin S. Mills and Byung-Nak Song, *Urbanization and Urban Problems*
89. Sung Hwan Ban, Pal Yong Moon, and Dwight H. Perkins, *Rural Development*
*90. Noel F. McGinn, Donald R. Snodgrass, Yung Bong Kim, Shin-Bok Kim, and Quee-Young Kim, *Education and Development in Korea*
*91. Leroy P. Jones and Il SaKong, *Government, Business, and Entrepreneurship in Economic Development: The Korean Case*
92. Edward S. Mason, Dwight H. Perkins, Kwang Suk Kim, David C. Cole, Mahn Je Kim et al., *The Economic and Social Modernization of the Republic of Korea*
93. Robert Repetto, Tai Hwan Kwon, Son-Ung Kim, Dae Young Kim, John E. Sloboda, and Peter J. Donaldson, *Economic Development, Population Policy, and Demographic Transition in the Republic of Korea*
94. Parks M. Coble, Jr., *The Shanghai Capitalists and the Nationalist Government, 1927–1937*
95. Noriko Kamachi, *Reform in China: Huang Tsun-hsien and the Japanese Model*
96. Richard Wich, *Sino-Soviet Crisis Politics: A Study of Political Change and Communication*
97. Lillian M. Li, *China's Silk Trade: Traditional Industry in the Modern World, 1842–1937*
98. R. David Arkush, *Fei Xiaotong and Sociology in Revolutionary China*
*99. Kenneth Alan Grossberg, *Japan's Renaissance: The Politics of the Muromachi Bakufu*
100. James Reeve Pusey, *China and Charles Darwin*
101. Hoyt Cleveland Tillman, *Utilitarian Confucianism: Chen Liang's Challenge to Chu Hsi*
102. Thomas A. Stanley, *Ōsugi Sakae, Anarchist in Taishō Japan: The Creativity of the Ego*
103. Jonathan K. Ocko, *Bureaucratic Reform in Provincial China: Ting Jih-ch'ang in Restoration Kiangsu, 1867–1870*
104. James Reed, *The Missionary Mind and American East Asia Policy, 1911–1915*
105. Neil L. Waters, *Japan's Local Pragmatists: The Transition from Bakumatsu to Meiji in the Kawasaki Region*
106. David C. Cole and Yung Chul Park, *Financial Development in Korea, 1945–1978*
107. Roy Bahl, Chuk Kyo Kim, and Chong Kee Park, *Public Finances During the Korean Modernization Process*
108. William D. Wray, *Mitsubishi and the N.Y.K, 1870–1914: Business Strategy in the Japanese Shipping Industry*
109. Ralph William Huenemann, *The Dragon and the Iron Horse: The Economics of Railroads in China, 1876–1937*
*110. Benjamin A. Elman, *From Philosophy to Philology: Intellectual and Social Aspects of Change in Late Imperial China*

111. Jane Kate Leonard, *Wei Yüan and China's Rediscovery of the Maritime World*
112. Luke S. K. Kwong, *A Mosaic of the Hundred Days:. Personalities, Politics, and Ideas of 1898*
*113. John E. Wills, Jr., *Embassies and Illusions: Dutch and Portuguese Envoys to K'ang-hsi, 1666–1687*
114. Joshua A. Fogel, *Politics and Sinology: The Case of Naitō Konan (1866–1934)*
*115. Jeffrey C. Kinkley, ed., *After Mao: Chinese Literature and Society, 1978–1981*
116. C. Andrew Gerstle, *Circles of Fantasy: Convention in the Plays of Chikamatsu*
117. Andrew Gordon, *The Evolution of Labor Relations in Japan: Heavy Industry, 1853–1955*
*118. Daniel K. Gardner, *Chu Hsi and the "Ta Hsueh": Neo-Confucian Reflection on the Confucian Canon*
119. Christine Guth Kanda, *Shinzō: Hachiman Imagery and Its Development*
*120. Robert Borgen, *Sugawara no Michizane and the Early Heian Court*
121. Chang-tai Hung, *Going to the People: Chinese Intellectual and Folk Literature, 1918–1937*
*122. Michael A. Cusumano, *The Japanese Automobile Industry: Technology and Management at Nissan and Toyota*
123. Richard von Glahn, *The Country of Streams and Grottoes: Expansion, Settlement, and the Civilizing of the Sichuan Frontier in Song Times*
124. Steven D. Carter, *The Road to Komatsubara: A Classical Reading of the Renga Hyakuin*
125. Katherine F. Bruner, John K. Fairbank, and Richard T. Smith, *Entering China's Service: Robert Hart's Journals, 1854–1863*
126. Bob Tadashi Wakabayashi, *Anti-Foreignism and Western Learning in Early-Modern Japan: The "New Theses" of 1825*
127. Atsuko Hirai, *Individualism and Socialism: The Life and Thought of Kawai Eijirō (1891–1944)*
128. Ellen Widmer, *The Margins of Utopia: "Shui-hu hou-chuan" and the Literature of Ming Loyalism*
129. R. Kent Guy, *The Emperor's Four Treasuries: Scholars and the State in the Late Chien-lung Era*
130. Peter C. Perdue, *Exhausting the Earth: State and Peasant in Hunan, 1500–1850*
131. Susan Chan Egan, *A Latterday Confucian: Reminiscences of William Hung (1893–1980)*
132. James T. C. Liu, *China Turning Inward: Intellectual-Political Changes in the Early Twelfth Century*
*133. Paul A. Cohen, *Between Tradition and Modernity: Wang T'ao and Reform in Late Ching China*
134. Kate Wildman Nakai, *Shogunal Politics: Arai Hakuseki and the Premises of Tokugawa Rule*
*135. Parks M. Coble, *Facing Japan: Chinese Politics and Japanese Imperialism, 1931–1937*
*136. Jon L. Saari, *Legacies of Childhood: Growing Up Chinese in a Time of Crisis, 1890–1920*
137. Susan Downing Videen, *Tales of Heichū*

138. Heinz Morioka and Miyoko Sasaki, *Rakugo: The Popular Narrative Art of Japan*
139. Joshua A. Fogel, *Nakae Ushikichi in China: The Mourning of Spirit*
140. Alexander Barton Woodside, *Vietnam and the Chinese Model: A Comparative Study of Vietnamese and Chinese Government in the First Half of the Nineteenth Century*
*141. George Elison, *Deus Destroyed: The Image of Christianity in Early Modern Japan*
142. William D. Wray, ed., *Managing Industrial Enterprise: Cases from Japan's Prewar Experience*
*143. T'ung-tsu Ch'ü, *Local Government in China Under the Ching*
144. Marie Anchordoguy, *Computers, Inc.: Japan's Challenge to IBM*
145. Barbara Molony, *Technology and Investment: The Prewar Japanese Chemical Industry*
146. Mary Elizabeth Berry, *Hideyoshi*
147. Laura E. Hein, *Fueling Growth: The Energy Revolution and Economic Policy in Postwar Japan*
148. Wen-hsin Yeh, *The Alienated Academy: Culture and Politics in Republican China, 1919–1937*
149. Dru C. Gladney, *Muslim Chinese: Ethnic Nationalism in the People's Republic*
150. Merle Goldman and Paul A. Cohen, eds., *Ideas Across Cultures: Essays on Chinese Thought in Honor of Benjamin L Schwartz*
151. James M. Polachek, *The Inner Opium War*
152. Gail Lee Bernstein, *Japanese Marxist: A Portrait of Kawakami Hajime, 1879–1946*
*153. Lloyd E. Eastman, *The Abortive Revolution: China Under Nationalist Rule, 1927–1937*
154. Mark Mason, *American Multinationals and Japan: The Political Economy of Japanese Capital Controls, 1899–1980*
155. Richard J. Smith, John K. Fairbank, and Katherine F. Bruner, *Robert Hart and China's Early Modernization: His Journals, 1863–1866*
156. George J. Tanabe, Jr., *Myōe the Dreamkeeper: Fantasy and Knowledge in Kamakura Buddhism*
157. William Wayne Farris, *Heavenly Warriors: The Evolution of Japan's Military, 500–1300*
158. Yu-ming Shaw, *An American Missionary in China: John Leighton Stuart and Chinese-American Relations*
159. James B. Palais, *Politics and Policy in Traditional Korea*
*160. Douglas Reynolds, *China, 1898–1912: The Xinzheng Revolution and Japan*
161. Roger R. Thompson, *China's Local Councils in the Age of Constitutional Reform, 1898–1911*
162. William Johnston, *The Modern Epidemic: History of Tuberculosis in Japan*
163. Constantine Nomikos Vaporis, *Breaking Barriers: Travel and the State in Early Modern Japan*
164. Irmela Hijiya-Kirschnereit, *Rituals of Self-Revelation: Shishōsetsu as Literary Genre and Socio-Cultural Phenomenon*
165. James C. Baxter, *The Meiji Unification Through the Lens of Ishikawa Prefecture*
166. Thomas R. H. Havens, *Architects of Affluence: The Tsutsumi Family and the Seibu-Saison Enterprises in Twentieth-Century Japan*

167. Anthony Hood Chambers, *The Secret Window: Ideal Worlds in Tanizaki's Fiction*
168. Steven J. Ericson, *The Sound of the Whistle: Railroads and the State in Meiji Japan*
169. Andrew Edmund Goble, *Kenmu: Go-Daigo's Revolution*
170. Denise Potrzeba Lett, *In Pursuit of Status: The Making of South Korea's "New" Urban Middle Class*
171. Mimi Hall Yiengpruksawan, *Hiraizumi: Buddhist Art and Regional Politics in Twelfth-Century Japan*
172. Charles Shirō Inouye, *The Similitude of Blossoms: A Critical Biography of Izumi Kyōka (1873–1939), Japanese Novelist and Playwright*
173. Aviad E. Raz, *Riding the Black Ship: Japan and Tokyo Disneyland*
174. Deborah J. Milly, *Poverty, Equality, and Growth: The Politics of Economic Need in Postwar Japan*
175. See Heng Teow, *Japan's Cultural Policy Toward China, 1918–1931: A Comparative Perspective*
176. Michael A. Fuller, *An Introduction to Literary Chinese*
177. Frederick R. Dickinson, *War and National Reinvention: Japan in the Great War, 1914–1919*
178. John Solt, *Shredding the Tapestry of Meaning: The Poetry and Poetics of Kitasono Katue (1902–1978)*
179. Edward Pratt, *Japan's Protoindustrial Elite: The Economic Foundations of the Gōnō*
180. Atsuko Sakaki, *Recontextualizing Texts: Narrative Performance in Modern Japanese Fiction*
181. Soon-Won Park, *Colonial Industrialization and Labor in Korea: The Onoda Cement Factory*
182. JaHyun Kim Haboush and Martina Deuchler, *Culture and the State in Late Chosŏn Korea*
183. John W. Chaffee, *Branches of Heaven: A History of the Imperial Clan of Sung China*
184. Gi-Wook Shin and Michael Robinson, eds., *Colonial Modernity in Korea*
185. Nam-lin Hur, *Prayer and Play in Late Tokugawa Japan: Asakusa Sensōji and Edo Society*
186. Kristin Stapleton, *Civilizing Chengdu: Chinese Urban Reform, 1895–1937*
187. Hyung Il Pai, *Constructing "Korean" Origins: A Critical Review of Archaeology, Historiography, and Racial Myth in Korean State-Formation Theories*
188. Brian D. Ruppert, *Jewel in the Ashes: Buddha Relics and Power in Early Medieval Japan*
189. Susan Daruvala, *Zhou Zuoren and an Alternative Chinese Response to Modernity*
*190. James Z. Lee, *The Political Economy of a Frontier: Southwest China, 1250–1850*
191. Kerry Smith, *A Time of Crisis: Japan, the Great Depression, and Rural Revitalization*
192. Michael Lewis, *Becoming Apart: National Power and Local Politics in Toyama, 1868–1945*
193. William C. Kirby, Man-houng Lin, James Chin Shih, and David A. Pietz, eds., *State and Economy in Republican China: A Handbook for Scholars*
194. Timothy S. George, *Minamata: Pollution and the Struggle for Democracy in Postwar Japan*

195. Billy K. L. So, *Prosperity, Region, and Institutions in Maritime China: The South Fukien Pattern, 946–1368*
196. Yoshihisa Tak Matsusaka, *The Making of Japanese Manchuria, 1904–1932*
197. Maram Epstein, *Competing Discourses: Orthodoxy, Authenticity, and Engendered Meanings in Late Imperial Chinese Fiction*
198. Curtis J. Milhaupt, J. Mark Ramseyer, and Michael K. Young, eds. and comps., *Japanese Law in Context: Readings in Society, the Economy, and Politics*
199. Haruo Iguchi, *Unfinished Business: Ayukawa Yoshisuke and U.S.-Japan Relations, 1937–1952*
200. Scott Pearce, Audrey Spiro, and Patricia Ebrey, *Culture and Power in the Reconstitution of the Chinese Realm, 200–600*
201. Terry Kawashima, *Writing Margins: The Textual Construction of Gender in Heian and Kamakura Japan*
202. Martin W. Huang, *Desire and Fictional Narrative in Late Imperial China*
203. Robert S. Ross and Jiang Changbin, eds., *Re-examining the Cold War: U.S.-China Diplomacy, 1954–1973*
204. Guanhua Wang, *In Search of Justice: The 1905–1906 Chinese Anti-American Boycott*
205. David Schaberg, *A Patterned Past: Form and Thought in Early Chinese Historiography*
206. Christine Yano, *Tears of Longing: Nostalgia and the Nation in Japanese Popular Song*
207. Milena Doleželová-Velingerová and Oldřich Král, with Graham Sanders, eds., *The Appropriation of Cultural Capital: China's May Fourth Project*
208. Robert N. Huey, *The Making of 'Shinkokinshū'*
209. Lee Butler, *Emperor and Aristocracy in Japan, 1467–1680: Resilience and Renewal*
210. Suzanne Ogden, *Inklings of Democracy in China*
211. Kenneth J. Ruoff, *The People's Emperor: Democracy and the Japanese Monarchy, 1945–1995*
212. Haun Saussy, *Great Walls of Discourse and Other Adventures in Cultural China*
213. Aviad E. Raz, *Emotions at Work: Normative Control, Organizations, and Culture in Japan and America*
214. Rebecca E. Karl and Peter Zarrow, eds., *Rethinking the 1898 Reform Period: Political and Cultural Change in Late Qing China*
215. Kevin O'Rourke, *The Book of Korean Shijo*
216. Ezra F. Vogel, ed., *The Golden Age of the U.S.-China-Japan Triangle, 1972–1989*
217. Thomas A. Wilson, ed., *On Sacred Grounds: Culture, Society, Politics, and the Formation of the Cult of Confucius*
218. Donald S. Sutton, *Steps of Perfection: Exorcistic Performers and Chinese Religion in Twentieth-Century Taiwan*
219. Daqing Yang, *Technology of Empire: Telecommunications and Japanese Expansionism in Asia, 1883–1945*
220. Qianshen Bai, *Fu Shan's World: The Transformation of Chinese Calligraphy in the Seventeenth Century*
221. Paul Jakov Smith and Richard von Glahn, eds., *The Song-Yuan-Ming Transition in Chinese History*

222. Rania Huntington, *Alien Kind: Foxes and Late Imperial Chinese Narrative*
223. Jordan Sand, *House and Home in Modern Japan: Architecture, Domestic Space, and Bourgeois Culture, 1880–1930*
224. Karl Gerth, *China Made: Consumer Culture and the Creation of the Nation*
225. Xiaoshan Yang, *Metamorphosis of the Private Sphere: Gardens and Objects in Tang-Song Poetry*
226. Barbara Mittler, *A Newspaper for China? Power, Identity, and Change in Shanghai's News Media, 1872–1912*
227. Joyce A. Madancy, *The Troublesome Legacy of Commissioner Lin: The Opium Trade and Opium Suppression in Fujian Province, 1820s to 1920s*
228. John Makeham, *Transmitters and Creators: Chinese Commentators and Commentaries on the Analects*
229. Elisabeth Köll, *From Cotton Mill to Business Empire: The Emergence of Regional Enterprises in Modern China*
230. Emma Teng, *Taiwan's Imagined Geography: Chinese Colonial Travel Writing and Pictures, 1683–1895*
231. Wilt Idema and Beata Grant, *The Red Brush: Writing Women of Imperial China*
232. Eric C. Rath, *The Ethos of Noh: Actors and Their Art*
233. Elizabeth Remick, *Building Local States: China During the Republican and Post-Mao Eras*
234. Lynn Struve, ed., *The Qing Formation in World-Historical Time*
235. D. Max Moerman, *Localizing Paradise: Kumano Pilgrimage and the Religious Landscape of Premodern Japan*
236. Antonia Finnane, *Speaking of Yangzhou: A Chinese City, 1550–1850*
237. Brian Platt, *Burning and Building: Schooling and State Formation in Japan, 1750–1890*
238. Gail Bernstein, Andrew Gordon, and Kate Wildman Nakai, eds., *Public Spheres, Private Lives in Modern Japan, 1600–1950: Essays in Honor of Albert Craig*
239. Wu Hung and Katherine R. Tsiang, *Body and Face in Chinese Visual Culture*
240. Stephen Dodd, *Writing Home: Representations of the Native Place in Modern Japanese Literature*
241. David Anthony Bello, *Opium and the Limits of Empire: Drug Prohibition in the Chinese Interior, 1729–1850*
242. Hosea Hirata, *Discourses of Seduction: History, Evil, Desire, and Modern Japanese Literature*
243. Kyung Moon Hwang, *Beyond Birth: Social Status in the Emergence of Modern Korea*
244. Brian R. Dott, *Identity Reflections: Pilgrimages to Mount Tai in Late Imperial China*
245. Mark McNally, *Proving the Way: Conflict and Practice in the History of Japanese Nativism*
246. Yongping Wu, *A Political Explanation of Economic Growth: State Survival, Bureaucratic Politics, and Private Enterprises in the Making of Taiwan's Economy, 1950–1985*
247. Kyu Hyun Kim, *The Age of Visions and Arguments: Parliamentarianism and the National Public Sphere in Early Meiji Japan*

248. Zvi Ben-Dor Benite, *The Dao of Muhammad: A Cultural History of Muslims in Late Imperial China*
249. David Der-wei Wang and Shang Wei, eds., *Dynastic Crisis and Cultural Innovation: From the Late Ming to the Late Qing and Beyond*
250. Wilt L. Idema, Wai-yee Li, and Ellen Widmer, eds., *Trauma and Transcendence in Early Qing Literature*
251. Barbara Molony and Kathleen Uno, eds., *Gendering Modern Japanese History*
252. Hiroshi Aoyagi, *Islands of Eight Million Smiles: Idol Performance and Symbolic Production in Contemporary Japan*
253. Wai-yee Li, *The Readability of the Past in Early Chinese Historiography*
254. William C. Kirby, Robert S. Ross, and Gong Li, eds., *Normalization of U.S.-China Relations: An International History*
255. Ellen Gardner Nakamura, *Practical Pursuits: Takano Chōei, Takahashi Keisaku, and Western Medicine in Nineteenth-Century Japan*
256. Jonathan W. Best, *A History of the Early Korean Kingdom of Paekche, together with an annotated translation of* The Paekche Annals *of the* Samguk sagi
257. Liang Pan, *The United Nations in Japan's Foreign and Security Policymaking, 1945–1992: National Security, Party Politics, and International Status*
258. Richard Belsky, *Localities at the Center: Native Place, Space, and Power in Late Imperial Beijing*
259. Zwia Lipkin, *"Useless to the State": "Social Problems" and Social Engineering in Nationalist Nanjing, 1927–1937*
260. William O. Gardner, *Advertising Tower: Japanese Modernism and Modernity in the 1920s*
261. Stephen Owen, *The Making of Early Chinese Classical Poetry*
262. Martin J. Powers, *Pattern and Person: Ornament, Society, and Self in Classical China*
263. Anna M. Shields, *Crafting a Collection: The Cultural Contexts and Poetic Practice of the* Huajian ji 花間集 *(Collection from Among the Flowers)*
264. Stephen Owen, *The Late Tang: Chinese Poetry of the Mid-Ninth Century (827–860)*
265. Sara L. Friedman, *Intimate Politics: Marriage, the Market, and State Power in Southeastern China*
266. Patricia Buckley Ebrey and Maggie Bickford, *Emperor Huizong and Late Northern Song China: The Politics of Culture and the Culture of Politics*
267. Sophie Volpp, *Worldly Stage: Theatricality in Seventeenth-Century China*
268. Ellen Widmer, *The Beauty and the Book: Women and Fiction in Nineteenth-Century China*
269. Steven B. Miles, *The Sea of Learning: Mobility and Identity in Nineteenth-Century Guangzhou*
270. Lin Man-houng, *China Upside Down: Currency, Society, and Ideologies, 1808–1856*
271. Ronald Egan, *The Problem of Beauty: Aesthetic Thought and Pursuits in Northern Song Dynasty China*
272. Mark Halperin, *Out of the Cloister: Literati Perspectives on Buddhism in Sung China, 960–1279*

273. Helen Dunstan, *State or Merchant? Political Economy and Political Process in 1740s China*
274. Sabina Knight, *The Heart of Time: Moral Agency in Twentieth-Century Chinese Fiction*
275. Timothy J. Van Compernolle, *The Uses of Memory: The Critique of Modernity in the Fiction of Higuchi Ichiyō*
276. Paul Rouzer, *A New Practical Primer of Literary Chinese*
277. Jonathan Zwicker, *Practices of the Sentimental Imagination: Melodrama, the Novel, and the Social Imaginary in Nineteenth-Century Japan*
278. Franziska Seraphim, *War Memory and Social Politics in Japan, 1945–2005*
279. Adam L. Kern, *Manga from the Floating World: Comicbook Culture and the* Kibyōshi *of Edo Japan*
280. Cynthia J. Brokaw, *Commerce in Culture: The Sibao Book Trade in the Qing and Republican Periods*
281. Eugene Y. Park, *Between Dreams and Reality: The Military Examination in Late Chosŏn Korea, 1600–1894*
282. Nam-lin Hur, *Death and Social Order in Tokugawa Japan: Buddhism, Anti-Christianity, and the* Danka *System*
283. Patricia M. Thornton, *Disciplining the State: Virtue, Violence, and State-Making in Modern China*
284. Vincent Goossaert, *The Taoists of Peking, 1800–1949: A Social History of Urban Clerics*
285. Peter Nickerson, *Taoism, Bureaucracy, and Popular Religion in Early Medieval China*
286. Charo B. D'Etcheverry, *Love After* The Tale of Genji*: Rewriting the World of the Shining Prince*
287. Michael G. Chang, *A Court on Horseback: Imperial Touring & the Construction of Qing Rule, 1680–1785*
288. Carol Richmond Tsang, *War and Faith:* Ikkō Ikki *in Late Muromachi Japan*
289. Hilde De Weerdt, *Competition over Content: Negotiating Standards for the Civil Service Examinations in Imperial China (1127–1279)*
290. Eve Zimmerman, *Out of the Alleyway: Nakagami Kenji and the Poetics of Outcaste Fiction*
291. Robert Culp, *Articulating Citizenship: Civic Education and Student Politics in Southeastern China, 1912–1940*
292. Richard J. Smethurst, *From Foot Soldier to Finance Minister: Takahashi Korekiyo, Japan's Keynes*
293. John E. Herman, *Amid the Clouds and Mist: China's Colonization of Guizhou, 1200–1700*
294. Tomoko Shiroyama, *China During the Great Depression: Market, State, and the World Economy, 1929–1937*
295. Kirk W. Larsen, *Tradition, Treaties and Trade: Qing Imperialism and Chosŏn Korea, 1850–1910*
296. Gregory Golley, *When Our Eyes No Longer See: Realism, Science, and Ecology in Japanese Literary Modernism*

297. Barbara Ambros, *Emplacing a Pilgrimage: The Ōyama Cult and Regional Religion in Early Modern Japan*
298. Rebecca Suter, *The Japanization of Modernity: Murakami Haruki between Japan and the United States*
299. Yuma Totani, *The Tokyo War Crimes Trial: The Pursuit of Justice in the Wake of World War II*
300. Linda Isako Angst, *In a Dark Time: Memory, Community, and Gendered Nationalism in Postwar Okinawa*
301. David M. Robinson, ed., *Culture, Courtiers, and Competition: The Ming Court (1368–1644)*
302. Calvin Chen, *Some Assembly Required: Work, Community, and Politics in China's Rural Enterprises*
303. Sem Vermeersch, *The Power of the Buddhas: The Politics of Buddhism During the Koryŏ Dynasty* (918–1392)
304. Tina Lu, *Accidental Incest, Filial Cannibalism, and Other Peculiar Encounters in Late Imperial Chinese Literature*
305. Chang Woei Ong, *Men of Letters Within the Passes: Guanzhong Literati in Chinese History, 907–1911*
306. Wendy Swartz, *Reading Tao Yuanming: Shifting Paradigms of Historical Reception (427–1900)*
307. Peter K. Bol, *Neo-Confucianism in History*
308. Carlos Rojas, *The Naked Gaze: Reflections on Chinese Modernity*
309. Kelly H. Chong, *Deliverance and Submission: Evangelical Women and the Negotiation of Patriarchy in South Korea*
310. Rachel DiNitto, *Uchida Hyakken: A Critique of Modernity and Militarism in Prewar Japan*
311. Jeffrey Snyder-Reinke, *Dry Spells: State Rainmaking and Local Governance in Late Imperial China*
312. Jay Dautcher, *Down a Narrow Road: Identity and Masculinity in a Uyghur Community in Xinjiang China*
313. Xun Liu, *Daoist Modern: Innovation, Lay Practice, and the Community of Inner Alchemy in Republican Shanghai*
314. Jacob Eyferth, *Eating Rice from Bamboo Roots: The Social History of a Community of Handicraft Papermakers in Rural Sichuan, 1920–2000*
315. David Johnson, *Spectacle and Sacrifice: The Ritual Foundations of Village Life in North China*
316. James Robson, *Power of Place: The Religious Landscape of the Southern Sacred Peak (Nanyue 南嶽) in Medieval China*
317. Lori Watt, *When Empire Comes Home: Repatriation and Reintegration in Postwar Japan*
318. James Dorsey, *Critical Aesthetics: Kobayashi Hideo, Modernity, and Wartime Japan*
319. Christopher Bolton, *Sublime Voices: The Fictional Science and Scientific Fiction of Abe Kōbō*
320. Si-yen Fei, *Negotiating Urban Space: Urbanization and Late Ming Nanjing*

321. Christopher Gerteis, *Gender Struggles: Wage-Earning Women and Male-Dominated Unions in Postwar Japan*
322. Rebecca Nedostup, *Superstitious Regimes: Religion and the Politics of Chinese Modernity*
323. Lucien Bianco, *Wretched Rebels: Rural Disturbances on the Eve of the Chinese Revolution*
324. Cathryn H. Clayton, *Sovereignty at the Edge: Macau and the Question of Chineseness*
325. Micah S. Muscolino, *Fishing Wars and Environmental Change in Late Imperial and Modern China*
326. Robert I. Hellyer, *Defining Engagement: Japan and Global Contexts, 1750–1868*
327. Robert Ashmore, *The Transport of Reading: Text and Understanding in the World of Tao Qian (365–427)*
328. Mark A. Jones, *Children as Treasures: Childhood and the Middle Class in Early Twentieth Century Japan*
329. Miryam Sas, *Experimental Arts in Postwar Japan: Moments of Encounter, Engagement, and Imagined Return*
330. H. Mack Horton, *Traversing the Frontier: The* Man'yōshū *Account of a Japanese Mission to Silla in 736–737*
331. Dennis J. Frost, *Seeing Stars: Sports Celebrity, Identity, and Body Culture in Modern Japan*
332. Marnie S. Anderson, *A Place in Public: Women's Rights in Meiji Japan*
333. Peter Mauch, *Sailor Diplomat: Nomura Kichisaburō and the Japanese-American War*
334. Ethan Isaac Segal, *Coins, Trade, and the State: Economic Growth in Early Medieval Japan*
335. David B. Lurie, *Realms of Literacy: Early Japan and the History of Writing*
336. Lillian Lan-ying Tseng, *Picturing Heaven in Early China*
337. Jun Uchida, *Brokers of Empire: Japanese Settler Colonialism in Korea, 1876–1945*
338. Patricia L. Maclachlan, *The People's Post Office: The History and Politics of the Japanese Postal System, 1871–2010*
339. Michael Schiltz, *The Money Doctors from Japan: Finance, Imperialism, and the Building of the Yen Bloc, 1895–1937*
340. Daqing Yang, Jie Liu, Hiroshi Mitani, and Andrew Gordon, eds., *Toward a History Beyond Borders: Contentious Issues in Sino-Japanese Relations*
341. Sonia Ryang, *Reading North Korea: An Ethnological Inquiry*
342. Susan Huang, *Picturing the True Form: Daoist Visual Culture in Traditional China*
343. Barbara Mittler, *A Continuous Revolution: Making Sense of Cultural Revolution Culture*
344. Hwansoo Ilmee Kim, *Empire of the Dharma: Korean and Japanese Buddhism, 1877–1912*
345. Satoru Saito, *Detective Fiction and the Rise of the Japanese Novel, 1880–1930*
346. Jung-Sun N. Han, *An Imperial Path to Modernity: Yoshino Sakuzō and a New Liberal Order in East Asia, 1905–1937*
347. Atsuko Hirai, *Government by Mourning: Death and Political Integration in Japan, 1603–1912*
348. Darryl E. Flaherty, *Public Law, Private Practice: Politics, Profit, and the Legal Profession in Nineteenth-Century Japan*

349. Jeffrey Paul Bayliss, *On the Margins of Empire: Buraku and Korean Identity in Prewar and Wartime Japan*
350. Barry Eichengreen, Dwight H. Perkins, and Kwanho Shin, *From Miracle to Maturity: The Growth of the Korean Economy*
351. Michel Mohr, *Buddhism, Unitarianism, and the Meiji Competition for Universality*
352. J. Keith Vincent, *Two-Timing Modernity: Homosocial Narrative in Modern Japanese Fiction*
353. Suzanne G. O'Brien, *Customizing Daily Life: Representing and Reforming Customs in Nineteenth-Century Japan*
354. Chong-Bum An and Barry Bosworth, *Income Inequality in Korea: An Analysis of Trends, Causes, and Answers*
355. Jamie L. Newhard, *Knowing the Amorous Man: A History of Scholarship on* Tales of Ise
356. Sho Konishi, *Anarchist Modernity: Cooperatism and Japanese-Russian Intellectual Relations in Modern Japan*
357. Christopher P.Hanscom, *The Real Modern: Literary Modernism and the Crisis of Representation in Colonial Korea*
358. Michael Wert, *Meiji Restoration Losers: Memory and Tokugawa Supporters in Modern Japan*
359. Garret P. S. Olberding, ed., *Facing the Monarch: Modes of Advice in the Early Chinese Court*
360. Xiaojue Wang, *Modernity with a Cold War Face: Reimagining the Nation in Chinese Literature Across the* 1949 *Divide*